English G 21

A2
für Gymnasien

Cornelsen

English G 21 • Band A 2

Im Auftrag des Verlages herausgegeben von
Prof. Hellmut Schwarz, Mannheim

Erarbeitet von
Laurence Harger, Wellington, Neuseeland
Barbara Derkow Disselbeck, Köln
Allen J. Woppert, Berlin
sowie Susan Abbey, Nenagh, Irland

unter Mitarbeit von
Wolfgang Biederstädt, Köln
Joachim Blombach, Herford
Helmut Dengler, Limbach
Jörg Rademacher, Ilvesheim
Jennifer Seidl, München
Sabine Tudan, Erfurt

in Zusammenarbeit mit der Englischredaktion
Kirsten Bleck (Projektleitung);
Dr. Christian v. Raumer (verantwortlicher Redakteur);
Susanne Bennetreu und Julie Colthorpe (Bildredaktion);
Christiane Bonk; Dr. Philip Devlin; Gareth Evans; Bonnie S. Glänzer; Uwe Tröger; Klaus G. Unger sowie Nathalie Schwering

Beratende Mitwirkung
Peter Brünker, Bad Kreuznach; Helga Estor, Darmstadt; Anette Fritsch, Dillenburg; Dr. Helga Hämmerling, Jena; Patrick Handschuh, Köln; Martina Kretschko-Ulbrich, Dresden; Dr. Annette Leithner-Brauns, Dresden; Dr. Ursula Mulla, Germering; Wolfgang Neudecker, Mannheim; Birgit Ohmsieder, Berlin; Albert Rau, Brühl; Angela Ringel-Eichinger, Bietigheim-Bissingen; Dr. Jana Schubert, Leipzig; Sieglinde Spranger, Chemnitz; Harald Weißling, Mannheim; Monika Wilkening, Wehretal

Illustration
Graham-Cameron Illustration, UK: Fliss Cary, Grafikerin sowie Roland Beier, Berlin

Fotos
Rob Cousins, Bristol

Layoutkonzept und technische Umsetzung
Aksinia Raphael; Korinna Wilkes

Umschlaggestaltung
Klein & Halm Grafikdesign, Berlin

Für die freundliche Unterstützung danken wir der Cotham School, Bristol.

www.cornelsen.de
www.EnglishG.de

Die Webseiten Dritter, deren Internetadressen in diesem Lehrwerk angegeben sind, wurden vor Drucklegung sorgfältig geprüft. Der Verlag übernimmt keine Gewähr für die Aktualität und den Inhalt dieser Seiten oder solcher, die mit ihnen verlinkt sind.

Dieses Werk berücksichtigt die Regeln der reformierten Rechtschreibung und Zeichensetzung.

Alle Drucke dieser Auflage sind inhaltlich unverändert und können im Unterricht nebeneinander verwendet werden. Einige der in diesem Druck verwendeten Bilder können sich von denen in vorherigen Drucken dieser Auflage unterscheiden. Der Austausch dieser Bilder war aus urheberrechtlichen Gründen notwendig, um Ihnen die Inhalte auch digital zur Verfügung stellen zu können.

© 2007 Cornelsen Verlag, Berlin
© 2017 Cornelsen Verlag GmbH, Berlin

Das Werk und seine Teile sind urheberrechtlich geschützt. Jede Nutzung in anderen als den gesetzlich zugelassenen Fällen bedarf der vorherigen schriftlichen Einwilligung des Verlages.
Hinweis zu §§ 60 a, 60 b UrhG: Weder das Werk noch seine Teile dürfen ohne eine solche Einwilligung an Schulen oder in Unterrichts- und Lehrmedien (§ 60 b Abs. 3 UrhG) vervielfältigt, insbesondere kopiert oder eingescannt, verbreitet oder in ein Netzwerk eingestellt oder sonst öffentlich zugänglich gemacht oder wiedergegeben werden. Dies gilt auch für Intranets von Schulen.

Soweit in diesem Lehrwerk Personen fotografisch abgebildet sind und ihnen von der Redaktion fiktive Namen, Berufe, Dialoge und Ähnliches zugeordnet oder diese Personen in bestimmte Kontexte gesetzt werden, dienen diese Zuordnungen und Darstellungen ausschließlich der Veranschaulichung und dem besseren Verständnis des Buchinhalts.

Druck und Bindung: Livonia Print, Riga

2. Auflage, 2. Druck 2019
ISBN 978-3-06-031305-1
broschiert

2. Auflage, 1. Druck 2019
ISBN 978-3-06-031355-6
gebunden

ISBN 978-3-06-033206-9 (E-Book)

PEFC zertifiziert
Dieses Produkt stammt aus nachhaltig bewirtschafteten Wäldern und kontrollierten Quellen.
www.pefc.de
PEFC/12-31-006

Dein Englischbuch enthält folgende Teile:

Welcome back	Einstieg in das Buch – hier triffst du die Lehrwerkskinder wieder.
Units	die sechs Kapitel des Buches
Topics	besondere Themen – z.B. die Geschichte von Robinson Crusoe
Skills File (SF)	Beschreibung wichtiger Lern- und Arbeitstechniken
Grammar File (GF)	Zusammenfassung der Grammatik jeder Unit
Vocabulary	Wörterverzeichnis zum Lernen der neuen Wörter jeder Unit
Dictionary	alphabetische Wörterverzeichnisse zum Nachschlagen

Die Units bestehen aus diesen Teilen:

Lead-in	Einstieg in das neue Thema
A-Section	neuer Lernstoff mit vielen Aktivitäten
Practice	Übungen
Text	eine spannende oder lustige Geschichte

In den Units findest du diese Überschriften und Symbole:

Looking at Language	Hier sammelst du Beispiele und entdeckst Regeln.
STUDY SKILLS	Einführung in Lern- und Arbeitstechniken
DOSSIER	Schöne und wichtige Arbeiten kannst du in einer Mappe sammeln.
Background File	Hier findest du interessante Informationen über Land und Leute.
GAME	Spiele für zwei oder für eine Gruppe – natürlich auf Englisch
GETTING BY IN ENGLISH	Alltagssituationen üben; Sprachmittlung
MEDIATION	Hier vermittelst du zwischen zwei Sprachen.
LISTENING	Aufgaben zu Hörtexten auf der CD
Now you	Hier sprichst und schreibst du über dich selbst.
POEM / SONG	Gedichte / Lieder zum Anhören und Singen
PRONUNCIATION	Ausspracheübungen
REVISION	Übungen zur Wiederholung
WORDS	Übungen zu Wortfamilien und Wortfeldern, Wortverbindungen
Checkpoint	Im Workbook kannst du dein Wissen überprüfen.
Extra	Zusätzliche Aktivitäten und Übungen
👥 👥👥	Partnerarbeit/Gruppenarbeit
🎧 🎧	nur auf CD / auf CD und im Schülerbuch
▷	Textaufgaben

Inhalt

Die folgenden Angebote sind nicht obligatorisch abzuarbeiten. Die Auswahl der Übungen und Übungsteile richtet sich nach den Schwerpunkten des schulinternen Curriculums.

Seite	Unit	Sprechabsichten	Sprachliche Mittel: • grammatische Strukturen • Wortfelder	STUDY SKILLS DOSSIER
6	**Welcome back** Die Lehrwerkskinder in den Sommerferien	Über die Ferien berichten; über das Wetter sprechen	Reisen, Verkehrsmittel, Urlaubsorte, Urlaubsaktivitäten zu Hause und unterwegs; Landschaft; Wetter	**STUDY SKILLS** REVISION Mind maps **DOSSIER** My holiday
10	**Unit 1** **Back to school** Das neue Schuljahr hat begonnen; die Lehrwerkskinder lernen eine neue Mitschülerin kennen	Bilder beschreiben; sagen, wo sich etwas befindet; über den Schulalltag sprechen; über Vergangenes berichten; neu in der Schule: sich gegenseitig vorstellen; Gefühle ausdrücken	• REVISION simple past positive and negative statements, questions and short answers • subject/object questions with *who* and *what* • Bildbeschreibung; Orts- und Zeitangaben; Schule, schulische Aktivitäten; Freizeit- und häusliche Aktivitäten	**STUDY SKILLS** Describing pictures Linking words and phrases **DOSSIER** A holiday adventure
24	**EXTRA Topic 1** **A trip to Jamaica**	Mr. Kingsley berichtet über seinen Urlaub auf Jamaica und erzählt eine Legende aus der Karibik		
26	**Unit 2** **What money can buy** Taschengeld und andere Geldfragen; ein Schulprojekt zum Thema „Kleidung"	Sagen, wofür man sein Taschengeld ausgibt oder ob man spart; über einen schlechten Tag sprechen; über Absichten und (Zukunfts-)Pläne sprechen; Dinge und Personen miteinander vergleichen; etwas vorschlagen; sagen, was man besser findet	• possessive pronouns (*mine, yours,...*) • REVISION *some/any* • compounds with *some/any* • *going to*-future • comparison of adjectives (*-er/-est, more/most*) • Taschengeld, Kleidung, Mode, Kaufhaus; *make/do*; *how much/how many*	**STUDY SKILLS** Learning words Mediation **DOSSIER** A different point of view
42	**EXTRA Topic 2** **Special days around the world**	Besondere Feste in der englischsprachigen Welt: Guy Fawkes Day in Großbritannien • Weihnachten in Neuseeland • Holi in Indien • Independence Day in den USA		
44	**Unit 3** **Animals in the city** Eine Fernsehsendung über Tiere in der Stadt; wie Ananda das Leben von Igelbabys rettet	Über Lieblingssendungen im Fernsehen sprechen; über Zukünftiges sprechen; sagen, was unter einer bestimmten Bedingung passieren wird; sagen, wie man bestimmte Dinge macht; über den Umgang mit Tieren sprechen; ein Telefongespräch führen	• *will*-future • conditional sentences (1) • adverbs of manner • EXTRA comparison of adverbs • REVISION comparison of adjectives • Fernsehsendungen, Haustiere, frei lebende Tiere in der Stadt, Zootiere; Adverbien der Art und Weise	**STUDY SKILLS** Listening Scanning Multiple-choice exercises **DOSSIER** Animals Pet of the day
58	**EXTRA Topic 3** **Animal songs and poems**	Lieder und Gedichte über Tiere		

Inhalt

Seite	Unit	Sprechabsichten	Sprachliche Mittel: • grammatische Strukturen • Wortfelder	STUDY SKILLS DOSSIER
60	**Unit 4** **A weekend in Wales** Dan und Jo sind zu Besuch bei den Großeltern; Dan wird krank und nicht alles läuft wie geplant.	Stadt/Land beschreiben, über Unterschiede sprechen; sagen, was man gerade/schon/noch nicht gemacht hat; sagen, dass man sich nicht wohl fühlt/was einem fehlt; sich nach dem Befinden anderer erkundigen; über ein Ereignis berichten	• REVISION word order (S–V–O) • word order *place – time* • present perfect • EXTRA present perfect and simple past in contrast • Stadt, Land, Reisen; Sehenswürdigkeiten; Körperteile, Krankheiten; technische Anweisungen (Computer); Verkehrsunfall; *be able to, be allowed to*	**STUDY SKILLS** Topic sentence **DOSSIER** Wales
75	**EXTRA Topic 4** **A weekend in Wales – Jo's e-mail to his mum**	Jo schreibt seiner Mutter eine E-Mail und berichtet ihr über das Wochenende in Wales. Dan hört sich eine walisische Sage an.		
76	**Unit 5** **Teamwork** Wie gut kennen die Lehrwerkskinder Bristol? Sie erkunden ihre Stadt, lösen ein Quiz und erstellen eine Broschüre.	Ein Brettspiel spielen; im Café/in der Eisdiele etwas bestellen; sagen und begründen, warum man etwas gut/nicht gut findet	• relative clauses • question tags • Spielewortschatz; Aktivitäten in der Stadt; Obstsorten; Speisekarte; Pläne	**STUDY SKILLS** Marking up a text Structuring a text **DOSSIER** Lesley's story
91	**EXTRA Topic 5** **Robinson Crusoe**	Die Abenteuer des Robinson Crusoe, der sich als einziger aus einem sinkenden Schiff auf eine unbewohnte Insel retten kann		
94	**Unit 6** **A trip to Bath** Die Klasse 8PK macht einen Ausflug ins benachbarte Bath und besucht historische Sehenswürdigkeiten.	Sagen, wie man etwas empfunden hat; Gespräche führen; nach dem Weg fragen und den Weg beschreiben; sagen, was man zu einem bestimmten Zeitpunkt in der Vergangenheit gemacht hat	• EXTRA contact clauses • EXTRA indirect speech • REVISION present progressive • past progressive • EXTRA conditional sentences (2) • Schulausflug; Fahrradtour; Wegbeschreibung; *mustn't/needn't*	**STUDY SKILLS** Having a conversation Correcting mistakes **DOSSIER** A school trip
108	**EXTRA Topic 6** **The twins' holiday trip**	Dan und Jo planen einen Besuch bei ihrer Mutter in Neuseeland.		

110 Partner B
114 Skills File
126 Grammar File (Grammatical terms S. 148–149; Lösungen S. 149)
150 Vocabulary
178 Dictionary (English – German)

200 **Dictionary (German – English)**
217 English sounds / The English alphabet
218 List of names
219 Countries and continents
220 Irregular verbs
222 Classroom English
223 Arbeitsanweisungen

Welcome back – After the holidays

1 🎧

15th Aug.

Dear Jack
Well, here we are by the sea in Cornwall. Dad didn't find a holiday flat. He was too late, so we're in a caravan by the sea. On Monday it was cold and windy and it rained.

Today it was hot and sunny. We went swimming and met a nice girl on the beach!

Dan   Jo :)

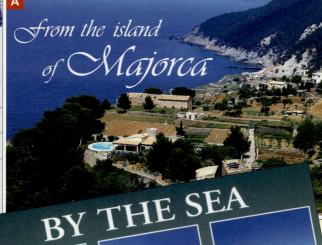

A

from the island of Majorca

B

BY THE SEA

2 🎧

Dear Sophie,
We didn't go away on holiday, but here's a funny postcard for you anyway! Last week it was warm and sunny, so I went to the pool in Portishead. It was great. There's a nice French family here at the moment. It was cool and rained a lot yesterday, so I took the boy (he's 12 too) to Explore-at-Bristol. It was fun.

Text me when you get back.
            Jack

3 🎧

Dear Danandjo!
This city is so great! This was the view of Manhattan from the plane as we flew in on Monday.
We went on a boat trip yesterday – all round the island. We saw a lot! It was cloudy, but that was good: it's <u>very very</u> hot when the sun shines!

See you soon.

Ananda

FREE E-Cards

To:
From:
Sent:

4

Dear Ananda,
It's great here. We've got a villa and our own pool! The weather is fantastic – blue sky and hot sun every day. On Sunday we travelled into the mountains by car. Yesterday we rode our bikes to the beach because Emily wanted to see 'something new' (boys of course!). I think it's more fun at our pool, so that's where I am today!

Lots of love

Sophie

1 The cards

a) Read the cards. Match the messages to the pictures. Give reasons for your choice.
Dan and Jo write about the sea and a beach in Cornwall. Card B shows a beach. So, I think card B is from Dan and Jo.

b) Collect words and phrases about holidays from the cards. Use headings like places, transport, weather, activities, ... Add more words and phrases you know.

▶ SF Learning words – Step 1 (p. 115) • WB 1–2 (p. 1)

2 Your holidays – at home or away?

Make appointments with three students.
Ask each other about the summer holidays.

1. Did you go away?
2. Who was with you?
3. What did you do?
4. What was the weather like?
5. Did you stay in a hotel/holiday flat/villa/caravan/...?

My appointments
1 o'clock   Marek
2 o'clock   ...
3 o'clock   ...

Welcome back

3 What's the weather like in …?

Partner B: Look at the map on page 110.
Partner A: Look at this weather map.
Answer B's questions. Then ask B about the weather in the red cities.

B: What's the weather like in Madrid/London/…?
A: It's hot and sunny in Madrid. / It's raining in … / There's a storm in … / It's foggy/cloudy in … / It's 15 degrees in …
Swap after three questions.

4 Holiday weather

a) Talk to your partner. What is good weather for … a boat trip? / … a day in town? / … a day on the beach? / … a walk in the country?
A: What is good weather for a boat trip?
B: Not too hot and no storm. What is good weather for a day in town?

b) The Millers are on their summer holidays. When they aren't at the beach, they like going on trips. Copy the chart. Then listen to the CD. Who wants to do what? Fill in a copy of the chart.

	Mum	Barry	Laura
day in the country			
day in town			
day on the beach			

c) Listen again. Take notes on the weather for today and tomorrow. Then look at a) and say what plans the three can make for these two days.

5 Extra ACTIVITY

Make a weather calendar for your classroom. When you change it, one student can give a short weather report to the class.

▶ WB 3–4 (p. 2)

Welcome back

6 A holiday diary

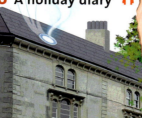

Dear Diary,
It's holiday time and the house is empty. My family isn't here. They went abroad, to sunny Spain. But I didn't go with them. I had to stay at home, alone. It's cold and rainy and very boring.
  Well, it isn't boring all the time … On Friday I went through the house and dropped things in every room and nobody grumbled. That was fun!
  On Saturday I spoke to Uncle Henry. Then we played tennis in the afternoon. That was fun too!
  Yesterday I tried on all Emily's clothes and put them in the fridge. I threw her CDs on the floor and then I went plate-surfing on the roof and dropped my plate down the

> What other fun things can Prunella do? Write a few more lines for her diary or draw a picture.

7 Now you

a) Collect ideas for a diary entry about your holidays. (They can be real or imaginary.) You can use your words and phrases from 1b), p.7.

b) Write about your holiday. You can add pictures or maps. You can put it in your DOSSIER.

DOSSIER My holiday

My family and I went to Italy on holiday. We went by car. We were by a little lake in the mountains and stayed in a big flat. It was hot and sunny, so I went swimming every day. And I ate lots of spaghetti! I met a nice girl from Holland – we often played tennis. Here is a picture of the lake. It's very beautiful.

STUDY SKILLS Mind maps

Denk daran: Mindmaps können dir helfen, Ideen zu sammeln und zu ordnen.

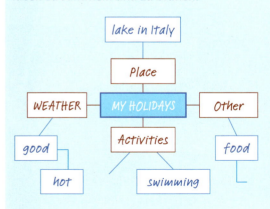

▶ SF Mind maps (p. 116) • WB 5 (p. 3)

DOSSIER My dream holiday

I flew to Mars. It was very hot and the people were very interesting: they were green, and their eyes …

Unit 1

Welcome to Cotham School

1

2

4

5

© Cotham School
All Rights Reserved.

Back to school

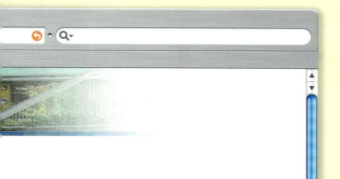

1 Talking about school

a) What can you remember about Cotham School? Make notes. Then look at the Cotham website on the left for more ideas.

b) 👥 Compare Cotham School with your school. What's the same, what's different?
At Cotham they've got a cafeteria but we haven't. Cotham has got a camera club and we have too.

2 `Extra` **Who are they?**

a) Do you remember much about the Bristol kids?
– Who lives in a bed and breakfast?
– Who shares her room with a poltergeist?
– Where does the twins' mum live?
– Who lives over a shop?

b) 👥 Ask your partner more questions.

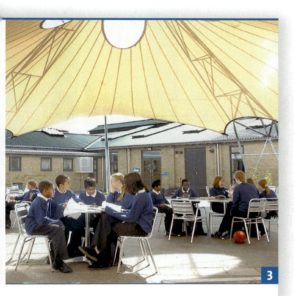

3

6

STUDY SKILLS Describing pictures

Um ein Bild zu beschreiben, musst du sagen können, wo genau sich die Personen und Gegenstände befinden. Am besten gehst du dabei in einer bestimmten Reihenfolge vor, z.B. von unten nach oben oder von vorne nach hinten.

3 Find the red balls
Say where the red balls are in the photos.
There's a red ball in picture ... It's in the background/on the left/behind the .../between ... and ...

▶ SF Describing pictures (p. 117) • P 1–3 (pp. 16–17) • WB 1–3 (pp. 4–5)

1 A-Section

1 Friends meet again 🎧

Jack	Thanks for the postcard, Ananda. Now, tell me all about New York.
Ananda	Oh, Jack, it was so fantastic. We stayed with my aunt and uncle – they were really great, the weather was great, the sights were great …
Jack	You were there with Dilip, right?
Ananda	Well, we flew there together, but he came back about a week before me.
Jack	How was the flight?
Ananda	It was my first time on a plane, so I was a bit nervous. But it wasn't scary. Not like the subway – that was scary!
Jack	Yeah, I heard that the underground is dangerous.
Ananda	No, not dangerous – just very fast.
Jack	Oh look, there's Sophie.

Sophie	Hi, you two. So what was the best thing about New York, Ananda?
Ananda	The Empire State Building! We took the elevator …
Jack	Subway, elevator? So you speak American English now!
Ananda	Sorry, we took the lift to the top. It's amazing! You can see for miles …

▶ What was so exciting about Ananda's trip to New York?

Extra | Background File

The Empire State Building
The building stands 443.2 metres high and has 102 floors, 73 lifts, 1,860 stairs and 6,500 windows. Lightning hits the ESB about 100 times a year.
It takes 50 seconds in a lift from the lobby to the 86th floor. There you can see over 120 kilometres on a clear day.
Every year there's a run up to the observatory. The best runners can do it in 10 minutes.
To find out more, visit the building's web site at www.esbnyc.com.

Looking at language

Revision
– Find the simple past forms of **(to) be** in **1**.
– Find the simple past of **(to) stay**. How do you make the simple past form of regular verbs?
– Find four irregular simple past forms (**flew, came, heard, took**). What are the infinitives?

▶ GF 1: Simple past: positive statements (p. 127) • P 4–6 (pp. 17–18) • WB 4–9 (pp. 6–8)

2 A new girl 🎧

When they got to their classroom, the friends saw a girl, alone at the back of the room.

Sophie	Hi! I'm Sophie and this is Ananda. Are you new?
Lesley	Of course I'm new.
Ananda	What's your name?
Lesley	Lesley.
Sophie	Hi, Lesley. Where are you from?
Lesley	Mind your own business. I didn't want to come here, you know.
Sophie	I'm not from Bristol, Lesley. I didn't want to come either, but I really like it here now.
Lesley	Oh, just go away!

Ananda and Sophie went back to the group.

Ananda	She doesn't like us, Sophie.
Jo	Why? What happened?
Sophie	Well, she didn't say much.
Ananda	And after she said 'Mind your own business' we didn't ask her much!
Jack	Wow! That was rude of her!
Dan	Maybe she was nervous or …
Jo	Yeah, yeah.
Jack	Hey, here comes Mr Kingsley.

▷ What can you say about the new girl?
Why do you think she is so rude?

Looking at language

Find all the negative sentences in **2** and put them in two lists like this:

simple present	simple past
She doesn't like us	I didn't want …
…	

How do you make the negative form of the **simple past**?

▶ GF 2: Simple past: negative statements (p. 128) •
P 7–9 (pp. 18–19) • WB 10–13 (pp. 9–11)

3 Now you

a) How are your school days different from your holidays? Think of at least three things. Make sentences like these: I usually get up early. I didn't get up early in the holidays.
Here are some more ideas:

> have a big breakfast • ride my bike every day • play computer games in the evenings • work in the afternoons • only watch TV for an hour • eat a big lunch • go to bed at 9 o'clock

b) 👥 Tell a partner.

4 Lunch break 🎧

Ananda	I can't find my lunch money. It was in my jacket, but it isn't there now.
Sophie	Do you want to borrow some? I can lend you £1.
Ananda	Thanks. But it's very strange. I'm sure I had it this morning.
	...
Dan	The food is better this year.
Jack	Do you really think so?
Dan	Yes, I do. This veggie burger is very good.
Sophie	It's fish, Dan.
Dan	Oh ... Hey, I can't see that new girl.
Jo	Well, she's right behind you.
Dan	Maybe she'd like to eat with us.
All	No way!
Dan	Why don't you give her a chance?
Jo	Did she give Sophie and Ananda a chance this morning? No, she didn't.
Dan	Did you try and understand her, Jo? No, you didn't. Or when we were on holiday – did *you* help when Jody was in trouble? No, you didn't. But you wanted to be the big hero anyway.
Jack	Hey Dan, calm down.
Dan	I don't want to calm down. I'm going outside.
Sophie	Why did Dan get so angry?
Jack	Yeah, and who's Jody?
Jo	Oh, it's nothing. Let's eat.

Looking at language

Find all the questions in **4**. Make two lists, one for the **simple present**, one for the **simple past** forms. What's the difference between the two?

5 Now you

a) What did you do on your last birthday? Write down three things.

b) 👥 Ask different partners what they did on their last birthday. Find somebody who did two of the same things as you.

▶ GF 3: Simple past: questions and short answers (p. 128) • P 10–13 (pp. 19–20) • WB 14–18 (pp. 11–13)

6 Prunella is unhappy 🎧

Prunella At last! You're back. You're never here and I'm alone all the time.
Sophie I'm sorry you're unhappy, Prunella, but I …
Prunella First you went to Spain for weeks. You came back a few days ago, and you were out again yesterday and all day today. You don't like me.
Sophie But I had to go to school!
Prunella School? Oh. How was it?
Sophie Well, it was nice at first. I saw all my friends again.
Prunella And then?
Sophie There was this new girl, so we went and talked to her and …
Prunella Who talked to her?
Sophie Ananda and me. But she was very unfriendly. She didn't talk to us.
Prunella Who did she talk to?
Sophie No one. And then there was an argument later.
Prunella An argument? Who did you have an argument with?
Sophie I didn't have an argument.
Prunella Well, who had an argument?
Sophie Dan and Jo.
Prunella What did they argue about? 
Sophie I'm not really sure. About the new girl and a girl on holiday and …
Prunella What happened on holiday?
Sophie Oh, Prunella, I can't explain it. I need a cup of tea.
Prunella See, you don't like me. What do you need? A cup of tea? Who needs me? Nobody! I haven't got any friends.

▷ Explain why Prunella is unhappy.
– Sophie can't explain what Dan and Jo's argument was about. Can you?

Looking at language

Copy the questions with *who* and *what* from **6** into lists like this:

Questions without do/does/did	Questions with do/does/did
Who talked to her?	Who did she talk to?
…	…

When is the question word (*what*, *who*) the subject of the sentence? When is it the object?

▶ GF 4: Subject/object questions (p. 129) • P 14–16 (p. 21) • WB 19 (p. 13)

7 Extra SONG Carole King: You've got a friend 🎧

When you're down and troubled
And you need some loving care
And nothing, nothing is going right,
Close your eyes and think of me
And soon I will be there
To brighten up even your darkest night.

You just call out my name
And you know wherever I am
I'll come running to see you again.
Winter, spring, summer or fall
All you have to do is call
And I'll be there,
You've got a friend.   *(by Carole King)*

1 WORDS School

a) Make lists like these. Use words and phrases from the box. Do you know any more words? Add them.

In my school bag	In the classroom	School subjects	What I do at school	Sports
book ...	CD player... ...	Art ...	answer questions ...	basketball ...

answer questions • Art • basketball • Biology • book • CD player • chair • cupboard • do an exercise • do a project • Drama • English • exercise book • football • French • Geography • History • hockey • listen to the CD • look at the board • Maths • Music • PE • pen • pencil • pencil case • play with my classmates • practise pronunciation • read • rubber • ruler • Science • sing songs • spell • swimming • talk to my friend • talk to the teacher • timetable • work with a partner

b) Check your lists with a partner. Ask your teacher when you are not sure.

c) Extra Write about one of these topics. Use lots of words from your lists.

'A day in the life of my school bag'
I'm Pia's school bag. This morning Pia put lots of books in me. Her mother gave me a sandwich box. Mmmm! Really good sandwiches! Then we went to ...

'Today at school'
A: Hi Ben. How was school today?
B: Oh, we had a really easy day. First, we had PE. And then we ...

2 LISTENING Aliens at school

You're playing a game with your friend – 'Aliens at school'.
You have to find all the aliens in the classroom.

a) Look at the picture. Say where you see aliens. There are two aliens on ... There's one alien next to ...

b) Your friend knows where there are more aliens. Listen to him and look.

c) Listen again. Draw the other aliens on a copy of the picture.

d) Extra Check with a partner. Don't show your picture. Say: *There's an alien in front of the ...*

3 STUDY SKILLS Describing pictures

Partner B: Go to p. 110.
a) *Partner A: Draw a picture with a house, two people, two trees, a cloud and a ball.*

b) *Describe your picture to your partner. (Do not show him/her your picture.)*
There's a house in the middle of my picture. On the right, there are …
Your partner draws the picture.
Then compare the two pictures.

c) *Now your partner describes his/her picture and you draw it. Then compare the pictures again.*

4 PRONUNCIATION (Vowel sounds)

a) How do you pronounce the words in the box? Make nine rhyming pairs from them. Then listen and check.

> their • we're • idea • shirt • where • were •
> they're • bird • ear • hair • heard • her • near •
> here • chair • year • hurt • fair

their – hair, …

b) Put the nine pairs into three sound (not spelling) groups.

[eə]	[ɪə]	[ɜː]
their – hair	we're – …	shirt – …
…	…	…

c) Extra Choose two rhyming pairs and write a little poem.

5 REVISION Ananda's holidays (Simple past/simple present)

a) Complete the dialogue with the verbs in brackets. Use the simple present or the simple past.

Ananda — Hello, Dan.
Dan — Ananda, great to hear from you. You … (be) back from New York!
Ananda — Yes, I … (come) back yesterday.
Dan — Well, how … (be) New York?
Ananda — Oh, it … (be) fantastic. But there just … (not be) enough time to see everything.
Dan — Tell me about all the sights.
Ananda — Well, we … (see) the Statue of Liberty, of course. And we … (go) on a great bus tour round Manhattan. We … (walk) through Central Park. And we … (go) up the Empire State Building. That … (be) my favourite. Oh Dan, I … (have got) something for you.
Dan — Wow, what … (be) it? A present?
Ananda — Well, maybe. Now, how … (be) your holidays?
Dan — Oh, we … (go) to Cornwall. It …

b) Extra Think of a good present for Dan. Say why it's a good present.

c) Extra Continue the dialogue from a) about Dan's holidays in Cornwall. (Look at p. 6 for help.)

6 WRITING Linking words and phrases

a) Copy the flow chart. Put the verbs in brackets in the simple past and complete the story.

| **After breakfast** Ms Travelot *rode* (ride) her ... to her ... | **At 10 o'clock** she ... (go) to Dover by ... | She ... (get on) a ... there and ... (take) it to Dover station. | She ... (be) late, so she ... (run) to the train. |

| **Then** she ... (go) to Bristol by ... and ... (be) home for dinner. | **An hour later** she ... (get on) a ... and ... (fly) to Leeds. | **After that** she ... (take) the ... | She ... (take) the ... to London and ... (get off) there. |

b) Make a flow chart with eight boxes. Use linking words to write what you did last Saturday. If you need ideas, look at the green box.

> help my mother • listen to music • make a model • call Eva • play basketball • meet my friends • ride my bike • go swimming

STUDY SKILLS | **Linking words and phrases**

*Wenn du beschreiben willst, in welcher Reihenfolge etwas passiert ist, helfen dir z. B. Zeitangaben (Englisch: **time phrases**) wie* after lunch, at 10 o'clock, after that, an hour later, then *usw.*

▶ SF Linking words and phrases (p. 123)

7 REVISION The Grumbles (Simple present: negative statements)

a) Greg, Griselda, Graham and Grandma Grumble are very negative. Write down their sentences.

1 Greg _____ The sun ☹ shine when we go out. *The sun doesn't shine when we ...*
2 Griselda _____ My friend ☹ call me.
3 Grandma _____ Griselda ☹ listen to nice music on the radio.
4 Graham _____ Dad ☹ take me to the disco on Saturdays.
5 Greg _____ But you ☹ say 'please' or 'thank you', Graham.
6 Grandma _____ The neighbours ☹ talk to us.
7 Griselda _____ Well, they ☹ like us, Grandma!

b) And the Grumbles grumble when they go on holiday too. Can you imagine what they say? Write some more sentences – here's some help: dog at hotel – like me; people at shop – speak English; bus – stop near our hotel; ...

8 REVISION Jobs for the Grumbles (Simple past: positive and negative statements) 🎧

a) Grandma Grumble was away in London yesterday. Before she went, she made a list of nine jobs. Listen. Which three jobs did Graham, Greg and Griselda do? Write them down.

b) Say what the Grumbles did – and what they didn't do.
Graham tidied the living room. But he didn't …

c) Extra Make two short lists.

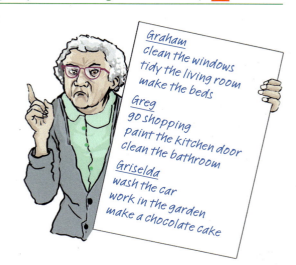

What I did last week	What I didn't do last week
I helped my dad in the garden.	I didn't go shopping.
…	…

9 REVISION Are you a good detective? (Simple past: negative statements)

a) Are you a good detective? Find out what's wrong. (You can check on pp. 12–13.)

1 Ananda went to London in her holidays.
   Ananda didn't go to London – she went to New York.
2 She went by boat.
3 She stayed with her grandparents.
4 Dilip went to Spain.
5 Sophie and Ananda talked to the new boy.
6 Lesley said 'Can we be friends?'.

b) Write some more sentences like this for your partner. Can he/she correct them?

10 REVISION Is your partner a music person? (Simple present: yes/no questions)

a) What do you think: Is your partner a music person? Fill in a copy of the chart. Does he/she …

1 … do his/her homework with music on?
2 … sometimes sing in the shower?
3 … read about pop stars in magazines?
4 … often take an MP3 player to school?
5 … play the piano or sing in a choir?
6 … sometimes listen to live music?

	I think	Partner's answer
1	Yes	No
2	…	…
3		
4		
5		
6		

b) 👥 Now ask your partner the questions. Fill in his/her answers in the chart. Were you right or wrong?
A: Do you do your homework with music on? – B: Yes, I do. / No, I don't.

11 REVISION Did your father watch TV yesterday? (Simple past: yes/no questions)

Use the chart and ask a partner at least ten questions. He/She answers with short answers.

| Did | you
your father
your mother
your grandparents
you and your ...
your pet
your ... | watch TV ...
play ...
listen to ...
phone ...
eat ...
wear ...
read ...
have ...
go to ...
do ... | yesterday?

the day before yesterday?

last Saturday?

in the holidays?
... |

A: Did your grandparents do sport yesterday?
B: Yes, they did. / No, they didn't. / I don't know. / I don't remember.
B: Did ...?
A: ...

12 REVISION Find somebody who ... (Simple past: yes/no questions)

a) *Find somebody in your class who ...*
1 ... went abroad in the holidays.
2 ... stayed at home in the holidays.
3 ... learned to play a new game in the holidays.
4 ... stayed in a hotel or a holiday flat.
5 ... did something for the first time.
You: Did you go abroad in the holidays?
Classmate: Yes, I did./No, I didn't.
Think of at least three more questions.

b) *Report to your neighbour.*
Oliver went abroad.
Anna went to the new swimming pool.
...

I learned to walk through doors in the holidays!

13 REVISION Yesterday afternoon (Simple past: wh-questions)

Partner B: Go to p. 110.
a) Partner A: Ask your partner about the gaps in your chart. Fill in a copy of the chart. Then answer your partner's questions.

	Where did ... go?	How ... go?	What ... do?	When ... go to bed?
Ananda		by bike	do homework + help her mum	
Jo	the Downs	by bike		9.30
Jack				9.30
Sophie	pet shop		buy food for the rabbits	
You				
Your partner				

b) *Write about your partner or one of the Bristol kids. Then swap and check.*

14 WORDS Word building

a) Copy the table and complete it.

happy	unhappy
...	unfriendly
clear	...
comfortable	...
fair	...
interesting	...
sure	...

b) Complete the sentences with the right words from a).
1. I can't sleep in this bed – it's really ...
2. It's ... My sister can go out but I have to stay at home and do all the work.
3. I didn't understand him on the phone. It was very ...
4. She never says good morning. A very ... girl!
5. It's an ... place, a very boring town.
6. He's new, so he's very nervous and ...
7. Why aren't you smiling? Are you ...?

15 More questions (Subject/object questions)

a) Ask Mr Hanson's questions about Jack's first day back at school.
Be careful – do you need *do/does/did* or not?
1. What – happen – at school today?
   What happened at school today?
2. Where – new girl – come from?
3. Who – talk to her?
4. What – she – say?
5. What – Sophie and Ananda - do – then?
6. Who – she – sit next to?
7. What – Mr Kingsley – say?
8. Who – go away on holiday?
9. Where – Sophie – go?

b) Answer these questions:
1. Where did you go at the weekend?
2. Who went with you?

c) Write two more pairs of questions for your partner, one with *do/does/did*, one without. Can he/she answer them? You can use these verbs:

> argue with • find • like •
> phone • see • talk to • ...

16 GETTING BY IN ENGLISH First day back at school

a) Anke made friends with an English girl, Tamsin, in her holidays. One day Tamsin phones from England. They talk about their first day back at school. Write the dialogue down in the right order.

Tamsin — Hello, this is Tamsin here.
Anke — Yes, school started here today too.
Tamsin — How was it?
Anke — Oh, it's different every day. At 11.15 today. Because it was the first day. One o'clock usually.
Tamsin — Oh, I'm OK. I'm back at school now.
Anke — School starts really early in Germany. Eight o'clock.
Tamsin — What time did you have to start?
Anke — Tamsin! Anke here. How are you?
Tamsin — Eight. That is early. I get up at eight on school days. When do you go home?
Anke — It was very nice. I saw all my friends again.
Tamsin — One o'clock! You call that 'a day at school'? We finish at 3.30 in the afternoon. I should live in Germany.

b) Make notes about your first day back at school. Now imagine a friend from England phones you and asks you about your first day. Prepare a dialogue. Act it out for the class.

Saved!

> Look at the pictures. Where and when do you think the story takes place?

The sun came through the window of the caravan. Dan opened his eyes and looked round. His dad was still asleep. From the top bunk Dan could hear the 'bleep bleep' of a
5 gameboy.
'Hi, Jo,' he whispered.
'Hi, Dan!' Jo jumped down. 'Breakfast?'
'Good idea!' said Dan.
Dan made the tea and some toast, Jo went and
10 got milk.
'Mmm, is that breakfast?' Mr Shaw sat up.
'Morning, Dad. Can we pull out the table?'
'Yes, please!'

After breakfast they went to Hayle Beach.
15 'Do you want to go swimming, boys?' Mr Shaw asked.
'Yeah!' Jo said.
'Come on, then! Let's go before the tide starts to go out – it's much too dangerous then.'

20 As they came out of the water, Dan saw Jody. He and Jo sometimes talked to her when they met her on the beach.
'Hi, Jody!' Dan called.
'Who's that?' Mr Shaw asked.
25 'That's Jody. She's really nice, Dad,' Dan said.
'She's staying in the village with her aunt,' Jo said. 'What about a game of football, Jody?' he called.
'Maybe, but I want to go swimming first. See
30 you!' She ran into the sea.

Jo went to get the football. Soon lots of other people joined the Shaws' game.
'Dan, what are you looking at?' shouted his dad. But it was too late: the ball flew past Dan and one of the others had it.   35

'Oh, Dan!' Jo grumbled.
'It's Jody,' Dan said. 'Look, she's so far away. And the tide is going out too.'
'So what? She's a good swimmer.' Jo went back to the game. But Dan looked out to sea again.   40
Suddenly, Jody started to wave.
'Oh, no! She's in trouble. Dad, Dad!' Dan shouted.
'Dan, the ball!' But Dan didn't hear him.
'Dad,' Dan shouted, 'We have to do something.   45
Look!'
Mr Shaw looked out to sea. Other people looked out to sea too. One man had binoculars.
'The boy's right. That swimmer is in trouble,' he said.   50
'Dad, where's your mobile? We have to call the lifeboat,' Dan said.
'Right,' Mr Shaw said. He dialled 999.
'Lifeboat, please,' he said.

55 A few minutes later the man with the binoculars shouted, 'There's the lifeboat! It's coming from St Ives, I can see it.'
'But where's Jody? I can't see Jody!' Dan was really scared.

60 'It's all right,' the man said. 'I can see her. But she isn't waving now. Maybe she's too tired. Now the lifeboat is almost there … it's there. Oh, I can't see her … Wait … they've got her, now they're pulling her out, but …'
65 'Dad, do you think Jody's OK?' asked Dan. 'Can we drive to St Ives and see her? Please, Dad.'
'Come on then,' said Mr Shaw.

Working with the text

1 Who was it?
Who …
1 … made breakfast?
2 … went and got the milk?
3 … went swimming together?
4 … went swimming alone?
5 … played football?
6 … saw Jody was in trouble?
7 … called the lifeboat?
8 … got Jody out of the water?

ST IVES TIMES & ECHO

Help in a twinpack
Bristol boys save swimmer

Photo: R. Cousins

On Tuesday, 21st August the St Ives lifeboat went out to save a young swimmer, 70 Jody Brooks, 14, from London.
'I'm a good swimmer,' the teenager said, 'But I didn't know about the tides.'
Jo Shaw, 13, from Bristol, said, 'I saw her swim out. And then I saw her wave. "She's in 75 trouble, because the tide is going out!" I said to my dad. So he called the lifeboat.'
The exciting story had a happy ending: the lifeboat got to Jody in time.
'The lifeboatmen saved my life,' Jody said, 80 'And the twins!'

2 What's different?
a) How is the story different from the newspaper report? Find examples and make a list:

The story	The newspaper report
Dan …	Jo …
…	

Now explain why Dan was angry with Jo.

b) Write a new, correct report.

DOSSIER A holiday adventure

Write a short story about a holiday adventure. It can be funny/exciting/not true/… First organize your ideas. Look back at the Study Skills box on p. 18. Remember: you can link your sentences with time phrases.

▶ SF Stop – Check – Go (p. 114) • WB 20 (p. 14)
Checkpoint 1 ▶ WB (p. 15)

Extra A trip to Jamaica

1 Mr Kingsley's talk 🎧
Mr Kingsley is telling Form 8PK about his trip to Jamaica in the Caribbean.

a) Listen to the CD. Make notes about Mr Kingsley's talk. Use these questions as headings.
- What sort of place is it?
- What is the weather like?
- What can you see there?
- Are the people rich or poor?

b) 👥 Compare your notes with a partner. Then check them with other students in class.

c) Grace Nichols comes from the Caribbean. Read her poem below. Then look again at the pictures. Which pictures go with the poem? Why? Which picture does not go with the poem? Describe it.

d) Learn the poem by heart. Choose some music to go with the poem and recite it to the music.

Sea Timeless Song

Hurricane come	Hibiscus bloom	Tourist come
and hurricane go	then dry-wither so	and tourist go
but sea … sea timeless	but sea … sea timeless	but sea … sea timeless
sea timeless	sea timeless	sea timeless
sea timeless	sea timeless	sea timeless
sea timeless	sea timeless	sea timeless
sea timeless	sea timeless	sea timeless

by Grace Nichols

2 Anansi and the calabash of wisdom – an Afro-Caribbean legend 🎧

a) Look at the pictures. Describe what Anansi the spider is doing. You can use words from the box.
Anansi the spider is sitting ...

sit • green and yellow calabash • ask • climb • front • talk • back • throw

b) Now listen to the CD.

c) Do you know any wise people? How can you become wise? What would you do with all your wisdom?

Unit 2
What money can buy

Where does your pocket money go?

Last month we asked our readers:
1 How do you spend your pocket money?
2 Do you save any of your pocket money?

Lots of readers answered our questions. Here are the results of the survey.

1 Our readers spend their money on …

Food and drink

Clothes

Free-time activities

2 Most readers save some money

35% I don't save any pocket money.

65% I save some pocket money.

Other

1 Talking about shopping
Look at the words in the box. Put them in these groups: food and drink, spare time, clothes, other. Add more words to the groups.

> blouse • cap • CD • cinema ticket • comic • crisps • fruit • jacket • magazine • make-up • mobile phone • (bottle of) orange juice • pens and pencils • present • pullover • skirt • sports gear • sweets • (pair of) trousers

STUDY SKILLS Learning words – Step 2

*Vokabeln kannst du dir besser merken, wenn du sie in **Wortfeldern** lernst. Um ein Wortfeld zusammen zu stellen, brauchst du erst einen Oberbegriff (**group word**). Bei red, green und blue zum Beispiel ist der Oberbegriff colours.*

▶ SF Learning words – Step 2 (p. 115)

2 Extra 👥 GAME
Choose something from the box in 1. Describe where it is in the picture. Can your partner find it?
A: What are they? They're under 'clothes', near the bottom. They're white.
B: The pair of trousers! – What is it: it's …

3 Where does your pocket money go?
a) 👥 Ask your partner questions.
– What do you buy with your pocket money?
– Who goes shopping with you?
– What do your parents buy for you?
– Do you save any of your pocket money? How much? What would you like to buy with it?

b) Tell the class about your partner.
Maria usually buys … with her pocket money. She saves … every week. …

▶ P 1–2 (p. 33) • WB 1–3 (pp. 16–17)

1 Who needs money? 🎧

Prunella   What's the matter, Sophie?
Sophie   I had an awful day!
Prunella   Mine was awful too.
Sophie   Oh, was it? Tell me all about it.
Prunella   No, tell me about yours first.
Sophie   Well, Jack's mum lost her job yesterday. So he was really sad. And then Ananda and Dilip had an argument about lunch money.
Prunella   Whose money – his or hers?
Sophie   Hers. It disappeared. So Dilip shouted at her: 'You lost your lunch money!' And Ananda shouted back: 'No, somebody took it!'
Prunella   Just like you and Emily!
Sophie   Don't make jokes about it, Prunella.
Prunella   Why not?
Sophie   My parents have got lots of money; theirs haven't, OK?
Prunella   OK, OK. But who needs money? I don't!
Sophie   Well I do! I want to buy a new book on Saturday but I haven't got much pocket money left.

> Why was Prunella's day awful? Think of two things.

2 SONG Chair rap 🎧

Do the rap in a group of four.

This chair is yours, that chair is mine.
Yeah, that's fine, yeah, that's fine!
This chair is hers, that chair is his.
Yes, it is, yes, it is!
These chairs are ours, those chairs are theirs.
Make new pairs, make new pairs!

Go on with a different partner. This bag/... is yours, that bag is ...

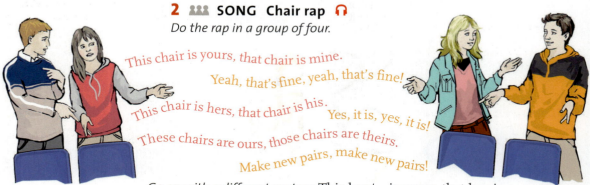

▶ GF 5: *Possessive pronouns (p. 130)* • P 3–4 (pp. 33–34) • WB 4–7 (pp. 17–19)

3 Now you

Make notes about a bad day. Then write a short dialogue with a partner. Act it out for the class. Look at 1) and on the right for ideas.

- I had an awful/ terrible/... day.
- Mine was ... too.
- What happened?

- I lost ... • I/... had an argument with ... • We had a ... test. • It was very difficult. • Somebody took ... • It was too hot/cold/...

4 Money problems 🎧

'Can I have some money, Mum?' Jack asked. Mrs Hanson looked up from her newspaper. 'What for, Jack?' she asked.
Jack didn't say anything for a moment. 'I'm sorry, Mum, but I need a new pair of trainers. My old ones are too small.'
'Don't be sorry, dear,' his mum said. 'Kids grow!'
'But I know we haven't got much money right now,' Jack said.
'Yes, we had more money when I had a job, but there's enough for most things.'
'Are you looking for a new one, Mum?' Jack pointed to the newspaper in his mother's hands. It was open at the job adverts. 'Are there any jobs for you in there?'
'Well, there aren't many interesting jobs,' his mum said. 'But there must be one somewhere. I'm sure I can find something soon.'

▶ GF 6: Compounds with some and any (p. 130) • P 5–8 (pp. 34–35) • WB 8–11 (pp. 19–21)

▷ What does Jack need? Why does he think it's a problem?

5 Extra How much can you buy for £10?

▷ What do Q and A mean on the magazine's problem page?
Can you save money too? Think of some ideas and tell the class.

6 Now you

a) Think: You've got €10 to spend with a partner. What do you want to buy? Write a list.

b) Pair: Compare your lists and agree on a new list together.

c) Share: Compare your shopping list with another pair. Do you really need everything on the list? How can you save some money?

7 Ananda's letter to her grandma 🎧

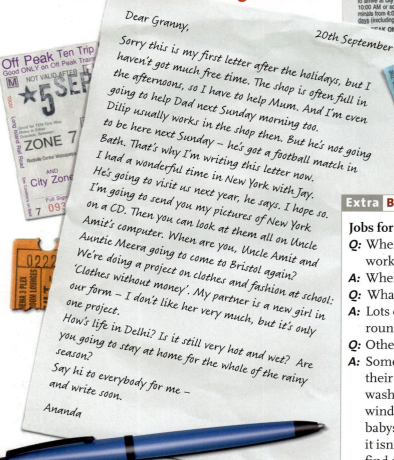

Dear Granny,
20th September

Sorry this is my first letter after the holidays, but I haven't got much free time. The shop is often full in the afternoons, so I have to help Mum. And I'm even going to help Dad next Sunday morning too. Dilip usually works in the shop then. But he's not going to be here next Sunday – he's got a football match in Bath. That's why I'm writing this letter now.

I had a wonderful time in New York with Jay. He's going to visit us next year, he says. I hope so. I'm going to send you my pictures of New York on a CD. Then you can look at them all on Uncle Amit's computer. When are you, Uncle Amit and Auntie Meera going to come to Bristol again?

We're doing a project on clothes and fashion at school: 'Clothes without money'. My partner is a new girl in our form – I don't like her very much, but it's only one project.

How's life in Delhi? Is it still very hot and wet? Are you going to stay at home for the whole of the rainy season?

Say hi to everybody for me – and write soon.

Ananda

Extra Background File

Jobs for kids
- **Q:** When can kids start work in Britain?
- **A:** When they're 13.
- **Q:** What jobs can they do?
- **A:** Lots of kids do a paper round before school.
- **Q:** Other things too?
- **A:** Some kids do jobs for their neighbours. They wash the car, clean the windows, or do some babysitting. Of course, it isn't always easy to find a job.

▶ What does the letter tell you about Ananda's family and where they live? Have you got any family in another country? Tell the class about them.

Looking at language

Find sentences in **7** where Ananda talks or asks about people's plans. Write them down like this:

	(Question word)	form of to be	going to	infinitive
+		I'm He's …	going to …	help
–		He's not	…	
?	When	… …		

How do you form the going to-future?

8 Who is it?

a) Which people in the book have got these plans?

- I'm going to repeat everything. Yes, I am! Yes, I am!
- We're going to phone New Zealand at the weekend.
- I'm going to ask Emily for a date at the weekend.
- I'm going to go surfing on the roof tonight.

b) 👥 Write some plans for some other Bristol people. Can your partner guess who they are?

▶ GF 7: going to-future (p. 131) • P 9–10 (pp. 35–36) • WB 12 (p. 21)

9 New clothes from old 🎧

Ananda and Sophie are in Sophie's room.

Sophie	When are you going to talk to Lesley about your clothes project?
Ananda	Tomorrow at lunch break.
Sophie	Jack's going to come here later for ours. And I've got an idea. Look.
Ananda	A photo album?
Sophie	Yes, photos of my mum when she was a teenager. We can compare teenagers' clothes then and now and make a poster. Look at this photo of her: 'Skirts were longer.'
Ananda	Well, that skirt is longer, but what about that short skirt in that photo?
Sophie	Wow! You're right. That's much shorter than skirts today.
Ananda	That red dress is nice. Your mum looks very pretty in that.
Sophie	This one with flowers is nicer. Look.
Ananda	No, it's not as nice as the red one. Your mum looks much prettier in the red dress.
Sophie	But that hat! It's too big – yuck!
Ananda	'Hats were bigger then.'
Sophie	Well, what do you think of my idea?
Ananda	Not bad. There are worse ideas.
Sophie	Well, I think it's really good.
Ananda	Yes, it's very good, Soph, but I think I've got a better one. Look at this advert for old clothes in your magazine. I think you should wear your mum's old clothes!
Sophie	She hasn't got them any more. But … wait a minute. Thanks Ananda. That's it!

▶ What is Sophie's first project idea? What do you think: is Ananda's idea better or worse? At the end Sophie says, 'That's it!' Has she got another idea? What can it be?

The Sixties Shop

Be the **coolest** girl in town with clothes from the past.

We Have:
- the **biggest** selection of dresses from the 60s
- the **shortest** skirts
- the **prettiest** tops and blouses
- the **wildest** colours
- the **cheapest** prices
- the **fastest** service
- the **best** website

www.sixties-shop.co…

Looking at language

Complete a copy of the chart.

short	shorter	shortest
nice	nicer	…
big	…	…
pretty	…	…
good	…	…
bad	…	…

How do you compare things in English? Look for comparisons in **9**.

▶ GF 8a, c, d: Comparison of adjectives (pp. 132–133) • P 11–14 (pp. 36–37) • WB 13 (p. 22)

10 Now you

a) 👥 Make comparisons. Here are some ideas:

hamsters/cats/… • English/Maths/… • Germany/England/… • text message/e-mail/…

big • cold • cool • easy • fast • good • hot • long • pretty • rainy • small • sunny

A: Cats are faster than hamsters.
B: Yes, but hamsters are cooler.
  English is …

b) Make as many comparisons as you can.

…	is	the best	band	in the world.
	are	the biggest	…	…
		the …		

11 Project ideas 🎧

Ananda — So, the project is 'Clothes without money'. Not very interesting.
Lesley — No.
Ananda — Why don't we do a report on cheap clothes at a charity shop?
Lesley — Boring.
Ananda — Then what about a poster?
Lesley — That's more boring.
Ananda — Maybe we can do something about clothes on the internet?
Lesley — That must be the most boring idea in the world! My project has to be the most interesting project in the form.
Ananda — OK, so what ideas have you got?
Lesley — Recycling.
Ananda — What about it?
Lesley — You are slow. Clothes with recycled stuff.
Ananda — Like a dress from old newspapers?
Lesley — Maybe.
Ananda — Mmm, I like that.
Lesley — So let's do it.

▶ Who has got more ideas for the project, Ananda or Lesley? Who do you think has got the best idea? Would you like to do this project? Why or why not?

▶ P 17–18 (p. 39) • WB 15–19 (pp. 23–25)

12 👥 A dangerous pet

Choose an adjective from the red box and a noun from the blue box, e.g. dangerous and pet. Think of three dangerous pets. Tell your group about them:

> beautiful • boring • dangerous • difficult •
> exciting • expensive • fantastic • interesting •
> terrible • wonderful

> book • city • holiday place • pet • subject •
> TV show

My words are 'dangerous' and 'pet'. I think an elephant is a dangerous pet. A ... is more dangerous than an elephant. But a ... is the most dangerous pet.

▶ GF 8b, d: Comparison of adjectives (pp. 132–133) • P 15–16 (p. 38) • WB 14 (p. 22)

13 Extra SONG The Kinks: Low budget 🎧

...
Excuse my shoes they don't quite fit
They're a special offer and they hurt me a bit
Even my trousers are giving me pain
They were reduced in a sale so I shouldn't complain
They squeeze me so tight so I can't take no more
They're size 28 but I take 34

I'm on a low budget
What did you say
I'm on a low budget
I thought you said that
I'm on a low budget
I'm a cut-price person in a low budget land
...

(by Ray Davies)

Practice **2** 33

1 STUDY SKILLS Wortfelder

a) Which of the four words is the group word?
1 cola • drink • juice • lemonade
2 dance • hobby • models • music
3 Art • Geography • PE • subject
4 dog • hamster • parrot • pet
5 apple • banana • fruit • orange
6 fish • food • fruit • meat
7 clothes • jeans • shoes • socks
8 bedroom • hall • kitchen • room

b) Put the words in order from small to large.
Find a group word from the box for each list.
1 cafeteria • classroom • desk
   desk • classroom • cafeteria: *school*
2 car • bus • train
3 bathroom • cupboard • living room
4 fridge • plate • sink
5 basketball • table-tennis ball • tennis ball
6 letter • sentence • word

> ball • building • English • food • house •
> kitchen • picture • room • school • sport •
> story • trip

2 WORDS Clothes

a) Read the sentences and find the right words. The pictures help you.
1 You wear them on your feet when you play football.
2 Girls wear them in summer – and sometimes to parties.
3 Boys and girls wear them when it's hot or when they do sport.
4 Every boy and girl has got a pair of these – usually they're blue.
5 When it's cold you can wear this over a shirt or blouse.
6 Your clothes are in here when you aren't wearing them.

b) Write one or two sentences like the sentences in a) for your partner. Can he/she guess the word?

c) Complete a copy of the network. You can put it in your DOSSIER.

shorts
pullover
dress
jeans
wardrobe
 trainers
 boots

my favourite clothes — Clothes and me — I often wear
today I'm wearing — I don't like
jeans — I need — I want

3 WORDS 'make' or 'do'?

a) Fill in the right form of the right verb.
1 I often … my bed before I go to school.
2 My brother sometimes … the dishes.
3 We both … our homework in the kitchen.
4 My homework today is to … a model.
5 We are … a project on pocket money.
6 But my brother is … a lot of noise.

b) Do the words in the box go with 'make' or with 'do'? Write four sentences with these words.

> tricks • an exercise • a list • a mistake •
> a report • a sandwich • dinner

4 A Geography lesson (Possessive pronouns)

a) In a Geography lesson the kids are talking about where their clothes and things are from.
Complete the sentences. Use *mine*, *yours*, *his*, *hers*, *ours*, *theirs*.

1 Ananda   My new T-shirt is from China. Where's … from, Sophie?
2 Sophie   … is from China too. What about Dan and Jo: Where do you think … are from?
3 Dan and Jo   Oh, … are from Thailand. And our MP3 players are from Japan. … too, Tom?
4 Tom   No, … is from the USA. And my new mobile is from Finland.
5 David   Simon has got a new mobile too. … is from Taiwan.
6 Jack   Bill's football boots are from Vietnam. Where are … from, Kevin?
7 Kevin   They're from Thailand. Ananda has got new hockey shoes. … are from India.

b) Collect ten things in your group. Swap them with another group. Find out whose they are.

- Yes, you're right. It's mine. It's from Japan.
- No, sorry, it's not mine.
- Is this your watch, Alex?
- I think it's Karla's. Am I right?

5 REVISION Shopping (some and any)

Dan and Jo are at the supermarket. They're doing the shopping for the weekend.
Complete the dialogue with *some* or *any*.

Jo   We need some bananas.
Dan   Yes, and we haven't got … oranges.
Jo   Yuck, I hate oranges. Let's get … apples.
Dan   And we have to get Dad's computer magazine. Did you see … magazines when we came in?
Jo   They haven't got … here. Let's ask that assistant. Maybe she knows where we can get …
Dan   And remember: we have to buy … glue for school.
Jo   School, school, school – it's always the same! I'd like to get … posters!
      We haven't got … new ones in our room.
Dan   You and your posters! We still need … bread and … milk. Have we got … sausages at home?
Jo   I don't know.
Dan   But you had … yesterday.
Jo   Oh, yes! No, we haven't got … left.

6 More shopping (some and any compounds)

Ananda and Sophie are out shopping too.
Complete the dialogue with *something*, *anything*, *somewhere*, …

Sophie   Are there any clothes shops *anywhere* near here?
Ananda   I don't know. But there's a book shop (somewhere) in this street. Let's go there.
Sophie   Ananda, I'm looking for some new clothes.
Ananda   Well, I don't want … to wear. Clothes shops are boring.
Sophie   Can't you look at … different? Shopping with you isn't much fun. Books, books, books.
Ananda   Thank you very much. Well, maybe you should go shopping with … like Jack, or Dan and Jo.
Sophie   But they all hate shopping. Please, let's look for a clothes shop. I need … new. Then we can go to the book shop. Please!

7 PRONUNCIATION Is Bob's pet a cat or a dog? (Consonants at the end of words) 🎧

a) Listen: what sound do you hear at the end of each word? Hold up a red or blue pen:

[b] or [p]   [g] or [k]   [d] or [t]

b) Say the words from the box. Are they *red* or *blue* words? Write them down. Use the right colour. Can you find any pairs? Listen and check.

> add • at • bed • board • date • heard • hurt • pet • played • ride • right • sport • step • web

c) Extra Say these tongue-twisters again and again. Be careful with the ends of the words.
- Ted's red pet has its head in the bed.
- I heard you hurt your head and I heard your head hurt you.
- Mad Cat and Bad Bat sat at the back.

8 How much TV, how many text messages? (much/many – more – most)

a) 👥 Partner B: Look at p. 111. Partner A: Read the information about Lennart. Then ask your partner about Christine. Write the answers in a copy of the chart. Now answer your partner's questions about Lennart.

	Lennart	Christine	You	Your partner
CDs – have got / has got	about 75			
time – need for homework	60 minutes			
hours – sleep at night	7			
text message – get every week	25 to 30			
friends – have / has got	7			
TV – watch every day	5 hours			
money – spend on sweets	€3			

A: How many books does Christine read?
B: One every week.
A: How much time does she …?

b) 👥 Fill in the answers for 'You' and 'Your partner' in your copy of the chart. Then ask your partner and correct your answers.

c) Extra Report to the class. Make comparisons. Use *more* and *most*.
My partner has got more CDs than Christine. I've got more than my partner. But Lennart has got the most. Christine needs more time …

9 8PK's Fashion show (going to-future)

What do you think: who's going to wear what at Form 8PK's fashion show?

Jack
Sophie
Dan
Jo
Ananda
Lesley

1 I think Jack's going to wear the …
2 …

Your class is going to have a fashion show. What are you going to wear? What about your best friend?

10 Lunch break (going to-future)

a) 👥 It's lunch break at Cotham.
What are the people going to do? Ask your partner.
A: What's Ananda going to do?
B: She's going to …
   What are …?
A: …

b) Make appointments for 1, 2 and 3 o'clock with three students in your class. Find out what they are going to do after school, at the weekend, in their next holidays. Report to the class.

11 What do you think? (Comparison of adjectives)

a) Compare the people and things in the pictures.

1 fast

2 funny

3 easy

4 cold

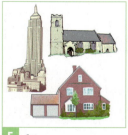
5 big

6 nice

7 pretty

8 clean

1   I think the skates are faster than the bike. But the car is the fastest.

b) 👥 Compare your answers with a partner.
Then, together, think of something faster than …,
funnier than …, … Who's got the fastest/funniest/
… ideas in the class?

12 As big as ... (Comparison of adjectives)

Two things are about the same – one is different. Make sentences:
1 big   Belgium, the Netherlands, the USA
   Belgium is about as big as the Netherlands. The USA is bigger.
2 sunny   England, Germany, Turkey
3 loud   disco, radio, CD player
4 warm   April, August, October
5 cold   Cologne, Paris, Stockholm
6 long   a story in a magazine, a newspaper article, a book
7 fast   a car, a bus, a plane
8 old   mum, dad, grandpa

13 Extra Writing an advert

a) Have you got a pair of inline skates? What can you say about them?

b) Look at the advert. What is new about the MEGA-WHIZZ inline skates?

c) Find all the adjectives. What do you see?

d) Write an advert for one of your favourite products. It can be something for one of your hobbies, a book, a TV show, something to eat or drink, ... Use words like best, fastest, newest, ...
Your advert should have:
– a picture
– a big headline
– information on why your product is so good

e) Present your advert to your class.

MEGA-WHIZZ INLINE SKATES *New model*

the fastest wheels
the best value for your money
the latest technology
the softest softboot

Be the happiest person in the world with **MEGA-WHIZZ INLINE SKATES**

14 LISTENING Quiz show

a) Make two teams. One student from each team goes to the front. Listen to the first question on the CD. Who can buzz first? After your buzz, you've got 10 seconds for your answer.
'What can you wear? Say three things.'
A Shoes, trousers and a cap.
– That's right. One point for Team A. / That's wrong. One point for Team B. Next pair please!

b) Extra Make more questions and have your own quiz show.

15 Jumble sale (Comparison of adjectives)

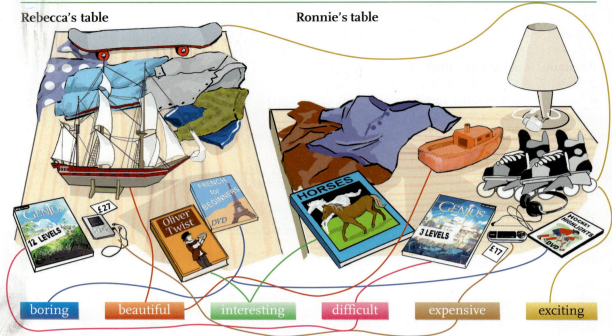

a) Compare the things on the two tables.
Rebecca's computer game is more difficult than Ronnie's.
Ronnie's MP3 player is not as ...

b) Which table do you think is better? Why?

c) Which three things do you think are most interesting/most beautiful/...? Why?
The ... on ...'s table is the most beautiful thing there. ... is my favourite colour.

16 What do you think? (Comparison of adjectives)

a) **Think:** Make questions for a group survey.
Then answer the questions. Make notes.
1 difficult – German / English
What do you think is more difficult – German or English?
2 good – a pet rabbit / a pet dog
What do you think is better – ...
3 exciting – a computer game/a football match
4 interesting – summer by the sea/summer in the mountains
5 nice – a red pullover/a blue pullover
6 boring – three hours in the car/three hours shopping
7 funny – Otto/Mr Bean
8 dangerous – to travel by car/to travel by plane

b) **Pair:** Compare your notes with a partner and discuss your answers.

c) **Share:** Make a group of four. Compare your results and then prepare a report for your class.
Our group thinks German is more difficult than English. Two of us think a pet cat is better ...

17 MEDIATION London shopping 🎧

a) *Imagine you're shopping with your little brother in London. He needs your help. Tell him what the assistant says.*

Assistant	Hi! Can I help you?
You	Yes, please. My brother wants to buy some souvenirs for his best friend.
Assistant	Well, T-shirts and baseball caps are on special offer in the sports department. Most of them are only £3.99 now.
You	Es gibt T-shirts …
Your brother	Langweilig. Ich brauche was Besonderes für Daniel.
You	My brother would like something really special for his friend.
Assistant	Let's see … What about a model? We've got a great model of Big Ben for example. Your brother's friend can put it together at home.
You	…

STUDY SKILLS | **Mediation**

Manchmal musst du zwischen zwei Sprachen vermitteln. Versuche nicht, alles wörtlich zu übersetzen. Gib nur das Wesentliche wieder.

▶ SF Mediation (p. 125)

b) *Now listen to the rest of the dialogue. Tell your little brother what the assistant says.*

c) **Extra** 👥 *Act out the dialogue. Your teacher can give you a copy of the complete text.*

18 GETTING BY IN ENGLISH Shopping for a birthday present

a) *How can you do these things in English? Find one or more phrases for each one.*
1. Jemandem einen Vorschlag machen:
   Let's (go to the cinema); …
2. Sagen, dass man etwas gut/schlecht findet: …
3. Sagen, dass etwas besser/größer/… ist als etwas anderes: …
4. Zustimmen: …

b) 👥 *Partner A: you want to buy a birthday present for your friend Emma. You phone your friend in Germany. Partner B: can you help your English friend? Prepare a dialogue and act it out for the class.*

Partner A

Du sagst, du möchtest Emma einen Fußball kaufen, denn sie mag Sport.

Den Vorschlag findest du gut. Du sagst, dass Taschen nicht billig sind und du gerade nicht viel Geld hast.

Den Vorschlag findest du auch gut. Du fragst B, ob du ihn/sie wieder anrufen kannst, wenn du ein Geschenk hast.

Partner B

Das findest du nicht gut. Du findest, eine Tasche wäre ein besseres Geschenk – die kann sie jeden Tag benutzen.

Du schlägst vor, dass A in einen Second-Hand-Laden geht.

Du bist einverstanden.

The Clothes Project

Part 1 At Sophie's house

> Sophie and Jack are working on 8PK's 'Clothes Project'. Who is with them?

It was Tuesday afternoon, after school. Jack was at Sophie's house. They wanted to work on their clothes project.
'"Clothes without money". What are we going to do?' Jack asked as he took another biscuit.
'I've got an idea.' Sophie said.
'Good!' Jack said. 'I've got ideas about lots of things, but not about clothes. Clothes are really boring!'
'No, they aren't!'
'Yes, they are!'
'Do you want to hear my idea?' Sophie asked.
'Oh, all right,' Jack answered.
'Well,' Sophie said, 'Rachel and Tom want to do a fashion show. And Ananda and Lesley are going to join them and I thought we ...'
'What?!' Jack said. 'Me in a fashion show? No way!'
'Not you. Me. You can be the presenter,' Sophie said.
'Oh – OK. So what's your idea?'
'Come up to the attic and see,' Sophie said.
Prunella floated over to Sophie. 'Oh good! We're going up to the attic!' she said.
'No, we aren't!' Sophie whispered. 'You're staying here.'
'What did you say?' asked Jack.
'Nothing,' Sophie said. 'Come on!'
Prunella was the first in the attic. She went to the shelf with Grandma's plates.
'I love plates!' Prunella said. She took one.
'Careful!' Sophie whispered.
'Oops!' Prunella said and dropped the plate. Crash!
'What was that?' said Jack.
'Er – something fell down, I suppose,' Sophie said. 'Never mind.' She opened a wardrobe and took out a beautiful long blue dress.
'Look at this dress. Isn't it lovely? My grandma made it. She wore it to balls and dances.

And here's a hat and a jacket ... It's all very old, but still beautiful. What do you think?'
'Fashion from Grandma's wardrobe? That's a nice idea. We can say a bit about when she lived and ...'
Suddenly Prunella took the hat from Sophie and floated over to a mirror. She put the hat on. Of course Jack didn't see Prunella – he only saw the hat. He stood there with his mouth open.
'No! I don't like it!' said Prunella and dropped the hat on the floor.
'Ooops! The wind in here!' Sophie said as she ran over to the mirror to get the hat. 'Well then, let's take the stuff down and start work, Jack.' She hurried to the door.
'What about shoes?' Prunella asked.
'Oh, no!' said Sophie.
Crash! A pair of black shoes landed at Jack's feet. Bang! A pair of red shoes followed.
'I don't understand,' said Jack. Wallop! A pair of blue shoes landed in front of him.

'Hey, Sophie, maybe there's a poltergeist in your house.'
Sophie laughed: 'You and your mad ideas, Jack! Now hurry up: we have to prepare our presentation and it has to be ready tomorrow.'
'Hee! Hee! Hee!' laughed Prunella as Sophie took a very puzzled Jack downstairs.

▶ How does Sophie explain the noises and the hat in the attic? How can she explain the shoes?

Part 2 The fashion show 🎧
Now listen to the end of the story. Which person goes with the first part, which person goes with the second part? Which presentation do you think is more interesting?

Working with the text

1 Heads and tails
a) Match the heads and tails of three sentences. Then find a tail for the fourth.

1 Ananda was the model …	… Prunella tried on the hat.
2 When Sophie showed Jack the dress …	… when she wore Grandma's dress.
3 Jack liked Sophie's idea but …	… but Lesley designed the outfit.
4 Sophie looked lovely at the fashion show …	

b) 👥 Write three more heads and tails sentences for your partner. Can he/she put them together?

DOSSIER *A different point of view*

Write the scene in the attic (ll. 29–68) from Jack's point of view. Describe what the attic looks like and what happened. You can start like this:
I went up to the attic with Sophie.
It was great. There were lots of …

---

2 Extra ACTIVITY A fashion show
a) Collect clothes words (e.g. skirt) and useful adjectives (e.g. long/short/brown …). Use a list or a mind map.

b) Prepare your show: collect clothes, choose music, write the presentation, … Then rehearse. Here are some ideas:

Welcome to our fashion show.

We want to show you …   Our topic is …

Please welcome our first/second/… model.

He's/She's wearing …

We found this dress/sweater/… in …

We made this hat/sweater/… from …

c) Put your show on for your class.

▶ WB 20 (p. 26) • Activity page 1   **Checkpoint 2** ▶ WB (pp. 27–29)

2 Topic

Extra Special days around the world

A

- **Fawkes, Guy (1570–1606)** _____

Most famous person in the 'Gunpowder Plot'. On the night of 4 to 5 Nov, 1605, the Catholic Fawkes and his men put 30 barrels of gunpowder under the Parliament building in London. They wanted to blow up the Protestant King James I and his ministers when they met there on 5 Nov. The King's men arrested Fawkes and saved the King. The English celebrate this every year on 5 Nov, 'Guy Fawkes Day': they burn 'Guys' on bonfires and enjoy fireworks.

Guy Fawkes, or 'Bonfire Night', is very popular in Britain.

B

AN E-CARD FROM CATHERINE THOMPSON SHAW

Dan and Jo
Merry Christmas from Down Under

To:
From:
Sent:

The card shows the 'New Zealand Christmas tree'. Its other name is the pohutukawa tree, and it blooms in the summer – at Christmas time. Yes, we aren't going to celebrate at home in front of a fire – we're going to the beach for Christmas! Father Christmas comes on a surfboard every year. That reminds me – did my parcel arrive in time for the holidays? Lots of love – from Pat too!

1 Special days

a) Work in groups of four. Each group reads about one of the four special days and takes notes about these questions:
– What is the special day called?
– Where, when, why and how do people celebrate it?

b) Make a new group with students who read about the other days. Use your notes to tell them about your special day.

2 Now you

Write to a friend in England about a special day in your family. Think about these questions:
1 Why do people celebrate this special day?
2 How does your family celebrate?
3 What do you do/eat/drink/wear/play/...?
4 What are the best things about the celebrations?
5 ...
Ask your teacher for help or use a dictionary.

C

Dear Ananda,

Thank you for your last letter about Valentine's Day. It's always a joy to hear from my granddaughter.

It's spring in Delhi, and it's so beautiful! The sky is clear, and the sun looks wonderful in the morning. And the flowers!

The city seems so quiet after a week of Holi. Do you celebrate Holi in Bristol? The young people have so much fun! They go out in the morning in white clothes and then the fun starts. They throw coloured water and powders till everybody looks like the flowers around us.

At night there's much singing and dancing in the streets. It's very pretty to see the people dance with the colours everywhere. That's what Holi is: the Festival of Colour. It is a day of big bonfires too

D

★ New York City Star ★ July 5

Queens celebrates on a beautiful day

People in Queens celebrated Independence Day yesterday with all the traditions: a morning parade, an afternoon barbecue and evening fireworks.

"It was perfect Fourth of July weather," said Mike Ekster of the National Weather Service. "A clear blue sky and summer temperatures."

The traditional parade began with a band from Benjamin Cardozo High School. Two open cars followed. They were full of tall young men – Cardozo's champion basketball team, including team captain Jay Gupta. Next were about 100 children on bikes and two trucks full of red, white and blue flowers, one with a giant Statue of Liberty.

Photo: Cardozo High School band at the Fourth of July Parade

▶ WB Activity page 4

Unit 3
Animals in the city

Thursday   18 November

7.00 pm BBC 1
Animals in the City

The fox

David Lee-Bingham and the BBC's Natural History Unit in Bristol present this new series about wild animals in the city.
Tonight: The fox and how it survives in our cities. The first in another fine series of animal programmes from the BBC.

BBC 1	CBBC (Children)	ITV 1
5.00 pm **Dance Factory** Finding new dance stars	4.00 pm **The Batman** Cartoon	3.50 pm **Art Attack** Art ideas for young Picassos
5.25 pm **Newsround** News for children	4.30 pm **Raven** Fantasy game show	4.00 pm **Clever Heads** Quiz show
5.35 pm **Ready, Steady, Cook** Who can cook the best meal in 20 minutes?	5.00 pm **The Basil Brush Show** Comedy series with TV's favourite fox	4.30 pm **My Parents are Aliens** Series Mel and Josh argue
6.00 pm **BBC News and Weather**	5.30 pm **Jonny Wilkinson's Hotshots** Learn to play with the rugby superstar	5.00 pm **The Paul O'Grady Show** Chat show
6.30 pm **Points West** News, sport and weather for the west of England	6.30 pm **Blue Peter** The children's magazine's Book of the Year show	6.00 pm **Around the West Country** Local News
7.00 pm **Animals in the City** Documentary series		

1 Now you

a) It's a special day and you can watch TV for an hour and a half. Which English TV programmes would you like to watch? Make a list.

b) 👥 Talk to your partner about your list.
A: I'd like to watch … at … pm.
B: Oh, no, I hate …
A: I'm going to watch …
B: Yes, I'm going to watch … too.
A: I love sport programmes/quiz shows/…
Then I'm going to …

c) Think of your three favourite programmes on German TV and make notes on them:
– When is the programme on?
– What sort of programme is it: documentary, news, game show, quiz, comedy, sports, cartoon, series, chat show, …?
– How long is it?

d) 👥 Tell your group about your programme but don't say its name. Can they guess what it is?

2 Talking about animals 🎧

a) 👥 Look at the photos. Can you see these animals where you live? What other animals can you see? Talk to a partner.

A: There are hedgehogs in the park near our flat. You don't often see them.
B: I saw a deer in the park last month. It …

b) Make notes or a mindmap about an animal. It can be an animal from the photos or a different one. Use these headings:
– Where does it live?   – What does it eat?
– When does it sleep?   – …

c) Use your notes and tell the class about your animal.
Frogs live in or near water. They make lots of noise at night, so I think they sleep in the day. I don't know what they eat. They can jump very far.

d) Listen to the radio interview with the presenter of 'Animals in the City'. What animals does he name? What's their order in the series?

Programme	1	2	3	4	5
Animals	foxes	…			

▶ P 1 (p. 50) • WB 1 (p. 30)

STUDY SKILLS Listening

Vielleicht fällt es dir manchmal schwer, einen Hörtext zu verstehen. So kannst du dir helfen:
– Lies dir die Aufgabe gut durch, um dich einzustimmen. Worum geht es in dem Hörtext? Was genau sollst du herausfinden?
– Bereite deine Notizen vor. In Aufgabe 2 d) oben kannst du z.B. die Tabelle vorschreiben. Weitere Tipps findest du auf S. 119.

▶ SF Listening (p. 119)

Woodpecker

Grey squirrel

Frog

Deer

Hedgehog

Mole

1 Hello hedgehogs!

Ananda opened the back door, walked over to the dustbin and put the rubbish in. Suddenly she saw two baby hedgehogs.
'You poor little things. Where's your mum? You'll be very cold tonight without her.'
She looked round the yard. Their mother wasn't there. Ananda went inside.
'Sophie knows all about animals,' she thought. So she called her.

'You'll have to wait,' Sophie said. 'Maybe their mother will come and get them.'
'Maybe she won't come back tonight,' Ananda said. 'Then what? Will they need milk?'
'No, they won't need milk. It's bad for them. But they'll need water.'
'OK. What about food? Will they be hungry?'
'Yes, they'll probably be hungry. But they won't eat. They'll be too scared, I think.'
'Oh, Sophie, they won't survive without their mum! I know they won't.'
'I think they will, Ananda. I know: mail that TV programme "Animals in the City". Their Animal Hotline will help.'

> Write Ananda's e-mail to the Animal Hotline.

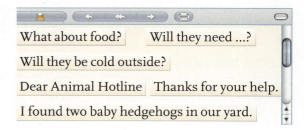

What about food?   Will they need …?
Will they be cold outside?
Dear Animal Hotline   Thanks for your help.
I found two baby hedgehogs in our yard.

2 Now you

a) Finish these sentences for yourself.
In 20 years I'll probably … / I probably won't …

> be a pop star • be married • have a family •
> have a horse • like the same music •
> live abroad • live at home • travel to the moon •
> …

b) 👥 Compare with a partner.
A: What do you think? Will you be a pop star in 20 years?
B: Yes, I will. / No, I won't. Will you?

Looking at language

Collect statements and questions with **'ll**, **will**, **won't**:
'You'll be very cold tonight …'
'Will they …?'
'But they won't …'

Look again at **1.** *What time are Sophie and Ananda talking about when they use* **will** *and* **won't**? *When do you use* **'ll/will**? *When do you use* **won't**?

▶ GF 9: will-future (p. 134) • P 2–4 (pp. 50–51) • WB 2–3 (p. 31)

3 Animal Hotline's answer 🎧

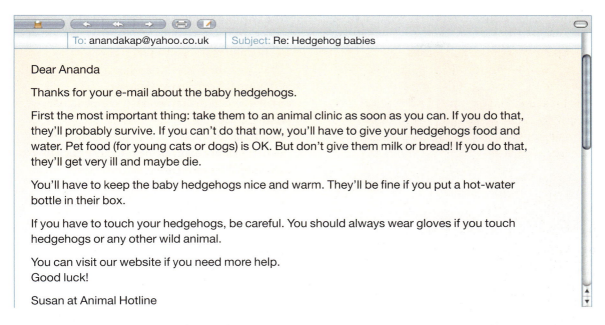

To: anandakap@yahoo.co.uk | Subject: Re: Hedgehog babies

Dear Ananda

Thanks for your e-mail about the baby hedgehogs.

First the most important thing: take them to an animal clinic as soon as you can. If you do that, they'll probably survive. If you can't do that now, you'll have to give your hedgehogs food and water. Pet food (for young cats or dogs) is OK. But don't give them milk or bread! If you do that, they'll get very ill and maybe die.

You'll have to keep the baby hedgehogs nice and warm. They'll be fine if you put a hot-water bottle in their box.

If you have to touch your hedgehogs, be careful. You should always wear gloves if you touch hedgehogs or any other wild animal.

You can visit our website if you need more help.
Good luck!

Susan at Animal Hotline

> What will happen if …
… Ananda puts a hot-water bottle in the hedgehogs' box?
… Ananda gives the baby hedgehogs cat food?
… Ananda takes the hedgehogs to an animal clinic?

👥 Write down two more 'What will happen if …' questions and swap them with your partner.

Looking at language

Find all the sentences with **if** in **3**. Write them down like this. Use different colours for the clauses.

if-clause	main clause
If you do …, …	they'll probably … …

main clause	if-clause
They'll be … …	if you put … …

What different verb forms are there in the two clauses?

4 Now you
a) Think what you'll do if …
– it rains tomorrow
If it rains tomorrow, I'll go to school by bus.
– you can't understand your Maths homework
– you see a deer in your garden
– there's a great film on TV at 11 tonight
– you win 500 euros in a quiz

b) 👥 Ask your partner questions and find out what he/she will do.
A: What will you do if it rains tomorrow?
B: I'll stay in bed.

▶ GF 10: Conditional sentences 1 (p. 135) • P 5–8 (pp. 52–53)
• WB 4–10 (pp. 32–35)

5 Dilip killed my hedgehogs 🎧

'So,' Ananda explained, 'first I fed the hedgehogs. Then I took them slowly and carefully back to the yard. But this morning, when I went out very quietly with some water, the yard was empty.'
'Empty?' asked Sophie.

'Yes,' Ananda said sadly, 'Dilip put all the old boxes out for the rubbish collection. He killed my hedgehogs!'
'That's terrible!' said Jack.
'I'm sure there's an explanation,' said Dan.
Jo sat down at the table. 'Hey, people, guess what?!'
'What?' asked Jack.
'Simon's new pen disappeared at break,' Jo said. 'And guess who was in the classroom at break?'
'Who?' asked Ananda.
'Lesley, of course!' he went on quietly. 'Do you know what I think …?'
Just then Sophie jumped up. 'Look, there's Dilip,' she said. She walked over to him quickly. 'You horrible person: you killed Ananda's hedgehogs,' she shouted angrily.
'No, I didn't!' said Dilip. 'I put them in the garage. They're warm and safe.'

Looking at language

a) How do people do or say things?
In your exercise book, write down phrases from **5** like 'Then I took them slowly …'. What word describes **how** somebody does something? Underline it.

b) What adjectives do these adverbs come from?
slowly   slow
carefully   …
angrily   …
quietly   …

---

6 👥 ACTIVITY The funniest sentence

a) Form groups of three. Fold a piece of paper into three columns. In the left-hand column write a list of five people/animals. Then fold the column so that nobody can see it and pass the piece of paper to your left.

b) Now write five verbs in the middle column. Fold the middle column back and pass the piece of paper to your left again.

c) Write five adverbs from the box in the right-hand column. Open up the piece of paper. Read the sentences to each other. Who's got the funniest?

d) Read your group's funniest sentence to the class.

My mum	tells jokes	dangerously.
Our teacher	sings	fantastically.
Jennifer	paints	strangely.
Brad Pitt	dances	rudely.
The elephant	eats pizza	angrily.

angrily • badly • beautifully • boringly • clearly • cleverly • dangerously • easily • fantastically • funnily • happily • loudly • madly • nervously • nicely • prettily • quickly • quietly • rudely • sadly • strangely • sweetly • terribly • wonderfully

▶ GF 11a–b, d: Adverbs of manner: use (p. 136) • P 9–10 (p. 53) • WB 11–13 (pp. 36–37)

7 Goodbye hedgehogs 🎧

'You did a good job with the hedgehogs,' said the woman at the RSPCA Animal Clinic. 'You looked after them well.'

'Really?' Ananda asked.

'The babies will be fine – you did well. Now, if you want to see the clinic, one of our volunteers can show you everything.'

Steve showed Ananda the small animals: 'This rabbit came with a broken leg. She still can't run fast, but she's moving more quickly now. Rabbits have to be fast if they want to survive. In a week or two she'll be back in the woods again.'

'I'd like to help animals too,' Ananda said. 'Is it hard work?'

'Well yes, I work hard,' Steve answered. 'But I enjoy it. I'm afraid you have to be 16 to be a volunteer. But you can collect money for the RSPCA. We're planning a fun run: you run, and for each mile, people give you money. Then you give the money to the RSPCA.'

▷ Do people have fun runs where you live?

8 More about animals

Complete a copy of the chart. Scan these web pages for the missing information. Who can finish first?

www.EnglishG.de/A2/fox
www.EnglishG.de/A2/squirrel
www.EnglishG.de/A2/hedgehog

	foxes	squirrels	hedgehogs
food			
number of babies			
enemies			

STUDY SKILLS Scanning

Wenn du nach bestimmten Informationen suchst, brauchst du meist nicht den ganzen Text zu lesen. Suche statt dessen nach einem Schlüsselwort und lies nur dort genauer.

▶ SF Scanning (p. 120) • P 12 (p. 54) • WB 16 (p. 39)

Extra Background File

The Royal Society for the Prevention of Cruelty to Animals (RSPCA)

Most people in Britain love animals, but it wasn't always like that. Back in 1824, lots of people were cruel to animals. That's why a small group of animal lovers started the Society for the Prevention of Cruelty to Animals. (The 'Royal' came later.) Today the RSPCA is a big organization. If somebody is cruel to an animal anywhere in Britain, an RSPCA inspector will soon be there. For more information, visit their website at:
www.rspca.org.uk

Looking at language

You did a good job. – You did well.
Which one is an adjective, which is an adverb?
Find the words fast and hard in 7. Are they adjectives or adverbs?

▶ GF 11c: Adverbs of manner: irregular forms (p. 136) • P 11 (p. 54) • WB 14–15 (pp. 37–38)

▶ **Extra** GF 11e: Comparison of adverbs of manner (p. 137)

DOSSIER Animals

Write a short report about one of the animals. The phrases below can help you.
Add pictures. You can put your report in your dossier.

… lives in the woods/…
It eats …
The female has her babies in the spring/…
She usually has one/two/…
It has no/a few/… natural enemies.
Its biggest enemy is …

▶ P 13–16 (pp. 54–55) • WB 17–18 (p. 40)

3 Practice

1 WORDS Animals

a) *Put the animals in two groups:* **pets** *and* **wild animals**. *Can any go in both groups?*

> budgies • cats • deer • dogs • elephants • fish • foxes • frogs • guinea pigs • hamsters • hedgehogs • horses • mice • moles • parrots • rabbits • squirrels • tortoises • woodpeckers

b) *Which adjectives go with which animals? Match them.*

> beautiful • big • clever • dangerous • fast • little • pretty • quiet • scary • slow • strange • sweet • ...

c) *Use some of the adjectives and write a sentence or two about an animal. Don't use the animal's name. Can your partner guess what it is?*
A: My animal is little and fast and very sweet.
B: Is it a guinea pig?
A: Yes, it is./No, it isn't.

2 In 2050 (will-future)

a) *What will probably happen in 2050? Write out a caption for each picture with* **will** *or* **won't**.

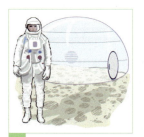
1 live – on Mars

2 not use – computers

3 not live – in hotels

4 be warm – in winter

5 fly – to work

6 not read – books

7 not need – shops

8 live – under the sea

1. In 2050 people will probably live on Mars.   2. In 2050 babies probably won't ...

b) **Extra** *Do you and your partner agree with the captions?*
A: Caption 1 says: 'In 2050 people will probably live on Mars'. I think that's wrong.
B: I don't agree with you. I really think people will live on Mars then. What about caption 2?

3 Fifi the fortune-teller (will-future)

a) *Prunella wants to know about Sophie's future. So she goes to Fifi the fortune-teller. Fill in the correct forms of the will-future.*

1 ... Sophie ... (be) a doctor, like her mum?
– No, she ... (not be) a doctor. Maybe she ... (be) a teacher.
Will Sophie be a doctor, like her mum?
– No, she ...
2 ... she ... (have) children?
– Oh, yes. She ... (have) at least three children.
3 Where ... she (live)? ... she still ... (live) in this house in 20 years?
– I don't know where she ... (live), but she ... (not be) here.
4 When ... she ... (go away)?
– She ... (go away) when she's twenty.
5 Oh! But ... I (see) Sophie again?

b) *Your partner is a fortune-teller. Write down five questions for him/her. Swap questions and answer them. You can use some of Prunella's questions.*

4 READING A book: No Small Thing

Read about the book on the right. Then answer the questions.

1 No Small Thing is a book for ...
A just boys.
B just girls.
C old people.
D young people.

2 Life is difficult for Nathaniel and his sisters. The reason is ...
A a dangerous fire.
B a single parent.
C no money.
D no horse.

3 Nathaniel and his sisters read that somebody wants to ...
A give away a horse.
B buy a horse.
C sell a horse.
D ride a horse.

4 Nathaniel's mother says the children can ...
A buy a horse.
B get a free horse.
C not buy a horse.
D not have a horse.

5 It is *not* sure that the children ...
A are good to the horse.
B have fun with it.
C sell it.
D ride it.

6 After the fire ...
A Smokey is dead.
B Smokey is hurt.
C Smokey is not there.
D Smokey is OK.

7 Later the family sells ...
A the barn.
B the house.
C newspapers.
D Smokey.

STUDY SKILLS Multiple-choice exercises

Lies bei Multiple-Choice-Aufgaben erst alle Lösungen durch, bevor du dich entscheidest.

No Small Thing • by Natale Ghent
Ages 10–14, 256 pages

Life isn't easy for Nathaniel and his two sisters, Queenie and Cid. Their father left them and they live with their single mother. They all want something to make them a happy family again. One day, the children see an advert in the newspaper for a free horse. First they don't tell their mother. They're sure she will say no. But, when they tell her, she agrees. With Smokey, the children feel happy again. They ride him, take care of him, and share many happy hours together. Then one day there's a fire in Smokey's barn. Luckily, Smokey survives. But things get worse when the family has to sell their house and somebody wants to buy Smokey.
No Small Thing is a great horse story, warm and funny. Put it on your book list and read it soon!

▶ *SF Multiple-choice exercises (p. 118)*

3 Practice

5 If you see a baby hedgehog ... (Conditional sentences 1)

Match and complete.

1 If you see a baby hedgehog,			have what it needs.
2 If you give it water and keep it warm,			tell you where you can get more help.
3 If you give milk to the hedgehog,	you	'll	have to be very careful.
4 If you touch the hedgehog	he/she		have to look for its mother.
5 If you don't take it to an animal clinic,	it	won't	tell you more about hedgehogs.
6 If you ask your Biology teacher,			have a good chance of survival.
7 If you go to the Animal Hotline website,			get very ill.

If you see a baby hedgehog, you'll have to look for its mother.

6 What will they do if ...? (Conditional sentences 1)

a) Partner B: Look at p. 111. Partner A: Make a copy of the chart.
Ask your partner for the missing information and take notes.
Then answer his or her questions.

A: What will Maike do if she finds a baby squirrel?
B: She'll ...
A: What will you do if ...
B: I'll ...

	find a baby squirrel	get a 5 in English	need a new mobile
Maike		practise every day	
Jan	put it in a box		buy one with his pocket money
Christoph	ask the Biology teacher for help	talk to the teacher	
Your partner			

b) Write three sentences: one about one of the people, one about your partner and one about yourself.
If Maike finds a baby squirrel, she'll ...
If my partner Finn gets a 5 in English, he must ...
If I need a new mobile, I can ...

c) Can you help your partner? Finish these sentences. Does he/she agree with your ideas?
1 If you find a baby animal, take it ...
2 If you like good films, go and see ...
3 If you get a lot of money for your birthday, ...

7 WORDS Fourth word

Find the fourth word.
1 frogs – jump
   birds – ?
2 invite – invitation
   survive – ?
3 fox – foxes
   mouse – ?
4 as big ... – ... as
   bigger ... – ...?
5 do – don't
   will – ?
6 left – right
   background – ?
7 meet – met
   hear – ?
8 documentary – interesting
   comedy – ?
9 Maths – subject
   apple – ?

8 WRITING Pet of the day (Linking ideas)

Link the sentences with the words in brackets. Together, they make an e-mail to the website
www.petoftheday.com

1 Hi, this is Rosie. She is a sweet, 7-month-old cat. I love her very much. (and)
   Hi, this is Rosie. She is a sweet, 7-month-old cat and I love her very much.
2 I get up in the mornings. She wants to play. (after)
   After I get up in the mornings, she ...
3 She follows me happily. She likes playing with my feet. (because)
4 I feed her. She wants to sit with me. She wants to sleep. (after, and)
5 Sometimes I want to play. I can't find her. (but)
6 She likes going outside. The window is usually open for her. (so)
7 I call her. She won't come. (if)
8 Cats are like that. That's OK. I love Rosie very much. (but, because)

DOSSIER Pet of the day

Write an e-mail to ⟶ pet@petoftheday.com
about your pet, a friend's pet or an imaginary pet. Add a photo. Print out your e-mail and put it in your Dossier. Write your pet's name and how old it is, what sort of animal it is, where your pet lives, what you like about your pet, ...

9 GAME Act the adverbs (Adverbs of manner)

a) Each group writes five activities on green cards and five adverbs on blue cards. Here are some ideas:

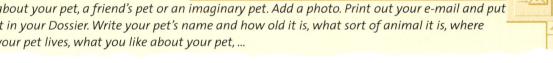

b) Put all the cards together. Your teacher reads all the cards to the class. Then one person takes a green card and a blue card and mimes what is on them. The others guess what he/she is doing:

– I think Marie is cleaning the board madly.
– Yes, that's right. Your turn./
  No, that's wrong. Try again.

10 PRONUNCIATION [f] – [v] – [w] 🎧

a) What sound do you hear at the beginning of each word? Is the first letter **f**, **v** or **w**? Write the words into your exercise book with the correct first letter.

_ery • _eek • _illage • _ind • _eed • _ater • _isit •
_ord • _ith • _iew • _irst • _alk • _ace • _oman •
_olleyball • _hite • _ood • _ind • _oodpecker

b) Say the words from a).

c) Extra Now try these tongue-twisters:
Willy Walter won't wear white in winter, will he?
Fiona's got a very funny visitor from Valencia.
Where's the village with the very wild view?
Val fell on the floor when Vinny phoned Will.

11 LISTENING She's talking loudly (Adverbs of manner)

a) Make adverbs from the adjectives in the box.

angry • careful • fast • happy • loud • quiet • slow

b) Listen to the CD. Write down how the people are talking. Use your adverbs.
1 The first person is talking ...
2 The second person is talking ...
3 ...

Are you all sitting comfortably? Then I'll begin.

12 STUDY SKILLS Scanning

Read the questions, then scan the TV magazine page on p. 44. Write down the answers. Shout 'Stop!' when you've got them all. Check with your teacher. All correct? You're the winner. Not all correct? You're out.

▶ SF Scanning (p. 120)

1 Where is the BBC's Natural History Unit?
2 Where can you find very good animal programmes?
3 When and where can you see news for children?
4 What can you watch if you like food?
5 Which programme is a comedy programme?
6 Which programme is about books?
7 How many quiz shows are there?

13 MEDIATION Longleat Safari Park

a) Imagine you want to go to Longleat Safari Park with your parents. Look at this information on the park. Tell them in German:
– what animals are in each part of the park
– how much it costs for you and your parents
– what you have to do in Tiger Territory
– when you have to be there.

Remember: only say what's important. You don't have to understand every word. Don't try to translate. Start like this: Im East Africa Reserve gibt's Giraffen und ...

Welcome to Longleat

East Africa Reserve
As in Africa, our herd of giraffes and zebras graze happily together in this 25-hectare reserve.

Monkey Jungle
A drive through the Monkey Jungle is great fun. The monkeys like playing with your car.

Tiger Territory
Perhaps one of the most interesting animals at Longleat. Make sure your car windows are closed, as these beautiful animals can be very dangerous!

Wolf Wood
Longleat is famous for its wolves. If you are lucky, you will hear them howling.

Open **10** am, last entry at **4** pm (**5** pm weekends)

Prices **£10** adult **£7** child (**3–14** yrs)

b) **Extra** You phone Longleat for more information. Listen to the message. Your parents want to know how you can get to the park. Which number should you press? Then they want to speak to somebody at the park. What number should you press now?

14 WORDS Word building

a) *Make nouns from the verbs.*

+ -er	+ -r	+ n/m + -er	+ -or
work	dance	run	act
sing	explore	swim	collect
listen	write	win	visit
paint			

c) **Extra** 👥 *Choose three more words from a) and make sentences like the ones in b). Swap. Can your partner find the missing words?*

b) *Complete the sentences with words from a).*
1 Will Smith is my favourite … I try to see all his films.
2 Ananda talked to Steve, a … at the animal clinic.
3 If I see a book by Stephen King, I'll buy it. He's a really scary …
4 Jody was a good …, but she didn't know about the tides.
5 You're a fantastic …! Why aren't you in the choir?

15 REVISION Three cities (Comparison of adjectives)

a) *There was a survey on British cities. Here are the results for London (**L**), Bristol (**B**) and Manchester (**M**).*

1 Is … pretty?

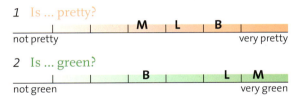

3 Is … exciting?

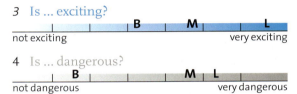

2 Is … green?

4 Is … dangerous?

Which city do you want to visit? Explain why.
I want to visit …. It's not as … as/It's -er than …/It's more … than …/ It's the -est …/It's the most …

b) *Where does your town/city/village go in the charts? Compare it with the British cities.*

16 GETTING BY IN ENGLISH Poor little cat

You're on holiday in England in your family's caravan. One night you find this cat under the caravan. You phone the RSPCA. Complete the dialogue.

RSPCA   RSPCA here. How can I help you?
You   Sage, dass du gestern eine Katze gefunden hast.
RSPCA   Oh, OK. Can you give me your name, address and telephone number, please?
You   Gib deinen Namen an. Sage, dass du nur im Urlaub in England bist.
RSPCA   That's all right. Now what colour is the cat?
You   Beantworte die Frage.
RSPCA   Can you say how old the cat is?
You   Schätze das Alter.
RSPCA   Now, has the cat got anything with its name and address on?
You   Verneine dies.
RSPCA   OK. Thank you. Now, what time did you find the cat?
You   Sage, gestern Abend um ca. 21.00 Uhr.
RSPCA   OK. And where?
You   Sage, unter eurem Wohnwagen.
RSPCA   All right, dear. Now, what would you like to do with the cat?
You   Frag, ob ihr sie zur RSPCA bringen könntet.
RSPCA   Yes, of course you can. Now, our …

El's best friend 🎧

> Look at the pictures and scan the text. Who is El's 'best friend'? Now read the story.

Everybody called the four girls the Black Angels. They looked dangerous, but they weren't – they were OK. El was the youngest in the group. She was 12, but she looked older.

At their school in London, the Black Angels were always together – nobody bullied them! 'And if somebody tries to bully one of the little kids,' they said, 'we'll be there to help them.' At home El's best friend was her dog Scruffy. When her parents argued (and they argued a lot) she went to her room with Scruffy, and told him all her problems.

One day El came home from school and found two big bags in the hall. When she went to her bedroom her mother was there with a third bag.
'Quick, pack your things,' her mum said.
'We're leaving.'
'Leaving?' El didn't understand.

'Yes, I'm leaving your father! We argue too much, El. I can't stand it any more. We'll go and stay with my friend Milly. We'll find a flat there and a new school.'
'But what about my friends? What about Scruffy ... and Dad?'
'You'll make lots of new friends, dear. And Scruffy can come when we've got a place.'
'I don't want new friends, I want my old friends,' El said angrily. 'And I don't want to ...'
'Just pack, El. The train leaves in three hours and I've still got a lot to do.'
Her mum left the room. El sat down on the bed. Scruffy jumped up and sat next to her. He knew that there was something wrong. She looked at him sadly.
'Oh, Scruffy, I'll miss you so much. But I'll come and get you, I promise.'

A few weeks later:

Tuesday, 27th November

Dear Dad,

I hate the new school – it's full of boring kids – all neat and tidy in their school uniforms. I really want Scruffy – I need Scruffy! Please, please bring him to Milly's.

Love
El

Hi, sweetheart!

I had to move out of our flat. I've got a nice room, but I'm afraid they don't allow pets. So I had to take Scruffy to Battersea Dogs Home. I'm sure he'll be OK there.
Sorry, sweetheart.
I'll write again soon.
Love
Dad

'Battersea Dogs Home?' thought El. 'But that's where people go when they want a new dog. Maybe somebody will want Scruffy – and then I'll never see him again! We haven't got a flat, so Mum won't help. I have to call Dad!'

It was 5.30 in the morning. El's mum and her
friend Milly were still asleep. But El had a plan.
She left the house and closed the door very
quietly behind her. Three hours later, after a
bus ride to London, El got on a train to Battersea Park Station. Her dad was there to meet her.
They walked to the Dogs Home together. El was
very excited … and very scared. 'What will we do
if he's not there any more, Dad? What if he's
already in another family! Oh, Dad, if he's not
there I'll die!'
El's father tried to calm her down. 'Don't worry,
sweetheart. I only took him to the Dogs Home
last week. I'm sure he's still there.'
At Battersea Dogs Home, El's dad explained
why they were there. The woman there checked
on her computer. 'Now, let me see, ' she said.
'Ah, yes. Scruffy. He's still here, but some
people are looking at him right now.'
At the top of the stairs El could feel the tears in
her eyes. She called Scruffy's name. The dog
heard her and barked happily. 'Scruffy's mine,'
she shouted and ran towards the family in front
of the kennel. 'He's mine and you can't have
him!'

On the trip back to Bristol, Scruffy was very
good. He sat quietly at El's feet. But when they
got off at the bus station, he was really happy.
El counted her money. 'I haven't got enough for
the bus,' she said. 'We'll walk home.'
And so the two of them started the long walk.
After about 45 minutes they were near Milly's
house. Suddenly El heard somebody call.
'Hey, Lesley!'
El turned. It was Jack from her new school.
He came towards them. 'So you're a dog
person, Lesley. I didn't know that.'
She smiled at Jack.
'Yes, I love dogs. This is my dog Scruffy.'
'Hello Scruffy,' said Jack. 'That's a nice name.'
El said shyly: 'In London all my friends called
me El.'
'That's nice too. Can I call you El?' asked Jack.
'OK,' said Lesley.

Working with the text

1 The story in two sentences
Which sentences summarize the first part of the story (ll. 1–37) correctly?

1. When El and her mum came to Bristol, El tried to make new friends. She left her dog Scruffy with the Black Angels.
2. El's mum and dad argued a lot, so El and her mum moved to Bristol. El was sad because her dog Scruffy was still in London.
3. El and her mum moved to Bristol. El hated it and went back to London to live with her dad and Scruffy.

2 The story in sections
a) Match the titles to the sections of the story:

1	ll. 1–8	El and the new school
2	ll. 9–12	Scruffy at the dogs home
3	ll. 13–31	The Black Angels
4	ll. 32–37	Scruffy, El's best friend
5	letter 1	Leaving El's dad
6	letter 2	Goodbye Scruffy

b) *Find titles for these sections of the story:*
ll. 39–43; ll. 44–57; ll. 58–68; ll. 69–87

3 Extra El's feelings
Find at least one place in the story when El was:

afraid • angry • happy • sad

I think El felt afraid when she …

4 That evening …
What will happen when El gets back to her mum?
a) *Write a short dialogue.*
Mum — Where were you?
El — In London, Mum. I'm sorry.
b) *Write El's diary entry for the day.*

5 Extra In your area
What happens to unwanted animals in your area? What can you do if you want to help animals or another good cause?

Checkpoint 3 ▶ WB (p. 41)

Extra Animal songs and poems

Read, listen to and enjoy these animal songs and poems. Then choose one task.

1 SONG I know an old lady who swallowed a fly

I know an old lady who swallowed a fly.
I don't know why she swallowed the fly –
Perhaps she'll die.

I know an old lady who swallowed a spider
That wriggled and jiggled and tickled inside her.
She swallowed the spider to catch the fly.
But I don't know why she swallowed the fly –
Perhaps she'll die.

I know an old lady who swallowed a bird.
How absurd – to swallow a bird.
She swallowed the bird to catch the spider
That wriggled and jiggled and tickled inside her.
She swallowed the spider to catch the fly.
But I don't know why she swallowed the fly –
Perhaps she'll die.

I know an old lady who swallowed a cat.
Imagine that. She swallowed a cat.
She swallowed the cat to catch the bird.
She swallowed the bird to catch the spider
That wriggled and jiggled and tickled inside her.
She swallowed the spider to catch the fly.
But I don't know why she swallowed the fly –
Perhaps she'll die.

    I know an old lady who swallowed a dog.
      What a hog! To swallow a dog!
        She swallowed the dog to catch the cat.
          She swallowed the cat to catch the
          bird.
          …

I know an old lady who swallowed a goat.
Opened her throat and down went the goat!
She swallowed the goat to catch the dog.
She swallowed the dog to catch the cat.

I know an old lady who swallowed a horse –
She's dead of course!

by Rosemary Bedeau and Alan Mills

2 POEM The song of a mole

All I did this afternoon was
Dig, dig, dig,
And all I'll do tomorrow will be
Dig, dig, dig,
And yesterday from dusk till dawn
I dug, dug, dug.
I sometimes think I'd rather be
A slug, slug, slug.

　　　　　by Richard Edwards

3 POEM Undersea tea

by Tony Mitton

OLIVER THE OCTOPUS
UNDERNEATH THE SEA
SWIMMING VERY SLOWLY
LOOKING FOR HIS TEA
MAKES A LITTLE BUBBLE
GIVES A LITTLE GRIN
"HI THERE, FISHES!
COME ON IN..."

4 POEM Early bird

Oh, if you're a bird, be an early bird
And catch the worm for your breakfast plate.
If you're a bird, be an early bird –
But if you're a worm, sleep late.

by Shel Silverstein

Working with the songs and poems

1 *Write one more verse for the song (1) with a new animal. Where can it go in the song?*
I know an old lady who swallowed a cow.
I don't know how she swallowed a cow!

2 *Think of other irregular verbs like* **dig** *in the poem 'The song of the mole' (2):* **write/wrote**, **sit**/..., ...
And think of other animals like **goat**, **cat**, ...
Write a new poem.
All I did this afternoon was write, write, write.
...

3 *'Undersea tea' (3) is a shape poem. What's a good shape for a poem about love? And about rain? Can you write a shape poem?*

4 *There is a saying in English: 'The early bird catches the worm.' What do you think it means? How does the poem 'Early bird' play with the saying?*

5 *Do you know any other animal poems, songs, tongue-twisters, ...? Write one down and teach it to your group. You can sing or say it for the class.*

Unit 4
A weekend in Wales

1 👥 Talking about a weekend trip
What weekend trips can you go on near your home? Talk to a partner. Here is some help:
go shopping in town – visit relatives – go to a theme park – go on a bike tour with friends – go to an open-air concert – go to the coast …

2 Town and country
a) How many words from the box can you find in the photos? Put the words into three lists: *town* – *country* – *town and country*.
If you don't know the word and can't guess it, look it up.

> CD and DVD shop • church • cinema • clean • cow • dirty • factory • farm • field • forest • go shopping • green • hill • horse • house • lots of people • lots of traffic • noisy • quiet • ride your bike • river • sheep • station • valley • village

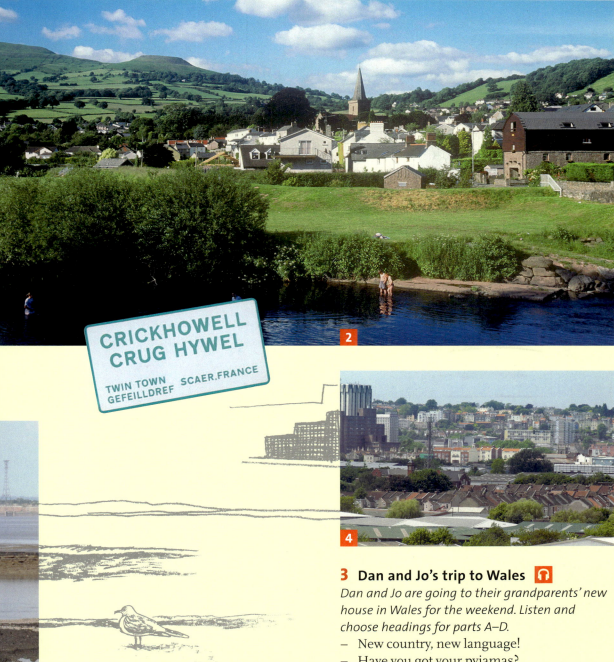

CRICKHOWELL
CRUG HYWEL
TWIN TOWN   SCAER, FRANCE
GEFEILLDREF

b) What do you like most about the town and the country? Write it down and tell the class.
– I love all the shops in towns. You can buy CDs and clothes there. That's fun.
– I like animals. If you wait very quietly in the forest near our town, you can see deer and rabbits.

3 Dan and Jo's trip to Wales 🎧
Dan and Jo are going to their grandparents' new house in Wales for the weekend. Listen and choose headings for parts A–D.
– New country, new language!
– Have you got your pyjamas?
– The beautiful Welsh village of Crickhowell
– Towns all look the same!
Then match photos 1–4 to your headings.

DOSSIER Wales

Listen again and take notes on Wales. Use your notes for a section of your dossier. You can also use information from other parts of the unit.

▶ P 1 (p. 66) • WB 1–2 (p. 42)

1 Friday dinner 🎧

It was late when the twins and their grandparents got to Crickhowell. 'Grandpa will show you your room, boys,' Grandma said. 'Dinner will be on the table in a few minutes.'
'It smells great,' Jo said when they came into the kitchen. 'What are you cooking?'
'Cawl mamgu,' Grandma answered. 'That's Welsh for "Grandma's soup". It's a leek soup.'

'You're very quiet, Daniel,' Grandpa Thompson said. 'Are you all right?'
'Yes, I'm fine.'
'That's good,' Grandpa Thompson said, 'because we've got big plans for tomorrow. We want to drive to the Brecon Beacons in the morning and go on the Brecon Mountain Railway. And we're going to have a picnic at Caerphilly Castle in the afternoon.'

▸ Where will Dan and Jo be when?
They'll be on … in the morning. They'll be …

▸ GF 12: Word order (p. 138) • P 2–3 (p. 66) • WB 3 (p. 43)

2 Caerphilly Castle 🎧

CAERPHILLY CASTLE
is an exciting place for visitors to South Wales. It's Britain's second biggest castle – as big as 30 football pitches! The castle is surrounded by water, beautiful on a sunny day. Plan to spend 3–4 hours. And don't miss the **leaning tower** – it leans more than the Leaning Tower of Pisa!

STUDY SKILLS | **Topic sentence**

In jedem Absatz (Englisch: **paragraph**) steht ein Satz, der die wichtigste Aussage dieses Absatzes enthält. Oft ist das der erste Satz. Man nennt ihn **topic sentence**. Alle anderen Sätze geben weitere Informationen oder Begründungen.

Welcher Satz ist der **topic sentence** im Prospekt für Caerphilly Castle (2)? Warum?

▸ SF Topic sentence (p. 123) • P 4 (p. 67) • WB 4 (p. 44)

3 Now you

a) Write a short paragraph about where you live.
1 Start with a topic sentence:
Berlin is the coolest city in Germany.
Friedewald is a lovely old village near …
2 Add two or three more sentences.
You can see and do lots of really exciting things there. For example, …

b) **Extra** Read your paragraph to the class. Then add a photo and put your paragraph in your DOSSIER.

4 'I've cooked your breakfast!' 🎧

Grandma   Daniel! Jonah! I've cooked your breakfast! Bacon and eggs. And Grandpa has already packed the picnic! Hurry up!
Grandpa   Don't worry, dear. I haven't cleaned the car yet, but I can do that now. Oh, look, here comes Gwyneth.
Gwyneth   Bore da!
Grandma   Bore da, Gwyneth! Hello, Emma.
Gwyneth   We've just made this pie for you.
Grandma   Thank you – the twins love pie!
Emma   But we haven't seen the twins yet.
Grandma   Here's one of them now. Jonah, this is Mrs Evans, our neighbour …
Jo   Hello … er, sorry, Grandma, can you come upstairs? Dan hasn't come down because, er … he doesn't feel well.

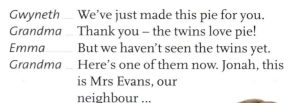

Looking at language

Find sentences in **4** with a form of **have**. Write them down. Underline the two parts of the verb form. What is the infinitive of the verb?
<u>I've cooked</u> your breakfast.   (to) cook

How do you make this verb form?

5 👥 GAME I've packed my bag

Play this game. Put ideas on the board. Here are some in the box.

> pack – my bag, the car, my rucksack, …
> finish – my homework, my picture, school, …
> wash – Dad's car, my hair, my clothes, …
> watch – a film, the news, the weather, …

A: I've packed my bag, so now we can go.
B: I've packed my bag and I've washed Dad's car, so now we can go.
C: I've packed my bag and I've washed Dad's car and I've … essay and I've …

▸ GF 13, 14a, b, 15: Present perfect (pp. 139–141) •
P 5–9 (pp. 67–69) • WB 5–8 (pp. 45–47)

Extra Background File

Croeso i Gymru!
That means 'Welcome to Wales' – in Welsh. One in five Welsh people speaks Welsh. All schoolchildren in Wales have to learn Welsh as their first or second language.
Welsh is a Celtic language. The Celts lived all over Britain before the Romans came in 43 AD. They were still there when the Romans left 400 years later. But then people from northern Europe and Germany started to move into Britain. Soon only Wales, Scotland and Ireland were Celtic. England was the new home of the Anglo-Saxons. There are almost no Celtic words in the English language now.

About 3 million people live in Wales.
The capital of Wales is Cardiff and this is the Welsh flag.

6 Poor Dan 🎧

'Poor Dan! What's the matter, dear?' Grandma asked. 'Are you feeling ill?'
'Yes, Grandma,' said Dan.
Grandma felt Dan's face. 'Oh dear!' she said.
'I think you have a temperature. Here, put the thermometer in your mouth. Now, do you have a sore throat?'
Dan took the thermometer out of his mouth.
'Yes I ...'
'No, no, dear, don't take it out. Just nod.'
Dan put the thermometer back and nodded.
'And a headache?'
Dan nodded.
'Move your arms and legs: do they hurt?'
Dan nodded again.
'Oh dear, maybe it's the flu,' said Grandma. 'It's a pity Bryn isn't at home.'
'Who?' Jo asked.
'Bryn Evans, our neighbour. He's a paramedic.'

> What's wrong with Dan?
He has a ... and a ... and his ... hurt.
And what does Grandma think it is?

7 What's the matter?

a) 👥 Tell your partner what's wrong with the boy. Take turns. You can use sentences from the box.

> He has a temperature. •
> He has broken his arm. •
> He has hurt his knee. • He has cut his finger •
> He has a headache. • He has hurt his foot.

1

2

3

4

5

6

b) Extra 👥👥👥 One student mimes something – a headache, a broken leg ... The others guess what's wrong.

A: You've broken your leg! C: You've broken your foot!
B: No, that's wrong. B: Yes, that's right. Your turn.

8 Extra Can you move your ...? 🎧

Imagine you have had an accident. Listen to the doctor. Move and bend and stretch when she tells you.

▶ P 10–11 (pp. 69–70) • WB 9–11 (pp. 47–48)

9 Grandma's new software 🎧

Grandma	I'm sorry I can't come on the trip, Jonah.
Jo	Yes, it's a pity, Grandma. But somebody has to stay with Dan.
Grandma	Jonah, have you ever installed software?
Jo	Yes, of course I have, Grandma.
Grandma	Well, I'd like to try this chat thing. Can you install it for me?
Jo	Well, Grandma, I've …
Grandma	I've already printed out the instructions. It says here: 'Download the software to your computer.' Have you downloaded the software, dear?
Jo	Yes, I have, Grandma. But –
Grandma	Good. Then it says: 'The installation will start.' Has it started?
Jo	Yes, it has, Grandma. But –

▶ Continue the dialogue.
Use numbers 3–6 on the right. 🎧

Grandma	Good. Then it says: 'Click on …' Have you …?
…	
Grandma	Very good, Jonah. Now we can chat with people all over the world!
Jo	I know, Grandma. I installed the software last night. I've already given you a chat name and I'm chatting with Mum in New Zealand now. She wants to talk to you!

Quick start instructions

1 Download the software to your computer.
2 The installation will start.
3 Click on 'Finish the installation'.
4 The computer will restart.
5 Start the software.
6 Enter a chat name and click 'OK'.

You can now chat with everybody – everywhere in the world. Have fun!

▶ GF 14c, 15: Present perfect: questions (pp. 140–141) • P 12–13 (p. 70) • WB 12 (p. 49)
Extra ▶ GF 16: Present perfect and simple past (p. 141) • P 14 (p. 71)

10 Grandma's first chat

WelshGranny	Hello, Catherine!
CathNZ	hi mum. how's the weather?
WelshGranny	Cool, dear. It's winter.
CathNZ	summer here. was 27° today!
WelshGranny	Why does it say 'WelshGranny' when I write something?
CathNZ	ask jo. lol
WelshGranny	What has Jonah done? And what does 'lol' mean?
CathNZ	lol = laughing out loud. don't worry, ur just starting. next we'll buy u a webcam :-)
WelshGranny	Please write in English, dear. I can't understand you.

▶ Write CathNZ's chat in complete sentences for Grandma Thompson. ▶ P 15–16 (p. 71) • WB 13–18 (pp. 49–52)

4 Practice

1 WORDS Travel

a) *Read the sentences and find the travel words.*
1. Lots of kids go to school together on one. b - - *bus*
2. Cars travel on this. r - - -
3. It travels from station to station, usually from town to town. t - - - -
4. Trains stop here. s - - - - - -
5. A road goes over a river on this. b - - - - -
6. You ride this to school. b - - -
7. If you go to an island you can travel on this. b - - -
8. You can fly to New York on this. p - - - -

b) *Copy and continue the networks.*

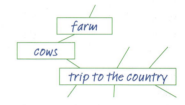

c) *Write about your last weekend trip to a town or the country. You can use ideas from b).*
In December I went on a trip to my Grandma's. She lives in the country. We went by car. When we ...

2 REVISION I can't go because ... (Word order in subordinate clauses)

Write about you, your family and friends. Remember the word order: subject – verb – object.

1 I can't go to the party this weekend	because	I can't go to the party
2 My dad usually has a shower	before	this weekend because
3 My mum sometimes gets angry with me	when	... I won't be at home.
4 My best friend often phones me	after	
5 I never eat	if	
6 I'll do badly in my next English test		

3 Where will they be tomorrow afternoon? (Word order: place before time)

a) *Say where they'll be tomorrow afternoon.*

1. Dan and Jo will be at Caerphilly Castle tomorrow afternoon.   2. Ananda ...

b) **Extra** *Everybody writes five where cards and three when cards. Put all the where cards together and the when cards together.*
A takes a where card and a when card and makes a suggestion: Let's go to the cinema tomorrow.
B takes a where card and answers:
Sorry, I'll be at my grandmother's tomorrow./
Great idea. I want to go to the cinema tomorrow too.
Now C takes a where card and a when card ...

4 STUDY SKILLS Topic sentence

a) Find the topic sentence in each group of sentences. Put the sentences in the right order to make a good paragraph. Remember: the topic sentence usually comes first.

1 Cardiff Castle

The Castle today is the result of many years of history, from the Romans 2000 years ago to the Bute family in the late 19th century. Cardiff Castle is the top sight in the city. Each room is different, and the gardens are wonderful too.

2 St Fagans Celtic Village

In this village you can see how the Celts lived over 2000 years ago. The Museum of Welsh Life opened St Fagans Celtic Village in 1992. It has three roundhouses just like those of the ancient Celts.

3 Techniquest

Techniquest is a science centre for young and old. There are 160 exhibits and live presentations for visitors to enjoy. The centre usually has interesting projects too, where you can learn about lots of things like police work or life on Mars.

4 Brecon Mountain Railway

It travels through the beautiful Brecon Beacons. From the train you have a fantastic view of the valley. The name of the locomotive is 'Graf Schwerin-Löwitz'. Brecon Mountain Railway is one of the finest small railways in Wales.

b) **Extra** *Write a short paragraph about a tourist attraction in your area. Make sure your paragraph has got a good topic sentence.*

5 LISTENING Accents

a) Listen to four different speakers and say where they are from: London (1), Scotland (2), Wales (3) or the West Country (4). Who was the easiest to understand? Who was the most difficult?

b) Listen again and find the right answers.
1. How many languages does Gwyneth speak?
2. Who are her new neighbours?
3. Has Thomas always lived in Bristol?
4. Thomas likes where he lives. Why?
5. Does Angus live on the east or west coast of the island?
6. What animals are there on Jura? Name two.
7. Caroline says London has got everything. Name two things.
8. What is her favourite activity in London?

6 Mr Shaw has painted the kitchen door (Present perfect: regular verbs)

a) Write about the pictures.

1 Mr Shaw
paint – kitchen door

2 The twins
pack – bags

3 Jack
tidy – desk

4 Mr Kingsley
finish – book

5 The Kapoors
count – money

6 Ananda and Sophie
watch – DVD

7 The Thompsons
cook – lunch

8 Prunella
drop – plates

1 *Mr Shaw has painted the kitchen door.*   2 *The twins have ...*

b) Match a sentence from a) to a sentence from the box.

> Now they can go up to the flat. • He really likes the new colour. •
> The Carter-Browns will need new ones • They're ready to go to the station. •
> Now it's time for bed. • Now he can start the next one. • Today they're having chicken and chips. •
> Now he can find everything again.

1 *Mr Shaw has painted the kitchen door. He really likes the new colour.*   2 *The twins have ...*

7 After dinner at Grandma Thompson's (Present perfect: irregular verbs)

Read the dialogue and put the verbs in brackets in the present perfect:
I (take) = I've taken, I (lose) = ... You can find the irregular forms on p. 220.

____ Grandma! I (take) some really good photos. Would you like to see them?
Gr. ____ Yes of course – oh no, I (lose) my glasses again.
Dan ____ Here they are! I (find) them.
Gr. ____ Thanks, Daniel. Have some chocolate!
Dan ____ No thank you. I'm not very hungry.
Jo ____ Chocolate! Mmmm!
Gr. ____ Not for you, Jonah. You (have) too much.

Jo ____ Oh, well! OK, the photos. This one is ...
Gr. ____ Wait for Grandpa, Jonah. He (go) to Gwyneth's for a few minutes. She's our neighbour.
Dan ____ Do you know many of the people here, Grandma?
Gr. ____ Well, we (meet) the Evans family, and we (speak) to a lot of the other ...
Jo ____ Hey, Grandpa's back. So now we can ...

8 They've already made their beds (Present perfect: negative sentences, already and not ... yet)

a) Mr and Mrs Kapoor have made lists of jobs for Ananda and Dilip. Say what they've already done.
Ananda and Dilip have already made their beds.
Ananda has already ...
Dilip ...

b) Now say what they haven't done yet.
Ananda and Dilip haven't tidied their rooms yet.
...

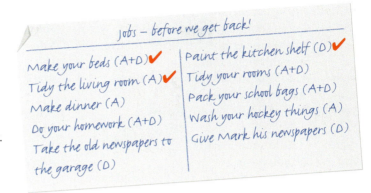

9 What's different? (Present perfect: just)

Partner B: Go to p. 112.
Partner A: Tell your partner about the people in the picture.
Ask about his/her picture. Take turns. Use ideas from the box.
A: In my picture Sophie has just made popcorn. And in your picture?
B: In my picture Sophie has just ...

drop • eat • find • make • open • take

10 WORDS The body

Draw a 'word body': you can use body words from the green box to draw a person, an animal, a monster, a ....

arm • ear • eye • finger • foot • hair • hand • head • knee • leg • mouth • nose • shoulder • stomach • toe • tooth • ...

11 MEDIATION Phoning a doctor

Imagine you've got an English guest, Sally, in your home. When she feels ill, you phone the doctor for her.

You	Guten Morgen, Frau Dr. Schwarz. Wir haben eine englische Gastschülerin. Sie fühlt sich krank.
Ärztin	Aha. Frag sie bitte, was ihr fehlt.
You	She wants to know what's …
Sally	Well, my eyes are quite sore.
You	…
Ärztin	Hat sie auch Fieber?
You	Do you have …
Sally	I think maybe a bit, yes. I felt cold last night.
You	…
Ärztin	Halsschmerzen auch?
You	…
Sally	Yes, a bit.
You	…
Ärztin	Und tun ihr auch die Arme und Beine weh?
You	…
Sally	Yes, my legs hurt.
You	…
Ärztin	Das klingt wie eine Grippe. Ich würde sie gerne sehen. Kann sie heute Nachmittag um 14.00 Uhr vorbeikommen?
You	Sally, she says it sounds like … She … Can …?

12 Have you done your homework? (Present perfect: questions)

a) *Complete the questions with the verbs in brackets. Then complete the answers.*
1. Mr Hanson: *Have you done* (you/do) your homework, Jack? – Jack: Yes, *I have,* Dad.
2. Mr Hanson: And … (Dan and Jo/finish) that project yet? – Jack: No, ….
3. Jack: What about dinner? … (Mum/cook) it yet? – Mr Hanson: No, …
4. Jack: Well, … (she/buy) the food? – Mr Hanson: Yes, …
5. Jack: And … (you/feed) Polly? – Polly: No, …. Hurry up! Hurry up!

b) 👥 *Ask your partner five more questions about what he/she has done this week/month/year. Use ideas from the box. Take notes and report to the class.*
A: Have you been late for school this month?
B: Yes, I have./No, I haven't.

> be late for school • cut your hair •
> feel ill • make breakfast for your parents •
> paint a picture • travel by plane •
> try any new food • …

13 👥 GAME Have you …? (Present perfect: questions)

a) *Make groups of three or four. One group goes out of the room. The others change five things, for example, they open a window, write on the board, … See the box for ideas.*

> close • hide • move • open • put • read •
> take • write • …

b) *The group comes back in. They have to ask questions and try to find out what has changed. They get one point for each change.*
A: Have you opened the cupboard?
Class: No, we haven't.
B: Have you written on the board?
Class: Yes, we have. One point.
The group with the most points wins.

14 Extra **Have you done it yet?** (Present perfect and simple past)

Complete these chat messages. Who are the people?
1 **WelshGranny** install/new chat software?
   Have you installed the new chat software yet?
   madtwin yesterday evening
   Yes, I have. I installed it yesterday evening.
2 **CathNZ** phone/dad/about your brother?
   madtwin after dinner
3 **SHoCKer** hear/Dan/ill?
   CBdancer Jo/send me/text message/at 7
4 **CBdancer** finish/your homework?
   SHoCKer after/my parents/go out
5 **KingDread** see/the new Beethoven film?
   snowwhite last weekend
6 **ghostlysir** see my head?
   PeePol 200 years ago

15 PRONUNCIATION Silent letters 🎧

In some English words you do not pronounce all the letters – they are silent.

a) *Read the words quietly. Then write them in your exercise book. Underline the silent letters.*
two, knee, talk, know, would, climb, wrong, calm, sandwich, answer, half, who, could, walk, knock.

b) 👥 *Check with your partner.*

c) *Listen and say the words. Did you underline the right letters?*

d) *Read the poem out loud:*
Who is knocking here today?
Writers climbing on their knees.
'This is wrong, don't walk away.
We would like a sandwich, please.'

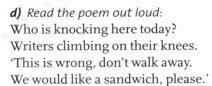

16 GETTING BY IN ENGLISH It's a pity

a) *Can you say these things in English?*
1 Ist bei dir alles OK? – Mir geht es gut. (p. 62)
2 Er fühlt sich nicht gut. (p. 63)
3 Was fehlt dir? (p. 64)
4 Es tut mir leid mit unserem Ausflug. (p. 65)
5 Das ist schade. (p.65)
6 Hast du schon mal etwas installiert? (p. 65)

b) 👥 *Partner A: You're in England. You go to your friend Mike's house. Partner B: You are Mike's brother/sister. Act out the dialogue.*

Partner A	Partner B
Du grüßt Partner B und fragst, ob Mike da ist.	Du grüßt zurück und erklärst, dass Mike im Bett ist.
Du fragst, was ihm fehlt.	Du sagst, dass Mike Halsschmerzen hat.
Schade. Du wolltest mit Mike ins Kino.	Es tut dir leid mit dem Kino. Du fragst, ob A schon mal einen Star-Wars-Film gesehen hat.
Das hast du noch nicht. Aber du möchtest gern einen sehen.	Du lädst A ein, eine DVD mit dir anzusehen.
Du sagst, du würdest sie gern ansehen, und bedankst dich.	

All in a day's work 🎧

> Look at the title and the pictures. What do you think the story is about?

Bryn hated his mobile. It always rang when he was really tired – like this morning. Before he picked it up, he looked at the clock: 6.25.

'Morning, Bryn. Elaine here. We need you on
5 the road to Tredegar – there's been a car accident. A bad accident.'
'Oh, Elaine,' Bryn said. 'Can't Mike and Drew go? I was on a rescue till after ten last night. I'm never allowed to sleep after a late night.'
10 'I know, I know. But Mike and Drew have just gone to another accident in Llanfoist. I'm afraid *you'll* have to go.'
Bryn put on his uniform and was in his car in four minutes. 'If Elaine says it's bad, it'll be *very*
15 bad,' Bryn thought.
When Bryn got to the accident, he saw a red car on its side. The driver was hurt, but Bryn was able to see that it wasn't too bad. 'They didn't call me for this,' he knew.

'Are you the paramedic?' It was one of the
20 firemen. 'A car has gone down there.' He pointed to the side of the hill. 'We're trying to secure it, but they need you down there – fast.' Bryn followed the fireman. He could see that the car was in some trees about ten metres
25 down. It was another 70 or 80 metres to the valley floor.
'Beth here will go down with you,' the fireman told him.
'Hi,' said Beth. 'Are you ready?'
30 'As ready as I'll ever be,' he answered. 'Let's just

hope those trees hold till we get there.'
Bryn and Beth quickly climbed down to the car. There they found four very scared people: a man, a woman and two children. 'We're here
35 to help you,' Beth said. 'Is everybody OK?'
The children and the woman weren't hurt, but the man had a broken leg. The bigger problem was that the trees weren't strong enough.

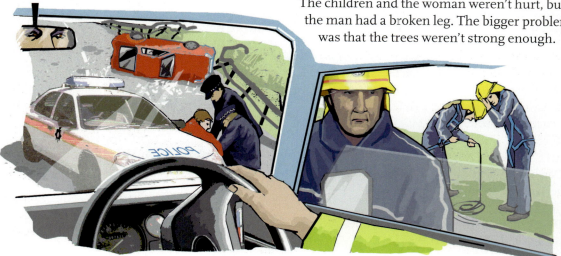

Text 4

'But, Bryn, you won't be allowed to go in till ...'
She didn't have time to finish.
'I hope the trees hold,' Bryn said and got into the car. Fifteen minutes later the driver was out of the car. Bryn started to climb out. He had one foot in the tree when the car fell.
'That was close,' Bryn thought. 'Too close.'

40 Bryn worked on the man, and Beth took the little boy up the hill, then the girl. Then she came back for the
45 woman.
'Beth,' Bryn said from the other side of the car, 'take her up fast. Then come back – I need your help here.'
50 'OK, I'll just ...'
But before Beth could finish her sentence, the car started to fall. It stopped after another three metres. When Beth and Bryn got to the car again, the man was unconscious. The woman
55 didn't want to leave her husband, but Beth said, 'Think of the children. They need you.'

'The helicopter is coming,' Beth said when she got back to Bryn and the man. 'If we can get him out, we'll have to get him to hospital fast!'
60 'But I can't get him out. You'll have to cut him out,' Bryn told Beth.
'We can't cut him out,' Beth answered. 'They haven't secured the car yet.'
'Well, I'll have to go inside the car,' Bryn said.
65 'Maybe I'll be able to get him out then.'

When Bryn got home at 5 pm, after one more car accident, a woman with a broken arm and a new baby, his wife Gwyneth came to the door.
'How was work, dear?' she asked.

'Well, there was a small problem with a car, but we were able to help. It was nothing special.'
'Oh good. Can you just go over to the Thompsons' and look at their grandson? Jonah – or is it Daniel? – well, one of the twins is ill.'
'Of course,' he said, and put on his jacket again. 'All in a day's work!'

Working with the text

1 The rescue
Find seven mistakes in the picture. Take turns.
In the story it says there was a red car on its side. In the picture it's a blue car.
In the story there were two ...

2 Extra Who said what?
Partner B: Go to p. 112.
Partner A: Ask your partner who said these things and when.

A: Who said 'Morning, Bryn' and when?
B: Elaine said that when ... That's in line ...
1 'Morning, Bryn' (Elaine, l. 4)
2 'Are you the paramedic?' (The fireman, l. 20)
3 'They need you.' (Beth, l. 56)
4 'We can't cut him out.' (Beth, l. 62)

Now listen to your partner's questions. Scan the text for the correct answers.
B: Who said 'Is everybody OK?'
A: Beth said that when ... That's in lines ...

▶ SF Scanning (p. 120)

3 Accident report
Imagine you're the radio reporter. Can you answer the presenter's questions?

Presenter — There's been a bad accident on the Tredegar Road. Here's our reporter, Jo Blake. How many cars were in the accident, Jo?
Reporter — ... in the accident. One of them went over the side of the road and stopped ...
Presenter — How many people were in the car?
Reporter — ...
Presenter — Have the firemen cut everybody out?
Reporter — Yes, but it was difficult. They couldn't ... So the paramedic went ... and ... Then the car ... It was very ...
Presenter — What about injuries?
Reporter — The driver of the car had ... The helicopter has just ...
Presenter — Thanks, Jo. We'll have more on that accident in the news. It's almost ...

Checkpoint 4   ▶ WB (pp. 53–55) • Activity page 2

Topic **4**

Extra A weekend in Wales – Jo's e-mail to his mum

Dear Mum,
I've attached a short report of our weekend with Grandma and Grandpa and some of my photos (one from the internet too). I hope you can open them without any problems!
I'll write again soon.
Lots of love – from Dan too.
Jo

Crug Hywel.jpg

Goodbye Crickhowell.jpg

Dan ill.jpg

Railway.jpg

1 Jo's photos and report

a) What do you think: what happened first, second, …?

b) Use the photos and Jo's notes and write Jo's report about the weekend in Wales. Write a paragraph about each photo. Put the topic sentence first. You can add your own ideas.

2 The red dragon and the white dragon
Dan listened to a Welsh legend in bed. Now you listen to the legend too.

– Dan: ill most of visit; had to stay in bed Sunday morning: couldn't eat

– Sat.: Grandma home with Dan; Grandpa & me: trip on Brecon Mountain Railway: beautiful country. Visited Crug Hywel (Welsh name of Crickhowell): Celtic hillfort, Iron Age: too high to go up ☺

– Sun. afternoon: back to Bristol, Dan better but not good – I packed his bag

Unit 5
Teamwork

👥 The Bristol Game
Play the game in groups. You will need a dice and counters. Agree on your rules first. Use phrases from the box.

- Can I have the dice, please?
- It's your turn. Throw the dice, please.
- Hey, you had a three, not a four.
- Wait, that's my counter. You're blue.

Bristol Tourist Information
Lots of good ideas for your time in Bristol!
Start here.

Explore-at-Bristol
You learn about science at this exciting museum.
Move on one space.

Llandoger Trow
You stop and look at this pub from 1664, where pirates met.
Name a pirate or miss a turn.

Temple Meads Station
Stop and look at the station. Britain's greatest engineer, Brunel, designed and built it.
Move on two spaces if you can say what stops there.

St Nicholas Market
You buy a healthy snack.
Move on two spaces if you can name some healthy food.

Cotham School
You want to visit the SHoCK Team, but the school is closed.
Move back two spaces.

The International Balloon Fiesta
You ride across the city in a balloon.
Take another turn.

28 Pretty Polly B&B
You go back to your room and sleep.
Miss a turn.

British Empire and Commonwealth Museum
You get angry when you find out how Bristol got rich from the slave trade. Close your eyes and count to ten to calm down.
Move on one space.

43 Georgian House
A family in the sugar trade built this house in 1791. They lived here with their black slaves. The tour is long.
Go back one space.

50 Cabot Tower
Arrive here first, and you're the

winner!

33 The Downs
You stop and look at the kites in this beautiful park.
Say the German word for kite or move back one space.

40 Aardman Studios
You want to see where they make the Wallace and Gromit films, but they don't have tours.
Name the title of one of their films or go back two spaces.

36 Clifton Suspension Bridge
You walk over the River Avon on this famous bridge.
Move on three spaces.

37 River Avon
Oops! You've fallen into the water.
Sing a song in English or miss a turn.

▶ P 1–2 (p. 82) •
WB 1–2 (p. 56)

1 The Bristol Quiz 🎧

Mr Kingsley has given his form a project which starts with a quiz. Ananda and her friends are working on it together.

The Bristol Quiz Project

Find the answers to the project questions. Make one A4 page of material for each answer. Add a title page to make a Bristol booklet.

Question 1
This is something that happens in August. It produces a lot of hot air. The people who come to it look up a lot. It begins at night.

Jo	Let's plan what we're going to do: I'll take all the photos that we need.
Ananda	Who says we need photos?
Sophie	Yes, it just says 'material' here.
Dan	Well, I'm not going to make a boring Bristol booklet without any photos.
Jo	Thanks, Dan. You're the only one who understands.
Jack	But I don't think you can take photos for question number one, Jo. It isn't August yet.
Jo	What? I don't get it.
Sophie	Read the question, Jo. Something that produces hot air …
Ananda	… yes, and people that have to look up a lot …
Dan	… oh, right: an event in August which begins at night. I know. It's …
Jo	… the International Balloon Fiesta! Well, I'll download all the photos that we need.

▷ What interesting events take place in your area?

▶ P 3–4 (pp. 82–83) • WB 3–5 (pp. 57–58)

2 Jo is the boy who …

Use the phrases on the right and write five sentences about the Bristol kids.

Jo is the boy who …   Dan is …   …

… can talk to Prunella. • … was ill in Wales. •
… knows when the Balloon Fiesta is. •
… likes taking photos. • … lives over a shop.

Looking at language

a) Look at these sentences from 1.
Mr Kingsley has given his form a project **which** starts with a quiz.
This is something **that** happens in August.
The people **who** come to it look up a lot.

Which words do the relative pronouns **who**, **which** and **that** refer to?

b) Find more sentences with relative pronouns in 1. Which relative pronouns can you use for people, which for things?

3 Now you   Project (Step 1)

Start a booklet on your area like Form 8PK's on Bristol.

a) Think: What's the most interesting event in your area? What do you know about it? (When does it take place? Where? How many people come? What happens? …)

b) 👥 **Pair:** Agree on one event.

c) 👥👥 **Share:** Agree on one event with your group. Start to collect material on this event.

▶ GF 17a: Relative clauses (p. 142) • P 5–8 (pp. 83–84) • WB 6 (p. 59)

4 Who is he? 🎧

> **Question 2**
> This is the man whose statue is outside a building near the station. He's one of the most famous people who ever lived in Bristol.
> Who is he? When did he live? Name at least three things which he built in Bristol.

'Well,' said Jack, 'we were right. It's Brunel.'
'And the dates are right here,' added Ananda.
'Now we have to find out what he built in Bristol,' said Jo.
'That's easy,' said Dan. 'He built the station.'
'And Clifton Suspension Bridge,' Sophie said.
'But what's the third thing?' asked Ananda.
'Don't ask me,' answered Jo. 'I'm just the photographer.'
'Well, let's go to the library and look in an encyclopedia, or on the internet,' said Sophie.

> What famous people have lived or worked in your area?

▶ GF 17b: Relative clauses: whose (p. 142) • WB 7 (p. 59)

5 Brunel – Bristol's engineer 🎧

Isambard Kingdom Brunel was a man with a dream. Born in Portsmouth in 1806, Isambard decided to become an engineer like his father. He worked with his father on the Thames Tunnel in London and almost died in an accident there. He went to Bristol to recover.

When he was in Bristol, Brunel had an idea for a bridge over the River Avon. Work started on the Clifton Suspension Bridge in 1831 but Brunel died in 1859, five years before the bridge opened.

But Brunel wanted to build more than a bridge! He wanted to link London with New York: with bridges, tunnels, hotels, stations – and of course ships. London's Paddington Station and Bristol's Temple Meads Station are two results of his dream. Another is one of the most famous ships that he built, the SS Great Britain. It was built in Bristol and the people of Bristol are still proud of the ship and of 'their' engineer, Isambard Kingdom Brunel.

STUDY SKILLS | **Marking up a text**

Wenn du einen Text mit vielen Fakten liest, kann es nützlich sein, wenn du die wichtigsten Informationen markierst.
Sieh dir einmal an, wie Sophie den Text links markiert hat. Sie sucht Antworten auf die folgende Fragen: Who was Brunel? When did he live? What did he build in Bristol?

▶ SF Marking up a text (p. 121) • P 9 (p. 85) • WB 8 (p. 59)

6 Now you Project (Step 2)

a) Think: *What interesting people live or have lived in your area? What do you know about them?*
b) 👥 Pair: *Agree on one person.*
c) 👥👥 Share: *Agree on one person with the other pair in your group. Start to collect material on your person.*

7 Healthy *and* delicious?! 🎧

Mr Kingsley's last quiz question was the hardest for the team.

> **Question 3**
> Time for a break! Find a healthy and delicious drink in St Nicholas Market. What is the smallest drink? The cheapest? The most interesting?

| Jo | A healthy and delicious drink – that's impossible! |
| Sophie | Don't be silly, Jo. Of course it's possible. |

So the team went to St Nicholas Market and looked ... and looked ... and looked. At last they found a place.

| Jack | That's the place, isn't it? |
| Ananda | The juice bar? Yes, it looks pretty cool, doesn't it? |

They all went in and ordered drinks.

Assistant	What can I get you?
Jo	You haven't got cola, have you?
Assistant	No, we haven't. We've got juices, smoothies, ...
Jo	OK, I'd like a smoothie, please.
Assistant	What flavour would you like?
Jo	Strawberry, please.

Dan had a smoothie too. Jack and Ananda both ordered apple juice. Sophie tried the smallest drink. 'Mum says it's really good for you,' she said.

That was good, wasn't it, Jo?

Yeah, healthy and delicious.

Delicious? You didn't try the wheatgrass juice, did you?

▷ What drinks did the kids order? Where can you get healthy food and drink in your area?

8 Now you Project (Step 3)

a) Think: Where can you go for a good snack, an ice cream or a drink in your area?
b) 👥 Pair: Agree on one place.
c) 👥👥👥 Share: Agree on one place with the other pair in your group.
Start to collect material on your snack/drink place.

▶ GF 18: Question tags (p. 143) • P 10–11 (p. 86) • WB 9–12 (pp. 60–61)

Looking at language

a) Find all the question tags in **7** and complete the chart:

	question tag
That's the place,	isn't it?
It looks pretty cool,	...
...	

When is the question tag positive? When is it negative?

b) Look at the question tags again. How can you say the same thing in German?

9 Ananda at the computer 🎧

Ananda was the last one at the computer club that evening. She now had the three pages of material for the team's Bristol booklet.
'I'm afraid I have to lock up now,' somebody said. It was Mrs Pitt, the IT teacher.
'Of course, Mrs Pitt,' Ananda said. She took her things and got up to leave. 'Oh, Mrs Pitt,' she remembered, 'have you seen a black and blue mobile anywhere?'
'No, Ananda. Why?'
'David has lost his. Or somebody has stolen it. Maybe there's a thief at school.'

> What are Ananda's three pages of material about?

10 A page from the booklet 🎧

The Bristol International Balloon Fiesta

The Bristol International Balloon Fiesta takes place in a park in Bristol every August. It is the biggest hot-air balloon festival in Europe, with hundreds of balloons.

There are lots of other fun things to do and see for all the family, with food and drink from all over the world. Everybody loves the 'Night Glow'. It takes place on the first night, with about 30 balloons in the night sky.

The fiesta began back in 1979. Balloonists from the west of England, Ireland, Luxembourg and Germany followed an invitation to Bristol. On a September weekend the International Balloon Fiesta was born when 27 balloons flew over the city.

That small fiesta has grown from year to year. Now, more than 500,000 people come to Balloon City Bristol. They have a great time as they watch more than a hundred balloons of all shapes, sizes and colours.

STUDY SKILLS — Structuring a text

Wenn du einen Sachtext schreibst, denk daran, ihn zu gliedern:
Beginning *(Einleitung): Hier beschreibst du, worum es geht.*
Middle *(Mittelteil): Hier schreibst du mehr über dein Thema.*
End *(Schluss): Hier kommst du zum Anfang zurück und rundest deinen Text ab.*
Finde Einleitung, Mittelteil und Schluss in Anandas Text über das Bristol International Balloon Festival (links). Schreib dir nützliche Ideen oder Redewendungen für eure Broschüre auf.

▶ SF Structuring a text (p. 123) • P 12 (p. 86)

11 👥 Now you   Project (Step 4)

Produce three pages of material for your booklet (event, person, snack/drinks place). First mark up the texts that you have found. Then write your text. It should have a beginning, a middle and an end. You can work on a computer and download or scan in pictures. Or you can write out your material and add drawings. Make a title page and put together your booklet.

▶ P 13–14 (p. 87) • WB 13–16 (pp. 62–63)

1 WORDS A Bristol mind map

a) Make a mind map about Bristol. Use as many words and phrases as you can. Here are some ideas.

b) Would you like to visit Bristol? Why/Why not?

c) **Extra** Start a mind map for your area. You can add to it as you go through the unit.

2 LISTENING The slave girl's story

a) On page 77 you found out that Bristol got rich from the slave trade. Now listen to Binta's story. Where did she come from? Where was she before she came to Bristol?

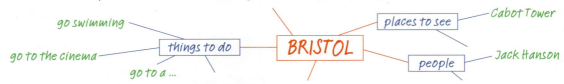

b) Listen again. Are these statements right or wrong? Correct the wrong ones.
1 Binta was twelve when she left Africa.
2 She was at sea for six weeks.
3 She saw her father again in the Caribbean.
4 When she arrived she sold sheep and sugar at a big market.
5 She's sure she'll die in Bristol.

3 WORDS Discussion

a) Agree in class on four statements like these to talk about:
1 English is the most interesting subject.
2 Students shouldn't bring mobiles to school.
3 Bristol is a very interesting city.
4 …

b) 👥 Talk to different partners about the statements. Use the following phrases to agree or disagree. Always give reasons.

– Yes, I agree with number one because it's interesting to hear about another country/…
– I agree with you. I think English is the most interesting subject too.
– Yes, you're right because …

– No, I disagree with number one. I think Art is more interesting because you can … /…
– Sorry, I disagree with you. I think Maths is more interesting.
– Sorry, I don't think that's right because …

c) **Extra** Tell the class about one of your partners and yourself.
Anna thinks Art is more interesting than English because you can do things with your hands.
I don't agree because I think it's interesting to hear about another country.
We both think number 2 is wrong because …

4 REVISION What have you done? (Present perfect)

a) Make three 'windows' like the one on the right. Fill in each window with a different partner. Here are some ideas – use different ideas with each partner.

A: I've visited Hamburg / seen a Wallace and Gromit film / eaten African food / read a Harry Potter book in English / ... What about you?
B: Yes, I've visited Hamburg too. / No, I haven't visited ...

b) Report to the class.

	My partner has ...	My partner hasn't ...
I have	... visited Hamburg. ...	... seen a Wallace and Gromit film. ...
I haven't	... eaten African food. ...	... read a Harry Potter book in English. ...

5 Bristol people and places (Relative clauses)

a) Link the sentence halves with **who** or **which**.
1 Sophie is the girl – she talks to a poltergeist.
  Sophie is the girl who talks to a poltergeist.
2 Cabot Tower is a building – it gives a good view of Bristol.
3 Dan is the twin – he misses his mother.
4 Dilip is the boy – he likes Sophie's sister.
5 Aardman is the name of the studios – they make Wallace and Gromit films.
6 Polly is the name of the parrot – she lives in a B&B.
7 Emily is the girl – she's not very nice to her sister.
8 Brunel is the engineer – he designed Temple Meads Station.

The only person who can talk to me is Sophie.

b) Make sentences like the ones in a) about other people or places in Bristol. Can your partner complete them with who or which?
Jack is the boy – he has mad ideas.
– Jack is the boy who ...

6 Extra My classmates (Relative clauses)

a) Write down some facts about five classmates and give them to your partner.
1 girl – plays football
2 boy – Mark's friend
3 ...

b) Your partner uses your notes and makes sentences with relative clauses about your classmates. Then he/she guesses their names. Are they right?

7 What are they called? (Relative clauses)

Partner B: Go to pages 112–113.
Partner A: Find out from your partner what the people and things in pictures 1–4 are called. Answer your partner's questions about pictures 5–8.
A: Who's the boy who is taking …? What's the name of the fish which …?

1
– take a photo
– listen to MP3s

2
– play tennis
– play with a cat

3
– eat a hamburger
– play basketball

4
– land on a field
– land on a lake

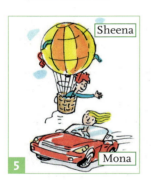  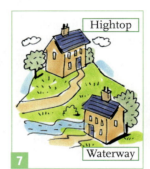 

5 Sheena / Mona
6 Brad / Tom
7 Hightop / Waterway
8 Fred / Ginger

8 Words that you don't know in English (Relative clauses)

Sometimes you really need a word, but you don't know it in English. Maybe you can explain what you mean with a relative clause. Try it with these pictures. The words in the boxes can help you.

1 Number 1 is a car that …
2 Number 2 …

be • drive • fit • help • look for • show • take away • work

dangerous • people when they're ill • in a church • pocket • rubbish • temperature • bank robbers • very fast

9 STUDY SKILLS Marking up a text

a) Use a copy of the text for these tasks. Work in groups of three.
Read the text. Try to understand new words before you look them up in the Dictionary.
- Student A marks up the most important information on Wallace and Gromit,
- student B on Nick Park,
- student C on the fire at Aardman Studios.

When you have finished, write down key words on your topic in your exercise book.

b) All the A students get together, all the B students and all the C students too.
Use your key words and give a short report to your group. Together decide on the best key words for the best report.

c) Use your best key words and give a report to the class.

Wallace & Gromit

Wallace and Gromit are the stars of three famous short films and one long one by Nick Park of Aardman Studios. But the two aren't like most stars – they're plasticine models! Everybody in the Wallace and Gromit films is a plasticine model.

Wallace lives at 62 West Wallaby Street in Wigan. He usually wears the same clothes. He loves cheese. He invents things all the time, but many of his ideas don't work. Wallace is a very nice man who believes everything will be fine in the future.

Gromit is a dog who lives with Wallace. He has no voice, his birthday is 12th February, and he's very clever. He even studied – at 'Dogwarts University'! (Do you know 'Hogwarts' from the Harry Potter books?) Gromit is cleverer than Wallace and often helps him with his work.

In 1976 Peter Lord and David Sproxton started Aardman Studios in Bristol. Nick Park came to Aardman in 1985, and he brought Wallace and Gromit with him. As a little boy Park liked drawing and making models with plasticine. He even used his parents' camera to make a film with his models.

When he left school, Park went to the National Film and Television School. He started his first Wallace and Gromit film, *A Grand Day Out*[1] (1989), there. Wallace and Gromit came back in *The Wrong Trousers*[2] in 1993, and two years later in *A Close Shave*[3]. Both films won Oscars. Nick Park got another Oscar for Wallace & Gromit: *The Curse of the Were-Rabbit*[4] (2005).

On 10 October, 2005, a fire destroyed the old warehouse where Aardman had most of their old models. They lost lots of models from the Wallace and Gromit films, but also the ones from Chicken Run (2000). The good news is: the Aardman films were safe in another building. Wallace and Gromit live on! ■

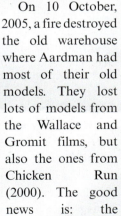

Deutsche Titel: [1] *Alles Käse*   [2] *Die Techno-Hose*   [3] *Unter Schafen*   [4] *Auf der Jagd nach dem Riesenkaninchen*

10 Nice weather today, isn't it? (Question tags)

Sir James has to take the bus today because his chauffeur is ill. He's very polite and tries to talk to Pete the punk. What does he say? Complete his sentences and use the right question tags in the right tense.

1 weather / very nice today
   The weather is very nice today, isn't it?
2 bus / not very full
3 Georgian House / lovely building
4 bus driver / drive carefully
5 Wallace and Gromit / the greatest
6 The Balloon Fiesta / going to start / tomorrow
7 we/not arrive at / the station/yet
8 they/sell/healthy food/at St Nicholas Market
9 you/not go to/Cotham School
10 you/enjoy/our chat
   Pete the punk — We didn't have a chat.
      I/not say/anything

aren't they? • did I? • don't they? • do you? •
haven't you? • have we? • is it? • isn't he? • isn't it? (2 x)

11 The greatest (Question tags)

Write the name of a person or an animal on a card. It can be a famous animal or person, a film star, a football player, … Your teacher collects all the cards and then puts one card on each student's back! Walk around, look at the other students' backs and make compliments. Can they guess who they are?

You're the best footballer in the world, aren't you?

Oh, am I Miroslav Klose?

Yes, you are./ No, you aren't.

You're the biggest animal, aren't you?

12 STUDY SKILLS Structuring a text

a) Read the three paragraphs below. Put them in the right order: beginning, middle and end.

1. Last year there were some really great things to see: a clown with a funny car and two jugglers from New Zealand. They were amazing. I learned to juggle from them. The festival always has lots of other interesting activities too.

2. My favourite event in Bristol is the Bristol Children's Festival. It takes place on the Downs every summer and is always great fun.

3. Everybody always has a great time at the Children's Festival and the best thing is: all the money goes to a children's charity. So kids can have fun and help other kids at the same time.

b) Look at the text in a) again. Collect useful phrases that you can use in your own text about an event.

The juggler

13 MEDIATION A tour of Bristol

a) The Meiers are guests at the Pretty Polly B&B. They see this brochure. Herr and Frau Meier don't understand much English. Answer their questions about the brochure. Remember: only give them the most important information.
1. Um wie viel Uhr geht die Tour los?
   You: Die Busse fahren …
2. Fahren sie auch am Sonntag?
3. Wie lange dauert die Tour?
4. Was kostet das für uns zwei?
5. Was müssen wir sonst noch wissen?

b) On the tour the Meiers don't understand the guide very well. Listen to the guide and to their questions. Can you help them?
Herr Meier — Was hat sie gesagt?
You — Sie heißt Carol und wünscht uns viel Spaß.
Herr Meier — Was ist mit …?
…

Come and join us…

…on our open-top buses for a tour of the fantastic city of Bristol. Tours run 7 days a week from 10 am to 4 pm and last 75 minutes. Get on and off where you like.

FARES
Adult …………………………£8.50 / €15
Child …………………………£4 / €7
Students/seniors …………£7.50 / €14

SAVE
£1 off with tickets from a different tour. Show this Bristol ticket to get 10% off tours.

14 GETTING BY IN ENGLISH At the juice bar

a) Can you say these things in English?
1. Das kapiere ich nicht. (p. 78)
2. Frag mich nicht. (p. 79)
3. Sei nicht albern. (p. 80)
4. Es sieht ziemlich cool aus. (p. 80)
5. Was darf ich dir bringen? (p. 80)
6. Welche Sorte hättest du gern? (p. 80)
7. Es ist unheimlich gesund. (p. 80)
8. Es tut mir leid, aber … (p. 81)

b) Imagine you are walking round Bristol with a friend when you see a juice bar. Prepare the dialogue and act it out.
A: Sag B, dass die Juice Bar recht gut aussieht. Schlag vor, dass ihr reingeht.
B: Antworte, dass A nicht albern sein soll. Saft ist gesund, aber langweilig.
A: Sag, dass du anderer Meinung bist. Saft kann sehr lecker sein.
B: Sag, das verstehst du nicht, aber okay, du wirst es probieren.
A: Sag B, er/sie soll sich an einen Tisch setzen, du kannst die Getränke holen. Frag, was du ihm/ihr bringen darfst.
B: Sag, dass du einen Smoothie möchtest. Sie sind sehr gesund. Frag, welche Sorten sie haben.
A: Sag, dass du keine Ahnung hast.
B: Bitte A, dir Erdbeere zu bringen.
(Du gehst an die Theke und bestellst.)
A: Es tut dir leid, aber Erdbeere haben sie nicht.
B: Sag, du hättest gern einen Bananen-Smoothie.

To catch a thief 🎧

'Well,' said Jack the next day, 'it was good teamwork on the booklet. Now we need good teamwork again: Who is stealing things from Form 8PK?'

'Well, it can only be one person,' Jo said.
'Who do you mean?' Sophie asked.
'Lesley, of course!' Jo said. 'I mean, before she came, nothing disappeared in our class. Now things disappear all the time, don't they? First there was Ananda's lunch money …'
'And then Simon's pen,' Ananda added.
'And now David's mobile. I think it's Lesley.'
Jack was angry: 'That's not fair, Jo. There's no proof.'
'But you're the one who told us about Lesley and how her mum hasn't got much money.'
'So? We haven't got much money,' said Jack, 'but you don't think I'm a thief, do you?'
'No, of course not,' said Dan. 'And I don't think Lesley's a thief!'
'This is the point, isn't it?' said Sophie. 'Somebody is stealing things and we don't know who.'
'No, we don't,' said Dan.
'So,' Sophie went on, 'We have to catch the thief – and we need proof.'

'Right!' said Jack.
'And how are we going to get proof?' asked Jo.
Jack smiled: 'We're going to set a trap.'
'And how are we going to do that?' asked Jo.
'Well,' said Jack, 'why don't we leave a purse in the classroom at break tomorrow?'
'But we have to go outside at break. So we can't watch it,' said Ananda.
'Hey,' said Sophie excitedly, 'I've got an idea. My mum always loses her keys. So my dad bought her a special key ring that bleeps when you whistle. So you can always find it.'
'Great idea!' said Jo. 'We put the key ring in the purse …'
'… we leave the purse in the classroom,' Dan added.
'And after break we whistle and Lesley's school bag bleeps!' Jo finished in a loud voice.
'Shut up, Jo!' they all said.

The next day Ananda brought an old purse to school, and Sophie brought her mum's key ring. At break, Sophie left the purse on her desk and they all went outside.
'Did you leave the purse inside?' asked Jack.
'Yes, I did,' said Sophie.

'And did you put the key ring in?' asked Jo.
'Yes, I did,' said Sophie.
'And yes, before you ask – I put some money in the purse too: five pounds,' said Ananda. 'Now all we have to do is wait.'

At the end of break, the SHoCK Team went to Sophie's desk.
'It has disappeared!' whispered Sophie.
'Right!' said Jo.
He started to whistle as he walked slowly towards Lesley's desk.

'Are you all right?' Lesley asked as Jo came nearer.
'I'm just looking for Ananda's purse – somebody has stolen it,' said Jo.
'And I suppose you think this "somebody" is me,' said Lesley angrily. Jo just whistled again. Nothing happened. No bleep.

'I told you it wasn't Lesley,' said Jack when Jo came back. 'I'm going to try over there.'
'And I'm going to try there,' said Ananda.
Just then Mr Kingsley came into the classroom.
'We'll have to look in other places at lunch break,' whispered Ananda.

So, at lunch break:

'And?' asked Jack as they all met outside.
'Nothing,' said Jo.
'Nothing,' said Dan. He started to whistle again.
'Wait a minute,' said Sophie. 'Listen, everybody.'
Jack smiled: 'A bleep! Whistle some more, Dan. Let's walk this way.'
They all walked towards the school. But the bleeps faded.
'We're going the wrong way. Let's go over there,' said Sophie.
They walked away from the school and …
'Bleep! Bleep!' the bleeps got louder and louder.
'Look!' said Jack. 'We're following Mr Smith.'
'But it can't be Mr Smith!' said Jo. 'He's the caretaker. He doesn't steal things!'
But, as they got nearer to Mr Smith, the bleeps got louder.
'Ah, there you are, Mr Kingsley!' The SHoCK Team stopped as Mr Smith started to talk to Mr Kingsley.
'Hello, Mr Smith,' said Mr Kingsley. 'What can I do for you?'
'It's your form – 8PK. They don't look after their things very well,' answered Mr Smith. He opened his bag and took out a mobile phone.
'The cleaners found this on the floor last night. And look …' He took out a purse.

'I found this purse when I went in to check the broken window at break this morning. Oh no, now it's bleeping!'

115 Jo stopped whistling. The rest of the SHoCK Team just stood there. Mr Kingsley turned. 'Ah, here's a group from 8PK. Who does this purse belong to? Do any of you know?'
'Er … me, Mr Kingsley,' said Ananda.
120 'And this mobile?'
'I think it's David's, Mr Kingsley,' said Jack.
'You really have to look after your things better, you know,' said Mr Smith. 'If thieves get into the school, it'll be very easy for them, won't it?'
125 'Mr Smith is right,' said Mr Kingsley. 'Remember how your lunch money disappeared, Ananda?'
'Yes, Mr Kingsley. And Simon's pen.'
'Right! So listen to Mr Smith or you'll really
130 lose something important. See you later.'
Mr Kingsley and Mr Smith walked away.

'Oh dear,' said Jack. 'Not one of the SHoCK Team's great cases, eh?'
'Well,' laughed Jo, 'You can't win them all!'
'No,' said Sophie, 'But we have learned something.' 135
'Er … have we?' asked Jo.
'Yes, we have,' she said. 'There isn't a bank robber or a spy behind every little mystery, is there Jack?' 140
'No, I suppose not.'
'Oh, yes,' added Dan, 'and you shouldn't go round and say people have stolen things before you're sure, right, Jo?'
'Er, … right.' Jo looked at the floor. 'I suppose I 145 should say sorry to Lesley then.'
'Yes,' said Jack. 'She's over there.'

Working with the text

1 The story – what happened?
Put these sentences in the right order.

1. So then Jo started to whistle and walked towards Lesley. There were no bleeps.
2. The purse disappeared at break.
3. They tried again at lunch break and the bleeps started when they followed Mr Smith.
4. So they set a trap to catch the thief.
5. Before Lesley came to Cotham School nothing disappeared. Jo thought Lesley was the thief.
6. Then Mr Smith explained: 'The cleaners found this mobile and I found this purse.' He gave them to Mr Kingsley.
7. At the end Jo had to say sorry to Lesley.
8. The SHoCK Team wanted to find out who was stealing things.
9. Mr Kingsley and Mr Smith said the SHoCK Team should look after their things better.
10. At break they left a purse with Sophie's mum's key ring in on a desk.

2 The end of the story
Write the end of the story. Use the box for help and begin like this:
So Dan told his brother, 'You should …'

> should say sorry • go over to Lesley •
> try to explain • Lesley very angry / not want to
> listen / not need friends like Jo •
> SHoCK Team try to help Jo •
> want to be friends • at the end • …

DOSSIER *Lesley's story*

Imagine you're Lesley. What will you tell your friends in London about what happened? Write a letter and put it in your dossier.
Dear Trish,
Today something mad happened after break. Jo Shaw came towards me and whistled …

3 Extra And at your school?
Do things ever 'disappear' in your school? What happens then? Who do you tell? What do they do?

▶ WB 17 (p. 64)   Checkpoint 5   ▶ WB (p. 65)

Extra EXTENSIVE READING Robinson Crusoe 🎧

1 Imagine you're going to live alone on an island. What five things do you want to take with you?
2 Read the story. Try to understand the new words from the context, from German or from other English words before you look them up in the Dictionary.

I was born in the year 1632 in the city of York. When I was 18, I wanted to go to sea. My father tried to stop me: 'If you go abroad, you will be the saddest man in the world.' But I did not listen to his words and when I was 19, I left home.

My travels took me to Africa, where I spent two years as a pirate's slave. I escaped and went to Brazil on a Portuguese ship. I bought a farm and after a few years I was very rich. But then some neighbours asked for my help. They wanted to get slaves from Africa for their farms. I knew that part of the world. So I went with them.

Our little ship left on 1 September 1659. After about ten days, there was a terrible storm. It went on for almost two weeks, and at the end we had no idea where we were.

Then one of the men saw land, but suddenly our ship hit a sandbank. 'The storm will break the ship soon,' we thought, so we decided to leave the ship in a small boat. We rowed towards the shore, when a wave like a mountain came down on our small boat and threw us into the sea.

Again and again the waves took me under the water, but I was getting nearer to shore. Suddenly I felt land under me, but the waves still pulled me out to sea.

The next time I felt land, I ran as fast and as far as I could. After three more times, I was safe at last. I looked up and thanked God for my life. I looked out to sea and saw the wreck of my ship. It was very far away. How did I get to shore? Now I was very afraid. I didn't know where I was, I was wet, I had no clothes and nothing to eat or drink.

I found a tree to sleep in for the night. But first I needed water, so I walked around a bit. I found a little river and drank. Then I went back to my tree, climbed it and slept.

The next morning I saw that the storm was over. But the biggest surprise was that my ship was now only about a mile away, on some rocks.

When the tide went out, I could walk most of the way to the ship. When I went on board, I thought of my dead friends and felt the tears in my eyes. Why didn't we all stay on the ship? I found food, guns, tools and clothes. I took a sail from the ship too. I wanted to make a tent with it. But how could I get everything to shore? I had to make a raft.

I used some of the tools. It wasn't a very good raft, but it helped me to take the things to shore.

I went to the ship eleven times in my first thirteen days and brought back lots of things. The twelfth time I even found lots of silver coins in the captain's cabin. I wanted to take

more, but I saw that there were clouds in the sky, and the wind was getting stronger.

I got to shore before the storm and took everything to my tent. The storm went on all night. When I looked the next morning, the ship was gone.

I still didn't know where I was. About a mile from my tent there were some hills. One was higher than the others, so I walked to it and climbed. It was very hard, but I got to the top.

There I could see that I was on an island. There were no houses or farms on the island, just trees, plants and wild animals.

'I'll be here a long time,' I thought. So I decided I had to build a house. But my house had to be a fort. I looked for a good place for a long time: I needed water, shelter from the sun and rain, a place where I could be safe from wild animals or cannibals, because I knew that cannibals lived in this part of the world. I also wanted to see the sea. 'If a ship comes, I have to see it and send a signal.'

It was hard work, but with the tools from the ship, I built my fort. After many weeks, I felt safe when I slept at night.

Over the next months and years I went to different parts of my island and found the best

place for fruits. I learned to kill or catch the wild goats on the island. I made clothes from the skins of the animals, candles from their fat. I learned to make pots, and I made my own tables and chairs. I even became a farmer and I built a small boat.

When I ate, I sat down with my pets. I had a parrot, a dog and two cats from the ship, and I had a baby goat. I wanted real friends, but my pets were better than nothing.

I even taught Poll – that was my name for the parrot – to talk. He learned to say his name, so the first word I heard on the island was 'Poll'.

Fifteen years came and went. And then ... one day, as I was walking to my boat, I suddenly saw a footprint. A man's footprint in the sand. I was very scared. I looked for more footprints, but there was only one.

I walked very quickly back to my house, my fort – I looked behind me all the time. When I got back to my house, I thought: 'How is this possible? Where is the ship that brought this man? Why is there only one footprint?'

After three days, I began to think that the footprint was really mine and felt better. But I had to go back and see. I went to the place, and the footprint was still there. I put my own foot next to it: my foot was much smaller!

Who was this man? Why was he on my island? I went back to my house and started work to make my fort stronger and safer.

A few years later I found something terrible: a place on the shore where there were people's bones in the sand – around a fire. Cannibals! I was very much afraid and didn't go back to that place for two years. I didn't want to be food for cannibals.

But later I visited the place to plan how I could wait for these terrible people and kill them when they came.

In my 24th year on the island about thirty cannibals came with two prisoners. They killed one and began to cook him. Just then the other prisoner ran. He ran, and three of the cannibals followed him.

When the prisoner got to the little river near my house, he quickly swam across it. Only two of the cannibals followed because the third couldn't swim. The prisoner was faster than the other men, and soon I was between him and the cannibals.

I had to kill one of the cannibals before he killed me. The prisoner killed the other one. Then he came to me and spoke to me in a strange language. I couldn't understand him, but I knew he wanted to thank me and be my servant.

I gave my servant the name Friday because that was the day when I saved him. Friday became not only my servant, but a friend. I taught him to speak our language and to use a gun. The time with Friday was my best time on the island.

Then one day a strange thing happened. I was asleep in my tent when Friday came in. 'They have come,' he shouted. 'They have come!'

I followed Friday to a place where we could watch the shore. There was a small boat – an English boat. And out at sea I saw an English ship. But something wasn't right.

The men were English, but they had prisoners. Friday thought they were cannibals, but I told him they weren't. 'Maybe they will kill the prisoners, but they won't eat them.'

That night, when the other men were drunk and asleep, I talked to the three prisoners.

Imagine their surprise when they saw me. They told me their story.

One of the prisoners was the captain of the ship. But a group of mutineers was now in control of the ship. 'I will help you,' I told the captain, 'if you promise to take me and my man Friday to England.' He quickly agreed.

I gave the captain and his men guns, and they killed one of the mutineers and injured one more. The others quickly agreed to help the captain to take back his ship.

When he was in control of his ship, the captain sent a boat for me and Friday.

I took with me a few souvenirs and the silver coins from my ship. It was 19 December 1686, when I left my island – after 27 years, two months and 19 days.

Background File

The real Robinson Crusoe

Daniel ... finished his book *Robinson Crusoe* in ...

Most people agree that the 'real' Robinson Crusoe was ... Selkirk. Selkirk was born in ... in ... He went to sea when he was 19.

In 1704 Selkirk worked on the ship ... When the ship stopped at a small island off the coast of ..., Selkirk said the ship was not safe and they should repair it. The captain said no. After an ..., Selkirk decided to stay on the island. He was there for ... years. An English ship, the ..., found him in 1709 and brought Selkirk back to England. He probably met Daniel ... at the ... Pub in Bristol and told him his story. You can still visit the pub today.

1 You are Robinson Crusoe

Imagine Robinson writes a message in a bottle about his life on the island and asks for help because he wants to go home. Write this message.

2 The 'real' Robinson

Find out about the 'real' Robinson Crusoe. Copy and complete the background file.

Unit 6

A trip to Bath

1 The Roman Baths
Talk about the drawing of the Roman Baths in the city of Bath. What can you see? What are the people doing there? The word boxes will help you.

| a big/round/… pool • mosaics • Roman clothes • slave • stairs • statue • stone walls/ floors • towel • water • … | chat • do exercises • have a bath/massage/ sauna • jump into • play games • relax • shout • sleep • swim • … |

▶ SF Describing pictures (p. 117) • WB 1 (p. 66)

2 A trip in a time machine 🎧

a) Close your eyes, relax and travel back in time to the Roman Baths. What can you see, hear, smell and feel?

b) What do you remember about your trip to the Baths? Which rooms did you go to? How did you feel? What did you like? Make notes in a mind map/list/….
Use your notes and talk to a partner.
First we went to the … / Then we …
I saw … / heard … / felt … / smelled … / liked …

Extra **Background File**

The Romans in Bath
The Romans came to Britain in 43 AD and stayed for about 400 years. They loved their public baths, and Bath, about 20 km south-east of Bristol, had the most famous public baths in Britain. They were huge and the hall of the great bath was 40 m high.

The Roman name for Bath was *Aquae Sulis*. That's Latin and means 'the waters of Sulis'. The name comes from the hot spring there, and the Celtic goddess of the spring, Sulis. The Romans called the goddess Sulis Minerva and built a temple to her next to the baths.

statue

mosaic floor

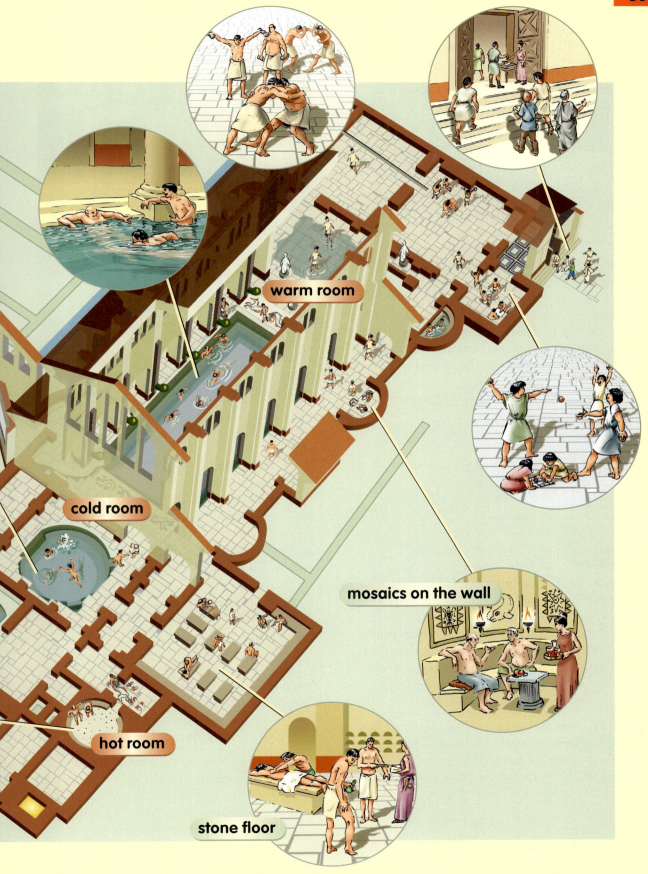

1 8PK's school trip to Bath 🎧

It was a beautiful, sunny day. Form 8PK cycled through Bristol and along the railway path which went to Bath. They were on a class trip with Mr Kingsley and Miss White.

Mr Kingsley	Hello, Sophie! How are you?
Sophie	Fine, Mr Kingsley. And this is a really nice bike ride.
Mr Kingsley	Yes, it's the nicest ride I know round Bristol. No traffic, very flat and a good cycle path. Well, Sophie, see you later.
Jack	It's a lovely day, isn't it?
Lesley	Yes, it is. I've never been to Bath. Do you know how far it is?
Jack	Mr Kingsley says it's about 14 miles. But we're only going to cycle half way, and then take the bus in Warmley. Look, here comes Jo.
Lesley	Oh, no! He's the last person I want to see.
Jo	Hi, Jack. Er … hello, Lesley.
Jack	Hi, Jo!
Jo	Dan wants to know when we get to Bath.
Jack	I'm not sure. Maybe 10.30.
Jo	Thanks. Er … Can I cycle with you guys?
Jack	What do you think, El?
Lesley	Well, I'm not sure …
Jack	Come on, El. You know Jo is sorry.
Lesley	Oh, all right then. Have you been to Bath before, Jo?
Jo	My grandma took us to the Theatre Royal when I was little.
Lesley	Oh, I love the theatre. I want to design clothes for the theatre one day. What was it like?

▶ P 1 (p. 100) • WB 2 (p. 67)

Extra ▶ GF 19 Contact clauses (p. 144) • P 2 (p. 100) • WB 3 (p. 67)

Extra ▶ GF 20 Indirect speech (p. 145) • P 3 (p. 100)

STUDY SKILLS | **Having a conversation**

Um mit jemandem ins Gespräch zu kommen, muss man ihn/sie freundlich ansprechen: **Hello! How are you?**
Zeige während des Gesprächs, dass dich interessiert, was die anderen denken oder fühlen: **What do you think?**
Finde andere nützliche Redewendungen in 1. Denk daran: Im Englischen gilt es meistens als unhöflich, nur mit einem Wort zu antworten.

▶ SF Having a conversation (p. 122) • P 4 (p. 101) • WB 4 (p. 68)

2 👥 Now you

On a school trip to a partner school in Britain, you visit a museum. Afterwards on the bus, you're sitting next to an English student. How can you get into a conversation with him/her? Write a dialogue. Look at the box for ideas. Try and use some of the phrases from 1. Act out your conversation.

A: Hi, I'm …
B: Oh, hi, my name's …
A: Did you like the museum?
B: …

You can talk about	who you are • how old you are • your hobbies • your favourite subjects • how long you've been in Bristol • the museum • your town • …
You can ask	your partner's name • what his/her favourite subjects are • what he/she liked about the museum • where he/she lives/goes to school • about his/her hobbies • …

3 Which way?

In Bath, they went to the Roman Baths in the morning. After lunch Mr Kingsley said, 'Let's get into our groups. Everybody for the Herschel Museum, Miss White is waiting for you opposite the Abbey. The others, stay here with me.'

The Herschel Museum sounds boring. I'm going with Mr Kingsley. Can you tell Miss White?

Sure, Dan, no problem.

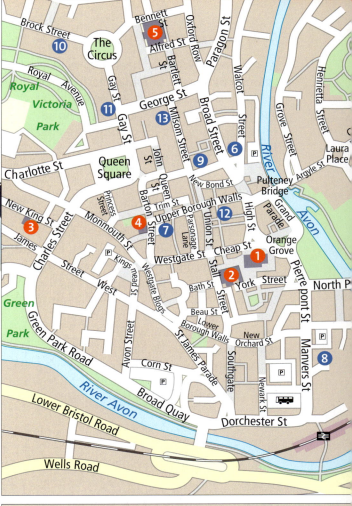

① Bath Abbey ② Roman Baths
③ Herschel Museum ④ Theatre Royal
⑤ Museum of Costume ⑥ church
⑦ hospital ⑧ police station ⑨ post office
⑩ chemist ⑪ café/restaurant
⑫ department store ⑬ supermarket

Some of the students left to go with Miss White. Mr Kingsley continued.
'Now, please look at your maps. The Museum of Costume is at the top. OK, you've learned to read a map. How can we get there? Lesley. You start.'
'Well,' Lesley said, 'we're at the Abbey. So, first we turn left into Cheap Street and walk to Union Street. We turn right into Union Street, cross Upper Borough Walls and go straight on past the post office to the end of Milsom Street.'
'Very good, Lesley,' Mr Kingsley said. 'Sophie, do you want to try?'
'Sure, Mr Kingsley,' said Sophie. 'From there we turn right into George Street, then left into Bartlett Street. We cross Alfred Street and the museum is on the left.'
'Very good, Sophie. Well then, let's go!'

4 Directions

a) How do Lesley and Sophie describe the route to the Museum of Costume? Collect the phrases and draw pictures to explain them.

Turn left. ⬑   Go past

b) Now find a route for Miss White from the Abbey to the Herschel Museum (number 3 on the map). Write down the directions. Use words and your drawings from a).

c) 👥 Choose two places on the map. Make notes and tell your partner how he or she can get from one to the other. Can he/she find the second place?
A: Start at the church. ... and then you go straight on. The place is on the left.
B: Oh, you mean the supermarket! My turn.

▶ P 5–6 (pp. 101–102) • WB 5–7 (pp. 68–70)

5 Who's missing?

At 1.30 Miss White and her group were walking through Bath. At Beauford Square, Miss White stopped. 'I must check that everybody's here,' she said. 'Hmm, I only count 15. Who's missing? – Where's your brother?' she asked Jo.
'Dan?' Jo said. 'Oh, er … we were going past the theatre when Dan stopped and looked at the posters. You needn't worry, Miss White – Dan is always slow. Oh, I can see him. He's coming.'
'All right then, but please stay together.'
A bit later, Miss White counted again: 14. She was just counting a second time when Jo came round the corner. 'Jo, I said, "Stay together."'
'Jo? I'm Dan. I'm sorry. I was looking in a shop window, and then I saw you were gone.'
'You're Dan? But then where's Jo?'
'I don't know, Miss White.'
Ananda and some of the other kids were laughing quietly. 'This isn't funny!' Miss White said. She took out her mobile and made a call.

Hello, Paul? This is Isabel. We've lost Jo!

Oh dear. What were you doing when he disappeared?

We weren't doing anything. We were just walking. And then Dan told me …

Did you say Dan? Isabel, listen: Dan is with me. Your 'Dan' is really Jo. He's playing one of his tricks.

A trick? Jo! Jo, where are you? You're in trouble now!

6 Now you

Write down six different times, like *at 8 o'clock on Saturday night, at 3.30 yesterday afternoon,* … Ask six different partners what they were doing then.
A: What were you doing at …?
B: I was watching …/talking to …/…

▶ GF 21: Present progressive (p. 146) • GF 22: Past progressive (p. 146) • P 7–9 (pp. 102–103) • WB 8–9 (pp. 71–72)

Looking at language

a) *What were Miss White and her group doing at 1.30?* They were walking through Bath.
Find more examples of this verb form in **5**. How do you make this verb form?
What were they doing when 'Dan' stopped?
They were … past the theatre.

b) Now look at the diagram. When do you use this verb form, when do you use the simple past?

They were going past the theatre
···▶
                    when Dan stopped ⬆

7 What planets can you name? 🎧

Miss White was in the museum with her group. Nicola, from the museum, was talking to the students.

'Right, now before we go round William Herschel's house, let's see what you know about astronomy. First, what planets can you name?'

'Mars!' called Jo. 'And Saturn, Venus ... and Jupiter.'

'Wow!' said Ananda. 'You really know about space.'

'Yes,' said Jo. 'I love astronomy. If we did astronomy at school, that would be really great. Then we could ...'

'Sssh, Jo!' whispered Miss White. 'If you didn't talk all the time, that would be really great too. Listen, please!'

Nicola went on: 'Now, does anybody know what planet William Herschel discovered?'

'Uranus!' said Jo.

'Very good! OK then, let's look at the telescope that Herschel used when he discovered Uranus. But please remember: you mustn't touch it. This way!'

Herschel's telescope

> Are you as good at astronomy as Jo?
> Name the planets in the right order from the sun.

Extra ▶ GF 23: Conditional sentences 2 (p. 147) • P 10–11 (pp. 103–104)

8 Extra The father of British astronomy 🎧

a) Look at the words in the box. Do you know or can you guess what they mean? Lots are like German words.
Check in the Dictionary (pp. 180–202).

b) At the museum, Form 8PK watch a film about William Herschel. Listen and answer these questions.
1 When did Herschel discover Uranus?
2 Who helped him?
3 How did he know it could be a planet?
4 What happened after he discovered Uranus?

astronomer • comet • galaxy • play the organ • solar system • star

The planet Uranus from the Hubble Space Telescope

9 Jo's report 🎧

Our class trip went to Bath. We cycled half way and then took a bus. We visited the famous Roman Baths. Too much history, but it was OK.

After lunch we divided into two groups. My group went to the Herschel Museum. I played a trick on Miss White on the way and she got really angry. It wasn't a good idea. But I really enjoyed the museum anyway. It was all about my favourite subject, the stars and planets.

We had to cycle half way home too. I was really tired but it was still a great day out.

DOSSIER A school trip

Write about a school trip.
1 First collect ideas.
2 Then start with a sentence like this:
   Last year/two years ago/... I went on a class trip to ...
3 Write about what happened on the trip. Say why it was funny/exciting/interesting/...
4 Finish with a sentence like this:
   It was a great/fantastic/... trip and I'll remember it for a long time.

Read your report to the class. Put it in your dossier.

▶ P 12–13 (p. 104) • WB 10–13 (pp. 73–74)

6 Practice

1 WORDS Word building

a) *Which parts go together?*

family	machine	dish	bin
felt	bag	dust	shirt
form	room	rail	chair
jumble	tree	skate	way
living	teacher	sweat	board
pocket	tip	time	washer
school	money	tooth	ache
washing	sale	wheel	table

family tree, felt ...

dishwasher, ...

b) 👥 *Choose six words from a). Write a sentence about each of them. Leave a gap for the word, then give the sentences to your partner. Can he/she guess the right words?*

> dishwasher -->
> *I've put all the dirty cups in the ...*

2 Extra On the cycle path (Relative clauses: contact clauses)

Read the sentences. Which ones don't need a relative pronoun? Write them down as contact clauses.

1. Bath is the city which Form 8PK are visiting.
   Bath is the city Form 8PK are visiting.
2. They're taking the cycle path that goes from Bristol to Bath.
3. The teacher who Sophie talks to is Mr Kingsley.
4. Jack is the boy who is riding with Lesley.
5. Jo is the boy that Lesley doesn't want to see.
6. The only place in Bath that Jo knows is the Theatre Royal.
7. It's the place which he visited with his grandma.
8. The first place which they are going to visit is the Roman Baths.
9. Most tourists who go to Bath visit them.
10. Miss White was the other teacher who went on the trip.

3 Extra Mr Kingsley says ... (Indirect speech)

1. Mr Kingsley: I love this cycle path, Sophie.
   Mr Kingsley says he loves this cycle path. / ... tells Sophie that he loves this cycle path.
2. Mr Kingsley: How are you, Sophie?
   Mr Kingsley wants to know how Sophie is. / ... asks how Sophie is doing.
3. Sophie: It's a really nice bike ride.
4. Jack: We're going to take the bus in Warmley.
5. Lesley: What do you know about Bath, Jo?
6. Lesley: I want to design clothes one day.
7. Dan: When do we get to Bath?
8. Lesley: What was the Theatre Royal like?

> I've never been to Bath. I can't go anywhere!

4 STUDY SKILLS Having a conversation 🎧

a) Listen to two more conversations on the cycle path to Bath. Which goes well? Which doesn't? Say why.
The first/second conversation goes/doesn't go well because …
– the first/second conversation is longer/shorter.
– … wants to know / doesn't want to know what Mr Kingsley/Miss White thinks.
– … asks/doesn't ask any questions.
– … answers with just one word.

b) Look at the phrases in the box. Listen again. Which phrases do you hear?

> What do you think of …? • What about you? •
> Do you? • That's nice. My … •
> … haven't you?/isn't it? •
> That sounds interesting. •
> Have you got any …? • Have you … before? •
> How are you? • Does she? •
> Why's that? • See you later. • All right then. •
> What was it like?

c) Write a short conversation between two people about their favourite hobby/sport/… Use as many phrases from the box as you can. You can also think of some phrases of your own.

5 WORDS Where in Bristol?

a) Partner B: Go to p. 113. Partner A: Look at your map. The names of some places are missing. Ask your partner where they are: ice rink • church • post office • internet café.
Then answer your partner's questions. The phrases in the box can help you.

> It's in … Street/Road/… •
> near/next to/… •
> opposite/in front of/behind … •
> between … and … •
> on the corner of … and …

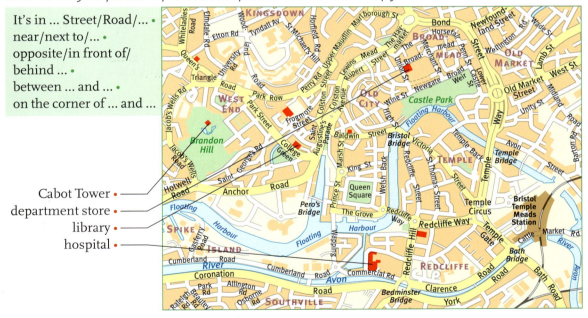

Cabot Tower •
department store •
library •
hospital •

b) [Extra] Now compare your maps.

c) You are at the station (at the bottom on the right of the map) when a tourist (your partner) asks you the way to five places on the map. Help him/her.
Tourist   Excuse me please, can you tell me the way to …?
You   First go along … Then turn left/right into … Cross … Then go straight on/… The … is on the left/right/corner of … and …

d) Now you're the tourist. Ask your partner the way to five places too.

6 MEDIATION Telling the way

Imagine you're on holiday in Bristol with your family. You are going to Bath to see the Roman Baths. You've got the directions (below) in a brochure. Answer your mother's questions.

By car from Bristol:
Take the A4 into Bath. For a day visit to Bath go to Newbridge Park and Ride, which is on the A4 just after the bridge across the River Avon. From there you can take a bus to the centre, where you will see signs to the Baths.
To park in the city centre, continue along the A4 to Charlotte Street car park. This is the largest car park in Bath and is clearly marked on approach roads – follow the 'All Attractions' signs. When you leave your car, follow the black pedestrian finger posts to the Baths.

Mother — Also, welche Straße nehmen wir nach Bath?
You — …
Mother — Steht da, wo wir parken können?
You — …
Mother — Park and Ride? Wie kommen wir dann in die Stadt?
You — …
Mother — Mit dem Bus? Nicht so schön. Können wir nicht näher parken?
You — …
Mother — Und wie finde ich den Parkplatz?
You — …
Mother — Und wie geht's dann zu den Römischen Bädern?
You — …

7 REVISION What are they doing? (Present progressive)

a) Write action cards like the ones here.

| walk | ride a bike | look for something |
| talk on the phone | eat an ice cream | cut out a photo |

b) Collect all the cards. One student chooses a card and mimes the action. The others guess what he/she is doing.
– I think you're singing a song.
– Yes, I am. Your turn. /
  No I'm not.
  Guess again, please.

8 What were you doing yesterday evening? (Past progressive)

a) Somebody killed Mr Big yesterday evening. The detective is asking questions. What do the people answer?

b) Did you kill Mr Big? What were you doing at 6 pm yesterday evening? Tell the class.

1 Jo Bloggs: 'I was watching …'
2 Ms Mabel: …
3 …

9 What were they doing when Mrs Harper came home? (Past progressive)

a) Write notes on what the people in the picture are doing. The words in the box will help you.

Sandra – talk on phone
Bobby – ...

build • do • feed •
play • read • ride • sleep •
take • talk • watch

b) Close your books. Use your notes to tell your partner what the different people in your picture were doing when Mrs Harper came home.

10 WORDS A school trip

a) Find words and phrases in the word snake. You can use all of them when you write a text about a school trip.

b) Put the words and phrases from a) into groups:
Getting there • What we did • How it was

11 Extra What would they do if ...? (Conditional sentences 2)

a) What would they do if ...?
Match the people (1–6) to the right phrases (a–f) and complete the sentences.

1 Jo – be older,
   If Jo was older, he'd learn all about astronomy.
2 Dan – have his mum at home,
3 Jack – be a detective,
4 Sophie – have a horse,
5 Ananda – go to India,
6 Prunella – be a real person

a catch a lot of thieves.
b go riding every day.
c go to Sophie's parties.
d learn all about astronomy.
e visit her aunt and uncle.
f be much happier.

b) Tell the class. What would you do
1 ... if you went to Bath?
2 ... if you won an elephant?

12 STUDY SKILLS Correcting mistakes

a) There are twelve spelling mistakes in the text. You can see the first two. Find the other mistakes and write the correct text in your exercise books.

> **STUDY SKILLS Correcting mistakes**
>
> Ein Text ist noch nicht „fertig", wenn du ihn zu Ende geschrieben hast. Du solltest ihn noch zweimal nach Fehlern durchsehen:
> – einmal, um zu sehen, ob dein Text vollständig und gut verständlich ist,
> – noch einmal langsam, Wort für Wort, um Fehler zu finden bei der Rechtschreibung, der Wortwahl, der Grammatik, ...

▶ SF Correcting mistakes (p. 124) • WB 11 (p. 73)

8PK's trip to Bath

On a beautiful <u>suny</u> morning 8PK cycled <u>happyly</u> from Bristol to a village on the way to Bath. There they left <u>there</u> bikes and took the bus into Bath, where they first visited the roman Baths. They <u>where</u> there for about ninety minutes. <u>Than</u> they had lunch at a great <u>sanwich</u> place. Most of them <u>tryd</u> the 'Roman sandwich'.
Later Miss White went with her group of <u>forteen pupils</u> to the Herschel Museum. On the way <u>their</u> Jo <u>dissapeared.</u>
Miss White started to worry. She <u>stoped</u> and phoned Mr Kingsley. He told her, 'Jo is playing a trick on you.'

b) 👥 Swap texts with a partner and check.

13 WORDS Prepositions

1 Dan and Jo live in/at/near 7 Hamilton Street.
2 They are students at/on/in Cotham School.
3 They're both under/on/in Form 8PK.
4 They usually go to school with/by/on bike.
5 They don't like waiting on/for/with the bus.
6 School starts at/on/for 8.45 and finishes at/on/for 3.30.
7 They've got PE with/under/by Mr Kingsley.
8 Jo plays football at/on/for Mondays.
9 At/In/By the weekends he often goes to/on/after the pool with his brother Dan.
10 He also listens at/on/to music.

A trip to Bath – a play for the end of term 🎧

> Look at the pictures. What do you think will happen in the play?

Jack	Hello, I'm Jack …
Lesley	I'm Lesley …
Jo	I'm Jo …
Ananda	I'm Ananda …
Dan	I'm Dan …
Sophie	And I'm Sophie. We're all students at Cotham School in Bristol.
Jack	Welcome to our little play:
Lesley	'A trip to Bath'.
Jo	Not 'bath' as in 'I have a bath every evening' … *(He mimes.)*
Ananda	Do you really have a bath every evening, Jo? I only have a bath every second evening. But I like a shower better anyway. I …
Jack	When you two have finished, maybe we can go on?
Ananda	Oh, sorry. Right.
Dan	The city of Bath is just 14 miles from Bristol, so our teacher …
Sophie	Mr Kingsley, our teacher, *(she points)* said:
'Mr Kingsley'	Let's cycle to Bath! *(All grumble.)*
Sophie	Luckily our Music teacher, Miss White, *(she points)* had a good idea. *('Miss White' walks over to 'Mr Kingsley'.)*
'Miss White'	Paul, dear, let's cycle to Warmley. That's only seven miles. We can leave our bikes there and take the bus into Bath.
'Mr Kingsley'	What a good idea, Isabel.
All	Good idea!
'Mr Kingsley'	Everybody here? Then let's go! *(Each actor sits on a chair and mimes cycling.)*
Jack	We cycled … *(very fast)*
Lesley	… and cycled *(fast)*
Jo	… and cycled *(slower)*
Ananda	… and cycled *(and slower)*
Dan	… and … cycled … *(He stops and falls off.)*

Sophie	And then we arrived in Warmley … *(all get up)* … and got on the bus.

50		*(All sit the other way round on their chairs. They mime the movement of the bus and wave. The bus stops and all jump up and take their chairs to the back. They make a group round 'Mr Kingsley'.)*
55	'Mr Kingsley'	Now here we are in the Roman Baths. The Romans built them almost two thousand years ago. They were a bit like our leisure centres – you know, swimming pools, saunas, cold pools ...
60	Sophie	*(shivering)* Very healthy!
	Ananda	Very nice.
	Dan	Very interesting.
65	Jo	Very old! *(He yawns.)* We were in there for two hours! And then, at last, Miss White said:
	'Miss White'	Time for lunch, Paul?
	All	Yes! Hooray! Lunch!
70	'Mr Kingsley'	I know a great sandwich place. Follow me!
		(They walk, they choose, they pay, they sit down on the floor and eat.)
75	Lesley	There were sandwiches with brown bread with salad ...
	Sophie	Very healthy!
	Lesley	... tomato, cheese and lettuce ...
	Ananda	Very nice!
	Lesley	... chicken tikka in a brown roll ...
80	Dan	Very interesting ...
	Lesley	... tuna and mayonnaise ...
	Jo	Very old! Hey Dan, that bread really looks very old!
	Dan	It's a Roman sandwich!
85		*(They all get up and make two groups, Miss White's group walks to one corner.)*
	Jack	After lunch we divided into two groups ... and we walked ... *(fast)*
90	Lesley	... and walked ... *(slower)*
	Dan	... and walked ... *(very slowly)*
	Jack	... and walked ... *(He falls to the floor.)*
	'Mr Kingsley'	Come on, everybody!
95	Lesley	We went to the Museum of Costume ...
	Sophie	And that's when things started to get interesting.
100	'Mr Kingsley'	Now, let's start here with the clothes from the 18th century.
	Lesley	There was so much work in these dresses – look.
	Dan	Hey, what are those things? Look!
	Sophie	They're corsets.
105	Dan	Corsets?
	Lesley	Yes, corsets. In those days all the women wore corsets under their clothes, poor things.
	Dan	But not the men, right!
110	Sophie	No, not the men.
	Dan	I wonder what they feel like ...
		(Dan tries to put on a corset. Jack helps him, then moves back to look at Dan. They all laugh.)
115	Dan	Lesley is right: the poor women. Get me out of here!

		(He tries to get out of the corset.)
	Dan	Help!
		(Jack tries to help.)
120	'Mr Kingsley'	Come on there! Hurry up!
	Lesley	We're coming, Mr Kingsley!
	Dan	You can't leave me here!
	Lesley	*(smiling)* Can't we?
	Dan	Please! Jack, Lesley, Sophie ...

Text **6**

125 Sophie	Did we leave Dan? Well … *(she laughs)* … No, we didn't. Here's the rest of the story – in pictures – Jo's pictures, of course. *(Jo comes on to the stage with his camera. Lesley is opening Dan's corset. They freeze.)*	

	('Mr Kingsley' looks into 'Miss White's' eyes.)
'Mr Kingsley'	Tired, Isabel?
'Miss White'	Yes, Paul.
Sophie	Sweet.
	(They freeze.)
Jo	Click!
'Mr Kingsley'	Jo Shaw!
Sophie	And then we cycled home … Click!
Jo	End of trip!
Lesley	Click!
Jo	End of term!
Jack	Click!
Jo	Happy holidays!
All	*(They sing.)*

Jo	Click!
Sophie	'Lesley saves Dan.'
Dan	Thank you, Lesley.
Lesley	You're welcome, Dan.
Sophie	After the museum there was ice cream …
	(All come on stage and cheer.)
All	Hooray! Chocolate for me! I'd like strawberry!
Jo	OK, say ice C R E E E E A M!
All	Ice C R E E E E E A M!
Jo	Click!
Sophie	And then we all took the bus back to Warmley. Miss White sat with Mr Kingsley.

We're all going on a summer holiday.
No more working for a week or two.
Fun and laughter on a summer holiday.
No more worries for me and you.
For a week or two.
We're going where the sun shines brightly.
We're going where the sea is blue.
We've seen it in the movies.
Now let's see if it's true.
Everybody has a summer holiday
Doing things they always wanted to
So we're going on a summer holiday
To make our dreams come true
For me and you.   *(by Bruce Welch, Brian Bennett)*

Working with the text

1 One play, seven scenes
Read the play. Divide it into seven scenes. Here are titles for three scenes. Which scenes do they go with? Find four more titles for the other scenes.

- Welcome to 'A trip to Bath'
- Great! The summer holidays
- At the Roman Baths

2 Extra   Act out the play
Divide into groups of eight. Think about what you need for the play: costumes, lighting, chairs, a corset, …
Learn the words.
Act out the play or your favourite scene(s).

Checkpoint 6 ▶ WB (pp. 75–77) • Activity page 3

6 Topic

Extra The twins' holiday trip

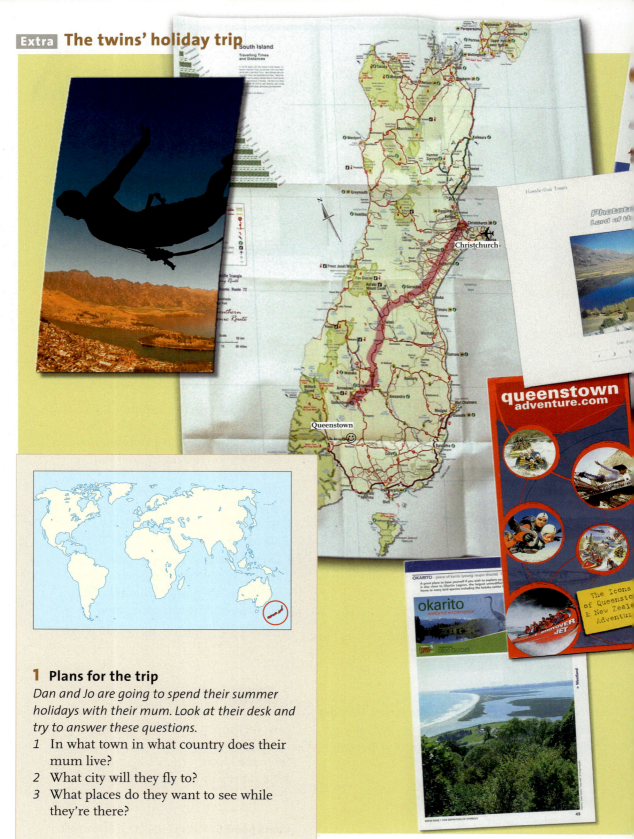

1 Plans for the trip
Dan and Jo are going to spend their summer holidays with their mum. Look at their desk and try to answer these questions.
1 In what town in what country does their mum live?
2 What city will they fly to?
3 What places do they want to see while they're there?

Topic **6**

2 Talking to Dad about the trip

a) Dan and Jo are talking to their dad about the trip. Make a chart like this and take notes on the places that they are going to visit and what they are going to do there.

Place	Activity
Christchurch	arrive – mum fetches them
Queenstown	spend time with ...
...	...
...	...

b) What's most important about the trip for Jo? And for Dan?

c) Choose one place/activity that you would most like to visit/do. Find out more about the place or activity and write an info card on it.

▶ Read more about Dan and Jo's trip in
A trip to New Zealand (Cornelsen English Library).

B Partner

Welcome Back

3 👥 What's the weather like in …?

Partner B: Look at the map on the right. Ask Partner A questions about the weather in the red cities. Then answer A's questions.

B: What's the weather like in Munich/…?
A: It's warm and stormy in Munich. / It's raining in … / There's a storm in … / It's foggy/cloudy in … It's 15 degrees in …
Swap after three questions.

Unit 1

3 SKILLS Describing pictures

a) Partner B: Draw a picture with a man, a table and a chair, a cupboard, a lamp and a tortoise.

b) Now your partner describes his/her picture and you draw it. Compare the two pictures.

c) Describe your picture to your partner. (Do not show him/her your picture.)
There's a table and chair in the foregound of my picture. A man is …
Your partner draws the picture. Then compare the pictures again.

15 Yesterday afternoon (Simple past: wh-questions)

a) Partner B: Answer your partner's questions. Then ask him/her about the information missing from your chart. Fill in a copy of the chart.

	Where did … go?	How … go?	What … do?	When … go to bed?
Ananda	home			10.00
Jo			play football	
Jack	home	by bus	do his homework / write a story	
Sophie		by car		9.15
You				
Your partner				

b) Now write a few sentences about your chart.   **c)** Swap with your partner and check.

Partner **B** 111

Unit 2

8 How much TV, how many text messages? (much/many – more/most – less)

a) Read the information about Christine. Answer your partner's questions about her. Then ask your partner about Lennart. Write the answers in a copy of the table.

	Lennart	Christine	You	Your partner
CDs – have / has got		about 30		
time – need for homework		90 minutes		
hours – sleep at night		8		
text message – get every week		10 to 15		
friends – have / has got		10		
TV – watch every day		4 hours		
money – spend on sweets		€5		

A: How many CDs has Christine got?
B: She's got about 30 CDs.
A: How much time does …?
B: …

b) Fill in the answers for 'You' in your copy of the table. Then ask your partner and add his/her answers.

c) **Extra** Report to the class. Make comparisons. Use more and most.
My partner has got more CDs than Christine. I've got more than my partner. But Lennart has got the most.

Unit 3

6 What will they do if …? (Conditional sentences 1)

a) Make a copy of the chart. Answer your partner's questions. Then ask your partner for the missing information and take notes.
A: …
B: What will Jan do if he finds a baby squirrel?
A: …
B: What will you do if

B: He'll …

I'll …

	find a baby squirrel	get a 5 in English	need a new mobile
Maike	take it to the clinic		ask her parents for one
Jan		get help from his dad	
Christoph			wait till his birthday
Your partner			

Unit 4

9 What's different? (Present perfect: just)

Partner B: Answer your partner's question about the people in the picture. Then ask about his/her picture. Take turns. Use the verbs in the box.
A: In my picture Sophie has just made some popcorn. What about in your picture?
B: In my picture Sophie has just ... And in my picture Ananda has just ...

drop • eat • find • make • open • take

Unit 4 Working with the text

2 Who said what?

Listen to your partner's questions. Scan the text for the correct answers.
A: Who said 'Morning, Bryn' and when?
B: Elaine said that when ... That's in lines ...

Now ask your partner who said these things and when.
1 'Is everybody OK?' (Beth, l. 36)
2 'We're trying to secure it.' (The fireman, ll. 22–23)
3 'I hope the trees hold.' (Bryn, l. 68)
4 'All in a day's work!' (Bryn, l. 84)

B: Who said 'Is everybody OK?'
A: Beth said that when ... That's in line ...

Unit 5

7 What are they called? (Relative clauses)

Partner B: Answer your partner's questions about pictures 1–4. Find out from your partner what the people and things in pictures 5–8 are called.
A: Who's the woman who's riding ...? What's the name of the house which ...?

Partner **B** 113

5
– ride in a balloon
– drive a car

6
– be asleep in bed
– look at the moon

7
– be on a hill
– be next to a river

8
– climb a tree
– eat an apple

Unit 6

5   WORDS   Where in Bristol?

a) Partner A: Go to p. 101. Answer your partner's questions. The phrases in the box can help you. Some places are missing in your map too. Ask your partner where they are: department store • library • Cabot Tower • hospital

> It's in ... Street/Road/... •
> near/next to/... •
> opposite/in front of/ behind ... •
> between ... and ... •
> on the corner of ... and ...

post office •
ice rink •
internet café •
church •

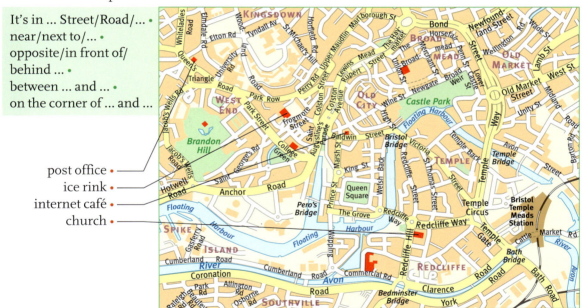

b) Extra Now compare your maps.

c) You're a tourist. You're at the station (at the bottom on the right of the map).
Ask your partner the way to five places.
You ———— Excuse me please, can you tell me the way to ...?
Your partner ———— ...

d) Now your partner is the tourist. Help him/her.
First go along ... Then turn left/right into ... Cross ... Then go straight on/ ... The ... is on the left/right/ corner of ...

Skills File

Skills File – Inhalt

	Seite
STUDY AND LANGUAGE SKILLS	
REVISION Stop – Check – Go	114
REVISION Learning words – Step 1	115
Learning words – Step 2	115
REVISION Mind maps	116
REVISION Understanding new words	116
REVISION Working with a dictionary	117
Describing pictures	117
Multiple-choice exercises	118
REVISION Giving a presentation	118
LISTENING AND READING SKILLS	
Listening	119
Scanning	120
REVISION Taking notes	121
Marking up a text	121
SPEAKING AND WRITING SKILLS	
Having a conversation	122
Linking words and phrases	123
Topic sentence	123
Structuring a text	123
Correcting mistakes	124
MEDIATION SKILLS	
Mediation	125

Im **Skills File** findest du Tipps zu Arbeits- und Lerntechniken. Was du in den Skills-Kästen der Units gelernt hast, wird hier näher erläutert.

Tipps, die du bereits aus Band 1 von English G 21. kennst, sind mit **REVISION** gekennzeichnet, z.B.
– **REVISION   Stop – Check – Go**, Seite 114
– **REVISION   Learning words – Step 1**, Seite 115.

Viele neue Tipps helfen dir bei der Arbeit mit Hör- und Lesetexten, beim Sprechen, beim Schreiben von eigenen Texten, bei der Sprachmittlung und beim Erlernen von Methoden.

Bei manchen Tipps gibt es auch Aufgaben.

STUDY AND LANGUAGE SKILLS

SF   REVISION   Stop – Check – Go

Fehler bei den Hausaufgaben? Falsche oder keine Antworten im Unterricht? Die nächste Englischarbeit steht bevor? – Höchste Zeit für STOP – CHECK – GO!

Stop
Mindestens einmal pro Unit, besser häufiger.

Check
Überprüfe, ob du den Stoff der Unit verstanden hast. Was zum Stoff einer Unit gehört, kannst du z.B. im Inhaltsverzeichnis sehen oder deine/n Lehrer/in fragen. Der **Checkpoint** ▶ im *Workbook* hilft dir am Ende jeder Unit bei der Überprüfung. Dort findest du Testaufgaben.

Go
Überlege, was du besser machen kannst. Du könntest
– deine/n Lehrer/in um Rat fragen,
– dir das, was du nicht verstanden hast, von einem Mitschüler/einer Mitschülerin erklären lassen,
– Übungen im Buch wiederholen,
– dir einzelne Abschnitte im *Grammar File* oder *Skills File* anschauen,
– die *Listening*-CD zum Schülerbuch oder das *Workbook* benutzen.

SF REVISION Learning words – Step 1

Worauf solltest du beim Lernen und Wiederholen von Vokabeln achten?

- Führe dein Vokabelverzeichnis, dein Vokabelheft oder deinen Karteikasten aus Klasse 5 weiter.
- Lerne immer 7–10 Vokabeln auf einmal.
- Lerne neue und wiederhole alte Vokabeln regelmäßig – am besten jeden Tag 5–10 Minuten.
- Es macht mehr Spaß, wenn du die Vokabeln mit jemandem zusammen lernst. Fragt euch gegenseitig ab.
- Finde heraus, welcher Lernertyp du bist, mit welchen Methoden du am besten Vokabeln lernen kannst: durch Hören, durch Bilder, am Computer (mit deinem *e-Workbook* oder dem *English Coach*) oder indem du dir eigene Geschichten um die neuen Vokabeln ausdenkst. Am besten lernst du, wenn du verschiedenen Methoden anwendest.

I walked round the car and looked in it, but the ball wasn't there. Then I looked under the car. There it was. But how did it get under the car? The ball was too big for that!

SF Learning words – Step 2 ▶ Unit 2 (p. 27) • P 1 (p. 33)

Wörter kannst du besser behalten, wenn du sie in Wortgruppen sammelst und ordnest. Dazu gibt es verschiedene Möglichkeiten.

Du kannst

- **Gegensatzpaare** sammeln, z.B.
  sunny – rainy,
  happy – sad,
  top – bottom,
  foreground – background;

- Wörter in **Wortfamilien** sammeln, z.B.
  (to) sing – song – singer;

- Wörter in **Wortfeldern** sammeln – dabei schreibst du alle Wörter unter Oberbegriffen (**group words**) auf;

- Wörter in **Wortnetzen** (*networks*) sammeln und ordnen.

SF REVISION Mind maps

Wozu dienen Mindmaps?

Mithilfe von Mindmaps kannst du Ideen sammeln und ordnen, wenn du etwas vortragen sollst oder einen Text vorbereiten willst.

Wie mache ich eine Mindmap?

1. Schreib das Thema in die Mitte eines leeren, unlinierten Blattes Papier. Male einen Kreis oder eine Wolke drum herum.
2. Überlege dir, welche Oberbegriffe zu deiner Sammlung von Ideen passen. Verwende unterschiedliche Farben.
3. Ergänze jede Idee, die zu einem Oberbegriff passt, auf einem Nebenast. Nimm dafür nur wichtige Schlüsselwörter. Du kannst statt Wörtern auch Symbole verwenden und Bilder ergänzen.

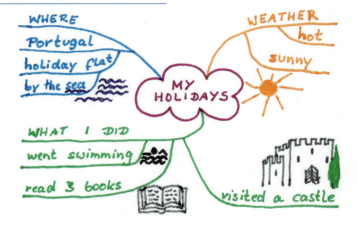

SF REVISION Understanding new words

Immer gleich im Wörterbuch nachschlagen?

Das Nachschlagen unbekannter Wörter im Wörterbuch kostet Zeit und nimmt auf Dauer den Spaß am Lesen. Oft kannst du die Bedeutung von Wörtern ohne Wörterbuch herausfinden.

Was hilft mir, unbekannte Wörter zu verstehen?

1. Bilder sind eine große Hilfe. Sie zeigen oft die Dinge, die du im Text nicht verstehst. Schau sie dir deshalb vor dem Lesen genau an.
2. Oft helfen dir die Wörter, die vor oder nach dem unbekannten Wort stehen, die Bedeutung eines Wortes aus dem Textzusammenhang zu erschließen.
   z.B. *We must hurry. Our train* **departs** *in ten minutes.*
3. Viele englische Wörter werden ähnlich wie im Deutschen geschrieben oder klingen ähnlich,
   z.B. **discussion**, **statue**, **margarine**.
4. Andere englische Wörter kannst du verstehen, weil sie einem Wort aus einer anderen Sprache ähnlich sind,
   z.B. **voice** (*French:* **voix**), **invitation** (*Latin:* **invitatio**).
5. Manchmal stecken in unbekannten Wörtern bekannte Teile,
   z.B. **sunshine**, **bottle opener**, **skater**.

> • Alles klar? Dann überlege, was diese Wörter bedeuten.
>   **energy • discovery • builder • winner • telescope • unfair • friendly • milkshake • sprinter • utilise**

SF REVISION Working with a dictionary

Du verstehst ein Wort nicht und kannst es auch nicht erschließen? Du brauchst ein englisches Wort, das du nicht kennst? Dann hilft Dir ein Wörterbuch weiter. In diesem Buch findest du das **English-German dictionary** auf den Seiten 178–199 und das **German-English dictionary** auf den Seiten 200–217.

Wörter nachschlagen: Wie benutze ich ein Wörterbuch?

Denk daran:
- Stichwörter sind alphabetisch geordnet: **f** vor **g**, **fa** vor **fe** und **fle** vor **fli** usw.
- Zusammengesetzte Wörter und längere Ausdrücke findest du oft unter mehr als einem Stichwort, z.B. **ask sb. the way** unter **ask** und unter **way** und **Geh ein Feld vor.** unter **gehen** und unter **Feld**.
- In eckigen Klammern steht, wie das Wort ausgesprochen und betont wird.
- Die Ziffern 1., 2. usw. zeigen, dass ein Stichwort mehrere Bedeutungen hat.

> - Suche im *Dictionary* (Seiten 178–199 und 200–217) die Bedeutung der Wörter rechts heraus ...
> - ... und sprich sie deinem Partner/deiner Partnerin oder der Klasse richtig vor.
>
> bottom • rude • service • Flug • gefährlich • Insel

Dictionary (English – German)
art [ɑːt] Kunst I
as [əz, æz]
  1. als, während II 2 (38)
  2. **as old as** so alt wie II 2 (30)
ask [ɑːsk] fragen I • **ask about sth.** nach etwas fragen I • **ask questions** Fragen stellen I • **ask sb. the way** jn. nach dem Weg fragen II 6 (95/170)

Dictionary (German – English)
Feld 1. field [fiːld] • **auf dem Feld** in the field
  2. *(bei Brettspielen)* **Geh ein Feld vor.** Move on one space. [speɪs] • **Geh ein Feld zurück.** Move back one space.
Fleisch meat [miːt]
fliegen fly [flaɪ]
Flug flight [flaɪt]

SF Describing pictures ▶ Unit 1 (p. 11) • P 3 (p. 17)

Wenn du ein Bild beschreibst, geht es viel besser, wenn du die folgenden Dinge beachtest.

Was?
- Du sagst zuerst, was du beschreiben willst:
  a photo • a painting • a poster • a drawing

Wo?
- Um zu sagen, wo etwas abgebildet ist, benutze:
  at the top/bottom • in the foreground/background • in the middle • on the left/right
- Du kannst diese *phrases* auch kombinieren:
  at the bottom on the left • at the top on the right
- Diese Präpositionen sind auch hilfreich:
  behind • between • in front of • next to • under

Wie?
Geh bei der Beschreibung in einer bestimmten Reihenfolge vor, z.B. von links nach rechts, von oben nach unten oder vom Vordergrund zum Hintergrund.

> **Tipp**
>
> Um zu sagen, was gerade passiert, benutzt du das **present progressive**:
> *Sophie **is showing** Jo a book. Ananda **is talking** to Jack.*

> - Alles klar? Dann beschreibe das Foto oben und mach Übung 3 auf S. 17.

SF Multiple-choice exercises ▶ Unit 3 (p. 51) • P 4 (p. 51)

Was sind Multiple-Choice-Aufgaben?

Bei Multiple-Choice-Aufgaben werden mehrere Antworten – meist sind es drei oder vier – zur Auswahl angeboten.

Wie sollte ich bei Multiple-Choice-Aufgaben vorgehen?

- Lies die Frage sehr genau durch.
- Bevor du dir die Lösungsangebote ansiehst, überlege dir, wie die richtige Antwort lauten könnte. Wenn diese dann auch als Lösung angeboten wird, könnte es die richtige sein.
- Lies aber erst alle vorgegebenen Lösungen, bevor du dich entscheidest.
- Sprich die Sätze mit den verschiedenen Lösungsmöglichkeiten leise nach. Oft hört man heraus, was richtig ist.
- Achte darauf, dass du nur **eine** Antwort ankreuzt (es sei denn, es heißt, dass mehrere Antworten richtig sein können).
- Mach erst die Aufgaben, die dir leicht fallen. Dann gehe zu den Fragen zurück, bei denen du unsicher bist.

• Nun probiere die Aufgabe 4 auf Seite 51.

1 What did Ananda find in her yard?
  A two cats
  B a fox
  C two hedgehogs
  D three mice

2 Hedgehog babies can drink:
  A orange juice
  B water
  C milk
  D iced tea

SF REVISION Giving a presentation

Wie mache ich eine gute Präsentation?

Vorbereitung
- Überlege, welche Form der Präsentation am besten zu dir und deinen Zuhörern passt (Poster, Folie, Musik, Tafel, …).
- Mach dir Notizen, z.B. auf nummerierten Karteikarten oder als Mindmap (vgl. SF **Mind maps**, S. 116).
- Bereite deine Medien vor (Poster, Folie, CD-Spieler, …). Schreib groß und für alle gut lesbar.
- Übe deine Präsentation zu Hause vor einem Spiegel. Sprich laut, deutlich und langsam.

Durchführung
- Kümmere dich zunächst um die Medien (Poster aufhängen, Folie auf den ausgeschalteten Projektor legen, CD in CD-Spieler schieben) und ordne deine Vortragskarten.
- Warte, bis es ruhig ist. Schau die Zuhörer an.
- Erkläre, worüber du sprechen wirst.
- Lies nicht von deinen Karten ab, sondern sprich frei.

> This picture/photo/… shows …

> My presentation is about …
> First, I'd like to talk about …
> Second, …

Schluss
- Sag, dass du fertig bist, und bedanke dich fürs Zuhören.
- Frag die Zuhörer, ob sie Fragen haben.

> That's the end of my presentation. Thank you for listening. Now, have you got any questions?

LISTENING AND READING SKILLS

SF Listening ▸ Unit 3 (p. 45)

Du brauchst nicht jedes Wort zu verstehen

Bei einem Hörtext sollst du oft nur allgemein verstehen, worum es geht.

1. Bevor es losgeht, frag dich: Was weiß ich schon über das Thema? Worum wird es in dem Hörtext gehen?
2. Lies die Aufgabe zum Hörtext durch. Was sollst du ganz allgemein herausfinden?
3. Denk daran: Wie jemand etwas sagt, verrät dir viel darüber, was die Person sagt. Klingt er oder sie fröhlich, traurig, aufgeregt, gelangweilt …?
4. Auch Nebengeräusche sind eine Hilfe: Du hörst einen pfeifenden Teekessel? Dann weißt du, dass sich der Dialog, den du hörst, in der Küche abspielt.
5. Vor allem: Lass dich nicht verunsichern, wenn du mal einen Satz nicht verstehst. Das geht jedem so.

Was sollte ich beim *Listening* noch beachten?

Oft willst du aus einem Hörtext Einzelinformationen heraushören, z.B. auf S. 45, in welcher Reihenfolge die Fernsehsendungen ausgestrahlt werden. Das ist nicht so schwer, wenn du die folgenden Tipps beachtest.

1. **Bereite dich gut vor**
   Lies die Aufgabe zum Hörtext gut durch und bereite deine Notizen vor. Leg z.B. eine Tabelle oder Liste an.

2. **Und wenn ich eine wichtige Information nicht verstehe?**
   Auch hier gilt: keine Panik! Denk an die Aufgabe und hör weiter zu. Oft werden wichtige Informationen auch wiederholt.

3. **Stimme und Betonung helfen dir**
   Achte darauf, was der Sprecher oder die Sprecherin besonders betont – das ist wichtig!

4. **Aufgepasst!**
   Die Informationen, die du suchst, kommen vielleicht in einer anderen Reihenfolge vor, als du erwartest.

5. **Notizen machen: gewusst wie**
   Mach während des Hörens nur kurze Notizen oder verwende Symbole. Du kannst sie hinterher ergänzen. (Vgl. SF **Taking notes**, S. 121).

SF Scanning ▶ Unit 3 (p. 49) • P 12 (p. 54)

Lesen, um nach Informationen zu suchen

Du musst einen Text manchmal gar nicht ganz lesen, wenn du nur bestimmte Informationen brauchst. Stattdessen kannst du den Text nach Schlüsselwörtern (**key words**) absuchen und nur dort lesen, wo du sie findest.

Wie gehe ich vor?

Schritt 1: Bevor du auf den Text schaust
Denk an das Schlüsselwort, nach dem du suchst. Es hilft dir, wenn du es aufschreibst.

Schritt 2: Die Schlüsselwörter finden
Geh mit deinen Augen sehr schnell durch den Text. Dabei hast du das Schriftbild oder das Bild der Wörter, nach denen du suchst, vor Augen. Die gesuchten Wörter werden dir sofort „ins Auge springen".
Du kannst auch mit dem Finger in breiten Schlingen oder Bewegungen wie bei einem „S" durch die Mitte des Texts von oben bis unten gehen.
Wenn du die Schlüsselwörter gefunden hast, lies nur dort weiter, um Näheres zu erfahren.

- Probiere das *Scanning* aus:
  Suche nach der fehlenden Information im Text über Maulwürfe (zuerst *food*, dann *number of babies* und *enemies*) und vervollständige die Tabelle auf einem Blatt Papier.

	moles
food	
number of babies	
enemies	

MOLES

Moles are about 17 cm long and weigh about 100 grams. They have sharp teeth, very small eyes and ears, and a hairless snout. They live underground – in tunnels in gardens, parks and woods. They don't usually come out during the day.
But at night they come out to look for food. Every day they eat 70 to 100 grams of worms and insects. They can't see colours very well, but they can see when something moves. And they can smell and hear very well. So it isn't difficult for them to find something to eat.
Female moles usually have three to five babies a year. The babies are born without any fur and are quite helpless. At first they stay underground. Then, at the age of three months, they are almost as large as their parents and are able to leave the tunnel. Moles can live up to three years. They have only a few enemies, like dogs and cats. These animals catch and kill them, but they don't eat them.

- Alles klar? Dann mach die Aufgabe 8 auf Seite 49.

SF REVISION Taking notes

Worum geht es beim Notizen machen?

Wenn du beim Lesen oder Zuhören Notizen machst, kannst du dich später besser daran erinnern, wenn du etwas vortragen, nacherzählen oder einen Bericht schreiben sollst.

Wie mache ich Notizen?

In Texten oder Gesprächen gibt es immer wichtige und unwichtige Wörter. Die wichtigen Wörter werden Schlüsselwörter (**key words**) genannt und nur die solltest du notieren. Meist sind das Substantive und Verben, manchmal auch Adjektive oder Zahlen.

Hmm, da hab ich wohl ein paar Symbole zu viel benutzt …

> **Tipp**
> - Verwende Ziffern (z.B. „7" statt „seven").
> - Verwende Symbole und Abkürzungen, z.B. ✔ (für „Ja") und + (für „und") oder GB für Great Britain, A. für Ananda.
>   Du kannst auch eigene Symbole erfinden.
> - Verwende **not** oder ✗ statt „doesn't" oder „don't".

SF Marking up a text ▶ Unit 5 (p. 79) • P 9 (p. 85)

Wann sollte ich einen Text markieren?

Du hast einen Text mit vielen Fakten vor dir liegen und sollst später über bestimmte Dinge berichten. Dann wird es dir helfen, die für dich wichtigen Informationen im Text zu markieren.

Wie gehe ich am besten vor?

Lies den Text und markiere nur die für dein Thema wichtigen Informationen – hier *What was Brunel's job? Name one of his famous ships*. Nicht jeder Satz enthält Wörter, die für deine Aufgabe wichtig sind, und oft reicht es aus, nur ein oder zwei Wörter in einem Satz zu markieren.

– Du kannst wichtige Wörter einkreisen.

– Du kannst sie unterstreichen.

– Du kannst sie mit einem Textmarker hervorheben.

ABER:
Markiere nur auf Fotokopien von Texten oder in deinen eigenen Büchern.

Isambard Kingdom Brunel was born in Portsmouth in 1806. He became an (engineer).
Brunel built many things: bridges, tunnels, stations and of course ships. Visitors can see one of his famous ships, the (SS Great Britain)

Isambard Kingdom Brunel was born in Portsmouth in 1806. He became an engineer.
Brunel built many things: bridges, tunnels, stations and of course ships. Visitors can see one of his famous ships, the SS Great Britain

Isambard Kingdom Brunel was born in Portsmouth in 1806. He became an engineer.
Brunel built many things: bridges, tunnels, stations and of course ships. Visitors can see one of his famous ships, the SS Great Britain

> • Alles verstanden? Dann probiere Aufgabe 9 auf S. 85.

SPEAKING AND WRITING SKILLS

SF Having a conversation ▶ Unit 6 (p. 96) • P 4 (p. 101)

Wie kann ich mich freundlich auf Englisch unterhalten?

Wenn du dich auf Englisch unterhalten willst, helfen dir ein paar einfache Redewendungen:

1. Fang nett an …	2. … und antworte nicht nur mit einem Wort.	3. Zeig, dass du wissen willst, was die anderen denken …	4. … und erzähle etwas von dir.	5. Verabschiede dich freundlich.
Hello! How are you? Can I sit with you?	Fine, thank you. Yes, of course. Yes, it is. No, I can't. Yes, thank you.	What about you? And you? What do you think? Do you like …?	I'm interested in … I often … I like … very much	Bye then. See you later. See you tomorrow. Goodbye.

Am folgenden Beispiel kannst du sehen, welchen Unterschied es macht, ob man diese Redewendungen verwendet oder nicht.

a) Jan aus Mainz ist Austauschschüler in England und spricht mit Jenny, der Tochter seiner Gasteltern.

Jenny — Hi Jan.
Jan — Hi.
Jenny — Is this your first time in England?
Jan — Yes.
Jenny — When did you arrive?
Jan — Yesterday.
Jenny — Mmm … Do you like music and dancing?
Jan — Yes.
Jenny — Well, … would you like to come to the student disco this evening?
Jan — OK.
Jenny — Well, let's meet at 7 pm then.
Jan — OK.
Jenny — Bye then, Jan.
Jan — Bye.

b) Malte ist auch zum ersten Mal in England.

Debbie — Hi Malte.
Malte — Oh, hi Debbie.
Debbie — Is this your first time in England?
Malte — Yes, it is. It's really great here.
Debbie — When did you arrive?
Malte — We arrived yesterday. So I'm a bit tired.
Debbie — Do you like music and dancing?
Malte — Oh yes, I like music a lot. What about you?
Debbie — Me too! Well, … would you like to come to the student disco this evening?
Malte — Yes, that sounds great.
Debbie — Well, let's meet at 7 pm then.
Malte — OK. Thank you.
Debbie — See you later.
Malte — Bye, Debbie. See you.

• Nun probiere das **Now you** auf S. 96 und Übung 4 auf S. 101.

SF Linking words and phrases ▶ Unit 1 (p. 18) • P 6 (p. 18)

Eine Geschichte klingt viel interessanter, wenn man die Sätze mit **linking words** miteinander verbindet. Eine Möglichkeit dazu sind **time phrases** wie at 2 o'clock, a few minutes later, before, in the morning, next, suddenly, then, …

> At 2 o'clock … David walked downstairs and opened the front door. Tim was outside. 'Follow me,' he whispered.
> … the two boys were in the garden of the old house. 'We can hide behind these trees,' Tim said. They waited and watched. … somebody opened one of the windows. … they saw a man and a woman. … the woman climbed out and jumped down. … the man threw out a big box … he jumped down too.
> 'What are they doing?' David asked.

- Copy the story. Add the linking words at the right places.

SF Topic sentence ▶ Unit 4 (p. 62) • P 4 (p. 67)

Wenn du einen Text schreibst, sind kurze einleitende Sätze (**topic sentences**) gut, weil sie den Lesern sofort sagen, worum es in einem Absatz geht. So lesen sie deinen Bericht mit mehr Interesse weiter.
Folgende Wendungen können dir helfen, einen *topic sentence* zu formulieren:
1. Orte: **Bristol is famous for … / … is a great place. / There are lots of reasons to visit …**
2. Personen: **… is/was one of the greatest/most interesting …**
3. Aktivitäten: **… is great fun. / Lots of people … every day.**

- Alles verstanden? Dann probiere Übung 4 auf S. 67.

SF Structuring a text ▶ Unit 5 (p. 81) • P 12 (p. 86)

Warum sollte ich meine Texte gliedern?

Ein Text ist viel besser zu verstehen, wenn er nicht einen „Textbrei", sondern mehrere Absätze enthält.

Wie sollte ich meine Texte gliedern?

Unterteile deinen Text in:
- eine Einleitung (**beginning**) – hier schreibst du, worum es in dem Text geht (vgl. SF **Topic sentence**),
- einen Mittelteil (**middle**) – hier schreibst du mehr über dein Thema,
- einen Schluss (**end**) – hier bringst du den Text zu einem interessanten Ende.

> ▶ Wuppertal is famous for its overhead monorail, the 'Schwebebahn'.
> ▶ The 'Schwebebahn' is over 100 years old. It's 13.5 km long and follows the River Wupper. The people of Wuppertal built it over the river because there wasn't much room in the Wupper valley. The 'Schwebebahn' isn't very fast, but it's very safe. Lots of people use it every day.
> ▶ When you're in Wuppertal, travel by 'Schwebebahn'. It's great fun!

- Nun probiere Übung 12 auf S. 86.

SF Correcting mistakes ▶ Unit 6 (p. 104) • P 12 (p. 104)

Warum sollte ich einen Text überarbeiten?

Ein Text ist noch nicht „fertig", wenn du ihn zu Ende geschrieben hast. Du solltest ihn immer mehrmals durchlesen:
Lies ihn noch einmal, um zu sehen, ob er vollständig und gut verständlich ist.

Lies ihn erneut, um ihn auf Fehler zu überprüfen. Das können unterschiedliche Fehler sein, z.B. **Rechtschreibfehler** *(spelling mistakes)*. Achte bei jedem Lesen nur auf eine bestimmte Fehlerart, z.B. 3. Person Singular-s.

Wie erkenne ich Rechtschreibfehler?

Lies deinen Text langsam, Wort für Wort, Buchstabe für Buchstabe. Wenn du unsicher bist, hilft dir ein Wörterbuch.
Einige **spelling mistakes** kannst du vermeiden, wenn du folgende Regeln beachtest.

> **Tipp**
>
> Einige Wörter haben Buchstaben, die geschrieben, aber nicht gesprochen werden,
>   z.B. **walk**, **grandma**.
>
> Manchmal ändert sich die Schreibweise, wenn ein Wort eine Endung erhält,
>   z.B. **take** —> **taking**,
>   **grumble** —> **grumbled**,
>
>   z.B. **happy** —> **happily**,
>   **fly** —> **flies**,
>   **ABER** **stay** —> **stays**,
>
>   z.B. **run** —> **running**,
>   **plan** —> **planned**.
>
> Beim Plural reicht manchmal ein *-s* als Endung nicht aus, es muss noch ein *-e* dazu,
>   z.B. **box** —> **boxes**,
>   **potato** —> **potatoes**.

tomato [təˈmɑːtəʊ], *pl* **tomatoes**
Tomate II 6 (104)

wife [waɪf], *pl* **wives** [waɪvz]
Ehefrau II 4 (71)

drop (-pp-) [drɒp] fallen lassen I

forget (-tt-) [fəˈget] vergessen I

• Alles verstanden? Dann probiere auch Aufgabe 12 auf S. 104.

Häufig sind es aber auch **Wortfehler**. Zum Beispiel hast du vielleicht eine falsche **Präposition** verwendet.

um drei Uhr – **at** three o'clock
im Moment – **at** the moment
zu Hause – **at** home

> **Tipp**
>
> • Lerne Wörter immer mit der dazugehörigen **Präposition**, z.B. nicht nur **wait**, sondern **wait for**, oder **am** Abend – **in** the evening.

• Alles klar? Dann probiere Aufgabe 13 auf S. 104.

MEDIATION SKILLS

SF Mediation ▶ Unit 2 (p. 39) • P 17 (p. 39)

Wann muss ich zwischen zwei Sprachen vermitteln?

Manchmal musst du zwischen zwei Sprachen vermitteln; das nennt man **mediation**.

1. Du gibst englische Informationen auf Deutsch weiter:
   Du fährst z.B. mit deiner Familie nach Großbritannien und deine Eltern oder Geschwister wollen wissen, was jemand in einem Café gesagt hat oder was an einer Informationstafel steht.

2. Du gibst deutsche Informationen auf Englisch weiter:
   Vielleicht ist bei dir zu Hause eine Austauschschülerin aus England oder Dänemark zu Gast, die kein Deutsch spricht und Hilfe braucht.

3. In schriftlichen Prüfungen musst du manchmal in einem englischen Text gezielt nach Informationen suchen und diese auf Deutsch wiedergeben. Oder du sollst Informationen aus einem deutschen Text auf Englisch wiedergeben.

Worauf muss ich bei *mediation* achten?

Übersetze nicht alles wörtlich, gib nur das Wesentliche wieder. Du kannst Unwichtiges weglassen und Sätze anders formulieren.

Well, let's go to the show by car. We can't walk there because of the children. They can't walk so far.

Er will mit dem Auto fahren. Die Kinder können nicht so weit laufen.

> **Tipp**
> - Verwende kurze und einfache Sätze.
> - Wenn du ein Wort nicht kennst, umschreibe es oder ersetze es durch ein anderes mit ähnlicher Bedeutung.

> - Alles verstanden? Dann probiere die Aufgabe 17 auf S. 39.

Grammar File

Grammar File – Inhalt

				Seite
Unit 1	GF 1	REVISION	**The simple past: positive statements** Die einfache Form der Vergangenheit: bejahte Aussagesätze	127
	GF 2	REVISION	**The simple past: negative statements** Die einfache Form der Vergangenheit: verneinte Aussagesätze	128
	GF 3	REVISION	**The simple past: questions and short answers** Die einfache Form der Vergangenheit: Fragen und Kurzantworten	128
	GF 4		**Subject and object questions with *who* and *what*** Subjekt- und Objektfragen mit *who* und *what*	129
Unit 2	GF 5		**Possessive pronouns** Possessivpronomen	130
	GF 6		**Compounds with *some* and *any*** Zusammensetzungen mit *some* und *any*	130
	GF 7		**The *going to*-future** Das Futur mit *going to*	131
	GF 8		**The comparison of adjectives** Die Steigerung der Adjektive	132
Unit 3	GF 9		**The *will*-future** Das Futur mit *will*	134
	GF 10		**Conditional sentences (type 1)** Bedingungssätze (Typ 1)	135
	GF 11		**Adverbs of manner** Adverbien der Art und Weise	136
Unit 4	GF 12		**Word order** Wortstellung	138
	GF 13		**The present perfect: use** Das *present perfect*: Gebrauch	139
	GF 14		**The present perfect: form** Das *present perfect*: Form	139
	GF 15		**The present perfect with adverbs of indefinite time** Das *present perfect* mit Adverbien der unbestimmten Zeit	141
	GF 16	Extra	**The present perfect and the simple past in contrast** Das *present perfect* und das *simple past* im Vergleich	141
Unit 5	GF 17		**Relative clauses** Relativsätze	142
	GF 18		**Question tags** Frageanhängsel	143
Unit 6	GF 19	Extra	**Contact clauses** Relativsätze ohne Relativpronomen	144
	GF 20	Extra	**Indirect speech** Indirekte Rede	145
	GF 21	REVISION	**The present progressive** Die Verlaufsform der Gegenwart	146
	GF 22		**The past progressive** Die Verlaufsform der Vergangenheit	146
	GF 23	Extra	**Conditional sentences (type 2)** Bedingungssätze (Typ 2)	147
Grammatical terms (Grammatische Fachbegriffe)				148
Lösungen der Grammar-File-Aufgaben				149

Im **Grammar File** (S. 126–149) wird zusammengefasst, was du in den sechs Units über die englische Sprache lernst.

In der **linken Spalte** findest du **Beispielsätze** und **Übersichten**, z.B.

How did Dan help her?

Fragen

Merke:

Simple present   Do you get up early?   Does Lesley get
Simple past   Did you get up earl   Did

In der **rechten Spalte** stehen **Erklärungen** und nützliche **Hinweise**. Das rote **Ausrufezeichen** (**!**) macht dich auf besondere Fehlerquellen aufmerksam.

Hinweise wie ▶ *Unit 1 (p. 12)* • *P 5–6 (pp. 17–18)* zeigen dir, zu welcher Unit und welcher Seite ein **Grammar-File**-Abschnitt gehört und welche Übungen du dazu im Practice-Teil findest.

Die **grammatischen Fachbegriffe** *(grammatical terms)* kannst du auf den Seiten 148/149 nachschlagen.

Am Ende der Abschnitte stellt dir Polly wieder kleine Aufgaben zur Selbstkontrolle. Schreib die Lösungen in dein Heft. Überprüfe sie dann auf Seite 149.

Unit 1

GF 1 REVISION The simple past: positive statements
Die einfache Form der Vergangenheit: bejahte Aussagesätze

We **were** in Spain **last summer**.
It **was** great. We **went** swimming a lot and **played** volleyball on the beach.
Wir waren letzten Sommer in Spanien / sind letzten Sommer in Spanien gewesen ...

Mit dem *simple past* kannst du über Vergangenes berichten, z.B. wenn du eine Geschichte erzählst. Das *simple past* steht häufig mit Zeitangaben wie *last summer, yesterday, three weeks ago, in 2004*.

a) (to) be and regular verbs

Our holiday **was** fantastic.
We **were** in New York.
We **stayed** for two weeks.
And Jay **played** basketball every day!

1 It was great for Prunella without the Carter-Browns. Nobody **grumbled**.
  Dan and Jo **argued** a lot.

2 Prunella **dropped** Emily's CDs on the floor.

3 Prunella **tried** on Emily's clothes too.

4 In August the Shaws **painted** their kitchen.
  After that they **needed** a holiday.

(to) be und regelmäßige Verben

– Beim *simple past* von *be* gibt es nur zwei Formen:
  I, he/she/it **was**   you, we, they **were**

– Bei **regelmäßigen Verben** wird **ed** an den Infinitiv angehängt: stay → stay**ed**, play → play**ed**
  Es gibt für **alle** Personen nur eine Form.

! Merke aber:

1 Ein stummes *e* fällt weg:
  grumb**le** → grumb**led**, argu**e** → argu**ed**.

2 Einige Konsonanten werden verdoppelt:
  drop → dro**pp**ed, fit → fi**tt**ed.

3 *y* nach einem Konsonanten wird zu **ied**:
  tr**y** → tr**ied**.
  (Aber **y** nach einem **Vokal** bleibt: pla**y** → pla**yed**.)

4 Nach **t** und **d** wird die **ed**-Endung [ɪd] ausgesprochen: pain**ted**, nee**ded**.

b) Irregular verbs

The Carter-Browns **went** to Majorca.
(Infinitiv: **go**)

Dan and Jo **met** a nice girl in Cornwall.
(Infinitiv: **meet**)

The Carter-Browns **had** a very nice holiday.
(Infinitiv: **have**)
Their villa **had** a swimming pool.
(Infinitiv: **have got**)

▶ Unit 1 (p. 12) • P 5–6 (pp. 17–18)

Unregelmäßige Verben

Wie im Deutschen gibt es auch im Englischen eine Reihe von unregelmäßigen Verben, deren *simple past*-Formen du einzeln lernen musst.

▶ *Unregelmäßige Verben (pp. 220–221)*

! *had* ist die *simple past*-Form von *have* und von *have got*.

Welche dieser Formen sind simple past-Formen?

1 has • 2 met • 3 sit • 4 go • 5 travelled • 6 heard
7 were • 8 hear • 9 had • 10 sat • 11 went • 12 meet

1 Grammar File

GF 2 REVISION The simple past: negative statements
Die einfache Form der Vergangenheit: verneinte Aussagesätze

Sophie Lesley **didn't want** to come to Bristol.
Ananda She **didn't say** much.
But we **didn't ask** her much.

Eine Aussage im *simple past* verneinst du immer mit **didn't** + **Infinitiv** (Langform: *did not*).
! (Nicht: *Lesley didn't wanted ...*)

Verneinte Aussagesätze

Merke:			
	Simple present	I **don't get up** early.	Lesley **doesn't get up** early.
	Simple past	I **didn't get up** early.	Lesley **didn't get up** early.

▶ Unit 1 (p. 13) • P 8–9 (p. 19)

Sieh dir die Bilder an und vervollständige die Sätze im *simple past*.

1 This morning Jo **didn't** ... his bed. (not – make)

2 Last week Dan ... ... his bike. (not – clean)

3 Yesterday Jack ... ... his homework. (not – do)

GF 3 REVISION The simple past: questions and short answers
Die einfache Form der Vergangenheit: Fragen und Kurzantworten

Did Jo **help** Jody?
– Yes, he **did**. / No, he **didn't**.

Did the girls **talk** to Lesley?
– Yes, they **did**. / No, they **didn't**.

Why **did** Jody **need** help?
How **did** Dan **help** her?

Fragen im *simple past* bildest du immer mit **did**:
Did Jo **help**?
! (Nicht: *Did Jo helped?*)

Das Fragewort steht wie immer am Anfang.

Fragen

Merke:			
	Simple present	**Do** you **get up** early?	**Does** Lesley **get up** early?
	Simple past	**Did** you **get up** early?	**Did** Lesley **get up** early?

▶ Unit 1 (p. 14) • P 11–13 (p. 20)

Vervollständige die Fragen.
1 Why ... Jody go swimming?
2 ... Jo help Jody?
3 What ... Dan do?

GF 4 Subject and object questions with *who* and *what*
Subjekt- und Objektfragen mit *who* und *what*

Who liked the new girl, Sophie?
And **what happened** on holiday?

Wer mochte das neue Mädchen, Sophie?
Und was geschah in den Ferien?

Who did you **see** in school, Sophie?
And **what did** you **do**?

Wen hast du in der Schule gesehen, Sophie?
Und was habt ihr gemacht?

<u>Who</u> did Lesley talk <u>to</u>?
Mit wem hat Lesley geredet?

<u>What</u> did she talk <u>about</u>?
Worüber/Über was hat Lesley geredet?

Mit *who* und *what* kannst du nach dem Subjekt oder nach dem Objekt eines Satzes fragen:

◀ **Subjektfragen** („Wer oder was?"-Fragen) bildest du <u>ohne</u> *do/does/did*. Die Wortstellung bei Subjektfragen ist wie in Aussagesätzen. Das Fragewort ist das Subjekt des Fragesatzes:

	S	V	O
Fragesatz:	Who	liked	the new girl? (**Wer** …?)
Aussagesatz:	Nobody	liked	the new girl.

◀ **Objektfragen** („Wen/Wem oder was?"-Fragen) bildest du im *simple present* mit *do/does* und im *simple past* mit *did*. Das Fragewort ist das Objekt des Fragesatzes:

	O		S	
	Who	did	you	see? (**Wen** …?)
	What	did	you	do?

❗ Im Englischen steht eine **Präposition** *(to, about)* in Objektfragen **am Ende der Frage** – anders als im Deutschen.

Subject and object questions

Subject questions

Who loves Polly?
Wer liebt Polly?

Object questions

Who does Polly love?
Wen liebt Polly?

Kein *do/does/did*, wenn *who?* = „wer?"

▶ Unit 1 (p. 15) • P 15 (p. 21)

Ordne die Sätze den Übersetzungen zu.

1 Who do you know?
2 Who did you phone?
3 Who knows you?
4 Who phoned you?

A Wer hat dich angerufen?
B Wer kennt dich?
C Wen kennst du?
D Wen hast du angerufen?

Unit 2
GF 5 Possessive pronouns   Possessivpronomen

Wörter wie *mine, yours, ours* sind Possessivpronomen (besitzanzeigende Pronomen). Sie zeigen an, wem etwas gehört.

Anders als die Possessivbegleiter *my, your, our* usw. stehen sie ohne Nomen:
It's **my dress**.   – It's **mine**.   („meins")
It isn't **your dress**. – It isn't **yours**. („deins")

Du kannst ein Possessivpronomen verwenden, wenn du ein schon genanntes Nomen nicht wiederholen willst:
Statt   This is my dress, not **your dress**.
lieber   This is my dress, not **yours**.

Possessivpronomen (Besitzanzeigende Pronomen)					
my dog	mine	meiner, meine, meins	**our** room	ours	unserer, unsere, unseres
your dog	yours	deiner, deine, deins	**your** room	yours	eurer, eure, eures
his dog	his	seiner, seine, seins	**their** room	theirs	ihrer, ihre, ihrs
her dog	hers	ihrer, ihre, ihrs			

▶ Unit 2 (p. 28) • P 4 (p. 34)

Wo kannst du mine, yours *usw. verwenden?*
Schreibe die Sätze neu.

1 Is this my money or your money?
2 This isn't your dress. It's my dress.
3 That is Jo's pen, but that ruler isn't his ruler.
4 The food is for the rabbits, and the water is their water too.

GF 6 Compounds with *some* and *any*   Zusammensetzungen mit *some* und *any*

Für die Zusammensetzungen mit *some-* und *any-* gelten dieselben Regeln wie für *some* und *any*:

– *somebody, something, somewhere* verwendest du vor allem in bejahten Aussagesätzen

– *anybody, anything, anywhere* verwendest du vor allem in verneinten Aussagesätzen und in Fragen.

(Siehe auch Vocabulary, Seite 158).

There's somebody at the door.   jemand
I can't find anything to eat.   nichts
Is there anything in the fridge?   (irgend)etwas
Let's go somewhere where it's hot. irgendwohin
I don't want to go anywhere.   nirgendwohin

▶ Unit 2 (p. 29) • P 6 (p. 34)

GF 7 The *going to*-future   Das Futur mit *going to*

I'm going to help Dad in the shop next Sunday.

Ich werde nächsten Sonntag Vater im Laden helfen. /
Ich habe vor, ... zu helfen.

Wenn du über **Absichten** und **Pläne** für die Zukunft sprechen willst, verwendest du das Futur mit ***going to***. Es wird mit ***am/are/is going to*** + **Infinitiv** gebildet. Die Kurzformen heißen *I'm/you're/he's going to* usw.

! *going to* hat hier nichts mit „gehen" zu tun. Es bedeutet „werden", „wollen", „vorhaben".

Well, I'm not going to help – I've got a football match.

Ich werde nicht helfen ...

◀ Die verneinten Formen heißen *I'm not going to/ you aren't going to/he isn't going to* usw.

Jay, **are** you **going to visit** us next year? **When are** you **going to come?**

Jay, wirst/willst du uns nächstes Jahr besuchen? Wann wirst du kommen?

◀ Fragen kannst du **mit Fragewort** (When ...?) oder **ohne Fragewort** (Are you ...?) stellen.

Are you going to visit us? –   **Yes, I am. / No, I'm not.**

◀ Die Kurzantworten sind *Yes, I am / No, I'm not* usw.

The *going to*-future

Positive statements		Negative statements		Questions and short answers
I'm going to You're going to He's/She's going to We're going to You're going to They're going to	read.	I'm not going to You aren't going to He/She isn't going to We aren't going to You aren't going to They aren't going to	play.	Are you going to watch TV? – Yes, I am. / No, I'm not. Is Jo going to watch TV? – Yes, he is. / No, he isn't.

▶ Unit 2 (p. 30) • P 9–10 (p. 35–36)

Sieh dir die Bilder an. Was haben Sophie, Jo und Dan vor? Was werden sie nicht tun? Schreib zwei Sätze mit *going to* und zwei Sätze mit *not going to* in dein Heft.

1 Sophie is ...

2 She isn't ...

3 Dan and Jo ...

4 They ...

GF 8 The comparison of adjectives — Die Steigerung der Adjektive

a) Comparison with -er/-est

How old are the Carter-Brown children?
– Well, Sophie is young. She's twelve now.
Toby is younger. He's nine.
Baby Hannah is the youngest,
and Emily is the oldest.

Prunella thinks Sophie is nicer than Emily.
Emily is bigger, but is she prettier?

▶ Unit 2 (p. 31) • P 11 (p. 36)

Steigerung mit -er/-est

Steigerungsformen verwendest du, um Personen oder Dinge miteinander zu vergleichen, z.B.:

young [jʌŋ]	jung
younger [ˈjʌŋɡə]	jünger
(the) youngest [ˈjʌŋɡɪst]	der/die/das jüngste …; am jüngsten
old	alt
older	älter
(the) oldest	der/die/das älteste …; am ältesten

Die Steigerung mit **-er/-est** verwendest du für
– einsilbige Adjektive (young, full, nice, big, …) und
– zweisilbige Adjektive mit der Endung **-y** (pretty, funny, easy, …).

! Merke: nice – nicer – nicest
           big – bigger – biggest
           pretty – prettier – prettiest

b) Comparison with more/most

I think tennis is **boring**. But basketball is even **more boring**. And mum's yoga is the **most boring** thing of all.

▶ Unit 2 (p. 32) • P 15 (p. 38)

Steigerung mit more/most

Andere Adjektive werden mit **more** und **most** gesteigert:

boring	langweilig
more boring	langweiliger
(the) most boring	der/die/das langweiligste …; am langweiligsten

Weitere Beispiele:
expensive – more expensive – most expensive
difficult – more difficult – most difficult

c) Irregular comparison

Ananda has got a good idea, but Sophie's idea is better. Lesley has got the best idea.

Jo hasn't got much money this week. Dan has got more, but Dilip has got the most.
Jo hat diese Woche nicht viel Geld. Dan hat mehr, aber Dilip hat das meiste/am meisten.

Unregelmäßige Steigerung

Einige Adjektive werden unregelmäßig gesteigert:

good   – better   – best
bad   – worse [wɜːs] – worst [wɜːst]
much/many – more   – most

Die Steigerung der Adjektive

Mit -er/-est:

Einsilbige Adjektive:
old – older – oldest

Adjektive auf -y:
happy – happier – happiest

Mit more/most:

Andere zwei- und mehrsilbige Adjektive:
boring – more boring – most boring
terrible – more terrible – most terrible
exciting – more exciting – most exciting

Unregelmäßig:

good – better – best

bad – worse – worst

much/many – more – most

▶ Unit 2 (pp. 31–32) • P 16 (p. 38)

d) bigger than – as big as

 Sophie, Hip is so big. I think your rabbit is **bigger than** my cat.

 But your cat is **faster than** Hip.

Is your cat **as fast as** my rabbit?
Ist deine Katze so schnell wie mein Kaninchen?

I think she's faster. But she is**n't as big as** your rabbit.
... Aber sie ist nicht so groß wie dein Kaninchen.

Sophie is twelve. Emily is **older than** her.
Sophie ist zwölf. Emily ist älter als sie.

Is Sophie as old as Dan and Jo?
No, she isn't **as old as** them.
... Nein, sie ist nicht so alt wie sie.

▶ Unit 2 (pp. 31–32) • P 11–12, 15–16 (pp. 36–38)

„größer als" – „so groß wie"

◀ Wenn Personen oder Dinge **unterschiedlich** groß/schnell/alt/... sind, vergleichst du sie mit der 1. Steigerungsform + **than** („als"):

Your rabbit is bigger than my cat.   (... größer als ...)
Your cat is   faster than Hip.   (... schneller als ...)
                  ↑
             1. Steigerungsform

❗ (Nicht: ... bigger/faster ~~as~~ ...)

◀ Wenn Personen oder Dinge **gleich** groß/schnell/alt/... sind, vergleichst du sie mit **as** big/fast/old/... **as**.
(Verneint: not as big/fast/old/... as)

❗ Merke:
Nach Vergleichen mit **than** und **as ... as** stehen die Personalpronomen me/him/her usw. (nicht: ~~I/he/she~~ usw.):
older than me/him/her/us/them
älter als ich/er/sie/wir/sie

 Sieh dir an, wie alt die drei Jungen in der Zeichnung sind. Schreib Vergleiche mit old auf.

1 Ali is ... ... Ben and Chris. He is the ...
2 Ben is ... ... Chris, but he isn't ... ... Ali.

Ali (13)   Ben (12)   Chris (12)

I'm faster than them.

Unit 3
GF 9 The *will*-future Das Futur mit *will*

The hedgehogs **will be** cold tonight. **I'll have to** take them inside.

Maybe their mother **will come**. But maybe she **won't**.

Ananda — **What will they need**? Do you know? **Will they want** milk?
Sophie — **No, they won't**.

Sophie — **I think they'll need** water.
Ich glaube, sie werden Wasser brauchen. /
Ich glaube, sie brauchen Wasser.
(Vermutung)

Ananda — **It will be** cold tonight.
Es wird heute Nacht kalt (werden).
(Vorhersage)

Um auszudrücken, was in der Zukunft geschehen wird, benutzt du **will** + **Infinitiv**.
Es gibt für **alle** Personen nur eine Form.
Die Kurzform von *will* ist *'ll*: *I'll, you'll* usw.

Das *will-future* steht häufig mit Zeitangaben wie *tomorrow, next month, soon, in a few weeks*.

Die **verneinte Form** von *will* heißt **won't**.
(Langform: *will not*).

Fragen kannst du **mit Fragewort** (*What will they ...?*) oder **ohne Fragewort** (*Will they ...?*) stellen.

Die Kurzantworten lauten: *Yes, I will / No, I won't* usw.

Mit *will* kannst du eine **Vermutung** oder eine **Vorhersage** ausdrücken:

◂ Eine **Vermutung** fängt oft mit *I think, I'm sure* oder *maybe* an.

◂ Bei einer **Vorhersage** geht es oft um Dinge, die man nicht beeinflussen kann, z.B. um das Wetter.

❗ Im Deutschen benutzen wir oft das Präsens, wenn wir Vermutungen äußern oder Vorhersagen machen:
Vielleicht kommt ihre Mutter bald.

Im Englischen steht das *will-future*:
Maybe their mother will come soon.

Ananda — **I want to** help the hedgehogs.
I will mail the Animal Hotline.
Ich will den Igeln helfen. Ich werde eine E-Mail an die *Animal Hotline* schicken.

▸ Unit 3 (p. 46) • P 2–3 (pp. 50–51)

❗ Nicht verwechseln:
– *I want to* heißt „ich will".
– *I will* heißt „ich werde".

Ergänze diese Vorhersagen und Vermutungen.
Verwende will *oder* 'll *und diese Verben:*

be – like – be – survive

1 I... ... 13 next month.
2 Come and visit me! I think you... ... it here.
3 I'm sure the weather ... ... fine in August.
4 What do you think? ... the baby hedgehogs ...?

GF 10 **Conditional sentences (type 1)**   Bedingungssätze (Typ 1)

If you **give** a hedgehog water, it**'ll be** happy.

Wenn du einem Igel Wasser gibst, wird er zufrieden sein.

If you **don't keep** it warm, it **won't survive**.

Wenn du ihn nicht warm hältst, wird er nicht überleben.

Bedingungssätze (Typ 1) sind „Was ist, wenn ..."-Sätze: Sie beschreiben, was unter bestimmten Bedingungen geschieht oder nicht geschieht.

Die Bedingung steht im *if*-Satz, die Folge davon steht im Hauptsatz:

if-Satz (Bedingung) ↓	Hauptsatz (Folge für die Zukunft) ↓
If you **give** a hedgehog water, If you **don't keep** it warm,	it**'ll be** happy. it **won't survive**.
Im *if*-Satz steht das *simple present*.	Im Hauptsatz steht meist das *will-future*.

You'll find more help **if you visit our website**. **If you visit our website**, you'll find more help.

◀ Wenn der Hauptsatz am Anfang steht, brauchst du kein Komma vor dem *if*-Satz.

If I **see** Jack, I**'ll show** him the babies.

Ananda:
When I see Jack, I'll tell him about the babies.
Sobald ich Jack sehe, ...

If I see Jack, I'll tell him about the babies.
Falls ich Jack sehe, ...

❗ Verwechsle nicht *when* und *if*:
– *when* = „sobald", „dann wenn"

– *if* = „falls", „wenn"

If you visit Ananda, you **can help** her with the hedgehogs.
If you need more information, **write** to the Animal Hotline.

◀ Im Hauptsatz können auch *can, must, should* oder ein Imperativ (Befehl, Aufforderung) stehen.

▶ Unit 3 (p. 47) • P 5–6 (p. 52)

Schreib die Sätze mit der richtigen Verbform in dein Heft.

1 If Jack sees the babies, he **(wants / will want)** to help them too.
2 What will happen if their mum **(won't come / doesn't come)** back?
3 If Ananda **(takes / will take)** the babies to the clinic, they **(have / will have)** a better chance of survival.

Extra   If you add blue to yellow, you **get** green.
If the bus is late, I always **walk** home.
Immer dann, wenn ...

Wenn etwas immer der Fall ist, kann im Hauptsatz auch das *simple present* stehen.

GF 11 Adverbs of manner — Adverbien der Art und Weise

a) Use — Gebrauch

Hedgehogs are **slow** and **quiet**.
This is Sleepy. He's a very **slow** hedgehog.
Be **careful** if you have to touch a hedgehog.

◀ Ein **Adjektiv** beschreibt ein **Nomen** näher.
Es sagt aus, wie etwas oder jemand **ist**.

Hedgehogs walk slowly and quietly.
Igel gehen langsam und leise.

Ananda took them carefully back to the yard.
Ananda brachte sie vorsichtig zurück auf den Hof.

◀ Ein **Adverb der Art und Weise** beschreibt ein **Verb** näher.
Es sagt aus, wie jemand etwas **tut** oder wie etwas **geschieht**.

b) Regular forms — Regelmäßige Formen

Adjektiv		Adverb
slow	→	slow**ly**
quiet	→	quiet**ly**
careful	→	careful**ly**

Die meisten Adverbien der Art und Weise entstehen durch Anhängen von **-ly** an das Adjektiv.

Ananda was **angry** with Dilip. (Adjektiv)
Sophie shouted at Dilip angrily. (Adverb)

❗ Merke aber:
1. **y** wird zu **i**: angr**y** → angr**i**ly
   happ**y** → happ**i**ly
2. **le** wird zu **ly**: terrib**le** → terrib**ly**
   horrib**le** → horrib**ly**
3. Nach **ic** wird **ally** angehängt:
   fantast**ic** → fantast**ically**

▶ Unit 3 (p. 48) • P 9 (p. 53)

c) Irregular forms — Unregelmäßige Formen

Einige Adverbien haben eine unregelmäßige Form, die du auswendig lernen musst:

She did a **good** job with the babies. (Adjektiv)
She did the job well. (Adverb)

– Das Adverb zu *good* heißt *well*.

Jo — The rabbits are very **fast**. (Adjektiv)
Dan — Of course! All rabbits can run fast. (Adverb)

– Bei *fast* und *hard* sind Adjektiv und Adverb gleich.

Ananda — It's **hard** work at the clinic. (Adjektiv)
Steve — That's right. The volunteers at the clinic work very hard. (Adverb)

▶ Unit 3 (p. 49) • P 11 (p. 54)

d) Word order — Wortstellung

'You killed the hedgehogs,' she shouted angrily.

Das Adverb der Art und Weise steht direkt **nach dem Verb**.

Steve fed **the babies** carefully.
Steve fütterte vorsichtig die Babys.

❗ In Sätzen mit Objekt steht es **nach dem Objekt**.

Welches Wort ist richtig, Adjektiv oder Adverb?

1 When you pick up a small animal, you have to be very **careful / carefully**.
2 Squirrels and rabbits can run very **quick / quickly**.
3 Hedgehogs walk **slow / slowly** and **quiet / quietly**.
4 Ananda did a **good / well** job with the hedgehogs.
5 The woman at the animal clinic said Ananda did **good / well**.

e) Extra The comparison of adverbs of manner

Die Steigerung der Adverbien der Art und Weise

Du kannst nicht nur Adjektive, sondern auch Adverbien steigern:

◀ Adverbien, die auf **-ly** enden, steigerst du mit **more/most**:

quickly	more quickly	most quickly
schnell	schneller	am schnellsten

◀ Einsilbige Adverbien *(fast, hard)* steigerst du mit **-er/-est**:

fast	faster	fastest
schnell	schneller	am schnellsten

◀ Die Steigerungsformen von *well* und *badly* lernst du am besten auswendig:

well	better	best
gut	besser	am besten
badly	*worse*	*worst*
schlecht, schlimm	schlechter, schlimmer	am schlechtesten, am schlimmsten

▶ Unit 3 (p. 49)

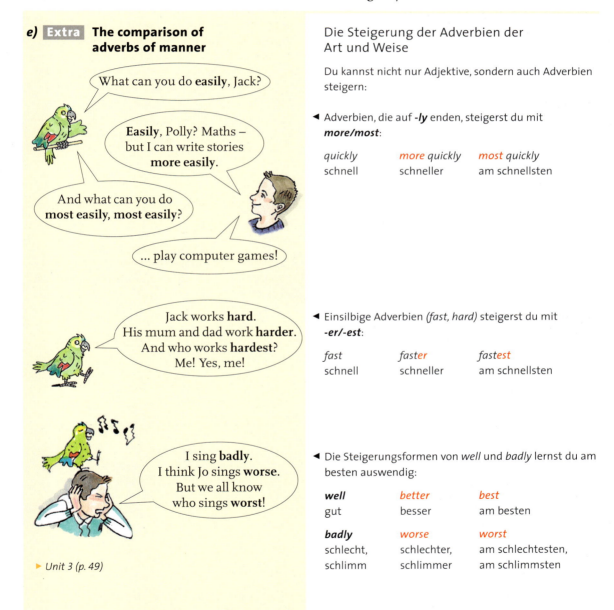

What can you do **easily**, Jack?

Easily, Polly? Maths – but I can write stories **more easily**.

And what can you do **most easily, most easily**?

… play computer games!

Jack works **hard**.
His mum and dad work **harder**.
And who works **hardest**?
Me! Yes, me!

I sing **badly**.
I think Jo sings **worse**.
But we all know who sings **worst**!

Unit 4
GF 12 Word order — Wortstellung

a) REVISION S – V – O

1. Jack **often** writes stories.
   Jack **schreibt** oft Geschichten.

2. Dilip **can play** the guitar.
   Dilip **kann** Gitarre **spielen**.

3. After school Jo **plays** football.
   Nach der Schule **spielt** Jo Fußball.

   When Jack comes home, he **feeds** Polly.
   Wenn Jack nach Hause kommt, **füttert** er Polly.

4. What do you do **when** you **come** home?
   Was machst du, **wenn** du nach Hause **kommst**?

▶ Unit 4 (p. 62) • P 2 (p. 66)

S – V – O

Die Wortstellung im Aussagesatz lautet
S – V – O (**S**ubjekt – **V**erb – **O**bjekt): *Jack writes stories.*

! Anders als im Deutschen …

1. … steht ein Häufigkeitsadverb *(often)* nie zwischen Verb und Objekt.

2. … dürfen Hilfsverb *(can)* und Vollverb *(play)* nicht durch ein Objekt *(the guitar)* getrennt werden.

3. … steht das Subjekt *(Jo, he)* auch dann vor dem Verb, wenn der Satz mit einer Zeitangabe *(after school)* oder einem Nebensatz *(when Jack comes home)* beginnt.

4. … ist auch im Nebensatz die Wortstellung **S – V – O**.

Denk dabei an die **Straßen-Verkehrs-Ordnung**, an die du dich immer halten musst!

b) Place before time

We can go **to the mountains in the morning.**

Wir können morgen Vormittag in die Berge fahren.

Great! And we can have a picnic **near the castle in the afternoon.**

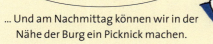

… Und am Nachmittag können wir in der Nähe der Burg ein Picknick machen.

▶ Unit 4 (p. 62) • P 3 (p. 66)

Ort vor Zeit

Wenn Ortsangaben *(to the mountains)* und Zeitangaben *(in the morning)* zusammen am Satzende stehen, dann gilt: **Ort vor Zeit**.

1	2
Ort	**Zeit**
… to the mountains	in the morning.
… near the castle	in the afternoon.

*Welcher Satz ist richtig, **1** oder **2**?*

1. We have to be at six o'clock at the station.
2. We have to be at the station at six o'clock.

GF 13 The present perfect: use   Das *present perfect*: Gebrauch

◀ Mit dem *present perfect* drückst du aus, dass jemand etwas getan hat oder dass etwas geschehen ist. Dabei ist **nicht wichtig**, **wann** es geschehen ist. Deshalb wird auch kein genauer Zeitpunkt genannt.

Wenn du aber den genauen Zeitpunkt angeben willst *(yesterday, last week, two years ago, in 2004)*, musst du das *simple past* verwenden.
(Zum *simple past* siehe GF 1–3, S. 127–128).

◀ Oft hat die Handlung Auswirkungen auf die Gegenwart oder die Zukunft:
Im Beispiel links hat Grandma das Frühstück gemacht. Ergebnis: Jetzt können alle frühstücken.

▶ Unit 4 (p. 63)

GF 14 The present perfect: form   Das *present perfect*: Form

a) The past participle

Das Partizip Perfekt

Das *present perfect* wird mit *have/has* und der 3. Form des Verbs gebildet. Die 3. Form des Verbs heißt **Partizip Perfekt** *(past participle)*.

1 Grandpa **has** packed a picnic.

1 Bei regelmäßigen Verben hängst du **ed** an den Infinitiv an: *pack* + *ed* → *packed*.

They **have** planned a day in the mountains.
Dan and Jo **haven't** tidied their room.

◀ Beachte die Besonderheiten der Schreibung und der Aussprache (siehe GF 1, S. 127).

2 The twins **haven't** seen Caerphilly Castle.
Dan doesn't feel well, so he **hasn't** eaten his breakfast.

2 Unregelmäßige Verben haben eigene Formen, die du einzeln lernen musst.
Unregelmäßige Verben werden immer so angegeben: *(to) see, saw,* **seen**
                                   (to) eat, ate, **eaten**
Die 2. Form ist die *simple past*-Form *(saw, ate)*, die 3. Form ist das *past participle (seen, eaten)*.

▶ Unregelmäßige Verben (pp. 220-221)

The Thompsons **have got** very nice neighbours.
Die Thompsons **haben** sehr nette Nachbarn.

! Merke:
have got („haben") ist keine *present perfect*-Form.

Welche dieser Formen sind past participles?

1 eaten • 2 went • 3 gone • 4 did • 5 ate • 6 done • 7 taken • 8 took

b) Positive and negative statements

1. The neighbours have made a pie for the Thompsons.
   Die Nachbarn haben einen Obstkuchen für die Thompsons gemacht.

2. Grandpa hasn't cleaned the car yet.
   Opa hat das Auto noch nicht sauber gemacht.

Dan hasn't come down.
Dan ist nicht nach unten gekommen.

Bejahte und verneinte Aussagesätze

1. Bejahte Aussagesätze im *present perfect*:
   have/has + **Partizip Perfekt**.

2. Verneinte Aussagesätze im *present perfect*:
   haven't/hasn't + **Partizip Perfekt**.

! Beim *present perfect* musst du immer **have/has** verwenden, egal ob im Deutschen „haben" oder „sein" steht.

Present perfect

Positive statements		Negative statements		Long forms
I've packed		I haven't seen		I/You/We/They have (not) packed
You've packed		You haven't seen		He/She has (not) packed
He's packed		He hasn't seen		
She's packed	a picnic.	She hasn't seen	Dan.	I/You/We/They have (not) seen
We've packed		We haven't seen		He/She has (not) seen
You've packed		You haven't seen		
They've packed		They haven't seen		

▶ Unit 4 (p. 63) • P 6–7 (p. 68)

Polly has cleaned her cage. Now she can watch TV.

c) Questions and short answers

Have the twins been to the Brecon Beacons?
– Yes, they have. / No, they haven't.

Has Jo installed the software?
– Yes, he has. / No, he hasn't.

Why has Grandma printed out the instructions?

▶ Unit 4 (p. 65) • P 12–13 (p. 70)

Fragen und Kurzantworten

Bei Fragen im *present perfect* werden Subjekt und *have/has* vertauscht.

Kurzantworten werden mit *have/has* gebildet.

Fragewörter stehen wie immer am Satzanfang.

! Merke:
Im *present perfect* gibt es **keine Fragen mit when**.
When fragt nach einem Zeitpunkt – und dafür verwendest du das *simple past*: When did …?

GF 15 The present perfect with adverbs of indefinite time

Das *present perfect* mit Adverbien der unbestimmten Zeit

Grandpa I've already packed the car.
Ich habe schon das Auto beladen.

Grandma Oh, good. Have the twins had breakfast yet?
Haben die Zwillinge schon gefrühstückt?

Grandpa I've just seen Jo in the kitchen. But Dan hasn't come down yet.
Ich habe Jo gerade in der Küche gesehen. Aber Dan ist noch nicht nach unten gekommen.

Jo I've always wanted to visit Caerphilly Castle. Grandma, Grandpa, have you ever been there?
Ich wollte schon immer ... besuchen. Oma, Opa, seid ihr jemals dort gewesen?

▶ Unit 4 (p. 63/p. 65) • P 8–9 (p. 69) / P 12 (p. 70)

Das *present perfect* drückt aus, dass etwas **irgendwann** geschehen ist.
Daher findest du oft **Adverbien der unbestimmten Zeit** in *present perfect*-Sätzen:

already	schon, bereits
always	(schon) immer
just	gerade (eben), soeben
never	(noch) nie
not ... yet	noch nicht
often	(schon) oft
ever?	jemals? / schon mal?
yet?	schon?

Die Adverbien der unbestimmten Zeit stehen **direkt vor** dem *past participle*.

! Ausnahme: *yet* steht am Satzende.

Sieh dir die Bilder an. Wie lauten die dazu passenden Sätze im *present perfect*?

1
Grandpa – just – wash – car

2
Dan – not eat – his breakfast – yet

3
The twins – already – make – their beds

GF 16 Extra The present perfect and the simple past in contrast

Das *present perfect* und das *simple past* im Vergleich

Jo Grandma, I've installed the chat software for you. You can chat with Mum now.

Grandma Thank you, Jo. When did you do it?

Jo I installed it last night when you were in bed.

▶ Unit 4 (p. 65) • P 14 (p. 71)

– Das **present perfect** drückt aus, **dass** jemand etwas **irgendwann** getan hat oder dass etwas **irgendwann** geschehen ist. Der Zeitpunkt ist nicht wichtig oder nicht bekannt.
Oft hat die Handlung Auswirkungen auf die Gegenwart oder Zukunft:
Jo hat irgendwann die Software installiert, sodass Oma jetzt chatten kann: *I've installed ...*

– Wenn du aber sagen oder fragen willst, **wann** etwas geschehen ist, musst du das **simple past** verwenden:
Oma fragt: *When did you do it?*
Jo antwortet: *I installed it last night.*

Unit 5

GF 17 Relative clauses — Relativsätze

a) who, which, that

1 **The student who likes taking photos** is Jo Shaw.
Der Schüler, der gern fotografiert, ist Jo Shaw.

2 8PK are doing **a project which starts with a quiz**.
Klasse 8PK macht ein Projekt, das mit einem Quiz beginnt.

3 **The people that come to the Fiesta** see some beautiful balloons.
Die Menschen, die zu dem Festival kommen, …

The Balloon Fiesta is **an event that takes place in August**.
… ein Ereignis, das im August stattfindet.

▶ Unit 5 (p. 78) • P 5–8 (pp. 83–84)

who, which, that

Mit Relativsätzen sagst du genauer, wen oder was du meinst.

1 Das Relativpronomen *who* steht in Relativsätzen, die **Personen** beschreiben:
*The **student/woman/people** who …*

2 Das Relativpronomen *which* steht in Relativsätzen, die **Dinge (und Tiere)** beschreiben:
*The **project/things/animals** which …*

3 Das Relativpronomen *that* kannst du für Personen und Dinge verwenden.

! Beachte die unterschiedliche **Wortstellung** in englischen und deutschen Relativsätzen:

a project **which** *starts* **with a quiz**
ein Projekt, **das** *mit einem Quiz* **beginnt**

b) whose

Brunel? That's **the man whose statue stands near the station**.
Brunel? Das ist der Mann, dessen Statue in der Nähe des Bahnhofs steht.

Who's the boy whose mother lives in New Zealand?
Wer ist der Junge, **dessen** Mutter in Neuseeland lebt?

▶ Unit 5 (p. 79)

whose

Das Relativpronomen *whose* („dessen", „deren") bezieht sich meist auf Personen, wird aber auch für Dinge (und Tiere) verwendet.
Auf *whose* folgt immer ein Nomen.

! Verwechsle *whose* nicht mit der Kurzform *who's (who is)!*

Ordne den Sätzen das richtige Relativpronomen zu.

1 Dan and Jo are the boys … grandparents live in Wales.
2 Brunel is the engineer … built the Clifton Suspension Bridge.
3 Temple Meads Station is another thing … Brunel built in Bristol.

A who
B which
C whose

I'm the parrot whose pet is a boy from Bristol. His name is Jack.

GF 18 Question tags — Frageanhängsel

a) Use

Jo The new pizza place **is** near here, **isn't it?** Let's go there.
Die neue Pizzeria ist doch hier in der Nähe, nicht? ...

Dan Wow! They**'ve got** really big pizzas, **haven't they?**
Sie haben wirklich große Pizzas, oder?

Jo Yes, and they **look** pretty cool, **don't they?**
Ja, und sie sehen ziemlich gut aus, nicht wahr?

Dan But wait. The place **doesn't look** very full, **does it?** And we **didn't look** at the prices before we came in, **did we?**

Jo Hmm. We **haven't got** much money with us, **have we?** Let's look at the prices before we sit down.

Gebrauch

Frageanhängsel *(isn't it? / haven't they? / did we?)* werden häufig in der gesprochenen Sprache verwendet. Mit Frageanhängseln signalisiert man, dass man vom Gesprächspartner Zustimmung erwartet.

Deutsche Frageanhängsel sind zum Beispiel „nicht?", „nicht wahr?" und „oder?", in manchen Gegenden auch „ne?", „gell?" oder „woll?".

The smoothies were great, weren't they?

b) Form

The new pizza place **is** near here, isn't it?

verneint — bejaht

We **haven't got** much money with us, have we?

They **look** pretty cool, don't they?
Sophie **likes** healthy food, doesn't she?
Jo **tried** a strawberry smoothie, didn't he?

▶ Unit 5 (p. 80) • P 10–11 (p. 86)

Form

Frageanhängsel bestehen aus **Hilfsverb** *(is, are, have, …)* + **Personalpronomen** *(I, you, he, they, …)*.

◀ Wenn der Aussagesatz bejaht ist, ist das Frageanhängsel verneint.

◀ Wenn der Aussagesatz verneint ist, ist das Frageanhängsel bejaht.

! Bejahte Aussagesätze mit Vollverben *(look, like, try, …)* enthalten im *simple present* und *simple past* kein Hilfsverb. In diesen Fällen steht im Frageanhängsel *don't / doesn't / didn't*.

Ordne die Frageanhängsel den Aussagen zu.

1 The smoothies are really good, …
2 We haven't got enough money for pizzas, …
3 Sophie's wheatgrass juice wasn't expensive, …
4 Jo and Dan's grandparents live in Wales, …
5 Brunel built the Clifton Suspension Bridge, …

A was it?
B don't they?
C have we?
D didn't he?
E aren't they?

Unit 6

GF 19 Extra Contact clauses Relativsätze ohne Relativpronomen

Die Relativpronomen *who, which, that* können entweder **Subjekt** oder **Objekt** des Relativsatzes sein. Vergleiche:

1

	subject	
Jo is the boy	**who**	didn't like Lesley.
Jo ist der Junge,	**der**	Lesley nicht mochte.
That's the bus	**which**	goes to Bath.
Das ist der Bus,	**der**	nach Bath fährt.

2

	object	subject	
Jo is the boy	[who]	**Lesley**	didn't like.
Jo ist der Junge,	den	**Lesley**	nicht mochte.
That's the bus	[which]	**we**	have to take.
Das ist der Bus,	den	**wir**	nehmen müssen.

Bath is one of the nicest **cities I know**. Look, that's the **bus we have to take**. And here comes Jo.

Oh no! He's the last **person I want to see**.

Wenn *who, which* oder *that* Objekt des Relativsatzes ist, kannst du es weglassen.
◀ In den Beispielen links sind die Relativpronomen weggelassen worden.
Relativsätze ohne Relativpronomen nennt man *contact clauses*.

That's the bus which goes to Bath.
(*not:* That's  the bus goes to Bath.)

! Achtung:
Wenn das **Relativpronomen direkt vor dem Verb** steht, ist es Subjekt – dann darfst du es **nicht weglassen**!

The **girl** [who] Jack is talking **to** is Lesley.
Das Mädchen, mit dem Jack spricht, ist Lesley.

The **school** [that] Dan and Jo go **to** is in Bristol.
Die Schule, auf die Dan und Jo gehen, ist in Bristol.

▶ Unit 6 (p. 96) • P 2 (p. 100)

! Beachte die Stellung der Präposition in Relativsätzen mit Verben wie *talk to, go to, look at, stay with*. Die Präposition steht an derselben Stelle wie im Hauptsatz:
 Jack is **talking** *to* Lesley.
 The girl Jack is **talking** *to* is Lesley.

 Wo kannst du who, which, that weglassen? Schreibe die Sätze als contact clauses in dein Heft.

1 Which is the bus that goes to Bath?
2 Lesley is the girl who Jo didn't like.
3 Bath is the place which Form 8PK visited on their class trip.
4 Lesley: 'Jo is the last person that I want to see.'
5 Mr Kingsley: 'The building which we are looking at now is the Theatre Royal.'

GF 20 Extra Indirect speech Indirekte Rede

a) Indirect statements

Direkte Rede
(Direct speech)

Bath is a very nice city.

Indirekte Rede
(Indirect speech)

Mr Kingsley **says (that)** Bath is a very nice city.
Mr Kingsley sagt, dass Bath eine sehr schöne Stadt ist/sei.

Direkte Rede
(Direct speech)

I love the theatre.

Indirekte Rede
(Indirect speech)

Lesley **says (that)** she loves the theatre.
Lesley sagt, dass sie das Theater liebt/liebe.

Indirekte Aussagen

Wenn du berichtest, was jemand sagt (oder gesagt hat), benutzt du die indirekte Rede.
Die indirekte Rede leitest du mit Verben wie *say, tell sb., add, answer* ein.

! Merke:

1. *that* („dass") kannst du weglassen.
2. Vor der indirekten Rede steht kein Komma.
3. Wie im Deutschen musst du in der indirekten Rede Pronomen und Verbformen oft der Sicht des Sprechers anpassen:
   Lesley: '*I love* …' → Lesley says **she** loves …
4. Im Gegensatz zum Deutschen bleibt im Nebensatz die Wortstellung so wie im Aussagesatz: **S – V – O**.
   Lesley says (that) she **loves the theatre**.
   Lesley sagt, dass sie **das Theater liebt**.

b) Indirect questions

Direkte Rede
(Direct speech)

Jack, when are you going to feed me?

Indirekte Rede
(Indirect speech)

Polly **wants to know** when Jack is going to feed her.
Polly möchte wissen, wann Jack sie füttern wird.

Direkte Rede
(Direct speech)

When do we get to Bath?

Indirekte Rede
(Indirect speech)

Dan **asks** when they get to Bath.
Dan fragt, wann sie in Bath ankommen.

▶ Unit 6 (p. 96) • P 3 (p. 100)

Indirekte Fragen

Eine indirekte Frage kannst du mit *ask* oder *want to know* einleiten.

! Merke:

1. Auch in indirekten Fragen ist die Wortstellung wie im Aussagesatz: **S – V – O**.
   Polly wants to know when Jack **is going to feed** her.
   Polly möchte wissen, wann Jack **sie füttern wird**.
2. Es gibt in indirekten Fragen keine Umschreibung mit *do/does/did*. Vergleiche:
   Direkte Frage: When **do** we **get** to Bath?
   Indirekte Frage: Dan asks when they **get** to Bath.

Vervollständige die Sätze.

1. Jo: 'I'm hungry.'   Jo says …
2. Jo: 'When are we going to have lunch?'   Jo wants to know when …
3. Dan: 'What do you want to have for lunch, Jo?'   Dan asks …

GF 21 REVISION The present progressive Die Verlaufsform der Gegenwart

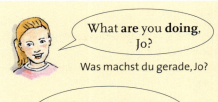

Du benutzt das *present progressive*, um auszudrücken, dass etwas gerade in diesem Moment geschieht.

Das *present progressive* wird mit *am/are/is* + *-ing*-Form des Verbs gebildet.
Die *-ing*-Form ist der Infinitiv + *-ing*:
do → *doing*, *wait* → *waiting*.
Beachte: *have* → *having*, *plan* → *planning*

▶ Unit 6 (p. 98) • P 7 (p. 102)

GF 22 The past progressive Die Verlaufsform der Vergangenheit

Yesterday at one o'clock …

Yesterday at one o'clock Form 8PK and their teachers **were having** lunch.
Gestern um ein Uhr aßen die Klasse 8PK und ihre Lehrer gerade zu Mittag.

Jack **was telling** jokes, but Jo **wasn't listening**.
Jack erzählte Witze, aber Jo hörte nicht zu.

What was Jo **doing**? **Was** he **talking** to Ananda?
Was machte Jo gerade? Redete er gerade mit Ananda?
– No, he **wasn't**. He **was planning** a trick.
– Nein. Er war gerade dabei, einen Streich zu planen.

The others **were** still **eating** and **chatting** when Jo suddenly **started** to laugh.
Die anderen waren noch dabei zu essen und sich zu unterhalten, als Jo plötzlich anfing zu lachen.

▶ Unit 6 (p. 98) • P 8–9 (pp. 102–103)

Du benutzt das *past progressive*, um auszudrücken, dass etwas zu einem bestimmten Zeitpunkt in der Vergangenheit gerade im Gange war. Die Handlung oder der Vorgang war noch nicht abgeschlossen.

Das *past progressive* wird mit *was/were* + *-ing*-Form gebildet.
Die verneinten Formen heißen *I wasn't listening/ you weren't listening/he wasn't listening* usw.

Fragen kannst du **mit Fragewort** (*What …?*) oder **ohne Fragewort** (*Was he …?*) stellen.
Die Kurzantworten sind *Yes, I was / No, I wasn't* usw.

Das *past progressive* wird oft benutzt, um auszudrücken, was gerade vor sich ging (*the others were still eating …*), als eine andere Handlung einsetzte (*Jo started to laugh*).
❗ Die zweite Handlung steht im *simple past*.

Welche Sätze drücken aus, dass jemand gerade dabei war, etwas zu tun?

1 At 6 o'clock yesterday evening Jack was reading a spy story.
2 Two days ago Sophie played tennis with Lesley.
3 At 8.30 this morning Lesley was cycling to school.
4 Last week Jo read two detective stories.
5 Emily cycled to school last Wednesday.
6 At 6.15 Jo and Dan were playing football in the park.

Grammar File 6

GF 23 Extra Conditional sentences (type 2) Bedingungssätze (Typ 2)

a) REVISION Conditional sentences (type 1)

If you give a hedgehog water, it will be happy.

Bedingungssätze (Typ 1)

Du kennst bereits **Bedingungssätze vom Typ 1** („Was **ist**, wenn ..."-Sätze).
Sie sagen aus, was unter bestimmten Bedingungen geschieht oder nicht geschieht:

if-Satz (Bedingung)	Hauptsatz (Folge)
If you **give** a hedgehog water,	it **will be** happy.
simple present	*will*-future

(Bedingungssätze vom Typ 1: siehe GF 10, S. 135).

b) Conditional sentences (type 2)

*If we **did** astronomy at school, that **would be** great.*

Wenn wir in der Schule Astronomie machen würden, das wäre toll.

*And if I **discovered** a planet, I'**d be** famous.*

Bedingungssätze (Typ 2)

Bedingungssätze vom Typ 2 sind „Was **wäre**, wenn ..."-Sätze. Sie drücken aus, dass es nicht sehr wahrscheinlich (oder sogar unmöglich) ist, dass die Bedingung aus dem *if*-Satz eintritt:

if-Satz (Bedingung)	Hauptsatz (Folge)
If Jo **discovered** a planet,	he **would be** famous.
simple past	*would* + infinitive

Es ist unwahrscheinlich, dass Jo einen Planeten entdeckt; also wird er wahrscheinlich auch nicht berühmt. Der Sprecher drückt nur aus, was wäre, wenn ...

! Merke:

1 Jo   If we **did** astronomy, we **could learn** about planets and stars.

    Miss White   Jo, if you **didn't talk** all the time, we **could hear** Nicola better.

2 Jo   If Grandma **were** here, she **would ask** lots of questions too.

3 Ananda   **If I were you**, Jo, I **would be** quiet now.

1 Im Hauptsatz kann auch *could* („könnte") + Infinitiv stehen.

2 Statt *was* steht im *if*-Satz manchmal *were*.

3 Für Ratschläge kannst du die Wendung **If I were you ...** verwenden („Wenn ich du wäre, ...").

▶ Unit 6 (p. 99) • P 11 (p. 104)

Welche Wörter gehören in welche Lücke?

1 Sophie: 'If we ... more sport at school, Jack wouldn't be happy.'
2 If we ... more time, we could go to the theatre to see a play.
3 Ananda: 'If I ... you, Jo, I would listen to Nicola now.'
4 Miss White: 'If you didn't talk so much, Jo, we ... all hear Nicola better.'
5 Dan: 'If Mum were here, I ... be much happier.'

A would
B could / would
C were
D did
E had

Grammatical terms (Grammatische Fachbegriffe)

English	Pronunciation	German	Example
adjective	[ˈædʒɪktɪv]	Adjektiv	*good, red, new, boring, …*
adverb	[ˈædvɜːb]	Adverb	
adverb of frequency	[ˌædvɜːb ɒv ˈfriːkwənsi]	Häufigkeitsadverb	*always, often, never, …*
adverb of indefinite time	[ɪnˌdefɪnət ˈtaɪm]	Adverb der unbestimmten Zeit	*already, ever, just, never, …*
adverb of manner	[ˈmænə]	Adverb der Art und Weise	*badly, happily, quietly, well, …*
comparison	[kəmˈpærɪsn]	Steigerung	*old – older – oldest*
compound	[ˈkɒmpaʊnd]	Zusammensetzung	*somebody, anything, …*
conditional sentence	[kənˌdɪʃənl ˈsentəns]	Bedingungssatz	*If I see Jack, I'll tell him.* *If I saw Jack, I'd tell him.*
conjunction	[kənˈdʒʌŋkʃn]	Konjunktion	*and, but, …; because, when, …*
contact clause	[ˈkɒntækt klɔːz]	Relativsatz ohne Relativpronomen	*I love the girl **I met in Bristol**.*
direct speech	[ˌdaɪrekt ˈspiːtʃ]	direkte Rede	*'I love the theatre.'*
future	[ˈfjuːtʃə]	Zukunft, Futur	
going to-future		Futur mit *going to*	***I'm going to watch** TV tonight.*
imperative	[ɪmˈperətɪv]	Imperativ (Befehlsform)	*Open your books. Don't talk.*
indirect speech	[ˌɪndərekt/ˌɪndaɪrekt ˈspiːtʃ]	indirekte Rede	*She says she loves the theatre.*
infinitive	[ɪnˈfɪnətɪv]	Infinitiv (Grundform des Verbs)	*(to) open, (to) see, (to) read, …*
irregular verb	[ɪˌregjələ ˈvɜːb]	unregelmäßiges Verb	*(to) go – went – gone*
negative statement	[ˌnegətɪv ˈsteɪtmənt]	verneinter Aussagesatz	*I don't like bananas.*
noun	[naʊn]	Nomen, Substantiv	*Sophie, girl, brother, time, …*
object	[ˈɒbdʒɪkt]	Objekt	*My sister is writing **a letter**.*
object form	[ˈɒbdʒɪkt fɔːm]	Objektform (der Personalpronomen)	*me, you, him, her, it, us, them*
object question	[ˈɒbdʒɪkt ˌkwestʃən]	Objektfrage, Frage nach dem Objekt	*Who did you talk to?*
past	[pɑːst]	Vergangenheit	
past participle	[ˌpɑːst ˈpɑːtɪsɪpl]	Partizip Perfekt	*cleaned, planned, gone, seen, …*
past progressive	[ˌpɑːst prəˈgresɪv]	Verlaufsform der Vergangenheit	*At 7.30 I **was having** dinner.*
person	[ˈpɜːsn]	Person	
personal pronoun	[ˌpɜːsənl ˈprəʊnaʊn]	Personalpronomen (persönliches Fürwort)	*I, you, he, she, it, we, they;* *me, you, him, her, it, us, them*
plural	[ˈplʊərəl]	Plural, Mehrzahl	
positive statement	[ˌpɒzətɪv ˈsteɪtmənt]	bejahter Aussagesatz	*I like oranges.*
possessive determiner	[pəˌzesɪv dɪˈtɜːmɪnə]	Possessivbegleiter (besitzanzeigender Begleiter)	*my, your, his, her, its, our, their*
possessive form	[pəˌzesɪv fɔːm]	s-Genitiv	*Jo's brother; my sister's room*
possessive pronoun	[pəˌzesɪv ˈprəʊnaʊn]	Possessivpronomen	*mine, yours, his, hers, ours, theirs*
preposition	[ˌprepəˈzɪʃn]	Präposition	*after, at, in, next to, under, …*
present	[ˈpreznt]	Gegenwart	
present perfect	[ˌpreznt ˈpɜːfɪkt]	present perfect	*We**'ve made** a cake for you.*
present progressive	[ˌpreznt prəˈgresɪv]	Verlaufsform der Gegenwart	*The Hansons **are having** lunch.*
pronoun	[ˈprəʊnaʊn]	Pronomen, Fürwort	
pronunciation	[prəˌnʌnsiˈeɪʃn]	Aussprache	
question	[ˈkwestʃən]	Frage(satz)	
question tag	[ˈkwestʃən tæg]	Frageanhängsel	*This place is great, **isn't it**?*
question word	[ˈkwestʃən wɜːd]	Fragewort	*what?, when?, where?, how?, …*
regular verb	[ˌregjələ ˈvɜːb]	regelmäßiges Verb	*(to) help – helped – helped*
relative clause	[ˌrelətɪv ˈklɔːz]	Relativsatz	*The man **who lived here** …*
relative pronoun	[ˌrelətɪv ˈprəʊnaʊn]	Relativpronomen	*who, which, that, whose*
short answer	[ˌʃɔːt ˈɑːnsə]	Kurzantwort	*Yes, I am. / No, I don't. / …*
simple past	[ˌsɪmpl ˈpɑːst]	einfache Form der Vergangenheit	*Jo **wrote** two letters yesterday.*

Grammar File

simple present [ˌsɪmpl ˈpreznt]		einfache Form der Gegenwart	I always **go** to school by bike.
singular [ˈsɪŋgjələ]		Singular, Einzahl	
spelling [ˈspelɪŋ]		Schreibweise, Rechtschreibung	
subject [ˈsʌbdʒɪkt]		Subjekt	**My sister** is writing a letter.
subject form [ˈsʌbdʒɪkt fɔːm]		Subjektform (der Personalpronomen)	I, you, he, she, it, we, they
subject question [ˈsʌbdʒɪkt ˌkwestʃən]		Subjektfrage, Frage nach dem Subjekt	Who likes bananas?
subordinate clause [səˌbɔːdɪnət ˈklɔːz]		Nebensatz	I like Scruffy **because I like dogs**.
verb [vɜːb]		Verb	hear, open, help, go, ...
will-future		Futur mit *will*	I think it **will be** cold tonight.
word order [ˈwɜːd ˌɔːdə]		Wortstellung	
yes/no question		Entscheidungsfrage	Are you 13? Do you like comics?

Lösungen der Grammar-File-Aufgaben

p.127   2, 5, 6, 7, 9, 10, 11

p.128/1   1 This morning Jo **didn't make** his bed.
2 Last week Dan **didn't clean** his bike.
3 Yesterday Jack **didn't do** his homework.

p.128/2   1 Why **did** Jody go swimming?
2 **Did** Jo help Jody?
3 What **did** Dan do?

p.129   1C, 2D, 3B, 4A

p.130   1 Is this my money or **yours**?
2 This isn't your dress. It's **mine**.
3 That is Jo's pen, but that ruler isn't **his**.
4 The food is for the rabbits, and the water is **theirs** too.

p.131   1 Sophie **is going to read** a book.
2 She isn't **going to watch** TV.
3 Dan and Jo **are going to play** football.
4 They **aren't going to take** photos.

p.133   1 Ali is **older than** Ben and Chris.
He is **the oldest**.
2 Ben is **as old as** Chris,
but he isn't **as old as** Ali.

p.134   1 I'll be 13 next month.
2 Come and visit me! I think you'll like it here.
3 I'm sure the weather will be fine in August.
4 ... Will the baby hedgehogs survive?

p.135   1 If Jack sees the babies, he **will want** to help them too.
2 What will happen if their mum **doesn't come** back?
3 If Ananda **takes** the babies to the clinic, they **will have** a better chance of survival.

p.137   1 When you pick up a small animal, you have to be very **careful**.
2 Squirrels and rabbits can run very **quickly**.
3 Hedgehogs walk **slowly** and **quietly**.
4 Ananda did a **good** job with the hedgehogs.
5 The woman at the animal clinic said Ananda did **well**.

p.138   2 (We have to be at the station at six o'clock.)

p.139   1, 3, 6, 7

p.141   1 Grandpa **has just washed** the car.
2 Dan **hasn't eaten** his breakfast **yet**.
3 The twins **have already made** their beds.

p.142   1C, 2A, 3B

p.143   1E, 2C, 3A, 4B, 5D

p.144   1 ("that" kann nicht weggelassen werden!)
2 Lesley is the girl Jo didn't like.
3 Bath is the place Form 8PK visited on their class trip.
4 Jo is the last person I want to see.
5 The building we are looking at now is the Theatre Royal.

p.145   1 Jo says (that) **he's hungry**.
2 Jo wants to know when **they are going to have lunch**.
3 Dan asks **what Jo wants to have for lunch**. / Dan asks Jo **what he wants to have for lunch**.

p.146   1, 3, 6

p.147   1D, 2E, 3C, 4B, 5A

Vocabulary

Diese Wörterverzeichnisse findest du in deinem Englischbuch:

- Das **Vocabulary** (Vokabelverzeichnis – S. 150–177) enthält alle Wörter und Wendungen, die du lernen musst. Sie stehen in der Reihenfolge, in der sie in den Units vorkommen.
- Das **Dictionary** besteht aus zwei alphabetischen Wörterlisten zum Nachschlagen:
  Englisch – Deutsch: S. 178–199 / Deutsch – Englisch: S. 200–217.

So ist das Vocabulary aufgebaut:

- Hier siehst du, wo die Wörter vorkommen.
  p. 31/A 11 = Seite 31, Abschnitt 11
  p. 35/P 11 = Seite 35, Übung 11
- Die Lautschrift zeigt dir, wie ein Wort ausgesprochen und betont wird.
  (→ Englische Laute: S. 217)
- Eingerückte Wörter lernst du am besten zusammen mit dem vorausgehenden Wort, weil die beiden zusammengehören.
- Diese Kästen solltest du dir besonders gut ansehen.

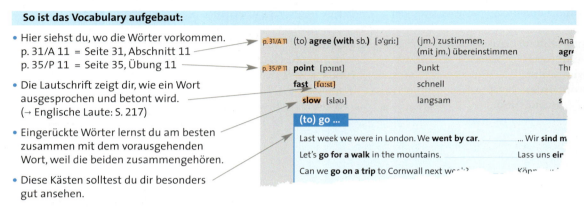

Tipps zum Wörterlernen findest du im Skills File auf Seite 115.

Abkürzungen:

n	= noun		v	= verb
adj	= adjective		adv	= adverb
prep	= preposition		conj	= conjunction
pl	= plural		no pl	= no plural
p.	= page		pp.	= pages
sb.	= somebody		sth.	= something
jn.	= jemanden		jm.	= jemandem

Symbole:

- ◄► ist das „Gegenteil"-Zeichen: **slow** ◄► **fast**
  (**slow** ist das Gegenteil von **fast**)
- ❗ Hier stehen Hinweise auf Besonderheiten, bei denen man leicht Fehler machen kann.

Welcome back – After the holidays

Remember?

p. 6

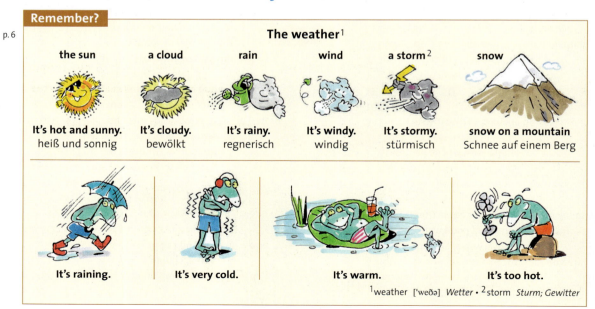

[1] weather [ˈweðə] Wetter • [2] storm Sturm; Gewitter

Vocabulary Welcome back

by the sea [baɪ]	am Meer	
caravan ['kærəvæn]	Wohnwagen	a **caravan by the sea** *French:* la caravane

Irregular simple past forms

(to) buy	**bought** [bɔːt]	kaufen	(to) read [riːd]	**read** [red]	lesen
(to) drink	**drank** [dræŋk]	trinken	(to) ride	**rode** [rəʊd]	reiten; *(Rad)* fahren
(to) eat	**ate** [et, eɪt]	essen	(to) swim	**swam** [swæm]	schwimmen
(to) meet	**met** [met]	(sich) treffen	(to) throw	**threw** [θruː]	werfen

on the beach [biːtʃ]	am Strand	
(to) **be on holiday** / (to) **go on holiday**	in Urlaub sein / in Urlaub fahren	John isn't at home. Maybe he**'s on holiday**. We **went on holiday** to Italy this summer.
anyway ['eniweɪ]	trotzdem	It was cold, but we went swimming **anyway**.
pool [puːl], **swimming pool** ['swɪmɪŋ puːl]	Schwimmbad, Schwimmbecken	
(to) **text** sb. [tekst]	jm. eine SMS schicken	Have a good trip. **Text** me when you get there.
text message ['tekst ˌmesɪdʒ]	SMS	
view [vjuː]	Aussicht, Blick	This postcard shows the **view** from our hotel. *French:* la vue
plane [pleɪn]	Flugzeug	❗ **im** Flugzeug = **on** the plane
as [əz, æz]	als, während	I ate my sandwiches **as** I waited for the bus.
(to) **fly** [flaɪ], simple past: **flew** [fluː]	fliegen	
round [raʊnd]	um … (herum); in … umher	**round** the car Walk **round** the classroom and talk to different partners.
island ['aɪlənd]	Insel	
(to) **shine** [ʃaɪn], simple past: **shone** [ʃɒn]	scheinen *(Sonne)*	Most people are happy when the sun **shines**.
villa ['vɪlə]	Ferienhaus; Villa	*Latin:* villa
our **own** pool [əʊn]	unser eigenes Schwimmbecken	❗ I've got **my own** room. (Never: ~~an own~~ room)
sky [skaɪ]	Himmel	❗ It was a sunny day. There wasn't a cloud **in the sky**. (= am Himmel)
(to) **travel** ['trævl] (-ll-)[1]	reisen	Last year we **travelled** to Turkey in the holidays.
(to) go **by car/bike/…**	mit dem Auto/Rad/… fahren	

(to) go … (simple past: went)

Last week we were in London. We **went by car**.	… Wir **sind mit dem Auto gefahren**.
Let's **go for a walk** in the mountains.	Lass uns **einen Spaziergang** in den Bergen **machen**.
Can we **go on a trip** to Cornwall next week?	Können wir … **einen Ausflug** nach Cornwall **machen**?
We **went on holiday** to Italy this summer.	Wir sind diesen Sommer nach Italien **in Urlaub gefahren**.

What was the weather like?	Wie war das Wetter?

[1] Die Angabe **(-ll-)** zeigt, dass der Endkonsonant bei der Bildung von *-ing*-Form und *-ed*-Form verdoppelt wird: **travel** — **travelling** / **travelled**.

1 Vocabulary

	(to) **stay** [steɪ]	bleiben; wohnen, übernachten	It rained all day so I **stayed** at home. In the holidays we **stayed** at a hotel in Cornwall.
p. 8	**foggy** ['fɒgi]	neblig	
	fog [fɒg]	Nebel	noun: **fog** – adjective: **foggy**
	degree [dɪ'griː]	Grad	It's 14 **degrees** (14°) and very cloudy in England. *French:* le degré
	country ['kʌntri]	Land *(auch als Gegensatz zur Stadt)*	Germany is a big **country**. ! The Millers live **in the country**. (= auf dem Land)
p. 9	(to) **go abroad** [ə'brɔːd]	ins Ausland gehen/fahren	
	through [θruː]	durch	He's climbing **through** the window.
	nobody ['nəʊbədi]	niemand	
	(to) **grumble** ['grʌmbl]	murren, nörgeln	'You never help me,' he **grumbled**.
	(to) **speak (to)** [spiːk], *simple past:* **spoke** [spəʊk]	sprechen (mit), reden (mit)	I **speak** German and English.
	(to) **go surfing** ['sɜːfɪŋ]	wellenreiten gehen, surfen gehen	(to) **go surfing** — surfboard
	roof ['ruːf]	Dach	
	lake [leɪk]	(Binnen-)See	mountains — the sea — an island — a lake
			! the **lake** = <u>der</u> See • the **sea** = <u>die</u> See, das Meer

Unit 1: Back to school

p. 11	**cafeteria** [ˌkæfə'tɪəriə]	Cafeteria, Selbstbedienungsrestaurant	
	(to) **describe** sth. **(to** sb.**)** [dɪ'skraɪb]	(jm.) etwas beschreiben	! **Describe** the picture **to your partner**. = **Beschreibe** das Bild **deinem Partner**. *Latin:* describere; *French:* décrire
	description [dɪ'skrɪpʃn]	Beschreibung	*French:* la description
	background ['bækgraʊnd]	Hintergrund	In this picture, Dan and Jo are in the **foreground**. In the **background** you can see a lake.
	foreground ['fɔːgraʊnd]	Vordergrund	
	at the bottom (of) ['bɒtəm]	unten, am unteren Ende (von)	Now do the exercise **at the bottom of** the page. ↓ **at the bottom (of)** ◄► **at the top (of)** ↑
	between [bɪ'twiːn]	zwischen	Sweden is **between** Norway and Finland.
p. 12/A 1	**sights** *(pl)* [saɪts]	Sehenswürdigkeiten	
	about [ə'baʊt]	ungefähr	There were **about** 300 people in the park. ! **about** = 1. über – a book **about** pets 2. ungefähr – **about** 300 people

Tipps zum Wörterlernen → S. 115 • Englische Laute → S. 217 • Alphabetische Wörterverzeichnisse → S. 178–199 / S. 200–217

Vocabulary 1

flight [flaɪt]	Flug		*verb:* (to) **fly** – *noun:* **flight**
time(s) [taɪm(z)]	Mal(e); -mal		We went surfing four **times** last week.
a bit [ə ˈbɪt]	ein bisschen, etwas		The tea was **a bit** hot, so I added some milk.
the underground [ˈʌndəɡraʊnd]	die U-Bahn		*American English:* **the subway** [ˈsʌbweɪ]

Irregular simple past forms

(to) find	**found** [faʊnd]	finden		(to) hear	**heard** [hɜːd]	hören
(to) get on/off	**got on/off**	ein-, aussteigen		(to) teach	**taught** [tɔːt]	unterrichten, lehren
(to) give	**gave** [ɡeɪv]	geben		(to) wear	**wore** [wɔː]	tragen *(Kleidung)*

dangerous [ˈdeɪndʒərəs]	gefährlich	*French:* dangereux, dangereuse
fast [fɑːst]	schnell	
slow [sləʊ]	langsam	fast ◄► slow
What was **the best thing about ...?**	Was war das Beste an ...?	**The best thing about** the film was the music.
building [ˈbɪldɪŋ]	Gebäude	**buildings**
lift [lɪft]	Fahrstuhl, Aufzug	*American English:* **elevator** [ˈelɪveɪtə]
amazing [əˈmeɪzɪŋ]	erstaunlich, unglaublich	
for miles [maɪlz]	meilenweit	You can see **for miles** from this tower.
mile [maɪl]	Meile (= ca. 1,6 km)	

p. 13/A 2	**at the back (of** the room**)** [bæk]	hinten, im hinteren Teil (des Zimmers)	
	Mind your own business. [ˌmaɪnd jər_ˌəʊn ˈbɪznəs]	Das geht dich nichts an! / Kümmere dich um deine eigenen Angelegenheiten!	How much was that mobile phone? – **Mind your own business.**
	not (...) either [ˈaɪðə, ˈiːðə]	auch nicht	I'm not going to Steve's party. – I'm **not** going **either**. John doesn't like zoos, and Jenny does**n't either**.
	after [ˈɑːftə]	nachdem	❗ after = 1. *(prep)* nach – **after** school 2. *(conj)* nachdem – **after** I came home
	before [bɪˈfɔː]	bevor	❗ before = 1. *(prep)* vor – **before** lunch 2. *(conj)* bevor – **before** we eat
	rude [ruːd]	unhöflich, unverschämt	It's **rude** to speak with your mouth full.
p. 14/A 4	**jacket** [ˈdʒækɪt]	Jacke, Jackett	❗ Betonung auf der 1. Silbe: **jacket** [ˈdʒækɪt]

Namen → S. 218–219 • Unregelmäßige Verben → S. 220–221 • Classroom English/Arbeitsanweisungen → S. 222–223

1 Vocabulary

(to) **borrow** sth. ['bɒrəʊ]	sich etwas (aus)leihen, etwas entleihen	❗ • You **borrow** something from somebody (= you **take** it): Can I **borrow** your CD player? • You **lend** somebody something (= you **give** it): OK, I can **lend** you my CD player. But be careful with it.
(to) **lend** sb. sth. [lend], *simple past:* **lent** [lent]	jm. etwas leihen	
Do you really think so?	Meinst du wirklich? / Glaubst du das wirklich?	Shopping is great fun. – **Do you really think so?** I think it's boring.
No way! [ˌnəʊ 'weɪ]	Auf keinen Fall! / Kommt nicht in Frage!	Mum, can you give me £80 for a new sweatshirt? – £80? **No way!** You can have £30.
chance [tʃɑːns]	Chance	
(to) **be in trouble** ['trʌbl]	in Schwierigkeiten sein; Ärger kriegen	My friends helped me when I **was in trouble**. Jo **is in trouble**. He hasn't got his homework.
hero ['hɪərəʊ], *pl* **heroes** ['hɪərəʊz]	Held, Heldin	*Latin:* heros; *French:* le héros, la héroïne
(to) **calm down** [ˌkɑːm 'daʊn]	sich beruhigen	Help! There's a mouse in the kitchen. – **Calm down.** It can't hurt you.
(to) **get angry/hot/...** (-tt-), *simple past:* **got**	wütend/heiß/... werden	It's **getting hot** in here. Can you open the window, please?
angry (**about** sth./**with** sb.) ['æŋgri]	wütend, böse (über etwas/auf jn.)	Let's be friends again. Or are you still **angry with** me?
nothing ['nʌθɪŋ]	nichts	**nothing** (nichts) **something** (etwas) **everything** (alles)
p. 15/A 6 **unhappy** [ʌn'hæpi]	unglücklich	**happy** ◂▸ **unhappy**
a few [fjuː]	ein paar, einige	We didn't have much money, just **a few** pounds.
unfriendly [ʌn'frendli]	unfreundlich	She isn't really rude, but she is a bit **unfriendly**.
friendly ['frendli]	freundlich	**friendly** ◂▸ **unfriendly**
Who did she talk to?	Mit wem hat sie geredet?	❗ **who** = 1. wer: **Who** loves Polly? – Jack. 2. wen: **Who** does Jack love? – Polly. 3. wem: **Who** did Polly help? – Jack.
argument ['ɑːgjumənt]	Streit, Auseinandersetzung	verb: (to) **argue** – noun: **argument** ❗ Betonung auf der 1. Silbe: **argument** ['ɑːgjumənt]
(to) **explain** sth. **to** sb. [ɪk'spleɪn]	jm. etwas erklären, erläutern	❗ *English:* Can you **explain** that **to me**? *German:* Kannst du **mir** das **erklären**? (*Not:* Can you explain me ...) *Latin:* explanare; *French:* expliquer
explanation [ˌekspləˈneɪʃn]	Erklärung	verb: (to) **explain** – noun: **explanation** *Latin:* explanatio; *French:* l'explication *(f)*
a cup of tea [kʌp]	eine Tasse Tee	
p. 17/P 4 **vowel sound** ['vaʊəl saʊnd]	Vokallaut	**vowel sounds**: [e], [æ], [ɜː], [aɪ], [əʊ], ...
p. 18/P 6 **linking word** ['lɪŋkɪŋ wɜːd]	Bindewort	
phrase [freɪz]	Ausdruck, (Rede-)Wendung	
Ms Travelot [mɪz, məz]	Frau Travelot	❗ Manche Frauen möchten lieber mit **Ms ...** angesprochen werden, weil am Wort **Ms** nicht zu erkennen ist, ob sie verheiratet sind oder nicht. (**Mrs ...** = verheiratet; **Miss ...** = unverheiratet)

Vocabulary 1

p. 19/P 10	(to) **be on**	eingeschaltet sein, an sein *(Radio, Licht usw.)*	I can't do my homework when the TV **is on**.
p. 20/P 12	**Find/Ask somebody who ...**	Finde/Frage jemanden, der ...	I don't know. **Ask somebody who** knows more about Bristol.
p. 21/P 14	**word building** [ˈwɜːd ˌbɪldɪŋ]	Wortbildung	
p. 21/P 16	**How are you?** [ˌhaʊ ˈɑː jʊ]	Wie geht es dir/Ihnen/euch?	**How are you**, Mr Kingsley? – I'm OK, thank you.

Saved!

p. 22	(to) **save** [seɪv]	retten	*Latin:* salvare; *French:* sauver
	(to) **be asleep** [əˈsliːp]	schlafen	**!** Wenn man mit **schlafen** meint, dass jemand **nicht wach** ist, benutzt man (to) **be asleep** (nicht ~~(to) sleep~~): It was 11 o'clock, but he **was** still **asleep**.
	bunk (bed) [bʌŋk]	Etagenbett, Koje	**bunk beds** — the top **bunk**
	he **could ...** [kəd, kʊd]	er konnte ...	My brother **could** ride a bike when he was four.
	(to) **jump** [dʒʌmp]	springen	Can you **jump** over your desk?
	(to) **get (-tt-)**, *simple past:* **got**	holen, besorgen	

(to) get (*simple past:* got)

1. gelangen, (hin)kommen	How can I **get** to the station, please?	**Remember:**	
2. werden	My mother **got** very angry last night.	(to) **get dressed**	sich anziehen
3. holen, besorgen	Can you **get** the tickets for the match?	(to) **get on/off**	ein-/aussteigen
4. bekommen, kriegen	Did you **get** nice birthday presents?	(to) **get up**	aufstehen

	(to) **sit up (-tt-)**, *simple past:* **sat up**	sich aufsetzen	(to) **sit up** („sich aufsetzen") ◄► (to) **sit down** („sich hinsetzen")

out („hinaus, heraus", „draußen")

There's a little cat in the water. We have to pull it **out**.	... Wir müssen sie **heraus**ziehen.
Dan saw a girl swim **out**.	Dan sah ein Mädchen **hinaus**schwimmen.
Where's Sheeba? – She's **out** there in the garden.	... Sie ist da **draußen** im Garten.

	Come on. [ˌkʌm ˈɒn]	Na los, komm.	
	tide [taɪd]	Gezeiten, Ebbe und Flut	The **tide** is **out**. (Es ist **Ebbe**.) The **tide** is **in**. (Es ist **Flut**.)

1–2 Vocabulary

	(to) **join** sb./sth. [dʒɔɪn]	sich jm. anschließen; bei jm./etwas mitmachen	We're going shopping. Do you want to **join** us? I like computers, so I **joined** the computer club.
	past [pɑːst]	vorbei (an), vorüber (an)	We walked **past** churches, cafés and shops.
	So what? [səʊ 'wɒt]	Und? / Na und?	We all hate you! – **So what?** I hate you too.
	(to) **wave** [weɪv]	winken	She's **waving**.
	(to) **dial** ['daɪəl] (-ll-)	wählen *(Telefonnummer)*	
p. 23	**all right** [ɔːl 'raɪt]	gut, in Ordnung	Let's meet tomorrow. – **All right**. Is 8.30 OK?
	almost ['ɔːlməʊst]	fast, beinahe	It's **almost** six.
	(to) **drive** [draɪv], simple past: **drove** [drəʊv]	(ein Auto/mit dem Auto) fahren	Does your mother **drive** to work? – No, she usually goes by bike.
	(to) **see** sb. [siː], simple past: **saw** [sɔː]	jn. besuchen, jn. aufsuchen	Why don't you come and **see** us next Sunday?
	(to) **know about** sth., simple past: **knew** [njuː]	von etwas wissen; über etwas Bescheid wissen	I didn't **know about** the party, so I couldn't go.
	exciting [ɪkˈsaɪtɪŋ]	aufregend, spannend	**exciting** ◄► **boring**
	happy ending [ˌhæpi_ˈendɪŋ]	Happyend	❗ In English you say **happy ending**. (*Not:* happy end)
	in time [ɪn 'taɪm]	rechtzeitig	We didn't get home **in time**, so we couldn't watch the film.
	adventure [ədˈventʃə]	Abenteuer	*French:* l'aventure (f)

Unit 2: What money can buy

p. 26	**pocket money** ['pɒkɪt mʌni]	Taschengeld	bags
	pocket ['pɒkɪt]	Tasche *(an einem Kleidungsstück)*	pockets
	(to) **spend money/time (on)** [spend], simple past: **spent** [spent]	Geld ausgeben (für) / Zeit verbringen (mit)	My brother **spends** a lot of money **on** clothes. We **spent** the weekend at my grandmother's in Rostock.
	(to) **save** [seɪv]	sparen	(to) **save** = 1. retten; 2. sparen
	survey (on) ['sɜːveɪ]	Umfrage, Untersuchung (über)	We're doing a **survey on** free-time activities.
p. 27	**blouse** [blaʊz]	Bluse	a pretty **blouse**
	(baseball) cap [kæp]	(Baseball-)Mütze	a **(baseball) cap**
	cinema ['sɪnəmə]	Kino	❗ **ins Kino** gehen = (to) go **to the cinema** *French:* le cinéma
	make-up ['meɪkʌp]	Make-up	❗ Betonung auf der 1. Silbe: **make-up** ['meɪkʌp]
	pullover ['pʊləʊvə]	Pullover	**pullover** ['pʊləʊvə] *French:* le pull-over, le pull
	skirt [skɜːt]	Rock	
	sports gear *(no pl)* ['spɔːts gɪə]	Sportausrüstung, Sportsachen	❗ Where **is** my **sports gear**? *(singular)* = Wo **sind** meine **Sportsachen**?
	a pair (of) [peə]	ein Paar	**a pair of** hockey shoes *French:* la paire

Tipps zum Wörterlernen → S. 115 • Englische Laute → S. 217 • Alphabetische Wörterverzeichnisse → S. 178–199 / S. 200–217

Vocabulary 2

| trousers *(pl)* ['traʊzəz] | Hose | ❗ • **eine** neue Hose = **a** new **pair of trousers**
• **Are** your **trousers** new? – Yes, **they are**.
(= **Ist** deine **Hose** neu?) |

Plural words: *glasses, jeans, shorts, trousers*

She wears **glasses**.	Sie trägt **eine Brille**.	❗ Wörter wie **glasses, jeans, shorts, trousers** sind Pluralwörter – also nie ~~a glasses~~, ~~two jeans~~, ~~this trousers~~!
Why does he need **two pairs of glasses**?	… **zwei Brillen**?	
Those **trousers** are great. Can I have **them**?	Die Hose da ist toll. Kann ich **sie** haben?	
I need **a new pair of trousers/some new trousers**.	… **eine neue Hose**.	

p. 28/A 1	**What's the matter?** ['mætə]	Was ist los? / Was ist denn?	
	awful ['ɔːfl]	furchtbar, schrecklich	very bad, terrible
	mine [maɪn]	meiner, meine, meins	 It's mine.
	(to) **lose** [luːz], *simple past:* **lost** [lɒst]	verlieren	(to) **lose a job** ◂▸ (to) **find a job** (to) **lose a match** ◂▸ (to) **win a match**
	sad [sæd]	traurig	**sad** 🙁 🙂 **happy**
	whose? [huːz]	wessen?	**Whose** CDs are these? Are they yours, Sophie? And **whose** are these? (= Wem gehören diese?)
	(to) **disappear** [ˌdɪsə'pɪə]	verschwinden	*French:* disparaître
	just like you	genau wie du	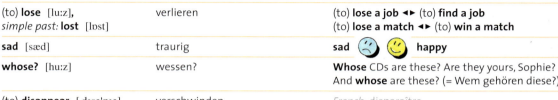 You look **just like** your father.
	(to) **be left** [left]	übrig sein	I can't buy the CD. I haven't got any money **left**.
p. 28/A 3	**test** [test]	Klassenarbeit, Test, Prüfung	*French:* le test
p. 29/A 4	**problem** ['prɒbləm]	Problem	❗ Betonung auf der 1. Silbe: **problem** ['prɒbləm] *Latin:* problema; *French:* le problème
	(to) **look up (from)**	hochsehen, aufschauen (von)	She heard a noise and **looked up from** her book.
	What for? [ˌwɒt 'fɔː]	Wofür?	I need £20. – **What for?**
	Jack did**n't** say **anything**. ['eniθɪŋ]	Jack sagte nichts.	
	trainers *(pl)* ['treɪnəz]	Turnschuhe	a pair of **trainers** 👟
	my old **ones** [wʌnz]	meine alten	There are three CDs on the table: a new **one** (= a new CD) and two old **ones** (= two old CDs).
	small [smɔːl]	klein	What a nice little house! But isn't it too **small** for your family?
	(to) **grow** [grəʊ], *simple past:* **grew** [gruː]	wachsen	Orange trees **grow** only in hot countries.
	(to) **look for** ['lʊk fɔː]	suchen	I'm **looking for** my keys. Do you know where they are?

Namen → S. 218–219 • Unregelmäßige Verben → S. 220–221 • Classroom English/Arbeitsanweisungen → S. 222–223

2 Vocabulary

(to) **point (at/to)** sth. [pɔɪnt]	zeigen, deuten (auf etwas)	He **pointed at/to** the clock. 'We're late,' he said.	
advert ['ædvɜːt]	Anzeige, Inserat; *(im Fernsehen)* Werbespot		

somebody – anybody / something – anything / somewhere – anywhere

Für die Zusammensetzungen mit **some-** und **any-** gelten dieselben Regeln wie für **some** und **any**:
- **somebody, something, somewhere** stehen vor allem in bejahten Aussagesätzen,
- **anybody, anything, anywhere** stehen vor allem in verneinten Aussagesätzen und in Fragen.

+	Listen. There's **somebody** at the door.	... Da ist **jemand** an der Tür.
–	I heard a noise in the garden, but I ca**n't** see **anybody**.	... aber ich kann **niemanden** sehen.
?	Can you see **anybody** in the garden?	Kannst du **(irgend)jemanden** im Garten sehen?
+	Let's go to the shops and get **something** to eat.	... **etwas** zu essen
–	I'm too nervous – I ca**n't** eat **anything** at the moment.	... ich kann im Moment **nichts** essen.
?	Do you need **anything** from the shops?	Brauchst du **(irgend)etwas** ...?
+	This summer I'd like to go **somewhere** where it's hot.	... **irgendwohin**, wo es warm ist.
–	I do**n't** want to go **anywhere**, I want to stay at home.	Ich möchte **nirgendwohin** fahren ...
?	Did you go **anywhere** last summer?	Bist du letzten Sommer **irgendwohin** gefahren?

p. 30/A 7	**letter (to)** ['letə]	Brief (an)	lots of **letters** a **letter**	*French:* la lettre
	even ['iːvn]	sogar	Everybody tried to help, **even** the children.	
	wonderful ['wʌndəfəl]	wunderbar	very nice, fantastic	
	(to) **visit** ['vɪzɪt]	besuchen, aufsuchen		
	I hope so.	Ich hoffe es.	Can you do it without me? – **I hope so.**	
	(to) **send** sb. sth. [send], *simple past:* **sent** [sent]	jm. etwas schicken, senden	My aunt **sends** me £10 every birthday.	
	fashion ['fæʃn]	Mode		
	I don't like her very much.	Ich mag sie nicht sehr.	**!** • (to) **like/love** sth. **very much** = etwas sehr mögen/sehr lieben • **Thanks very much.** = Danke sehr! / Vielen Dank!	
	wet [wet]	feucht, nass	My hair is **wet** because it is raining.	
	whole [həʊl]	ganze(r, s), gesamte(r, s)	We played cards the **whole** day. (= all day) John was in Berlin for the **whole** of 2006.	
	rainy season ['reɪni ˌsiːzn]	Regenzeit		
	season ['siːzn]	Jahreszeit	the four **seasons**: spring, summer, autumn, winter	*French:* la saison
	everybody ['evribɒdi]	jeder, alle	**nobody** (niemand) **somebody** (jemand) **everybody** (jeder, alle)	
p. 30/A 8	(to) **repeat** [rɪ'piːt]	wiederholen	What did you say? Please **repeat** it.	
	(to) **ask** sb. **for** sth.	jn. um etwas bitten	She **asked** her mother **for** help. He **asked** his father **for** some money.	

Tipps zum Wörterlernen → S. 115 • Englische Laute → S. 217 • Alphabetische Wörterverzeichnisse → S. 178–199 / S. 200–217

Vocabulary 2

p. 31/A 9	(to) **compare** [kəm'peə]	vergleichen	**Compare** your notes with a partner. *Latin:* comparare; *French:* comparer
	longer (than) ['lɒŋgə]	länger (als)	Mum's skirts are much **longer than** mine.
	(the) longest ['lɒŋgɪst]	der/die/das längste …; am längsten	Grandma's skirts are **the longest** in our family. **long – longer – (the) longest**
	flower ['flaʊə]	Blume; Blüte	*Latin:* flos; *French:* la fleur
	as nice/big/exciting **as**	so schön/groß/aufregend wie	Bristol is not **as big as** New York.
	then	damals	
	worse (than) [wɜːs]	schlechter, schlimmer (als)	The weather is **worse** today **than** yesterday.

good – better – best • bad – worse – worst

good	gut		**bad**	schlecht, schlimm
better	besser		**worse** [wɜːs]	schlechter, schlimmer
(the) **best**	am besten; der/die/das beste …		(the) **worst** [wɜːst]	am schlechtesten, schlimmsten; der/die/das schlechteste, schlimmste …

My computer is **better** than yours, but Mr Scott's computer is **the best**.
Our school uniform is **bad**, but theirs is **worse**.
What do you think: What's **the best** pop group at the moment? What's **the worst**?

	not (…) any more	nicht mehr	The Greens don't live here **any more**. They're in London now.
	(to) have [həv, hæv], *simple past:* **had** [həd, hæd]	haben, besitzen	❗ haben, besitzen = **1.** have got; **2.** (to) have (Im *simple present* wird *have got* häufiger verwendet. Das *simple past* von beiden ist *had*.)
	selection (of) [sɪ'lekʃn]	Auswahl (an)	That shop has a fantastic **selection** of old comics. *French:* la sélection
	dresses **from the 60s** ['sɪkstiz]	Kleider aus den 60ern / aus den 60er Jahren	
	wild [waɪld]	wild	❗ Pronunciation: **wild** [waɪld]
	cheap [tʃiːp]	billig, preiswert	**cheap** ◄► **expensive**
	service ['sɜːvɪs]	Dienst (am Kunden), Service	The **service** in this café is very slow. *French:* le service
p. 32/A 11	**charity** ['tʃærəti]	Wohlfahrtsorganisation	
	more boring **(than)**	langweiliger (als)	My home town is smaller and **more boring than** Bristol.
	(the) most boring [məʊst]	der/die/das langweiligste …; am langweiligsten	This village must be **the most boring** place in Britain.
	recycling [ˌriː'saɪklɪŋ]	Wiederverwertung, Recycling	
	recycled [ˌriː'saɪkld]	wiederverwertet, wieder- verwendet, recycelt	
p. 37/P 14	**point** [pɔɪnt]	Punkt	Three **points** for the right answer! *French:* le point

2 Vocabulary

The Clothes Project

'No, they aren't!' – 'Yes, they are!' (German „Doch!")

p. 40

Im Deutschen sagt man **„Doch!"**, wenn man einer verneinten Aussage widersprechen will.

Im Englischen benutzt man eine **Kurzantwort** mit Yes, z.B. *Yes, they are! / Yes, you can! / Yes, I do!*

Clothes are boring! – **No, they aren't!** – **Yes, they are!**	... – Sind sie nicht! – Sind sie doch!
Lesley **isn't** rude. – **Oh yes, she is!**	Lesley **ist nicht** unhöflich. – Ist sie doch!
I **can't** do this exercise! – **Yes, you can!**	... – Doch, kannst du!
You **don't** listen to me! – **Yes, I do!**	... – Doch!

presenter [prɪˈzentə]	Moderator/in	
over to ...	hinüber zu/nach ...	Dan saw Jo in the park and walked **over to** him.
(to) fall down [ˌfɔːl ˈdaʊn], *simple past:* **fell** [fel]	runterfallen; hinfallen	What happened to your leg? – I **fell down**, but it's OK.
Never mind. [ˌnevə ˈmaɪnd]	Kümmer dich nicht drum. / Macht nichts.	I haven't got any money. – **Never mind**, I can lend you some.
lovely [ˈlʌvli]	schön, hübsch, wunderbar	
mirror [ˈmɪrə]	Spiegel	a **mirror** — Don't I have **lovely** blue eyes? *French:* le miroir
(to) put sth. **on** [ˌpʊt ˈɒn] (-tt-), *simple past:* **put on**	etwas anziehen *(Kleidung)*; etwas aufsetzen *(Hut)*	
(to) take sth. **off** [ˌteɪk ˈɒf], *simple past:* **took off**	etwas ausziehen *(Kleidung)*; etwas absetzen *(Hut)*	(to) **take off** a pullover ◄► (to) **put on** a pullover
(to) stand [stænd], *simple past:* **stood** [stʊd]	stehen; sich (hin)stellen	Tom **is standing** on a chair. **Stand** on the chair, Tom.
(to) hurry [ˈhʌri]	eilen; sich beeilen	It was cold and windy so we **hurried** to the car. **Hurry (up)**, we haven't got much time.
(to) land [lænd]	landen	

p. 41

(to) prepare [prɪˈpeə]	vorbereiten; sich vorbereiten	(to) **prepare** a presentation / a show / a report ❗ sich vorbereiten **auf** = (to) **prepare for**: I can't help you. I have to **prepare for** a test. *Latin:* praeparare; *French:* préparer
puzzled [ˈpʌzld]	verwirrt	
outfit [ˈaʊtfɪt]	Outfit *(Kleidung; Ausrüstung)*	
point of view [ˌpɔɪnt əv ˈvjuː]	Standpunkt	❗ from my **point of view** = von meinem **Standpunkt** aus gesehen; aus meiner **Sicht**

Vocabulary 3

Unit 3: Animals in the city

p. 44	fox [fɒks]	Fuchs	a fox
	series, pl series ['sɪəriːz]	(Sende-)Reihe, Serie	It's my favourite **series**. I watch it every week.
	(to) survive [sə'vaɪv]	überleben	*Latin:* supervivere; *French:* survivre
	survival [sə'vaɪvl]	Überleben	verb: (to) **survive** — noun: **survival**
	fine [faɪn]	gut, ausgezeichnet; in Ordnung	If you want **fine** food, try our supermarket. Is my essay OK? – Yes, it's **fine**.
	sort (of) [sɔːt]	Art, Sorte	What **sort of** music do you like?
	documentary [ˌdɒkju'mentri]	Dokumentarfilm	! Betonung auf der 3. Silbe: **documentary** [ˌdɒkju'mentri]
	comedy ['kɒmədi]	Comedyshow, Komödie	*French:* la comédie
	chat show ['tʃæt ʃəʊ]	Talkshow	
p. 45	woodpecker ['wʊdpekə]	Specht	
	grey [greɪ]	grau	
	squirrel ['skwɪrəl]	Eichhörnchen	
	frog [frɒg]	Frosch	
	deer, pl deer [dɪə]	Reh, Hirsch	
	hedgehog ['hedʒhɒg]	Igel	
	mole [məʊl]	Maulwurf	
p. 46/A 1	dustbin ['dʌstbɪn], bin [bɪn]	Mülltonne	a dustbin — rubbish
	rubbish ['rʌbɪʃ]	(Haus-)Müll, Abfall	
	you'll be cold (= you will be cold) [wɪl]	du wirst frieren; ihr werdet frieren	! I'll (= I will) help Dan. = Ich **werde** Dan helfen. I **want to** help Dan. = Ich **will** Dan helfen.
	you won't be cold [wəʊnt] (= you will not be cold)	du wirst nicht frieren; ihr werdet nicht frieren	
	yard [jɑːd]	Hof	! *English:* **in the yard** — *German:* **auf dem Hof**
	probably ['prɒbəbli]	wahrscheinlich	*Latin:* probabiliter; *French:* probablement
	(to) mail sb. [meɪl]	jn. anmailen	
p. 46/A 2	moon [muːn]	Mond	
p. 47/A 3	important [ɪm'pɔːtnt]	wichtig	*French:* important, e
	clinic ['klɪnɪk]	Klinik	! Pronunciation: **clinic** ['klɪnɪk] (kurzes „i") *French:* la clinique
	as soon as [əz 'suːn_əz]	sobald, sowie	I'll call you **as soon as** I'm home.
	if [ɪf]	wenn, falls	! **If** I see him, I'll ask him. (Falls ich ihn sehe …) **When** I see him, … (Dann wenn … / Sobald …)
	ill [ɪl]	krank	Susan is **ill**.
	(to) die (of) [daɪ]	sterben (an)	! -ing form: **dying** — This tree is **dying**.
	(to) keep sth. warm/cool/open/… [kiːp], simple past: kept [kept]	etwas warm/kühl/offen/… halten	It's important to **keep** hedgehog babies **warm**. **Keep** your eyes **open** when you're on the road.

Namen → S. 218–219 • Unregelmäßige Verben → S. 220–221 • Classroom English/Arbeitsanweisungen → S. 222–223

3 Vocabulary

Irregular simple past forms

(to) bring	**brought** [brɔːt]	(mit-, her)bringen	(to) mean [miːn]	**meant** [ment]	meinen, sagen wollen
(to) choose	**chose** [tʃəʊz]	(aus)wählen, (sich) aussuchen	(to) sell	**sold** [səʊld]	verkaufen
(to) feed	**fed** [fed]	füttern	(to) sleep	**slept** [slept]	schlafen
(to) hide [haɪd]	**hid** [hɪd]	(sich) verstecken	(to) understand	**understood** [ˌʌndəˈstʊd]	verstehen
(to) lay the table	**laid** [leɪd]	den Tisch decken	(to) win	**won** [wʌn]	gewinnen
(to) let	**let** [let]	lassen	(to) write	**wrote** [rəʊt]	schreiben

fine [faɪn]	(gesundheitlich) gut	! I'm/He's **fine**. = Es geht mir/ihm gut.	
hot-water bottle	Wärmflasche		
gloves *(pl)* [glʌvz]	Handschuhe	a pair of **gloves**	
p. 48/A 5 **rubbish collection** [ˈrʌbɪʃ kəˌlekʃn]	Müllabfuhr		
Guess what! [ˌges ˈwɒt]	Stell dir vor! / Stellt euch vor!		
(to) **guess** [ges]	raten, erraten, schätzen	**Guess** how old I am. – 13? – No, I'm 14.	
at break	in der Pause *(zwischen Schulstunden)*		
just then	genau in dem Moment; gerade dann	At three o'clock we wanted to go swimming, and **just then** it started to rain.	
horrible [ˈhɒrəbl]	scheußlich, grauenhaft	a **horrible** day; **horrible** weather *Latin:* horribilis; *French:* horrible	
garage [ˈgærɑːʒ]	Garage	! Betonung auf der 1. Silbe: **garage** [ˈgærɑːʒ] *French:* le garage	
safe (from) [seɪf]	sicher, in Sicherheit (vor)	! Will the hedgehogs be **safe**? (= **in Sicherheit**) – **I'm sure** they'll be fine. (= **sicherlich**) *Latin:* salvus	
p. 49/A 7 (to) **do a good job**	gute Arbeit leisten	I like your essay. You **did a** really **good job**.	
(to) **look after** sth./sb. [ˌlʊk_ˈɑːftə]	sich um etwas/jn. kümmern; auf etwas/jn. aufpassen	Emily often **looks after** Baby Hannah.	
You looked after them **well**. *(adv)* [wel]	Du hast dich gut um sie gekümmert.	adjective: **good** – adverb: **well**	
broken *(adj)* [ˈbrəʊkən]	gebrochen; zerbrochen, kaputt	a **broken** arm a **broken** plate	
(to) **move** [muːv]	bewegen; sich bewegen	Don't **move**.	
woods *(pl)* [wʊdz]	Wald, Wälder	Let's go for a walk in the **woods**.	
wood [wʊd]	Holz	a piece of **wood**	
hard [hɑːd]	hart; schwer, schwierig	**hard** work; a **hard** piece of bread This exercise isn't **hard**. You can do it.	
(to) **work hard**	hart arbeiten		
I'm afraid [əˈfreɪd]	leider	! • I have to go, **I'm afraid**. = **Leider** muss ich … • He**'s afraid of** cats. = Er **hat Angst vor** Katzen.	

Tipps zum Wörterlernen → S. 115 • Englische Laute → S. 217 • Alphabetische Wörterverzeichnisse → S. 178–199 / S. 200–217

Vocabulary 3

	(to) **plan** [plæn] **(-nn-)**	planen	verb: (to) **plan** — noun: **plan**
p. 49/A 8	(to) **scan** a text [skæn] **(-nn-)**	einen Text schnell nach bestimmten Wörtern/ Informationen absuchen	
	enemy ['enəmi]	Feind/in	**enemy** ◄► **friend** *Latin:* inimicus; *French:* l'ennemi (m), l'ennemie (f)
	female ['fi:meɪl]	Weibchen	*Latin:* femella; *French:* la femelle
	male [meɪl]	Männchen	*Latin:* masculus; *French:* le mâle
	(to) **have a baby**	ein Baby/Kind bekommen	❗ ein Kind **bekommen** = (to) **have** a baby
	natural ['nætʃrəl]	natürlich, Natur-	❗ Pronunciation: **natural** ['nætʃrəl] *Latin:* naturalis; *French:* naturel, le

Remember?

1 **crocodile** ['krɒkədaɪl]
2 **monkey** ['mʌŋki]
3 **camel** ['kæml]
4 one **wolf** [wʊlf], two **wolves** [wʊlvz]
5 **zebra** ['zebrə]
6 **tiger** ['taɪgə]
7 **giraffe** [dʒə'rɑ:f]
8 **lion** ['laɪən]
9 **rhino** ['raɪnəʊ]
10 **hippo** ['hɪpəʊ]
11 **bear** [beə]
12 **elephant** ['elɪfənt]
13 **kangaroo** [ˌkæŋgə'ru:]

p. 51/P 4	**fire** ['faɪə]	Feuer, Brand	
	a single parent	ein(e) Alleinerziehende(r)	
	hurt [hɜ:t]	verletzt	❗ **hurt** = 1. *(v)* verletzen; wehtun; 2. *(adj)* verletzt
p. 55/P 16	**address** [ə'dres]	Anschrift, Adresse	What's your **address**? – 13 Alfred Street, Bristol. ❗ English: **address** — German: **Adresse** *French:* l'adresse (f)

El's best friend

p. 56	**angel** ['eɪndʒl]	Engel	*Latin:* angelus; *French:* l'ange (m)
	(to) **bully** ['bʊli]	einschüchtern, tyrannisieren	
	(to) **pack** [pæk]	packen, einpacken	
	(to) **leave** [li:v], *simple past:* **left** [left]	gehen, weggehen; abfahren	I said 'Goodbye' and **left**.

Namen → S. 218–219 • Unregelmäßige Verben → S. 220–221 • Classroom English/Arbeitsanweisungen → S. 222–223

3 Vocabulary

(to) leave (simple past: left)

1. (weg)gehen; abfahren	Get your suitcase. We're **leaving**. Hurry up, the train **leaves** in an hour.	
2. verlassen	El's mum wanted to **leave** her dad. I took my bags and **left** the room.	
3. zurücklassen	He **left** his dog in the car when he went into the shop.	

I **can't stand** it.	Ich kann es nicht ertragen/ aushalten/ausstehen.	I **can't stand** your music. Turn it off, please.
(to) **make friends (with)**	Freunde finden; sich anfreunden (mit)	He's a nice boy and **makes friends** easily. I **made friends with** John in 2002.
(to) **miss** [mɪs]	vermissen	It was great in England, but I **missed** my friends.
(to) **promise** ['prɒmɪs]	versprechen	I'll come and visit you. I **promise**. ! Ich verspreche **es**! = I **promise**! (*not*: I promise ~~it~~) *Latin:* promittere; *French:* promettre
neat and tidy [niːt], ['taɪdi]	schön ordentlich	My room is always **neat and tidy**.
neat	gepflegt	Your hair looks very **neat**, but isn't it a bit short?
tidy	ordentlich, aufgeräumt	verb: (to) **tidy** (aufräumen) – adjective: **tidy**
sweetheart ['swiːthɑːt]	Liebling, Schatz	
(to) **move out** [ˌmuːv_'aʊt]	ausziehen	(to) **move out** ◄► (to) **move in** We had to **move out** of our house, so we **moved to** London, **to** a small flat in Camden.
(to) **move (to)**	umziehen (nach, in)	
(to) **allow** [ə'laʊ]	erlauben, zulassen	NO DOGS **ALLOWED** IN THIS PARK

Verbs and nouns with the same form

p. 57

(to) **joke**	scherzen, Witze machen	(to) **name**	(be)nennen	(to) **ride** a bike	Rad fahren
joke	Witz	**name**	Name	(bike, bus) **ride**	(Rad-, Bus-)Fahrt
(to) **list**	auflisten, aufzählen	(to) **report (to)**	berichten	(to) **visit**	besuchen
list	Liste	**report**	Bericht	**visit**	Besuch

excited [ɪk'saɪtɪd]	aufgeregt, begeistert	! She was **excited** about the trip. (aufgeregt) It was an **exciting** trip. (aufregend)
already [ɔːl'redi]	schon, bereits	Are you leaving **already**? Can't you stay?
only ['əʊnli]	erst	Sorry I'm late. – That's OK, I **only** got here a minute ago. ! **only** = 1. nur, bloß; 2. erst
(to) **feel** [fiːl], *simple past:* **felt** [felt]	fühlen; sich fühlen	Take my hand. Can you **feel** how cold it is? I always **feel** good when I hear that song.
tear [tɪə]	Träne	He was so sad that his eyes were full of **tears**.
(to) **bark** [bɑːk]	bellen	
good	brav	If you're a **good** boy, you can have an ice cream. ! **good** = 1. gut – a **good** film/story 2. brav – a **good** boy/dog
(to) **count** [kaʊnt]	zählen	Jack **counted** his money. He had £6.50. *Latin:* computare; *French:* compter
the two of them	die beiden; alle beide	Sophie met Jack at the B&B, and then **the two of them** walked to the station.

Tipps zum Wörterlernen → S. 115 • Englische Laute → S. 217 • Alphabetische Wörterverzeichnisse → S. 178–199 / S. 200–217

(to) **turn** [tɜːn]	sich umdrehen	Jo **turned** and walked towards the door.	
shy [ʃaɪ]	schüchtern, scheu	Come on, ask that man over there. Don't be **shy**.	
section [ˈsekʃn]	Abschnitt, Teil	Can I have the sport **section** of the newspaper?	
line [laɪn]	Zeile	I don't know the second word in **line** 12. Abkürzung: **l.** 5 = **line** 5 • **ll.** 5–9 = **lines** 5–9 *French:* la ligne	

Unit 4: A weekend in Wales

p. 60	**relative** [ˈrelətɪv]	Verwandte(r)	aunts, uncles, cousins and other **relatives**
	theme park [ˈθiːm pɑːk]	Themenpark	I went to the *Wild West* **theme park** yesterday.
	open-air concert [ˌəʊpən ˈeə ˌkɒnsət]	Open-Air-Konzert, Konzert im Freien	❗ Betonung auf der 1. Silbe: **concert** [ˈkɒnsət]
	air [eə]	Luft	Please open the window and let some **air** in. *Latin:* aer; *French:* l'air *(m)*
	coast [kəʊst]	Küste	Aberdeen is a town on the **coast** of Scotland. *French:* la côte
	clean [kliːn]	sauber	verb: (to) **clean** – adjective: **clean**
	cow [kaʊ]	Kuh	
	dirty [ˈdɜːti]	schmutzig	**dirty** ◄► **clean**
	factory [ˈfæktri]	Fabrik	
	farm [fɑːm]	Bauernhof, Farm	*French:* la ferme
	field [fiːld]	Feld, Acker, Weide	❗ **auf** dem Feld = **in** the field
	forest [ˈfɒrɪst]	Wald	
	hill [hɪl]	Hügel	
	noisy [ˈnɔɪzi]	laut, lärmend	
	river [ˈrɪvə]	Fluss	
	sheep, *pl* **sheep** [ʃiːp]	Schaf	
	traffic [ˈtræfɪk]	Verkehr	
	valley [ˈvæli]	Tal	
p. 61	**pyjamas** *(pl)* [pəˈdʒɑːməz]	Schlafanzug	❗ Where **are** my **pyjamas**? (= Wo **ist** mein **Schlafanzug**?) *French:* le pyjama
	Welsh [welʃ]	walisisch; Walisisch	Some people in Wales speak English and **Welsh**.
p. 62/A 1	(to) **smell** [smel]	riechen	I could **smell** Mum's cake in the kitchen. 'Mmmm, that **smells** great,' I said.
	(to) **cook** [kʊk]	kochen, zubereiten	*Latin:* coquere

Verbs and nouns with the same form

(to) **call**	(an)rufen; nennen	(to) **glue**	(auf-, ein)kleben	(to) **smell**	riechen
call	Ruf, Schrei; Anruf	**glue**	Klebstoff	**smell**	Geruch
(to) **cook**	kochen, zubereiten	(to) **love**	lieben, sehr mögen	(to) **smile**	lächeln
cook	Koch, Köchin	**love**	Liebe	**smile**	Lächeln

Namen → S. 218–219 • Unregelmäßige Verben → S. 220–221 • Classroom English/Arbeitsanweisungen → S. 222–223

4 Vocabulary

	soup [suːp]	Suppe	*French:* la soupe
	railway ['reɪlweɪ]	Eisenbahn	
	picnic ['pɪknɪk]	Picknick	*French:* le pique-nique
	castle ['kɑːsl]	Burg, Schloss	a **castle**
p. 62/A 2	**south** [saʊθ]	Süden; nach Süden; südlich	north [nɔːθ] / north-west [ˌnɔːθ'west] / north-east [ˌnɔːθ'iːst] / west [west] / east [iːst] / south-west [ˌsaʊθ'west] / south-east [ˌsaʊθ'iːst] / south [saʊθ]
	football/hockey pitch [pɪtʃ]	Fußball-/Hockeyplatz, -feld	
	(to) be surrounded by [sə'raʊndɪd]	umgeben sein von	The house **is surrounded by** trees.
	(to) miss [mɪs]	verpassen	She got up late, so she **missed** the bus. ❗ (to) **miss** = 1. vermissen – I **miss** my friends. 2. verpassen – I **missed** the bus.
	topic sentence [ˌtɒpɪk 'sentəns]	*Satz, der in das Thema eines Absatzes einführt*	
	paragraph ['pærəgrɑːf]	Absatz *(in einem Text)*	❗ Betonung auf der 1. Silbe: p**a**ragraph ['pærəgrɑːf]
p. 63/A 4	**bacon** ['beɪkən]	Schinkenspeck	**bacon**
	not (...) yet [jet]	noch nicht	Are you ready? – **Not yet**. I'll be ready in ten minutes.
	just [dʒʌst]	gerade (eben), soeben	❗ **just** = 1. nur, bloß – Don't worry if you don't win. It's **just** a game. 2. gerade (eben) – I'm new in Berlin. I've **just** moved here.

The present perfect: statements

In Aussagesätzen im *present perfect* findet man oft diese unbestimmten Zeitangaben:

already	Please tidy your room. – But I've **already** tidied it.	schon
not ... yet	I've tidied my room, but I have**n't** finished my homework **yet**.	noch nicht
never	I often play football but I've **never** played basketball.	(noch) nie
just	Your room looks great. – Yes, I've **just** tidied it.	gerade (eben), soeben

	made [meɪd]	3. Form (Partizip Perfekt[1]) von „make"	(to) make – made – **made**
	pie [paɪ]	Obstkuchen; Pastete	
	seen [siːn]	*Partizip Perfekt von „see"*	(to) see – saw – **seen**
	come [kʌm]	*Partizip Perfekt von „come"*	(to) come – came – **come**

[1] Die dritte Form des Verbs nennt man **Partizip Perfekt** (Englisch: *past participle*).

Tipps zum Wörterlernen → S. 115 • Englische Laute → S. 217 • Alphabetische Wörterverzeichnisse → S. 178–199 / S. 200–217

Irregular past participles

(to) be	was/were	**been** [biːn]	sein		(to) hear	heard	**heard** [hɜːd]	hören
(to) do	did	**done** [dʌn]	tun, machen		(to) hurt	hurt	**hurt** [hɜːt]	wehtun; verletzen
(to) eat	ate	**eaten** [ˈiːtn]	essen		(to) lose	lost	**lost** [lɒst]	verlieren
(to) find	found	**found** [faʊnd]	finden		(to) meet	met	**met** [met]	(sich) treffen
(to) go	went	**gone** [gɒn]	gehen, fahren		(to) speak	spoke	**spoken** [ˈspəʊkən]	sprechen
(to) have (have got)	had	**had** [hæd]	haben, besitzen		(to) take	took	**taken** [ˈteɪkən]	nehmen, (weg-, hin)bringen

well (adj)	(gesundheitlich) gut; gesund, wohlauf	❗ **well** = 1. (adv) gut – She sang **well**. (Adverb zu „good") 2. (adj) gesund – He doesn't feel **well**. I'm **well** again.
p. 64/A6 **Oh dear!**	Oje!	
(to) **have a temperature** [ˈtemprətʃə]	Fieber haben	I feel very hot. I think I **have a temperature**. ❗ Betonung auf der 1. Silbe: **temperature** [ˈtemprətʃə]
temperature	Temperatur	*French:* la température
thermometer [θəˈmɒmɪtə]	Thermometer	❗ Betonung auf der 2. Silbe: **thermometer** [θəˈmɒmɪtə] *French:* le thermomètre
(to) **have a sore throat** [sɔː ˈθrəʊt]	Halsschmerzen haben	She **has a sore throat**.
(to) **be sore**	wund sein, wehtun	Your eyes are very red. **Are** they **sore**?
throat	Hals, Kehle	
(to) **nod** [nɒd] (-dd-)	nicken (mit)	❗ Er **nickte mit** dem Kopf. = He **nodded his head**.
headache [ˈhedeɪk]	Kopfschmerzen	I have a **headache**. I often get **headaches**.
flu [fluː]	Grippe	❗ German: Ich habe **eine** oder **die** Grippe. English: I've got **flu**. or I've got **the flu**. (not: I've got a̶ ̶f̶l̶u̶.)

What's wrong with you? („Was fehlt dir?")

(to) have **a headache / a toothache / an earache / a stomach[1] ache** (to) have **a cold**	Kopfschmerzen / Zahnschmerzen / Ohrenschmerzen / Magenschmerzen haben eine Erkältung haben, erkältet sein

I don't feel well. / I feel ill.
 – What's wrong with you?
 I have a terrible headache and my throat is sore.
 – Maybe you have a cold.
    Do you have a temperature too?
	Ich fühle mich nicht gut. / Ich fühle mich krank.
	 – Was fehlt dir?
	 Ich habe schreckliche Kopfschmerzen und mein Hals tut weh.
	 – Vielleicht hast du eine Erkältung / bist du erkältet.
	    Hast du auch Fieber?

Statt *I have a cold / a headache / a temperature* usw. kannst du auch *I've got a cold / a headache / a temperature* usw. sagen.	[1]stomach [ˈstʌmək] Magen

It's a pity (that ...) [ˈpɪti]	Es ist schade, dass ...	**It was a pity that** Mary wasn't there.
paramedic [ˌpærəˈmedɪk]	Sanitäter/in	❗ Englische Berufsangaben mit unbestimmtem Artikel: My dad is **a** paramedic / **a** teacher. (Mein Vater ist Sanitäter / Lehrer.)

Namen → S. 218–219 • Unregelmäßige Verben → S. 220–221 • Classroom English/Arbeitsanweisungen → S. 222–223

4 Vocabulary

p. 64/A 7	(to) **break** [breɪk], **broke** [brəʊk], **broken** ['brəʊkən]	(zer)brechen; kaputt machen; kaputt gehen	John fell down and **broke** his arm. Please be careful. Don't **break** my MP3 player. The plate fell down and **broke**.
	(to) **cut, cut, cut** [kʌt] (-tt-)	schneiden	**Cut** the paper into four pieces.
p. 65/A 9	**ever** ['evə]	je, jemals, schon mal	Have you **ever** visited England?

The present perfect: questions

In Fragen im *present perfect* findet man oft diese unbestimmten Zeitangaben:

ever?	Have you **ever** played tennis? – No, never.	**schon mal? / jemals?**
yet?	Have you done your homework **yet**? – Yes, I have.	**schon?**

	(to) **install** [ɪn'stɔːl]	installieren, einrichten	verb: (to) **install** –	*French:* installer
	installation [ˌɪnstə'leɪʃn]	Installation, Einrichtung	noun: **installation**	*French:* l'installation *(f)*
	(to) **chat** [tʃæt] (-tt-)	chatten, plaudern	We sat in the park and **chatted** for a few hours.	
	chat [tʃæt]	Chat, Unterhaltung		
	(to) **print** sth. **out** [ˌprɪnt_'aʊt]	etwas ausdrucken	If you've finished the letter, you can **print** it **out** now.	
	instructions *(pl)* [ɪn'strʌkʃnz]	(Gebrauchs-)Anweisung(en), Anleitung(en)	Read the **instructions** before you use the new dishwasher. *French:* les instructions *(f)*	
	It says here: ...	Hier steht: ... / Es heißt hier: ...		
	(to) **click on** sth. [klɪk]	etwas anklicken	What do I do next? – Just **click on** 'OK'.	
	(to) **enter** sth. ['entə]	etwas eingeben, eintragen	Please **enter** your name on this list.	

Irregular past participles

(to) buy	bought	**bought** [bɔːt]	kaufen	(to) put	put	**put** [pʊt]	legen, stellen
(to) feed	fed	**fed** [fed]	füttern	(to) read [riːd]	read	**read** [red]	lesen
(to) feel	felt	**felt** [felt]	(sich) fühlen	(to) say	said	**said** [sed]	sagen
(to) give	gave	**given** ['gɪvn]	geben	(to) send	sent	**sent** [sent]	senden, schicken
(to) hide	hid	**hidden** ['hɪdn]	(sich) verstecken	(to) think	thought	**thought** [θɔːt]	denken, glauben
(to) know	knew	**known** [nəʊn]	wissen; kennen	(to) write	wrote	**written** ['rɪtn]	schreiben

p. 65/A 10	(to) **mean** [miːn], **meant, meant** [ment]	bedeuten	What does 'classmate' **mean**? – It **means** somebody in your form.

Computer words and phrases

You can ...
- **surf** the internet and **download** music or pictures.
- **install** software on your computer.
- **chat** with friends in a chat room.
- **print out** pictures or texts.
- **copy** texts and pictures.
- **send** e-mails to your friends.

p. 67/P 5	**accent** ['æksənt]	Akzent	❗ Betonung auf der 1. Silbe: **accent** ['æksənt] *French:* l'accent *(m)*
p. 71/P 15	**silent letter** [ˌsaɪlənt 'letə]	„stummer" Buchstabe (nicht gesprochener Buchstabe)	You can't hear the 'w' in 'answer' – it's a **silent letter**.

All in a day's work

p. 72	(to) **ring** [rɪŋ], **rang** [ræŋ], **rung** [rʌŋ]	klingeln, läuten	Listen – I think the phone **is ringing**.
	(to) **pick up the phone** [pɪk]	den Hörer abnehmen	I **picked up the phone** and called the police.
	accident ['æksɪdənt]	Unfall	*French:* l'accident *(m)*
	(to) **be allowed to** do sth. [ə'laʊd]	etwas tun dürfen	**Were** you **allowed to** use dictionaries in your English tests?
	(to) **be able to** do sth. ['eɪbl]	etwas tun können; fähig sein/ in der Lage sein, etwas zu tun	Sandra **wasn't able to** come to my party last Saturday. (= Sandra **couldn't** come ...)

„können" und „dürfen"

Du kennst bereits **can** für „können" und **can** und **may** für „dürfen":

Ananda **can** play hockey very well.	Ananda kann sehr gut Hockey spielen.
You **can/may** go to the disco, but be home at 9, please.	Du darfst zur Disko gehen, ...

Wenn es um die **Vergangenheit** oder die **Zukunft** geht, verwende

– für „können" eine Form von **be able to** und
– für „dürfen" eine Form von **be allowed to**.

(to) **be able to:**	The museum was closed on Friday, but we **were able to** go on Saturday.[1]	..., aber wir konnten am Samstag hingehen.
	I **won't be able to** to meet you today.	Ich werde dich heute nicht treffen können.
(to) **be allowed to:**	**Were** you **allowed to** watch the film last night?	Durftest du den Film gestern Abend sehen?
	When I'm 18 I**'ll be allowed to** drive.	Wenn ich 18 bin, werde ich Auto fahren dürfen.

[1] Es gibt auch eine Vergangenheitsform *could* („konnte"): Bryn **could** see a red car on its side.

	side [saɪd]	Seite	How can we get to the other **side** of the river?
	fireman ['faɪəmən] **/ firewoman** ['faɪə‚wʊmən]	Feuerwehrmann/-frau	
	metre ['miːtə]	Meter	*French:* le mètre
	(to) **hold** [həʊld], **held**, **held** [held]	halten	That footbridge looks dangerous. Do you think it will **hold**? Can you **hold** my baby for a moment, please?
	strong [strɒŋ]	stark	He's very **strong**.
	weak [wiːk]	schwach	He's **weak**.
p. 73	(to) **fall** [fɔːl], **fell** [fel], **fallen** ['fɔːlən]	fallen, stürzen; hinfallen	Oh no! Toby **has fallen** into the pool. I **fell** and hurt my leg yesterday.
	unconscious [ʌn'kɒnʃəs]	bewusstlos	He isn't dead. He's just **unconscious**.
	husband ['hʌzbənd]	Ehemann	❗ mein **Mann** = my **husband** *(not: my man)*
	wife [waɪf], *pl* **wives** [waɪvz]	Ehefrau	❗ meine **Frau** = my **wife** *(not: my woman)*

Namen → S. 218–219 • Unregelmäßige Verben → S. 220–221 • Classroom English/Arbeitsanweisungen → S. 222–223

4–5 Vocabulary

(to) think		
think	I **think** you're right.	denken, glauben, meinen
think about	**Think about** these questions: ...	nachdenken über
think of	**Think of** the children. They need you.	denken an
	Think of a word with five letters.	sich ausdenken
think about/of	What do you **think about** / **think of** the story?	denken über, halten von

	hospital [ˈhɒspɪtl]	Krankenhaus	*French:* l'hôpital *(m)*
	That was close. [kləʊs]	Das war knapp.	❗ Pronunciation: (to) **close** („schließen") [kləʊz] **close** („knapp") [kləʊs]
	grandson [ˈɡrænsʌn] / **granddaughter** [ˈɡrændɔːtə]	Enkel/Enkelin	a son of your child / a daughter of your child
p. 74	injury [ˈɪndʒəri]	Verletzung	He died of his **injuries** after the accident.

Unit 5: Teamwork

p. 76	dice, *pl* dice [daɪs]	Würfel	
	counter [ˈkaʊntə]	Spielstein	
	Move on one space.	Geh ein Feld vor.	
	Move back one space.	Geh ein Feld zurück.	
	engineer [ˌendʒɪˈnɪə]	Ingenieur/in	
	(to) **build** [bɪld], **built**, **built** [bɪlt]	bauen	
	pub [pʌb]	Kneipe, Lokal	where people go to drink and talk
	Miss a turn. [tɜːn]	Einmal aussetzen.	
	Take another turn.	*hier:* Würfel noch einmal.	
	international [ˌɪntəˈnæʃnəl]	international	
	balloon [bəˈluːn]	Heißluftballon; Luftballon	*French:* le ballon
	across [əˈkrɒs]	(quer) über	All those cars! We can't get **across** the street.
	closed [kləʊzd]	geschlossen	**closed** ◄► **open** *Latin:* clausus
	market [ˈmɑːkɪt]	Markt	*Latin:* mercatus; *French:* le marché
	healthy [ˈhelθi]	gesund	It's very **healthy** to do sports.
	snack [snæk]	Snack, Imbiss	
p. 77	famous (for) [ˈfeɪməs]	berühmt (für, wegen)	Bristol is **famous for** the Clifton Suspension Bridge. *Latin:* famosus
	sugar [ˈʃʊɡə]	Zucker	Tea with milk and **sugar**? *French:* le sucre
	trade [treɪd]	Handel	the activity of buying and selling things
	slave [sleɪv]	Sklave, Sklavin	*French:* l'esclave *(m, f)*
	British [ˈbrɪtɪʃ]	britisch; Brite, Britin	There's a lot of **British** music on German radio. I'm German, but my mother is **British**.
	rich [rɪtʃ]	reich	**rich** ◄► **poor** *French:* riche

Vocabulary 5

	(to) **arrive** [əˈraɪv]	ankommen, eintreffen	(to) **arrive** ◄► (to) **leave** *French:* arriver
p. 78/A 1	a project **which** starts with a quiz	ein Projekt, das mit einem Quiz beginnt	
	material [məˈtɪəriəl]	Material, Stoff	We need a lot of **material** for our project. *Latin:* materia; *French:* le matériel
	booklet [ˈbʊklət]	Broschüre	
	something **that** happens in August	etwas, das im August passiert	
	(to) **produce** [prəˈdjuːs]	produzieren, erzeugen, herstellen	Germany **produces** more cheese than France. *Latin:* producere; *French:* produire
	the people **who** come ...	die Menschen, die ... kommen	
	I don't get it.	Das versteh ich nicht. / Das kapier ich nicht.	Look, it's very easy: if x is 52, y has to be 13. – **I don't get it.**
	event [ɪˈvent]	Ereignis	The first day at school is a big **event** in a child's life. *French:* l'événement *(m)*
p. 79/A 4	the man **whose** statue ...	der Mann, dessen Statue ...	
	statue [ˈstætʃuː]	Statue	*Latin:* statua; *French:* la statue
	photographer [fəˈtɒgrəfə]	Fotograf/in	❗ Betonung auf der 2. Silbe: **photographer** [fəˈtɒgrəfə] *French:* le/la photographe
	encyclopedia [ɪnˌsaɪkləˈpiːdiə]	Enzyklopädie, Lexikon	*French:* l'encyclopédie *(f)*
p. 79/A 5	(to) **be born** [bi ˈbɔːn]	geboren sein/werden	I **was** born in 1997. = Ich **bin** 1997 geboren. ❗ Never: I ~~am born~~ in 1997.
	(to) **decide (on** sth.**)** [dɪˈsaɪd]	sich entscheiden (für etwas), (etwas) beschließen	We **decided on** a project about the sea. (= We **decided** to do a project) *French:* décider
	(to) **become** [bɪˈkʌm], **became** [bɪˈkeɪm], **become**	werden	❗ Nicht verwechseln: (to) **become** = werden (to) **get** = bekommen

Irregular past participles

(to) drive	drove	**driven** [ˈdrɪvn]	(ein Auto) fahren		(to) ride	rode	**ridden** [ˈrɪdn]	reiten; *(Rad)* fahren
(to) get	got	**got** [gɒt]	bekommen; holen; werden; (hin)kommen		(to) run	ran	**run** [rʌn]	rennen, laufen
(to) grow	grew	**grown** [grəʊn]	wachsen		(to) sell	sold	**sold** [səʊld]	verkaufen
(to) leave	left	**left** [left]	(weg)gehen, abfahren; verlassen; zurücklassen		(to) sit	sat	**sat** [sæt]	sitzen; sich setzen
					(to) sleep	slept	**slept** [slept]	schlafen
					(to) win	won	**won** [wʌn]	gewinnen

	tunnel [ˈtʌnl]	Tunnel	❗ Pronunciation: **tunnel** [ˈtʌnl] *French:* le tunnel
	(to) **recover (from)** [rɪˈkʌvə]	sich erholen (von)	Has your mum **recovered**? – Yes, thanks.
	the ship **was built** in Bristol	das Schiff wurde in Bristol gebaut	Our house **was built** in three months.
	proud (of sb./sth.**)** [praʊd]	stolz (auf jn./etwas)	She's a very good student. We're **proud of** her.
	(to) **mark** sth. **up** [ˌmɑːk ˈʌp]	etwas markieren, kennzeichnen	
p. 80/A 7	**delicious** [dɪˈlɪʃəs]	köstlich, lecker	What's the pizza like? – Mmmm. It's **delicious**. *Latin:* deliciosus; *French:* délicieux, se

Namen → S. 218–219 • Unregelmäßige Verben → S. 220–221 • Classroom English/Arbeitsanweisungen → S. 222–223

5 Vocabulary

impossible [ɪmˈpɒsəbl]	unmöglich	It's **impossible** to run a mile in two minutes. *Latin:* impossibilis; *French:* impossible	
possible [ˈpɒsəbl]	möglich	**possible** ◄► **impossible** *Latin:* possibilis; *French:* possible	
silly [ˈsɪli]	albern, dumm	She's too **silly** – she can't understand the joke.	
pretty cool/good/… [ˈprɪti]	ziemlich cool/gut/…	❗ **pretty** = 1. *(adj)* hübsch – Polly is a **pretty** parrot. 2. *(adv)* ziemlich – This place looks **pretty** cool.	
(to) **order** [ˈɔːdə]	bestellen	We went into the bar and **ordered** drinks.	
What can I get you?	Was kann/darf ich euch/Ihnen bringen?	**What can I get you?** – Just a cup of coffee, please.	
smoothie [ˈsmuːði]	dickflüssiger Fruchtshake mit Milch, Joghurt oder Eiscreme		
flavour [ˈfleɪvə]	Geschmack, Geschmacksrichtung	Two ice creams, please. – What **flavour**? – Chocolate, please.	
strawberry [ˈstrɔːbəri]	Erdbeere		

p. 81/A 9

(to) **lock up** [ˌlɒk ˈʌp]	abschließen	Please **lock up** before you leave the building.	
IT [ˌaɪ ˈtiː] (**information technology**) [tekˈnɒlədʒi]	IT (Informationstechnologie)		
(to) **steal** [stiːl], **stole** [stəʊl], **stolen** [ˈstəʊlən]	stehlen	Where's your new bike? – Somebody **has stolen** it.	
thief [θiːf], *pl* **thieves** [θiːvz]	Dieb/in		

Irregular past participles

(to) bring	brought	**brought** [brɔːt]	(mit-, her)bringen	(to) swim	swam	**swum** [swʌm]	schwimmen
(to) choose	chose	**chosen** [ˈtʃəʊzn]	(aus)wählen, (sich) aussuchen	(to) teach	taught	**taught** [tɔːt]	unterrichten, lehren
(to) drink	drank	**drunk** [drʌŋk]	trinken	(to) tell	told	**told** [təʊld]	erzählen
(to) let	let	**let** [let]	lassen	(to) understand	understood	**understood** [ˌʌndəˈstʊd]	verstehen
(to) show	showed	**shown** [ʃəʊn]	zeigen				

p. 81/A 10

(to) **take place**	stattfinden	Our next school trip will **take place** next month.
from all over the world	aus der ganzen Welt	The band plays music **from all over the world**.

Numbers

500,000	= five hundred thousand	Im Englischen steht oft ein Komma in Zahlen, die größer als 1 000 sind.
11,400	= eleven thousand four hundred	
❗ 11.4	= eleven **point** four *(deutsch:* 11,4 = elf **Komma** vier*)*	
1,100,000	= one million one hundred thousand	
❗ 1.1 million	= one **point** one million *(deutsch:* 1,1 Millionen*)*	

shape [ʃeɪp]	Form, Gestalt	I like the colour, but not the **shape**.
(to) **structure** [ˈstrʌktʃə]	strukturieren, aufbauen	*Latin:* struere; *French:* structurer

p. 82/P 3

discussion [dɪˈskʌʃn]	Diskussion	❗ Betonung auf der 2. Silbe: **discussion** [dɪˈskʌʃn] *French:* la discussion

---

Tipps zum Wörterlernen → S. 115 • Englische Laute → S. 217 • Alphabetische Wörterverzeichnisse → S. 178–199 / S. 200–217

	(to) **disagree (with)** [ˌdɪsəˈɡriː]	anderer Meinung sein (als), nicht übereinstimmen (mit)	I'm sorry, but I **disagree with** you. (to) **agree** ◂▸ (to) **disagree**
p. 84/P 7	(to) **be called** [kɔːld]	heißen, genannt werden	Asterix has got a big friend. He**'s called** 'Obelix'. (= His name is 'Obelix'.)

To catch a thief

p. 88	(to) **catch** [kætʃ], **caught, caught** [kɔːt]	fangen; erwischen	You throw the ball and I'll **catch** it. The police are trying to **catch** a bank robber.
	proof *(no pl)* [pruːf]	Beweis(e)	Is she really a thief? We need **proof**. *Latin:* ❗ Never: a ~~proof~~ proba
	So?	Und? / Na und?	It's very cold today. – **So?** You can wear a pullover when you go out.
	(to) **set a trap (for** sb.**), set, set** [ˌset_ə ˈtræp] (-tt-)	(jm.) eine Falle stellen	
	purse [pɜːs]	Geldbörse	a **purse** *Latin:* bursa
	special [ˈspeʃl]	besondere(r, s)	Today is a very **special** day – it's my birthday! ❗ Betonung auf der 1. Silbe: **special** [ˈspeʃl] *Latin:* specialis; *French:* spécial, e
	ring [rɪŋ]	Ring	
	(to) **bleep** [bliːp]	piepsen	
	bleep [bliːp]	Piepton	
	(to) **whistle** [ˈwɪsl]	pfeifen	
	whistle [ˈwɪsl]	Pfiff; (Triller-)Pfeife	
	Shut up. [ˌʃʌtˈʌp]	Halt den Mund!	**Shut up,** Toby. I want to watch this film. ❗ (to) **shut – shut – shut**
p. 89	**all we have to do now …**	alles, was wir jetzt (noch) tun müssen, …	
	this way [ˈðɪs weɪ]	hier entlang, in diese Richtung	Excuse me. Where's 8PK's classroom? – **This way**, please. It's on the right.
	the wrong way	in die falsche Richtung	Stop! You're going **the wrong way.**
	caretaker [ˈkeəteɪkə]	Hausmeister/in	
	cleaner [ˈkliːnə]	Putzfrau, -mann	
p. 90	**rest** [rest]	Rest	*French:* le reste
	(to) **belong (to)** [bɪˈlɒŋ]	gehören (zu)	Who does this book **belong to**? – I think it's Jo's.
	case [keɪs]	Fall	'This will be a difficult **case**,' the detective said. *French:* le cas
	mystery [ˈmɪstri]	Rätsel, Geheimnis	My grandfather doesn't understand computers. They're a **mystery** to him. *Latin:* mysterium; *French:* le mystère

Unit 6: A trip to Bath

p. 94	**Roman** [ˈrəʊmən]	römisch; Römer, Römerin	*Latin:* Romanus; *French:* romain,e
	bath [bɑːθ]	Bad, Badewanne	❗ (to) **have a bath** = baden, ein Bad nehmen
	round [raʊnd]	rund	r**ound** *Latin:* rotundus; *French:* rond, e

6 Vocabulary

stone [stəʊn]	Stein	
wall [wɔːl]	Wand; Mauer	A room has got four **walls**. Can you climb that stone **wall**?
towel [ˈtaʊəl]	Handtuch	
(to) **have a massage** [ˈmæsɑːʒ]	sich massieren lassen	❗ Betonung auf der 1. Silbe: **massage** [ˈmæsɑːʒ]
(to) **have a sauna** [ˈsɔːnə]	in die Sauna gehen	
(to) **relax** [rɪˈlæks]	(sich) entspannen, sich ausruhen	
machine [məˈʃiːn]	Maschine, Gerät	*Latin:* machina; *French:* la machine

p. 96/A 1

(to) **cycle** [ˈsaɪkl]	(mit dem) Rad fahren	(to) ride a bike
along the road [əˈlɒŋ]	entlang der Straße / die Straße entlang	
path [pɑːθ]	Pfad, Weg	a **cycle path along** the river
flat [flæt]	flach, eben	The Netherlands is a very **flat** country.
I've never been **to** Bath.	Ich bin noch nie in Bath gewesen.	
half [hɑːf]	halbe(r, s)	❗ **half** an hour = eine **halbe** Stunde
way [weɪ]	Weg; Strecke	It's 14 miles, but we only have to cycle half **way**.

way („Richtung", „Weg")

Stop. You're going **the wrong way**. We have to go **this way**.	Halt! Du gehst **in die falsche Richtung**. Wir müssen **hier entlang / in diese Richtung**.
Which way is the station, please?	**In welcher Richtung liegt** der Bahnhof, bitte? / **Wo geht's** zum Bahnhof, bitte?
I don't know where we are. Let's **ask** somebody **the way**. 'Excuse me. Can you **tell** us **the way** to Bath?'	… Lass uns jemanden **nach dem Weg fragen**. „… Können Sie uns **den Weg** nach Bath **beschreiben**?"
The group had a lot of fun **on their way** to Bath.	… **auf ihrem Weg** nach Bath.

guy [gaɪ]	Typ, Kerl	❗ umgangssprachlich für „Mann" oder „Junge": Mike is a really nice **guy**. Der Plural **guys** („Leute") wird auch für Frauen und Mädchen verwendet: Hey, you **guys**! Wait for me. I'll come with you.
Come on. [ˌkʌm ˈɒn]	Ach komm! / Na hör mal!	Oh **come on** – you know that's wrong!
before [bɪˈfɔː]	(vorher) schon mal	Have you been to Bath **before** or is it your first visit?
theatre [ˈθɪətə]	Theater	❗ Betonung auf der 1. Silbe: **theatre** [ˈθɪətə] *Latin:* theatrum; *French:* le théâtre
royal [ˈrɔɪəl]	königlich, Königs-	Tourists love the British **royal** family. *Latin:* regalis; *French:* royal, e
conversation [ˌkɒnvəˈseɪʃn]	Gespräch, Unterhaltung	He loves **conversations** and can talk for hours. *French:* la conversation

p. 97/A 3

opposite [ˈɒpəzɪt]	gegenüber (von)	The bathroom is **opposite** the bedroom.
abbey [ˈæbi]	Abtei	*Latin:* abbatia; *French:* l'abbaye *(f)*

Tipps zum Wörterlernen → S. 115 • Englische Laute → S. 217 • Alphabetische Wörterverzeichnisse → S. 178–199 / S. 200–217

Vocabulary 6

(to) **continue** [kənˈtɪnjuː]	weitermachen (mit); weiterreden; weitergehen	(to) go on The teacher **continued** (to talk) after the bell rang. She **continued** with the lesson. I stopped to look at a poster, but Jo **continued**. *Latin:* continuere; *French:* continuer
map [mæp]	Landkarte, Stadtplan	*Latin:* mappa
(to) **turn left/right**	(nach) links/rechts abbiegen	Turn left. Turn right. *French:* tourner à gauche/à droite

(to) turn

The way to the station? No problem – **turn left** at the church, then **turn right** into Elm Street.	abbiegen
Suddenly the woman **turned** and looked at me.	sich umdrehen
Mrs Hanson **turned to** Jack and asked, 'Why?'	sich jm. zuwenden; sich an jn. wenden
Jo **turned off** the radio and **turned on** the TV.	aus-, einschalten

(to) **cross** [krɒs]	überqueren; (sich) kreuzen	Don't **cross** the road here. It's too dangerous. The two roads **cross** in the city centre.
straight on [streɪt ˈɒn]	geradeaus weiter	The hospital? Turn left here, and then go **straight on**.
post office [ˈpəʊst ˌɒfɪs]	Postamt	
police station [pəˈliːs steɪʃn]	Polizeiwache, Polizeirevier	
restaurant [ˈrestrɒnt]	Restaurant	! Betonung auf der 1. Silbe: **restaurant** [ˈrestrɒnt] *French:* le restaurant
chemist [ˈkemɪst]	Drogerie, Apotheke	
department store [dɪˈpɑːtmənt stɔː]	Kaufhaus	
p. 97/A 4 **directions** *(pl)* [dəˈrekʃnz]	Wegbeschreibung(en)	I couldn't find the station, but then a policeman gave me **directions**.

Irregular past participles

(to) fly	flew	**flown** [fləʊn]	fliegen	(to) shine	shone	**shone** [ʃɒn]	scheinen *(Sonne)*
(to) keep	kept	**kept** [kept]	*(warm/offen/...)* halten	(to) sing	sang	**sung** [sʌŋ]	singen
(to) lay the table	laid	**laid** [leɪd]	den Tisch decken	(to) throw	threw	**thrown** [θrəʊn]	werfen
				(to) wear	wore	**worn** [wɔːn]	tragen *(Kleidung)*

p. 98/A 5 (to) **be missing** [ˈmɪsɪŋ]	fehlen	Almost all my friends were at the party. Only Robbie **was missing**.
square [skweə]	Platz *(in der Stadt)*	
needn't do [ˈniːdnt]	nicht tun müssen, nicht zu tun brauchen	I can do the exercise. You **needn't** help me. **needn't** ◄► must
(to) **be gone** [gɒn]	weg sein, nicht da sein	Jo was looking for Sophie, but she **was gone**.
This is Isabel.	Hier spricht Isabel. / Hier ist Isabel. *(am Telefon)*	*(on the phone)* Am I speaking to Laura? – No, **this is** Emma.
(to) **play a trick on** sb.	jm. einen Streich spielen	

p. 99/A 7	**planet** ['plænɪt]	Planet	❗ Betonung auf der 1. Silbe: **planet** ['plænɪt] *Latin:* planeta; *French:* la planète
	space [speɪs]	Weltraum	*French:* l'éspace *(f)*
	we **could** ... [kəd, kʊd]	wir könnten ...	What can we do tonight? – We **could** watch TV. **Could** I have a hamburger with chips, please? ❗ **could** = 1. konnte(n); 2. könnte(n)
	(to) **discover** [dɪ'skʌvə]	entdecken; herausfinden	*French:* découvrir
	mustn't do ['mʌsnt]	nicht tun dürfen	You **mustn't** touch the plates. They're hot.

must – needn't – mustn't

must (müssen)	**needn't** (nicht müssen)	**mustn't** (nicht dürfen)
Mit **must** drückt man aus, dass jemand etwas tun muss:	Mit **needn't** drückt man aus, dass jemand etwas nicht zu tun braucht:	Mit **mustn't** drückt man aus, dass jemand etwas nicht tun darf:
I **must** clean the hamster's cage today. It's very dirty.	I **needn't** clean the rabbits' cage. It isn't dirty.	You **mustn't** give hedgehogs milk. It's bad for them.
(Ich muss ... sauber machen.)	(Ich muss ... nicht sauber machen / brauche ... nicht sauber zu machen.)	(Du darfst Igeln keine Milch geben.)

p. 99/A 9	(to) **divide (into)** [dɪ'vaɪd]	(sich) teilen (in), (sich) aufteilen (in)	**Divide into** groups and talk about the question. **Divide** the cake **into** eight parts. *Latin:* dividere; *French:* diviser
	star [stɑː]	Stern	*Latin:* stella a **star**
	still [stɪl]	trotzdem, dennoch	It was raining, but we **still** had a lot of fun. ❗ **still** = 1. (immer) noch; 2. trotzdem, dennoch
p. 101/P 5	**ice rink** ['aɪs rɪŋk]	Schlittschuhbahn	
p. 104/P 12	(to) **correct** [kə'rekt]	berichtigen, korrigieren	verb: (to) **correct** – adjective: **correct** *Latin:* corrigere; *French:* corriger

A trip to Bath – a play for the end of term

p. 105	**term** [tɜːm]	Trimester	The school year in Britain has three **terms**.
	as	wie	Traffic is a problem here, **as** in all big cities. **As** you know, Bristol is a town in England.
	(to) **mime** [maɪm]	vorspielen, pantomimisch darstellen	She had a sore throat and couldn't speak, so she had to **mime**.
	(to) **like** sth. **better**	etwas lieber mögen	Tim's favourite sport is tennis, but I **like** football **better**.
	luckily ['lʌkɪli]	zum Glück, glücklicherweise	I dropped a plate yesterday. **Luckily**, it wasn't very expensive.
	actor ['æktə]	Schauspieler/in	somebody who acts in a film or play *Latin:* actor; *French:* l'acteur *(m)*, l'actrice *(f)*
	(to) **fall off** [ˌfɔːl 'ɒf]	herunterfallen (von)	Liz **fell off** her horse, but luckily she wasn't hurt.
p. 106	**the other way round**	anders herum	So your name is John James. – No, **the other way round**: James John.
	movement ['muːvmənt]	Bewegung	*French:* le mouvement
	leisure centre ['leʒə sentə]	Freizeitzentrum, -park	
	(to) **shiver** ['ʃɪvə]	zittern	

Tipps zum Wörterlernen → S. 115 • Englische Laute → S. 217 • Alphabetische Wörterverzeichnisse → S. 178–199 / S. 200–217

(to) **yawn** [jɔːn]	gähnen		She**'s yawning**.
Hooray! [huˈreɪ]	Hurra!		
(to) **pay (for)** [peɪ], **paid, paid** [peɪd]	bezahlen	❗ (to) **pay for a sandwich** (ein Sandwich bezahlen) *French:* payer	
tomato [təˈmɑːtəʊ], *pl* **tomatoes**	Tomate		*French:* la tomate
		lettuce	**tomatoes**
lettuce [ˈletɪs]	(Kopf-)Salat		
roll [rəʊl]	Brötchen		
century [ˈsentʃəri]	Jahrhundert	Martin Luther was born in the 15th **century**.	
(to) **wonder** [ˈwʌndə]	sich fragen, gern wissen wollen	Do you know that boy over there? I **wonder** who he is.	
p. 107 (to) **cheer** [tʃɪə]	jubeln, Beifall klatschen	At the end of the play, they all **cheered** loudly.	
laughter [ˈlɑːftə]	Gelächter	verb: (to) **laugh** – noun: **laughter**	
worry [ˈwʌri]	Sorge, Kummer	verb: (to) **worry** – noun: **worry**	
bright [braɪt]	hell, leuchtend	It's a very **bright** room. It gets the sun all day.	
if	ob	❗ **if** = 1. I don't know **if** I can come to your party. (ob) 2. But I'll come **if** I can. (falls, wenn)	
true [truː]	wahr	The twins' mother lives in Australia. – That's not **true**. She lives in New Zealand.	
(to) **come true**	wahr werden	I hope your dreams will **come true**.	

Irregular past participles

(to) begin	began	**begun** [bɪˈgʌn]	beginnen, anfangen (mit)		(to) spend	spent	**spent** [spent]	*(Geld)* ausgeben; *(Zeit)* verbringen
(to) lend	lent	**lent** [lent]	(ver)leihen		(to) stand	stood	**stood** [stʊd]	stehen; sich (hin)stellen
(to) mean [miːn]	meant	**meant** [ment]	bedeuten; meinen, sagen wollen		(to) stick on	stuck	**stuck** [stʌk]	aufkleben

Dictionary (English – German)

Das Dictionary besteht aus zwei alphabetischen Wörterlisten:

Englisch – Deutsch (S. 178–199)
Deutsch – Englisch (S. 200–217).

Das **English – German Dictionary** enthält den Wortschatz der Bände 1 und 2 von *English G 21*.
Wenn du wissen möchtest, was ein Wort bedeutet, wie man es ausspricht oder wie es genau geschrieben wird, kannst du hier nachschlagen.

Im **English – German Dictionary** werden folgende **Abkürzungen** und **Symbole** verwendet:

sb. = somebody	jm. = jemandem	pl = plural	AE = American English
sth. = something	jn. = jemanden	no pl = no plural	

° Mit diesem Kringel sind Wörter markiert, die nicht zum Lernwortschatz gehören.
▶ Der Pfeil verweist auf Kästchen im Vocabulary (S. 150–177), in denen du weitere Informationen zu diesem Wort findest.

Die **Fundstellenangaben** zeigen, wo ein Wort zum ersten Mal vorkommt.
Die Ziffern in Klammern bezeichnen Seitenzahlen:

I	= Band 1
II Welc (6)	= Band 2, Welcome back, Seite 6
II Welc (6/150)	= Band 2, Welcome back, Seite 150 (im Vocabulary, zu Seite 6)
II 1 (22)	= Band 2, Unit 1, Seite 22
II 1 (22/155)	= Band 2, Unit 1, Seite 155 (im Vocabulary, zu Seite 22)

Tipps zur Arbeit mit dem Dictionary findest du im Skills File auf Seite 117.

A

a [ə] ein, eine I • **a bit** ein bisschen, etwas II 1 (12) • **a few** ein paar, einige II 1 (15) • **a lot (of)** eine Menge, viel, viele II 2 (33) **He likes her a lot.** Er mag sie sehr. I
abbey ['æbi] Abtei II 6 (97)
able ['eɪbl]: **be able to do sth.** etwas tun können; fähig sein/in der Lage sein, etwas zu tun II 4 (72)
▶ S. 169 „können" und „dürfen"
about [ə'baʊt]
1. über I
2. ungefähr II 1 (12)
ask about sth. nach etwas fragen I
know about sth. von etwas wissen; über etwas Bescheid wissen II 1 (23) • **learn about sth.** etwas über etwas erfahren, etwas über etwas herausfinden II 5 (76) • **This is about Mr Green.** Es geht um Mr Green. I • **What about ...? 1.** Was ist mit ...? / Und ...? I; **2.** Wie wär's mit ...? I • **What are you talking about?** Wovon redest du? I **What was the best thing about ...?** Was war das Beste an ...? II 1 (12)
abroad [ə'brɔːd] im Ausland II Welc (9) • **go abroad** ins Ausland gehen/fahren II Welc (9)
°**absurd** [əb'sɜːd] absurd, lächerlich
accent ['æksənt] Akzent II 4 (67)

accident ['æksɪdənt] Unfall II 4 (72)
across [ə'krɒs] (quer) über II 5 (76)
act [ækt] aufführen, spielen I
°**Act out ...** Spiele/Spielt ... vor.
°**action** ['ækʃn] Aktion, Handlung
activity [æk'tɪvəti] Aktivität, Tätigkeit I
actor ['æktə] Schauspieler/in II 6 (105)
°**AD** (*from Latin:* **Anno Domini**) [ˌeɪ'diː] nach Christus
add (to) [æd] hinzufügen, ergänzen, addieren (zu) I
address [ə'dres] Anschrift, Adresse II 3 (55)
adventure [əd'ventʃə] Abenteuer II 1 (23)
advert ['ædvɜːt] Anzeige, Inserat; (im Fernsehen) Werbespot II 2 (29)
afraid [ə'freɪd]
1. be afraid (of) Angst haben (vor) I
2. I'm afraid leider II 3 (49)
°**Afro-Caribbean** [ˌæfrəʊˌkærə'biːən] afro-karibisch
after ['ɑːftə] nach *(zeitlich)* I
after that danach I
after ['ɑːftə] nachdem II 1 (13)
afternoon [ˌɑːftə'nuːn] Nachmittag I • **in the afternoon** nachmittags, am Nachmittag I • **on Friday afternoon** freitagnachmittags, am Freitagnachmittag I
°**afterwards** ['ɑːftəwədz] danach

again [ə'gen] wieder; noch einmal I
against [ə'genst] gegen I
ago [ə'gəʊ]: **a minute ago** vor einer Minute I
agree [ə'griː]: **agree (on)** sich einigen (auf) I • **agree (with sb.)** (jm.) zustimmen I
air [eə] Luft II 4 (60/165)
alarm clock [ə'lɑːm klɒk] Wecker I
album ['ælbəm] Album II 2 (31)
°**alien** ['eɪliən] Außerirdische(r)
all [ɔːl] alle; alles I • **all day** den ganzen Tag (lang) I • °**all I did** alles, was ich tat • °**All in a day's work.** *etwa:* Mach ich doch gern. I °**all over Britain** in ganz Großbritannien • **all right** [ˌɔːl 'raɪt] gut, in Ordnung II 1 (23) • **all the time** die ganze Zeit I • **all we have to do now ...** alles, was wir jetzt (noch) tun müssen, ... II 5 (89) **from all over the world** aus der ganzen Welt II 5 (81) • **This is all wrong.** Das ist ganz falsch. I
allow [ə'laʊ] erlauben, zulassen II 3 (56) • **be allowed to do sth.** [ə'laʊd] etwas tun dürfen II 4 (72)
▶ S. 169 „können" und „dürfen"
almost ['ɔːlməʊst] fast, beinahe II 1 (23)
alone [ə'ləʊn] allein I
along the road [ə'lɒŋ] entlang der Straße / die Straße entlang II 6 (96)

Dictionary (English – German)

alphabet ['ælfəbet] Alphabet I
°**alphabetical** [ˌælfə'betɪkl] alphabetisch
already [ɔːl'redi] schon, bereits II 3 (57)
▶ S.166 The present perfect: statements
always ['ɔːlweɪz] immer I
am [eɪ 'em]: **7 am** 7 Uhr morgens/vormittags I
amazing [ə'meɪzɪŋ] erstaunlich, unglaublich II 1 (12)
American football [əˌmerɪkən 'fʊtbɔːl] Football I
an [ən] ein, eine I
°**ancient** ['eɪnʃənt] alt
and [ənd, ænd] und I • **nice and cool/clean/…** schön kühl/sauber/… I
angel ['eɪndʒl] Engel II 3 (56)
°**Anglo: the Anglo-Saxons** [ˌæŋgləʊ 'sæksnz] die Angelsachsen
angry (about sth./with sb.) ['æŋgri] wütend, böse (über etwas/auf jn.) II 1 (14)
animal ['ænɪml] Tier I
another [ə'nʌðə] ein(e) andere(r, s); noch ein(e) I • **another 70 metres** weitere 70 Meter, noch 70 Meter II 4 (72)
answer ['ɑːnsə] (be)antworten I
answer (to) ['ɑːnsə] Antwort (auf) I
any ['eni]: **any …?** (irgend)welche …? I • **not (…) any** kein(e) I • **not (…) any more** nicht mehr II 2 (31)
anybody ['enibɒdi]: **anybody?** (irgend)jemand? II 2 (29/158) • **not (…) anybody** niemand II 2 (29/158)
▶ S.158 somebody – anybody
anything ['eniθɪŋ]: **anything?** (irgend)etwas? II 2 (29/158) • **Did you do anything special?** Habt ihr irgendwas Besonderes gemacht? I • **not (…) anything** nichts II 2 (29/158)
▶ S.158 something – anything
anyway ['eniweɪ]
1. sowieso I
2. trotzdem II Welc (6)
anywhere ['eniweə]: **anywhere?** irgendwo(hin)? II 2 (29/158) • **not (…) anywhere** nirgendwo(hin) II 2 (29/158)
▶ S.158 somewhere – anywhere
apple ['æpl] Apfel I
appointment [ə'pɔɪntmənt] Termin, Verabredung I
April ['eɪprəl] April I
are [ɑː] bist; sind; seid I • **How are you?** Wie geht es dir/Ihnen/euch? II 1 (21) • **The pencils are 35p.** Die Bleistifte kosten 35 Pence. I

°**area** ['eərɪə] Gegend, Gebiet
argue ['ɑːgjuː] sich streiten, sich zanken I
argument ['ɑːgjumənt] Streit, Auseinandersetzung II 1 (15) • **have an argument** eine Auseinandersetzung haben, sich streiten II 1 (15)
arm [ɑːm] Arm I
armchair ['ɑːmtʃeə] Sessel I
°**around** [ə'raʊnd]: **around the world** in/auf der ganzen Welt • **around us** um uns herum
°**arrest** [ə'rest] festnehmen, verhaften
arrive [ə'raɪv] ankommen, eintreffen II 5 (77)
art [ɑːt] Kunst I
article ['ɑːtɪkl] (Zeitungs-)Artikel I
as [əz, æz]
1. als, während II Welc (6)
2. wie II 6 (105) • **as you know** wie du weißt II 6 (105/176)
3. **as nice/big/exciting as** so schön/groß/aufregend wie II 2 (31)
as soon as sobald, sowie II 3 (47)
°**4. as a little boy** als kleiner Junge **as their first language** als ihre erste Sprache
ask [ɑːsk] fragen I • **ask about sth.** nach etwas fragen I • **ask questions** Fragen stellen I • **ask sb. for sth.** jn. um etwas bitten II 2 (30) • **ask sb. the way** jn. nach dem Weg fragen II 6 (96/174)
asleep [ə'sliːp]: **be asleep** schlafen II 1 (22)
assistant [ə'sɪstənt] Verkäufer/in I
°**astronomer** [ə'strɒnəmə] Astronom/in
°**astronomy** [ə'strɒnəmi] Astronomie
at [ət, æt]: **at 7 Hamilton Street** in der Hamiltonstraße 7 I • **at 8.45** um 8.45 I • **at break** in der Pause (zwischen Schulstunden) II 3 (48) • **at home** daheim, zu Hause I • **at last** endlich, schließlich I • **at least** zumindest, wenigstens I • **at night** nachts, in der Nacht I • **at school** in der Schule I • **at sea** auf See II 5 (82) • **at that table** an dem Tisch (dort) / an den Tisch (dort) I • **at the back (of the room)** hinten, im hinteren Teil (des Zimmers) II 1 (13) • **at the bottom (of)** unten, am unteren Ende (von) II 1 (11) • **at the end (of)** am Ende (von) I • **at the moment** im Moment, gerade, zurzeit I • **at the Shaws' house** im Haus der Shaws / bei den Shaws zu Hause I • **at the station** am Bahnhof I • **at the top (of)** oben, am oberen Ende, an

der Spitze (von) I • **at the weekend** am Wochenende I • **at work** bei der Arbeit / am Arbeitsplatz I
ate [et, eɪt] siehe eat
°**attach** [ə'tætʃ] beifügen, beilegen, anhängen
°**attic** ['ætɪk] Dachboden
August ['ɔːgəst] August I
aunt [ɑːnt] Tante I • **auntie** ['ɑːnti] Tante II 2 (30)
autumn ['ɔːtəm] Herbst I
away [ə'weɪ] weg, fort I
awful ['ɔːfl] furchtbar, schrecklich II 2 (28)

B

baby ['beɪbi] Baby I • **have a baby** ein Baby/Kind bekommen II 3 (49)
°**babysitting** ['beɪbisɪtɪŋ]: **do babysitting** Babysitten gehen
back [bæk]
1. **at the back (of the room)** hinten, im hinteren Teil (des Zimmers) II 1 (13)
°2. Rücken
back door [ˌbæk 'dɔː] Hintertür II 3 (46)
back (to) [bæk] zurück (nach) I • °**Jo went back to the game.** Jo wandte sich wieder dem Spiel zu. • °**back in 1824** (damals) im Jahre 1824
background ['bækgraʊnd] Hintergrund II 1 (11) • **background file** etwa: Hintergrundinformation II (3)
bacon ['beɪkən] Schinkenspeck II 4 (63)
bad [bæd] schlecht, schlimm I
badminton ['bædmɪntən] Badminton, Federball I
bag [bæg] Tasche, Beutel, Tüte I
ball [bɔːl]
1. Ball (zum Sport) I
2. Ball (Tanz) II 2 (40)
balloon [bə'luːn] Heißluftballon; Luftballon II 5 (76)
°**balloonist** [bə'luːnɪst] (Heißluft-)Ballonfahrer/in
banana [bə'nɑːnə] Banane I
band [bænd] Band, (Musik-)Gruppe I
°**Bang!** [bæŋ] Peng!
bank [bæŋk] Bank, Sparkasse I
bank robber ['bæŋk ˌrɒbə] Bankräuber/in
bar [bɑː] Bar II 5 (80)
°**barbecue** ['bɑːbɪkjuː] Grillparty
bark [bɑːk] bellen II 3 (57)
°**barn** [bɑːn] Scheune

Dictionary (English – German)

°**barrel** ['bærəl] Fass, Tonne
baseball ['beɪsbɔːl] Baseball I •
 baseball cap Baseballmütze II 2 (27)
basket ['bɑːskɪt] Korb I • **a basket of apples** ein Korb Äpfel I
basketball ['bɑːskɪtbɔːl] Basketball I
°**bat** [bæt] Fledermaus
bath [bɑːθ] Bad, Badewanne II 6 (94) • **have a bath** baden, ein Bad nehmen II 6 (94)
bathroom ['bɑːθruːm] Badezimmer I
be [biː], **was/were, been** sein I
beach [biːtʃ] Strand II Welc (6) • **on the beach** [biːtʃ] am Strand II Welc (6)
bear [beə] Bär II 3 (49/163)
beautiful ['bjuːtɪfl] schön I
became [bɪˈkeɪm] siehe **become**
because [bɪˈkɒz] weil I
become [bɪˈkʌm], **became, become** werden II 5 (79)
bed [bed] Bett I • **Bed and Breakfast (B&B)** [ˌbed_ən 'brekfəst] Frühstückspension I • **go to bed** ins Bett gehen I
bedroom ['bedrum] Schlafzimmer I
been [biːn] siehe **be**
before [bɪˈfɔː] vor (zeitlich) I • **the day before yesterday** vorgestern II 1 (20)
before [bɪˈfɔː] bevor II 1 (13/153)
before [bɪˈfɔː] (vorher) schon mal II 6 (96)
began [bɪˈɡæn] siehe **begin**
begin (-nn-) [bɪˈɡɪn], **began, begun** beginnen, anfangen (mit) I
°**beginning** [bɪˈɡɪnɪŋ] Anfang, Beginn
begun [bɪˈɡʌn] siehe **begin**
behind [bɪˈhaɪnd] hinter I
bell [bel] Klingel, Glocke I
belong (to) [bɪˈlɒŋ] gehören (zu) II 5 (90)
°**below** [bɪˈləʊ] unten
bend [bend], **bent, bent** sich beugen
°**bent** [bent] siehe **bend**
best [best] am besten II 2 (31/159) • **the best ...** der/die/das beste ...; die besten ... I • **What was the best thing about ...?** Was war das Beste an ...? II (12)
better ['betə] besser I • **like sth. better** etwas lieber mögen II 6 (105)
°**between** [bɪˈtwiːn] zwischen II 1 (11)
big [bɪɡ] groß I
bike [baɪk] Fahrrad I • **bike tour** Radtour II 4 (60) • **ride a bike** Rad fahren I

bin [bɪn] Mülltonne II 3 (46)
°**binoculars** (pl) [bɪˈnɒkjələz] Fernglas
biology [baɪˈɒlədʒi] Biologie I
bird [bɜːd] Vogel I
birthday ['bɜːθdeɪ] Geburtstag I • **Happy birthday.** Herzlichen Glückwunsch zum Geburtstag. I • **My birthday is in May.** Ich habe im Mai Geburtstag. I • **My birthday is on 13th June.** Ich habe am 13. Juni Geburtstag. I • **When's your birthday?** Wann hast du Geburtstag? I
biscuit ['bɪskɪt] Keks, Plätzchen I
bit [bɪt]: **a bit** ein bisschen, etwas II 1 (12)
black [blæk] schwarz I
bleep [bliːp] piepsen II 5 (88)
bleep [bliːp] Piepton II 5 (89)
°**blew** [bluː] siehe **blow**
°**bloom** [bluːm] blühen
blouse [blaʊz] Bluse II 2 (27)
°**blow sth. up** [ˌbləʊ_'ʌp], **blew, blown** etwas in die Luft sprengen
°**blown** [bləʊn] siehe **blow**
blue [bluː] blau I
board [bɔːd]
 1. (Wand-)Tafel I • **on the board** an der/die Tafel I
 °2. **on board** an Bord
boat [bəʊt] Boot, Schiff I
body ['bɒdi] Körper I
°**bone** [bəʊn] Knochen
°**bonfire** ['bɒnfaɪə] (Freuden-)Feuer
book [bʊk] Buch I
booklet ['bʊklət] Broschüre II 5 (78)
boot [buːt] Stiefel I
boring ['bɔːrɪŋ] langweilig I
born [bɔːn]: **be born** geboren sein/werden II 5 (79)
borrow sth. ['bɒrəʊ] sich etwas (aus)leihen, etwas entleihen II 1 (14)
boss [bɒs] Boss, Chef/in I
both [bəʊθ] beide I
bottle ['bɒtl] Flasche I • **a bottle of milk** eine Flasche Milch I
bottom ['bɒtəm] unteres Ende II (11) • **at the bottom (of)** unten, am unteren Ende (von) II 1 (11)
bought [bɔːt] siehe **buy**
bowl [bəʊl] Schüssel I • **a bowl of cornflakes** eine Schale Cornflakes I
box [bɒks] Kasten, Kästchen, Kiste I
boy [bɔɪ] Junge I
°**bracket** ['brækɪt] Klammer (in Texten)
bread (no pl) [bred] Brot I
break [breɪk], **broke, broken** (zer)brechen; kaputt machen; kaputt gehen II 4 (64)

break [breɪk] Pause I • **at break** in der Pause (zwischen Schulstunden) II 3 (48)
breakfast ['brekfəst] Frühstück I • **have breakfast** frühstücken I
bridge [brɪdʒ] Brücke I
bright [braɪt] hell, leuchtend II 6 (107)
°**brighten sth. up** [ˌbraɪtn_'ʌp] etwas aufheitern
bring [brɪŋ], **brought, brought** (mit-, her)bringen I
British ['brɪtɪʃ] britisch; Brite, Britin II 5 (77)
°**brochure** ['brəʊʃə] Broschüre
broke [brəʊk] siehe **break**
broken ['brəʊkən] siehe **break**
broken ['brəʊkən] gebrochen; zerbrochen, kaputt II 3 (49)
brother ['brʌðə] Bruder I
brought [brɔːt] siehe **bring**
brown [braʊn] braun I
°**bubble** ['bʌbl] Blase, Bläschen
°**budget: be on a low budget** [ləʊ 'bʌdʒɪt] mit wenig Geld auskommen müssen
budgie ['bʌdʒi] Wellensittich I
build [bɪld], **built, built** bauen II 5 (76) • **the ship was built in Bristol** das Schiff wurde in Bristol gebaut II 5 (79)
building ['bɪldɪŋ] Gebäude II 1 (12)
built [bɪlt] siehe **build**
bully ['bʊli] einschüchtern, tyrannisieren II 3 (56)
bunk (bed) [bʌŋk] Etagenbett, Koje II 1 (22)
°**burn** [bɜːn] verbrennen; brennen
bus [bʌs] Bus I
business: Mind your own business. [ˌmaɪnd jər_ˌəʊn 'bɪznəs] Das geht dich nichts an! / Kümmere dich um deine eigenen Angelegenheiten! II 1 (13)
busy ['bɪzi] beschäftigt I
but [bət, bʌt] aber I • °**not only ... but (also)** nicht nur ..., sondern (auch)
buy [baɪ], **bought, bought** kaufen I
°**buzz** [bʌz] hier: den Summer/die Glocke betätigen
by [baɪ]
 1. von I
 2. an; (nahe) bei II Welc (6)
 3. **by car/bike/...** mit dem Auto/Rad/... II Welc (7)
Bye. [baɪ] Tschüs! I

Dictionary (English – German)

C

°**cabin** ['kæbɪn] Kajüte
café ['kæfeɪ] *(kleines)* Restaurant, Imbissstube, Café I
cafeteria [ˌkæfə'tɪəriə] Cafeteria, Selbstbedienungsrestaurant II 1 (11)
cage [keɪdʒ] Käfig I
cake [keɪk] Kuchen, Torte I
°**calabash** ['kæləbæʃ] Kalebasse *(aus einem Kürbis hergestelltes Gefäß)*
calendar ['kælɪndə] Kalender I
call [kɔːl] rufen; anrufen; nennen I
be called heißen, genannt werden II 5 (84)
call [kɔːl] Ruf, Schrei; Anruf II 4 (62/165) • **make a call** ein Telefongespräch führen, telefonieren II 6 (98)
calm down [ˌkɑːm 'daʊn] sich beruhigen II 1 (14) • **calm sb. down** jn. beruhigen II 3 (57)
came [keɪm] *siehe* **come**
camel ['kæml] Kamel II 3 (49/163)
camera ['kæmərə] Kamera, Fotoapparat I
can [kən, kæn]
1. können I
2. dürfen I
Can I help you? Kann ich Ihnen helfen? / Was kann ich für Sie tun? *(im Geschäft)* I
▶ S. 169 „können" und „dürfen"
°**candle** ['kændl] Kerze
°**cannibal** ['kænɪbl] Kannibale, Kannibalin
cap [kæp] Mütze, Kappe II 2 (27)
°**capital** ['kæpɪtl] Hauptstadt
°**captain** ['kæptɪn] Kapitän I
°**caption** ['kæpʃn] Bildunterschrift
car [kɑː] Auto I
caravan ['kærəvæn] Wohnwagen II Welc (6)
card [kɑːd] (Spiel-, Post-)Karte I
careful ['keəfl] vorsichtig I
caretaker ['keəteɪkə] Hausmeister/in II 5 (89)
°**Caribbean** [ˌkærə'biːən]: **in the Caribbean** in der Karibik
carrot ['kærət] Möhre, Karotte I
cartoon [kɑː'tuːn] Cartoon (Zeichentrickfilm; Bilderwitz) II 3 (44)
case [keɪs] Fall II 5 (90)
castle ['kɑːsl] Burg, Schloss II 4 (62)
cat [kæt] Katze I
catch [kætʃ], **caught, caught** fangen; erwischen II 5 (88)
°**Catholic** ['kæθlɪk] katholisch; Katholik/in
caught [kɔːt] *siehe* **catch**
°**cause** [kɔːz]: **a good cause** eine gute Sache

CD [ˌsiː'diː] CD I • **CD player** CD-Spieler I
°**celebrate** ['selɪbreɪt] feiern
°**celebration** [ˌselɪ'breɪʃn] Feier
°**Celt** [kelt] Kelte, Keltin
°**Celtic** ['keltɪk, 'seltɪk] keltisch
cent (c) [sent] Cent I
centre ['sentə] Zentrum, Mitte I
century ['sentʃəri] Jahrhundert II 6 (106)
°**chain** [tʃeɪn] Kette
chair [tʃeə] Stuhl I
champion ['tʃæmpiən] Meister/in, Champion I
chance [tʃɑːns] Chance II 1 (14)
change [tʃeɪndʒ] Wechselgeld I
°**chant** [tʃɑːnt] Sprechchor *(z.B. von Fußballfans)*
charity ['tʃærəti] Wohlfahrtsorganisation II 2 (32) • °**charity shop** Geschäft, in dem Sachen für eine Wohlfahrtsorganisation verkauft werden
°**chart** [tʃɑːt] Schaubild, Diagramm, Tabelle
chat (-tt-) [tʃæt] chatten, plaudern II 4 (65)
chat [tʃæt] Chat, Unterhaltung II 4 (65) • **chat show** Talkshow II 3 (44)
°**chauffeur** ['ʃəʊfə] Chauffeur/in, Fahrer/in
cheap [tʃiːp] billig, preiswert II 2 (31)
check [tʃek] (über)prüfen, kontrollieren I
checkpoint ['tʃekpɔɪnt] Kontrollpunkt *(hier: zur Selbstüberprüfung)* I
cheer [tʃɪə] jubeln, Beifall klatschen II 6 (107)
cheese [tʃiːz] Käse I
chemist ['kemɪst] Drogerie, Apotheke II 6 (97)
chicken ['tʃɪkɪn] Huhn; (Brat-)Hähnchen I • °**chicken tikka** [ˌtʃɪkɪn 'tɪkə] indisches Gericht *(mariniertes gegrilltes Hühnerfleisch)*
child [tʃaɪld], *pl* **children** ['tʃɪldrən] Kind I
chips *(pl)* [tʃɪps] Pommes frites I
chocolate ['tʃɒklət] Schokolade I
°**choice** [tʃɔɪs] (Aus-)Wahl
choir ['kwaɪə] Chor I
choose [tʃuːz], **chose, chosen** (sich) aussuchen, (aus)wählen I
chose [tʃəʊz] *siehe* **choose**
chosen ['tʃəʊzn] *siehe* **choose**
°**Christmas** ['krɪsməs] Weihnachten • °**Father Christmas** der Weihnachtsmann • °**Merry Christmas.** Frohe Weihnachten.

church [tʃɜːtʃ] Kirche I
cinema ['sɪnəmə] Kino II 2 (27)
go to the cinema ins Kino gehen II 2 (27/156)
°**circle** ['sɜːkl] Kreis
city ['sɪti] Stadt, Großstadt I
city centre [ˌsɪti 'sentə] Stadtzentrum, Innenstadt I
class [klɑːs] (Schul-)Klasse I
class teacher Klassenlehrer/in I
classmate ['klɑːsmeɪt] Klassenkamerad/in, Mitschüler/in I
classroom ['klɑːsruːm] Klassenzimmer I
clean [kliːn] sauber II 4 (60)
clean [kliːn] sauber machen, putzen I • **I clean my teeth.** Ich putze mir die Zähne. I
cleaner ['kliːnə] Putzfrau, -mann II 5 (89)
clear [klɪə] klar, deutlich I
clever ['klevə] klug, schlau I
click on sth. [klɪk] etwas anklicken II 4 (65)
climb [klaɪm] klettern; hinaufklettern (auf) I • **Climb a tree.** Klettere auf einen Baum. I
clinic ['klɪnɪk] Klinik II 3 (47)
clock [klɒk] (Wand-, Stand-, Turm-)Uhr I
close [kləʊs]: **That was close.** Das war knapp. II 4 (73) • °**a close shave** [ˌkləʊs 'ʃeɪv] *etwa:* Das ging beinahe ins Auge. *(wörtlich: eine glatte Rasur)*
close [kləʊz] schließen, zumachen I
closed [kləʊzd] geschlossen II 5 (76)
clothes *(pl)* [kləʊðz, kləʊz] Kleider, Kleidungsstücke I
cloud [klaʊd] Wolke II Welc (6/150)
cloudy ['klaʊdi] bewölkt II Welc (6/150)
clown [klaʊn] Clown/in I
club [klʌb] Klub; Verein I
coast [kəʊst] Küste II 4 (60)
°**coin** [kɔɪn] Münze
cola ['kəʊlə] Cola I
cold [kəʊld] kalt I • **be cold** frieren I
cold [kəʊld] Erkältung II 4 (64/167)
have a cold erkältet sein, eine Erkältung haben II 4 (64/167)
▶ S. 167 What's wrong with you?
collect [kə'lekt] sammeln I
collector [kə'lektə] Sammler/in II 3 (55)
colour ['kʌlə] Farbe I • **What colour is …?** Welche Farbe hat …? I
°**coloured** ['kʌləd] farbig, bunt
°**column** ['kɒləm] Spalte *(auf Buchseite)*

°**combination** [ˌkɒmbɪˈneɪʃn] Kombination, Verbindung
come [kʌm], **came, come** kommen I • **come home** nach Hause kommen I • **come in** hereinkommen I • **Come on. 1.** Na los, komm. II 1 (22); **2.** Ach komm! / Na hör mal! II 6 (96) • **come true** wahr werden II 6 (107)
comedy [ˈkɒmədi] Comedyshow, Komödie II 3 (44)
°**comet** [ˈkɒmɪt] Komet
comfortable [ˈkʌmftəbl] bequem I
comic [ˈkɒmɪk] Comic-Heft I
°**Commonwealth** [ˈkɒmənwelθ]: **the Commonwealth** Gemeinschaft der Länder des ehemaligen britischen Weltreichs
compare [kəmˈpeə] vergleichen II 2 (31)
comparison [kəmˈpærɪsn] Steigerung; Vergleich II 2 (31) / 2 (132)
°**make comparisons** Vergleiche anstellen, vergleichen
°**complain** [kəmˈpleɪn] sich beschweren
°**complete** [kəmˈpliːt] vervollständigen, ergänzen
°**complete** [kəmˈpliːt] vollständig, komplett
°**compliment** [ˈkɒmplɪmənt] Kompliment
computer [kəmˈpjuːtə] Computer I
concert [ˈkɒnsət] Konzert II 4 (60)
°**context** [ˈkɒntekst] Kontext, (Text-)Zusammenhang
continue [kənˈtɪnjuː] weitermachen (mit); weiterreden; weitergehen II 6 (97)
°**control** [kənˈtrəʊl]: **be in control of sth.** etwas unter Kontrolle haben; die Gewalt über etwas haben
conversation [ˌkɒnvəˈseɪʃn] Gespräch, Unterhaltung II 6 (96)
cook [kʊk] kochen, zubereiten II 4 (62)
cook [kʊk] Koch, Köchin II 4 (62/165)
cooker [ˈkʊkə] Herd I
cool [kuːl]
1. kühl I
2. cool I
copy [ˈkɒpi] kopieren II 4 (65/168)
°**copy** [ˈkɒpi] Kopie
corner [ˈkɔːnə] Ecke I • **on the corner of Sand Street and London Road** Sand Street, Ecke London Road II 6 (101)
cornflakes [ˈkɔːnfleɪks] Cornflakes I
correct [kəˈrekt] korrigieren, verbessern II 6 (104)
correct [kəˈrekt] richtig, korrekt II 6 (104/176)

°**corset** [ˈkɔːsɪt] Korsett
°**cost** [kɒst], **cost, cost** kosten
costume [ˈkɒstjuːm] Kostüm, Verkleidung I
could [kəd, kʊd]: **he could ...** er konnte ... II 1 (22)
could [kəd, kʊd]: **we could ...** wir könnten ... II 6 (99)
count [kaʊnt] zählen II 3 (57)
counter [ˈkaʊntə] Spielstein II 5 (76)
country [ˈkʌntri] Land (auch als Gegensatz zur Stadt) II Welc (8) • **in the country** auf dem Land II Welc (8/152)
course: of course [əv ˈkɔːs] natürlich, selbstverständlich I
cousin [ˈkʌzn] Cousin, Cousine I
cover [ˈkʌvə] (CD-)Hülle I
cow [kaʊ] Kuh II 4 (60)
°**Crash!** [kræʃ] Krach!
crisps (pl) [krɪsps] Kartoffelchips I
crocodile [ˈkrɒkədaɪl] Krokodil II 3 (49/163)
cross [krɒs] überqueren; (sich) kreuzen II 6 (97)
°**cruel** [ˈkruːəl]: **be cruel to animals** grausam zu Tieren sein; Tiere quälen
°**cruelty to animals** [ˈkruːəlti] Tierquälerei
cry [kraɪ] schreien I • **cry in pain** vor Schmerzen schreien I
cup [kʌp] Tasse II 1 (15) • **a cup of tea** eine Tasse Tee II 1 (15)
cupboard [ˈkʌbəd] Schrank I
°**curse** [kɜːs] Fluch
cut (-tt-) [kʌt], **cut, cut** schneiden II 4 (64) • °**a cut-price person** etwa: eine Person, die immer nach Sonderangeboten sucht
cycle [ˈsaɪkl] (mit dem) Rad fahren II 6 (96)
cycle path [ˈsaɪkl pɑːθ] Radweg II 6 (96/174)

D

dad [dæd] Papa, Vati; Vater I
dance [dɑːns] tanzen I
dance [dɑːns] Tanz I
dancer [ˈdɑːnsə] Tänzer/in II 3 (55)
dancing [ˈdɑːnsɪŋ] Tanzen I
dancing lessons Tanzstunden, Tanzunterricht I
danger [ˈdeɪndʒə] Gefahr I
dangerous [ˈdeɪndʒərəs] gefährlich II 1 (12)
dark [dɑːk] dunkel I
date [deɪt] Datum I
daughter [ˈdɔːtə] Tochter I
°**dawn** [dɔːn] (Morgen-)Dämmerung

day [deɪ] Tag I • **one day** eines Tages I • **days of the week** Wochentage I • **the day before yesterday** vorgestern II (20)
dead [ded] tot I
dear [dɪə] Schatz, Liebling I **Oh dear!** Oje! II 4 (64)
dear [dɪə]: **Dear Jay ...** Lieber Jay, ... I
December [dɪˈsembə] Dezember I
decide (on sth.) [dɪˈsaɪd] sich entscheiden (für etwas), (etwas) beschließen II 5 (79)
deer, pl **deer** [dɪə] Reh, Hirsch II 3 (45)
degree [dɪˈɡriː] Grad II Welc (8)
delicious [dɪˈlɪʃəs] köstlich, lecker II 5 (80)
department store [dɪˈpɑːtmənt stɔː] Kaufhaus II 6 (97)
describe sth. (to sb.) [dɪˈskraɪb] (jm.) etwas beschreiben II 1 (11)
description [dɪˈskrɪpʃn] Beschreibung II 1 (11/152)
design [dɪˈzaɪn] entwickeln, entwerfen I
desk [desk] Schreibtisch I
°**destroy** [dɪˈstrɔɪ] zerstören
detective [dɪˈtektɪv] Detektiv/in I
°**diagram** [ˈdaɪəɡræm] Diagramm, Schaubild
dial (-ll-) [ˈdaɪəl] wählen (Telefonnummer) II 1 (22)
°**dialogue** [ˈdaɪəlɒɡ] Dialog
diary [ˈdaɪəri] Tagebuch; Terminkalender I
dice, pl **dice** [daɪs] Würfel II 5 (76) **throw the dice** würfeln II 5 (76)
dictionary [ˈdɪkʃənri] Wörterbuch, (alphabetisches) Wörterverzeichnis I
did [dɪd] siehe **do** • **Did you go?** Bist du gegangen?/Gingst du? I **we didn't go** [ˈdɪdnt] wir sind nicht gegangen/wir gingen nicht I
die (of) (-ing form: **dying**) [daɪ] sterben (an) II 3 (47)
°**difference** [ˈdɪfrəns] Unterschied
different (from) [ˈdɪfrənt] verschieden, unterschiedlich; anders (als) I
difficult [ˈdɪfɪkəlt] schwierig, schwer I
°**dig (-gg-)** [dɪɡ], **dug, dug** graben
dining room [ˈdaɪnɪŋ ruːm] Esszimmer I
dinner [ˈdɪnə] Abendessen, Abendbrot I • **have dinner** Abendbrot essen I
directions (pl) [dəˈrekʃnz] Wegbeschreibung(en) II 6 (97)
dirty [ˈdɜːti] schmutzig II 4 (60)

disagree (with) [ˌdɪsəˈgriː] anderer Meinung sein (als), nicht übereinstimmen (mit) II 5 (82)
disappear [ˌdɪsəˈpɪə] verschwinden II 2 (28)
disco [ˈdɪskəʊ] Disko I
discover [dɪˈskʌvə] entdecken; herausfinden II 6 (99)
°**discuss** [dɪˈskʌs] diskutieren
discussion [dɪˈskʌʃn] Diskussion II 5 (82)
dishes (pl) [ˈdɪʃɪz] Geschirr I • **do the dishes** das Geschirr abwaschen I
dishwasher [ˈdɪʃwɒʃə] Geschirrspülmaschine I
divide (into) [dɪˈvaɪd] (sich) teilen (in), (sich) aufteilen (in) II 6 (99)
divorced [dɪˈvɔːst] geschieden I
do [duː], **did, done** tun, machen I **do a good job** gute Arbeit leisten II 3 (49) • **do an exercise** eine Übung machen II 1 (16) • °**do a paper round** Zeitungen austragen **do a project** ein Projekt machen, durchführen II 1 (16) • °**do babysitting** Babysitten gehen • **do sport** Sport treiben I • **do the dishes** das Geschirr abwaschen I
doctor [ˈdɒktə] Arzt/Ärztin, Doktor I
documentary [ˌdɒkjuˈmentri] Dokumentarfilm II 3 (44)
dog [dɒg] Hund I
°**dolphin** [ˈdɒlfɪn] Delphin
done [dʌn] siehe **do**
don't [dəʊnt]: **Don't listen to Dan.** Hör/Hören nicht auf Dan. I • **I don't like ...** Ich mag ... nicht. / Ich mag kein(e) ... I
door [dɔː] Tür I
doorbell [ˈdɔːbel] Türklingel I
dossier [ˈdɒsieɪ] Mappe, Dossier (des Sprachenportfolios) I
double [ˈdʌbl] zweimal, doppelt, Doppel- I
down [daʊn] hinunter, herunter, nach unten I • **down there** (nach) dort unten II 4 (72)
°**down** [daʊn] niedergeschlagen
download [ˌdaʊnˈləʊd] runterladen, downloaden II 4 (65)
downstairs [ˌdaʊnˈsteəz] unten; nach unten I
°**Down Under** [ˌdaʊn ˈʌndə] umgangssprachliche Bezeichnung für Australien und New Zealand
°**dragon** [ˈdrægən] Drache
drama [ˈdrɑːmə] Schauspiel, darstellende Kunst I
drank [dræŋk] siehe **drink**
°**draw** [drɔː] zeichnen

°**drawing** [ˈdrɔːɪŋ] Zeichnung
dream [driːm] Traum I • **dream house** Traumhaus I
dress [dres] Kleid I
dressed [drest]: **get dressed** sich anziehen I
drink [drɪŋk] Getränk I
drink [drɪŋk], **drank, drunk** trinken I
drive [draɪv], **drove, driven** (ein Auto/mit dem Auto) fahren II 1 (23)
driven [ˈdrɪvn] siehe **drive**
driver [ˈdraɪvə] Fahrer/in II 4 (72)
drop (-pp-) [drɒp]
1. fallen lassen I
2. fallen I
drove [drəʊv] siehe **drive**
drunk [drʌŋk] siehe **drink**
°**drunk** [drʌŋk] betrunken
°**dry-wither** [draɪ], [ˈwɪðə] Zusammensetzung der Autorin aus **dry** („trocken"; „trocknen") und **wither** („verdorren")
°**dug** [dʌg] siehe **dig**
°**dusk** [dʌsk] (Abend-)Dämmerung
dustbin [ˈdʌstbɪn] Mülltonne II 3 (46)
DVD [ˌdiː viː ˈdiː] DVD I

E

each [iːtʃ] jeder, jede, jedes (einzelne) I • °**Ask each other ...** Fragt euch gegenseitig ...
ear [ɪə] Ohr I
earache [ˈɪəreɪk] Ohrenschmerzen II 4 (64/167)
▶ S.167 What's wrong with you?
early [ˈɜːli] früh I • °**early bird** Frühaufsteher/in
earring [ˈɪərɪŋ] Ohrring I
east [iːst] Osten; nach Osten; östlich II 4 (62/166)
easy [ˈiːzi] leicht, einfach I
eat [iːt], **ate, eaten** essen I
eaten [ˈiːtn] siehe **eat**
°**e-card** [ˈiː kɑːd] elektronische (Ansichts-, Glückwunsch-)Karte
°**echo** [ˈekəʊ] Echo
e-friend [ˈiːfrend] Brieffreund/in (im Internet) I
°**e.g.** [ˌiːˈdʒiː] z.B. (zum Beispiel)
egg [eg] Ei I
either [ˈaɪðə, ˈiːðə]: **not (...) either** auch nicht II 1 (13)
elephant [ˈelɪfənt] Elefant I
elevator [ˈelɪveɪtə] (AE) Fahrstuhl, Aufzug II 1 (12)
e-mail [ˈiːmeɪl] E-Mail I
°**empire** [ˈempaɪə] (Welt-)Reich
empty [ˈempti] leer I

encyclopedia [ɪnˌsaɪkləˈpiːdɪə] Enzyklopädie, Lexikon II 5 (79)
end [end] Ende; Schluss I • **at the end (of)** am Ende (von) I
ending [ˌhæpiˈendɪŋ]: **happy ending** Happyend II 1 (23)
enemy [ˈenəmi] Feind/in II 3 (49)
engineer [ˌendʒɪˈnɪə] Ingenieur/in II 5 (76)
English [ˈɪŋglɪʃ] Englisch; englisch I
enjoy [ɪnˈdʒɔɪ] genießen I
enough [ɪˈnʌf] genug I
enter sth. [ˈentə] etwas eingeben, eintragen II 4 (65)
°**entry** [ˈentri] Eintrag (im Tagebuch)
°**escape** [ɪˈskeɪp] entkommen, fliehen
essay (about, on) [ˈeseɪ] Aufsatz (über) I
euro (€) [ˈjʊərəʊ] Euro I
even [ˈiːvn] sogar II 2 (30)
evening [ˈiːvnɪŋ] Abend I • **in the evening** abends, am Abend I **on Friday evening** freitagabends, am Freitagabend I
event [ɪˈvent] Ereignis II 5 (78)
ever? [ˈevə] je? / jemals? / schon mal? II 4 (65)
▶ S.168 The present perfect: questions
every [ˈevri] jeder, jede, jedes I
everybody [ˈevribɒdi] jeder, alle II 2 (30)
everything [ˈevriθɪŋ] alles I
everywhere [ˈevriweə] überall I
example [ɪgˈzɑːmpl] Beispiel I **for example** zum Beispiel I
excited [ɪkˈsaɪtɪd] aufgeregt, begeistert II 3 (57)
exciting [ɪkˈsaɪtɪŋ] aufregend, spannend II 1 (23)
Excuse me, ... [ɪkˈskjuːz miː] Entschuldigung, ... / Entschuldigen Sie, ... I
exercise [ˈeksəsaɪz] Übung, Aufgabe I • **do an exercise** eine Übung machen II 1 (16) • **exercise book** [ˈeksəsaɪz bʊk] Schulheft, Übungsheft I
°**exhibit** [ɪgˈzɪbɪt] Ausstellungsstück
expensive [ɪkˈspensɪv] teuer I
explain sth. to sb. [ɪkˈspleɪn] jm. etwas erklären, erläutern II 1 (15)
explanation [ˌekspləˈneɪʃn] Erklärung II 1 (15/154)
explore [ɪkˈsplɔː] erkunden, erforschen I
explorer [ɪkˈsplɔːrə] Entdecker/in, Forscher/in II 3 (55)
°**extensive reading** [ɪkˈstensɪv] extensives Lesen (das Lesen längerer Texte mit dem Ziel des

Dictionary (English – German)

allgemeinen Verständnisses, nicht des Detailverständnisses)
extra [ˈekstrə] zusätzlich I
eye [aɪ] Auge I

F

face [feɪs] Gesicht I
°**fact** [fækt] Fakt, Tatsache
factory [ˈfæktri] Fabrik II 4 (60)
°**fade** [feɪd] schwächer werden
°**fail** [feɪl] fehlschlagen, scheitern
fair [feə] fair, gerecht II 1 (17)
°**fall** [fɔːl] (AE) Herbst
fall [fɔːl], **fell, fallen** fallen, stürzen; hinfallen II 4 (73) • **fall down** runterfallen; hinfallen II 2 (40) • **fall off** herunterfallen (von) II 6 (105)
fallen [ˈfɔːlən] siehe **fall**
family [ˈfæməli]
1. Familie I • **family tree** (Familien-)Stammbaum I
°2. Verwandtschaft, Verwandte
famous (for) [ˈfeɪməs] berühmt (für, wegen) II 5 (77)
fantastic [fænˈtæstɪk] fantastisch, toll I
far [fɑː] weit (entfernt) I
farm [fɑːm] Bauernhof, Farm II 4 (60)
°**farmer** [ˈfɑːmə] Bauer, Bäuerin
fashion [ˈfæʃn] Mode II 2 (30)
fast [fɑːst] schnell II 1 (12) / II 3 (49)
°**fat** [fæt] Fett
father [ˈfɑːðə] Vater I
°**Father Christmas** [ˌfɑːðə ˈkrɪsməs] der Weihnachtsmann
favourite [ˈfeɪvərɪt] Lieblings- I • **my favourite colour** meine Lieblingsfarbe I
February [ˈfebruəri] Februar I
fed [fed] siehe **feed**
feed [fiːd], **fed, fed** füttern I
feel [fiːl], **felt, felt** fühlen; sich fühlen II 3 (57); sich anfühlen II 6 (106)
▶ S.167 What's wrong with you?
°**feeling** [ˈfiːlɪŋ] Gefühl
feet [fiːt] Plural von „foot" I
fell [fel] siehe **fall**
felt [felt] siehe **feel**
felt tip [ˈfelt tɪp] Filzstift I
female [ˈfiːmeɪl] Weibchen II 3 (49)
festival [ˈfestɪvl] Fest, Festival II 5 (81)
°**fetch** [fetʃ] (ab)holen
few [fjuː]: **a few** ein paar, einige II 1 (15)
field [fiːld] Feld, Acker, Weide II 4 (60) • **in the field** auf dem Feld II 4 (60/165)

°**fiesta** [fiˈestə] Festival; Fest
file [faɪl]: **background file** etwa: Hintergrundinformation II (3) **grammar file** Grammatikanhang I **skills file** Anhang mit Lern- und Arbeitstechniken I
°**fill in** [ˌfɪl ˈɪn]
1. einsetzen
2. ausfüllen
film [fɪlm] Film I • **film star** Filmstar I
find [faɪnd], **found, found** finden I **find out (about)** herausfinden (über) I
fine [faɪn]
1. gut, ausgezeichnet; in Ordnung II 3 (44)
2. (gesundheitlich) gut II 3 (47) **I'm/He's fine.** Es geht mir/ihm gut. II 3 (47/162)
finger [ˈfɪŋgə] Finger I
finish [ˈfɪnɪʃ] beenden, zu Ende machen; enden I
fire [ˈfaɪə] Feuer, Brand II 3 (51)
fireman [ˈfaɪəmən] Feuerwehrmann II 4 (72)
firewoman [ˈfaɪəˌwʊmən] Feuerwehrfrau II 4 (72)
°**fireworks** (pl) [ˈfaɪəwɜːks] Feuerwerk
first [fɜːst]
1. erste(r, s) I
2. zuerst, als Erstes I **be first** der/die Erste sein I • **for the first time** zum ersten Mal II 1 (20)
fish, pl **fish / fishes** [fɪʃ] Fisch I
fit (-tt-) [fɪt] passen I
°**flag** [flæg] Flagge, Fahne
flat [flæt] Wohnung I
flat [flæt] flach, eben II 6 (96)
flavour [ˈfleɪvə] Geschmack, Geschmacksrichtung II 5 (80)
flew [fluː] siehe **fly**
flight [flaɪt] Flug II 1 (12)
°**float** [fləʊt] schweben
floor [flɔː]
1. Fußboden I
°2. Stockwerk
flow chart [ˈfləʊ tʃɑːt] Flussdiagramm I
flower [ˈflaʊə] Blume; Blüte II 2 (31)
flown [fləʊn] siehe **fly**
flu [fluː] Grippe II 4 (64)
fly [flaɪ], **flew, flown** fliegen II Welc (6)
°**fly** [flaɪ] Fliege
fog [fɒg] Nebel II Welc (8/152)
foggy [ˈfɒgi] neblig II Welc (8)
°**fold** [fəʊld] falten, zusammenfalten
follow [ˈfɒləʊ] folgen; verfolgen I

food [fuːd] Essen; Lebensmittel; Futter I
foot [fʊt], pl **feet** [fiːt] Fuß I
football [ˈfʊtbɔːl] Fußball I **football boots** Fußballschuhe, -stiefel I • **football pitch** Fußballplatz, -feld II 4 (62)
°**footprint** [ˈfʊtprɪnt] Fußabdruck
for [fə, fɔː] für I • **for a moment** einen Moment lang II 2 (29) • **for breakfast/lunch/dinner** zum Frühstück/Mittagessen/Abendbrot I • **for example** zum Beispiel I • **for lots of reasons** aus vielen Gründen I • **for miles** meilenweit II 1 (12) • **for the first time** zum ersten Mal II 1 (20) • **for three days** drei Tage (lang) I • **just for fun** nur zum Spaß I • **What for?** [ˌwɒt ˈfɔː] Wofür? II 2 (29) • **What's for homework?** Was haben wir als Hausaufgabe auf? I
foreground [ˈfɔːgraʊnd] Vordergrund II 1 (11)
forest [ˈfɒrɪst] Wald II 4 (60)
°**forget (-tt-)** [fəˈget], **forgot, forgotten** vergessen
°**forgot** [fəˈgɒt] siehe **forget**
°**forgotten** [fəˈgɒtn] siehe **forget**
form [fɔːm]
1. (Schul-)Klasse I • **form teacher** Klassenlehrer/in I
°2. Form
°**form** [fɔːm] bilden
°**fort** [fɔːt] Fort
°**fortune-teller** [ˈfɔːtʃuːn telə] Wahrsager/in
found [faʊnd] siehe **find**
fox [fɒks] Fuchs II 3 (44)
free [friː]
1. frei I • **free time** Freizeit, freie Zeit I • **free-time activities** Freizeitaktivitäten II 2 (26)
2. kostenlos I
°**freeze** [friːz], **froze, frozen** erstarren, stillstehen
French [frentʃ] Französisch I
Friday [ˈfraɪdeɪ, ˈfraɪdi] Freitag I
fridge [frɪdʒ] Kühlschrank I
friend [frend] Freund/in I • **make friends (with)** Freunde finden; sich anfreunden (mit) II 3 (56)
friendly [ˈfrendli] freundlich II 1 (15/154)
frog [frɒg] Frosch II 3 (45)
from [frəm, frɒm]
1. aus I
2. von I **dresses from the 60s** Kleider aus den 60ern / aus den 60er Jahren II 2 (31) • **from all over the world** aus der ganzen Welt II 5 (81)

Dictionary (English – German) 185

from my point of view aus meiner Sicht; von meinem Standpunkt aus gesehen II 2 (41/160) • **I'm from …** Ich komme/bin aus … I • **Where are you from?** Wo kommst du her? I
°**front** [frʌnt] Vorderseite
front [frʌnt]: **in front of** vor *(räumlich)* I • **to the front** nach vorn I
front door [ˌfrʌnt ˈdɔː] Wohnungstür, Haustür I
°**froze** [frəʊz] *siehe* **freeze**
°**frozen** [ˈfrəʊzn] *siehe* **freeze**
fruit [fruːt] Obst, Früchte; Frucht I
fruit salad Obstsalat I
full [fʊl] voll I
fun [fʌn] Spaß I • **have fun** Spaß haben, sich amüsieren I • **Have fun!** Viel Spaß! I • **just for fun** nur zum Spaß I • **Riding is fun.** Reiten macht Spaß. I
funny [ˈfʌni] witzig, komisch I
future [ˈfjuːtʃə] Zukunft I

G

°**galaxy** [ˈgæləksi] Galaxie
game [geɪm] Spiel I • **a game of football** ein Fußballspiel II 1 (22)
°**gap** [gæp] Lücke
garage [ˈgærɑːʒ] Garage II 3 (48)
garden [ˈgɑːdn] Garten I
gave [geɪv] *siehe* **give**
gear: **sports gear** *(no pl)* [ˈspɔːts gɪə] Sportausrüstung, Sportsachen II 2 (27)
geography [dʒiˈɒgrəfi] Geografie, Erdkunde I
°**Georgian** [ˈdʒɔːdʒən] georgianisch *(aus der Zeit der britischen Könige Georg I–IV)*
German [ˈdʒɜːmən] Deutsch; deutsch; Deutsche(r) I
Germany [ˈdʒɜːməni] Deutschland I
get (-tt-) [get], **got, got**
1. bekommen, kriegen II 1 (22/155)
2. holen, besorgen II 1 (22)
3. gelangen, (hin)kommen I
4. **get angry/hot/…** wütend/heiß/… werden II 1 (14)
5. **get off (the train/bus)** (aus dem Zug/Bus) aussteigen I • **get on (the train/bus)** (in den Zug/Bus) einsteigen I
6. **get up** aufstehen I
I don't get it. Das versteh ich nicht. / Das kapier ich nicht. II 5 (78)
get dressed sich anziehen I
get ready (for) sich fertig machen (für), sich vorbereiten (auf) I • **get things ready** Dinge fertig machen, vorbereiten I • **What can I get you?** Was kann/darf ich euch/Ihnen bringen? II 5 (80)
▶ S.155 (to) get
getting by in English [ˌgetɪŋ ˈbaɪ] *etwa*: auf Englisch zurechtkommen I
°**geyser** [ˈgiːzə] Geysir
°**giant** [ˈdʒaɪənt] riesig
giraffe [dʒəˈrɑːf] Giraffe II 3 (49/163)
girl [gɜːl] Mädchen I
give [gɪv], **gave, given** geben I
give sth. back etwas zurückgeben I
given [ˈgɪvn] *siehe* **give**
°**glacier** [ˈglæsiə] Gletscher
glass [glɑːs] Glas I • **a glass of water** ein Glas Wasser I
glasses *(pl)* [ˈglɑːsɪz] (eine) Brille I
▶ S.157 Plural words
gloves *(pl)* [glʌvz] Handschuhe II 3 (47)
°**glow** [gləʊ] Leuchten, Glühen
glue [gluː] (auf-, ein)kleben II 4 (62/165)
glue [gluː] Klebstoff I • **glue stick** [ˈgluː stɪk] Klebestift I
go [gəʊ], **went, gone** gehen I; fahren II Welc (6) • **go abroad** ins Ausland gehen/fahren II Welc (9) • **go by car/bike/…** mit dem Auto/Rad/… fahren II Welc (7) • **go for a walk** spazieren gehen, einen Spaziergang machen II Welc (7/151)
go home nach Hause gehen I
go on weitermachen I • **Go on.** Mach weiter. / Erzähl weiter. I
go on a trip einen Ausflug machen II Welc (7/151) • **go on holiday** in Urlaub fahren II Welc (6) • **go out** weg-, raus-, ausgehen I • °**go right** gut laufen, (gut) klappen I
go riding/shopping/swimming reiten/einkaufen/schwimmen gehen I • **go surfing** wellenreiten gehen, surfen gehen II Welc (9)
go to führen nach *(Straße, Weg)* II 6 (96) • **go to bed** ins Bett gehen I • **go to the cinema** ins Kino gehen II 2 (27/156) • **go well** gut (ver)laufen, gutgehen II 6 (101)
°**go with** passen zu • **Let's go.** Auf geht's! (*wörtlich*: Lass uns gehen.) I • **What are you going to do?** Was wirst du tun? / Was hast du vor zu tun? I
▶ S.151 (to) go
°**goat** [gəʊt] Ziege
°**god** [gɒd] Gott
°**goddess** [ˈgɒdes] Göttin
gone [gɒn] *siehe* **go** • **be gone** weg sein, nicht da sein II 6 (98)
good [gʊd]
1. gut I • **Good afternoon.** Guten Tag. *(nachmittags)* I • **Good luck (with …)!** Viel Glück (bei/mit …)! I • **Good morning.** Guten Morgen. I
2. brav II 3 (57)
Goodbye. [ˌgʊdˈbaɪ] Auf Wiedersehen. I • **say goodbye** sich verabschieden I
got [gɒt] *siehe* **get**
got [gɒt]: **I've got …** Ich habe … I **I haven't got a chair.** Ich habe keinen Stuhl. I
grammar [ˈgræmə] Grammatik I
grammar file Grammatikanhang I
°**grand** [grænd] prachtvoll, großartig
grandchild [ˈgræntʃaɪld], *pl* **grandchildren** [ˈ-tʃɪldrən] Enkel/in I
granddaughter [ˈgrændɔːtə] Enkelin II 4 (73)
grandfather [ˈgrænfɑːðə] Großvater I
grandma [ˈgrænmɑː] Oma I
grandmother [ˈgrænmʌðə] Großmutter I
grandpa [ˈgrænpɑː] Opa I
grandparents [ˈgrænpeərənts] Großeltern I
grandson [ˈgrænsʌn] Enkel II 4 (73)
granny [ˈgræni] Oma II 2 (30)
great [greɪt] großartig, toll I
green [griːn] grün I
grew [gruː] *siehe* **grow**
grey [greɪ] grau II 3 (45)
°**grin** [grɪn] Grinsen
group [gruːp] Gruppe I • **group word** Oberbegriff II 2 (27)
grow [grəʊ], **grew, grown** wachsen II 2 (29)
grown [grəʊn] *siehe* **grow**
grumble [ˈgrʌmbl] murren, nörgeln II Welc (9)
guess [ges] raten, erraten, schätzen II 3 (48) • **Guess what!** [ˌges ˈwɒt] Stell dir vor! / Stellt euch vor! II 3 (48)
guest [gest] Gast I
°**guide** [gaɪd] Fremdenführer/in, Reiseleiter/in
guinea pig [ˈgɪni pɪg] Meerschweinchen I
guitar [gɪˈtɑː] Gitarre I • **play the guitar** Gitarre spielen I
°**gun** [gʌn] Schusswaffe, Pistole
°**gunpowder** [ˈgʌnpaʊdə] Schießpulver
guy [gaɪ] Typ, Kerl II 6 (96) • **guys** *(pl)* Leute II 6 (96)

H

had [hæd] *siehe* **have**
hair *(no pl)* [heə] Haar, Haare I
°**half** [hɑːf], *pl* **halves** [hɑːvz] Hälfte
half [hɑːf] halbe(r, s) II 6 (96) • **half an hour** eine halbe Stunde II 6 (96/174) • **half past 11** halb zwölf (11.30 / 23.30) I • °**an hour and a half** eineinhalb Stunden, anderthalb Stunden
hall [hɔːl]
1. Flur, Diele I
°2. Halle
hamburger [ˈhæmbɜːgə] Hamburger I
hamster [ˈhæmstə] Hamster I
hand [hænd] Hand I
happen (to) [ˈhæpən] geschehen, passieren (mit) I
happy [ˈhæpi] glücklich, froh I
Happy birthday. Herzlichen Glückwunsch zum Geburtstag. I
happy ending Happyend II 1 (23)
hard [hɑːd] hart; schwer, schwierig II 3 (49) • **work hard** hart arbeiten II 3 (49)
hat [hæt] Hut I
hate [heɪt] hassen, gar nicht mögen I
have [həv, hæv], **had, had** haben, besitzen II 2 (31) • **have an argument** eine Auseinandersetzung haben, sich streiten II 1 (15) • **have a baby** ein Baby/Kind bekommen II 3 (49) • **have a bath** baden, ein Bad nehmen II 6 (94) • **have a cold** erkältet sein, eine Erkältung haben II 4 (64/167) • **have a massage** sich massieren lassen II 6 (94) • **have a sauna** in die Sauna gehen II 6 (94) **have a shower** (sich) duschen I **have a sore throat** Halsschmerzen haben II 4 (64) • **have a temperature** Fieber haben II 4 (64) • **have breakfast** frühstücken I • **have dinner** Abendbrot essen I • **have ... for breakfast** ... zum Frühstück essen/trinken I • **have fun** Spaß haben, sich amüsieren I • **Have fun!** Viel Spaß! I • **have to do** tun müssen I
have got: I've got ... [aɪv gɒt] Ich habe ... I • **I haven't got a chair.** [ˈhævnt gɒt] Ich habe keinen Stuhl. I
he [hiː] er I
head [hed] Kopf I • °**heads and tails** [ˌhedz ənd ˈteɪlz] *wörtlich:* Köpfe und Schwänze; *hier:* (Satz-) Anfänge und Enden

headache [ˈhedeɪk] Kopfschmerzen II 4 (64)
▶ S.167 What's wrong with you?
°**heading** [ˈhedɪŋ] Überschrift
°**headline** [ˈhedlaɪn] Überschrift, Schlagzeile
healthy [ˈhelθi] gesund II 5 (76)
hear [hɪə], **heard, heard** hören I
heard [hɜːd] *siehe* **hear**
heart [hɑːt] Herz I • °**learn sth. by heart** etwas auswendig lernen
hedgehog [ˈhedʒhɒɡ] Igel II 3 (45)
held [held] *siehe* **hold**
helicopter [ˈhelɪkɒptə] Hubschrauber, Helikopter II 4 (73)
Hello. [həˈləʊ] Hallo. / Guten Tag. I
help [help] helfen I • **Can I help you?** Kann ich Ihnen helfen? / Was kann ich für Sie tun? *(im Geschäft)* I
help [help] Hilfe I
her [hə, hɜː]
1. ihr, ihre I
2. sie; ihr I
here [hɪə]
1. hier I
2. hierher I
Here you are. Bitte sehr. / Hier bitte. I
hero [ˈhɪərəʊ], *pl* **heroes** [ˈhɪərəʊz] Held, Heldin II 1 (14)
hers [hɜːz] ihrer, ihre, ihrs II 2 (128)
Hi! [haɪ] Hallo! I • **Say hi to Dilip for me.** Grüß Dilip von mir. I
°**hibiscus** [hɪˈbɪskəs] Hibiskus
hid [hɪd] *siehe* **hide**
hidden [ˈhɪdn] *siehe* **hide**
hide [haɪd], **hid, hidden** sich verstecken; *(etwas)* verstecken I
°**high** [haɪ] hoch
°**high school** [ˈhaɪ skuːl] *Gesamtschule in den USA mit den Klassen 7–12 für 13- bis 18-Jährige*
hill [hɪl] Hügel II 4 (60)
°**hillfort** [ˈhɪlfɔːt] auf einem Hügel gelegenes Fort (befestigte Wall- und Grabenanlage)
him [hɪm] ihn; ihm I
hippo [ˈhɪpəʊ] Flusspferd II 3 (49/163)
his [hɪz]
1. sein, seine I
2. seiner, seine, seins II 2 (128)
history [ˈhɪstri] Geschichte I
°**hit a sandbank** (-tt-) [hɪt], **hit, hit** auf eine Sandbank laufen *(Schiff)*
hobby [ˈhɒbi] Hobby I
hockey [ˈhɒki] Hockey I • **hockey pitch** Hockeyplatz, -feld II 4 (62)
hockey shoes Hockeyschuhe I
°**hog** [hɒɡ] Schwein
hold [həʊld], **held, held** halten II 4 (72) • °**hold up** hochhalten
hole [həʊl] Loch I

holiday(s) [ˈhɒlədeɪ(z)] Ferien I **be on holiday** in Urlaub sein II Welc (6) • **go on holiday** in Urlaub fahren II Welc (6)
home [həʊm] Heim, Zuhause I **at home** daheim, zu Hause I **come home** nach Hause kommen I • **get home** nach Hause kommen I • **go home** nach Hause gehen I
homework *(no pl)* [ˈhəʊmwɜːk] Hausaufgabe(n) I • **do homework** die Hausaufgabe(n) machen I • **What's for homework?** Was haben wir als Hausaufgabe auf? I
Hooray! [huˈreɪ] Hurra! II 6 (106)
hope [həʊp] hoffen I • **I hope so.** Ich hoffe es. II 2 (30)
horrible [ˈhɒrəbl] scheußlich, grauenhaft II 3 (48)
horse [hɔːs] Pferd I
hospital [ˈhɒspɪtl] Krankenhaus II 4 (73)
hot [hɒt] heiß I • **hot chocolate** heiße Schokolade I • **hot-water bottle** Wärmflasche II 3 (47)
hotel [həʊˈtel] Hotel II Welc (7)
hotline [ˈhɒtlaɪn] Hotline II 3 (46)
hour [ˈaʊə] Stunde I • **half an hour** eine halbe Stunde II 6 (96/174) °**an hour and a half** eineinhalb Stunden, anderthalb Stunden
house [haʊs] Haus I • **at the Shaws' house** im Haus der Shaws / bei den Shaws zu Hause I
how [haʊ] wie I • **How are you?** Wie geht es dir/Ihnen/euch? II 1 (21) **How do you know ...?** Woher weißt/kennst du ...? I • **how many?** wie viele? I • **how much?** wie viel? I • **How much is/are ...?** Was kostet/kosten ...? / Wie viel kostet/kosten ...? I • **How old are you?** Wie alt bist du? I • **How was ...?** Wie war ...? I
°**huge** [hjuːdʒ] riesig
hundred [ˈhʌndrəd] hundert I
hungry [ˈhʌŋɡri] hungrig I • **be hungry** Hunger haben, hungrig sein I
°**hurricane** [ˈhʌrɪkən] Hurrikan, Orkan
hurry [ˈhʌri] eilen; sich beeilen II 2 (40) • **hurry up** sich beeilen I
hurry [ˈhʌri]: **be in a hurry** in Eile sein, es eilig haben I
hurt [hɜːt], **hurt, hurt** wehtun; verletzen I
hurt [hɜːt] verletzt II 3 (51)
husband [ˈhʌzbənd] Ehemann II 4 (73)
hutch [hʌtʃ] (Kaninchen-)Stall I

Dictionary (English – German)

I

I [aɪ] ich I • **I'm** [aɪm] ich bin I • **I'm from ...** Ich komme aus ... / Ich bin aus ... I • **I'm ... years old.** Ich bin ... Jahre alt. I • **I'm sorry.** Entschuldigung. / Tut mir leid. I
ice [aɪs] Eis II 6 (101)
ice cream [ˌaɪsˈkriːm] (Speise-)Eis I
ice rink [ˈaɪs rɪŋk] Schlittschuhbahn II 6 (101)
idea [aɪˈdɪə] Idee, Einfall I
if [ɪf]
1. wenn, falls II 3 (47)
2. ob II 6 (107)
ill [ɪl] krank II 3 (47)
▶ S.167 What's wrong with you?
°**imaginary** [ɪˈmædʒɪnəri] imaginär *(nicht wirklich, nur vorgestellt)*
°**imagine sth.** [ɪˈmædʒɪn] sich etwas vorstellen I
important [ɪmˈpɔːtnt] wichtig II 3 (47)
impossible [ɪmˈpɒsəbl] unmöglich II 5 (80)
in [ɪn] in I • **in 2050** im Jahr 2050 II 3 (50) • **in ... Street** in der ...straße I • **in English** auf Englisch I • **in front of** vor *(räumlich)* I • **in here** hier drinnen I • **in the afternoon** nachmittags, am Nachmittag I • **in the country** auf dem Land II Welc (8/152) • **in the evening** abends, am Abend I • **in the field** auf dem Feld II 4 (60/165) • **in the morning** am Morgen, morgens I • **in the photo** auf dem Foto I • **in the picture** auf dem Bild I • **in there** dort drinnen I • **in the sky** am Himmel II Welc (7/151) • **in the world** auf der Welt II 2 (31) • **in the yard** auf dem Hof II 3 (46/161) • **in time** [ɪn ˈtaɪm] rechtzeitig II 1 (23) • °**one in five people** jede(r) Fünfte, eine(r) von fünf(en)
°**including** [ɪnˈkluːdɪŋ] einschließlich
°**independence** [ˌɪndɪˈpendəns] Unabhängigkeit
infinitive [ɪnˈfɪnətɪv] Infinitiv *(Grundform des Verbs)* I
information (about/on) *(no pl)* [ˌɪnfəˈmeɪʃn] Information(en) (über) I
°**injure** [ˈɪndʒə] (sich) verletzen I
injury [ˈɪndʒəri] Verletzung II 4 (74)
°**inline skates** *(pl)* [ˌɪnlaɪn ˈskeɪts] Inliner, Inlineskates
inside [ˌɪnˈsaɪd]
1. innen (drin), drinnen I
2. nach drinnen II 3 (46)
3. **inside the car** ins Auto(hinein), ins Innere des Autos II 4 (73)

°**inspector** [ɪnˈspektə] Inspektor/in, Kontrolleur/in
install [ɪnˈstɔːl] installieren, einrichten II 4 (65)
installation [ˌɪnstəˈleɪʃn] Installation, Einrichtung II 4 (65)
instructions *(pl)* [ɪnˈstrʌkʃnz] (Gebrauchs-)Anweisung(en), Anleitung(en) II 4 (65)
interesting [ˈɪntrəstɪŋ] interessant I
international [ˌɪntəˈnæʃnəl] international II 5 (76)
internet [ˈɪntənet] Internet I • **surf the internet** im Internet surfen II 4 (65/168)
°**interview** [ˈɪntəvjuː] Interview
into [ˈɪntə, ˈɪntʊ] in ... (hinein) I
°**invent** [ɪnˈvent] erfinden
invitation (to) [ˌɪnvɪˈteɪʃn] Einladung (zu) I
invite (to) [ɪnˈvaɪt] einladen (zu) I
°**Iron Age** [ˈaɪən_eɪdʒ] Eisenzeit
is [ɪz] ist I
island [ˈaɪlənd] Insel II Welc (6)
IT [ˌaɪ ˈtiː], **information technology** [tekˈnɒlədʒi] IT (Informationstechnologie) II 5 (81)
it [ɪt] er/sie/es I • **It's £1.** Er/Sie/Es kostet 1 Pfund. I
its [ɪts] sein/seine; ihr/ihre I

J

jacket [ˈdʒækɪt] Jacke, Jackett II 1 (14)
January [ˈdʒænjuəri] Januar I
jeans *(pl)* [dʒiːnz] Jeans I
▶ S.157 Plural words
°**jiggle** [ˈdʒɪgl] herumhampeln
job [dʒɒb] Aufgabe, Job I • **do a good job** gute Arbeit leisten II 3 (49)
join sb./sth. [dʒɔɪn] sich jm. anschließen; bei jm./etwas mitmachen II 1 (22)
joke [dʒəʊk] Witz I
joke scherzen, Witze machen II 3 (57/164)
°**joy** [dʒɔɪ] Freude
judo [ˈdʒuːdəʊ] Judo I • **do judo** Judo machen I
jug [dʒʌg] Krug I • **a jug of milk** ein Krug Milch I
°**juggle** [ˈdʒʌgl] jonglieren (mit)
°**juggler** [ˈdʒʌglə] Jongleur/in
juice [dʒuːs] Saft I
July [dʒuˈlaɪ] Juli I
jumble sale [ˈdʒʌmbl seɪl] Wohltätigkeitsbasar I
jump [dʒʌmp] springen II 1 (22)
June [dʒuːn] Juni I

junior [ˈdʒuːniə] Junioren-, Jugend- I
just [dʒʌst]
1. (einfach) nur, bloß I
2. gerade (eben), soeben II 4 (63) **just then** genau in dem Moment; gerade dann II 3 (48)
3. **just like you** genau wie du II 2 (28)
▶ S.166 The present perfect: statements

K

kangaroo [ˌkæŋgəˈruː] Känguru II 3 (49/163)
°**kayaking** [ˈkaɪækɪŋ]: **sea kayaking** Kajak fahren (auf dem Meer)
keep [kiːp], **kept, kept**: **keep sth. warm/cool/open/...** etwas warm/kühl/offen/... halten II 3 (47)
°**kennel** [ˈkenl] Hundehütte, Zwinger
kept [kept] *siehe* **keep**
key [kiː] Schlüssel I • **key word** Stichwort, Schlüsselwort I
kid [kɪd] Kind, Jugendliche(r) I
kill [kɪl] töten I
°**kilometre (km)** [ˈkɪləmiːtə, kɪˈlɒmɪtə] Kilometer (km)
king [kɪŋ] König I
kitchen [ˈkɪtʃɪn] Küche I
kite [kaɪt] Drachen I
knee [niː] Knie I
knew [njuː] *siehe* **know**
knock (on) [nɒk] (an)klopfen (an) I
know [nəʊ], **knew, known**
1. wissen I
2. kennen I
How do you know ...? Woher weißt du ...?/Woher kennst du ...? I **know about sth.** von etwas wissen; über etwas Bescheid wissen II 1 (23) • **..., you know.** ..., wissen Sie. / ..., weißt du. I • **You know what, Sophie?** Weißt du was, Sophie? I
known [nəʊn] *siehe* **know**

L

°**label** [ˈleɪbl] beschriften, etikettieren
°**ladder** [ˈlædə] *(die)* Leiter
°**lady** [ˈleɪdi] Dame
laid [leɪd] *siehe* **lay**
lake [leɪk] (Binnen-)See II Welc (9)
lamp [læmp] Lampe I
land [lænd] landen II 2 (40)
°**land** [lænd] Land

Dictionary (English – German)

language [ˈlæŋwɪdʒ] Sprache I
°**large** [lɑːdʒ] groß
lasagne [ləˈzænjə] Lasagne I
last [lɑːst] letzte(r, s) I • **the last day** der letzte Tag I • **at last** endlich, schließlich I
late [leɪt] spät; zu spät I • **be late** zu spät sein/kommen I • °**sleep late** lange schlafen • **Sorry, I'm late.** Entschuldigung, dass ich zu spät bin/komme. I
later [ˈleɪtə] später I
°**latest: the latest technology** [ˌleɪtɪst tekˈnɒlədʒi] die neueste Technologie
°**Latin** [ˈlætɪn] Latein; lateinisch
laugh [lɑːf] lachen I • **laugh out loud** laut lachen II 4 (65)
laughter [ˈlɑːftə] Gelächter II 6 (107)
lay the table [leɪ], **laid, laid** den Tisch decken I
°**lean** [liːn] sich neigen • °**leaning tower** schiefer Turm
learn [lɜːn] lernen I • **learn about sth.** etwas über etwas erfahren, etwas über etwas herausfinden II 5 (76) • °**learn sth. by heart** etwas auswendig lernen
least: at least [ət ˈliːst] zumindest, wenigstens I
leave [liːv], **left, left**
1. (weg)gehen; abfahren II 3 (56)
2. verlassen II 3 (56/164)
3. zurücklassen II 3 (56/164)
▶ S.164 (to) leave
°**leek** [liːk] Lauch
left [left] siehe **leave** • **be left** übrig sein II 2 (28)
left [left] linke(r, s) I • **look left** nach links schauen I • **on the left** links, auf der linken Seite I • **turn left** (nach) links abbiegen II 6 (97) °**the left-hand column** die linke Spalte
leg [leg] Bein I
°**legend** [ˈledʒənd] Legende, Sage
leisure centre [ˈleʒə sentə] Freizeitzentrum, -park II 6 (106)
lemonade [ˌleməˈneɪd] Limonade I
lend sb. sth. [lend], **lent, lent** jm. etwas leihen II 1 (14)
lent [lent] siehe **lend**
lesson [ˈlesn] (Unterrichts-)Stunde I • **lessons** (pl) Unterricht I
let [let], **let, let** lassen II 3 (47/162) **Let's …** Lass uns … / Lasst uns … I **Let's go.** Auf geht's! (wörtlich: Lass uns gehen.) I • **Let's look at the list.** Sehen wir uns die Liste an. / Lasst uns die Liste ansehen. I
letter [ˈletə]
1. Buchstabe I

2. **letter (to)** [ˈletə] Brief (an) II 2 (30)
lettuce [ˈletɪs] (Kopf-)Salat II 6 (106)
library [ˈlaɪbrəri] Bibliothek, Bücherei
life [laɪf], pl **lives** [laɪvz] Leben I
°**lifeboat** [ˈlaɪfbəʊt] Rettungsboot, -schiff
°**lifeboatmen** (pl) [ˈlaɪfbəʊtmən] die Besatzung eines Rettungsbootes
lift [lɪft] Fahrstuhl, Aufzug II 1 (12)
°**lighting** [ˈlaɪtɪŋ] Beleuchtung
°**lightning** (no pl) [ˈlaɪtnɪŋ] Blitz, Blitzschlag
like [laɪk] wie I • **just like you** genau wie du II 2 (28) • °**like this so** • °**like that** so • **What was the weather like?** Wie war das Wetter? II Welc (7)
like [laɪk] mögen, gernhaben I • **like sth. better** etwas lieber mögen II 6 (105) • **like sth. very much** etwas sehr mögen II 2 (30) • **I like swimming/dancing/…** Ich schwimme/tanze/… gern. I • **I'd like … (= I would like …)** Ich hätte gern … / Ich möchte gern … I • **I'd like to go (= I would like to go)** Ich würde gern gehen / Ich möchte gehen I • **I wouldn't like to go** Ich würde nicht gern gehen / Ich möchte nicht gehen I • **Would you like …?** Möchtest du …? / Möchten Sie …? I
line [laɪn] Zeile II 3 (57)
link [lɪŋk] verbinden, verknüpfen I
linking word [ˈlɪŋkɪŋ wɜːd] Bindewort II 1 (18)
lion [ˈlaɪən] Löwe II 3 (49/163)
list [lɪst] auflisten, aufzählen II 3 (57/164)
list [lɪst] Liste I
listen (to) [ˈlɪsn] zuhören; sich etwas anhören I
listener [ˈlɪsnə] Zuhörer/in II 3 (55)
little [ˈlɪtl] klein I
live [lɪv] leben, wohnen I • °**live on** weiterleben
live music [laɪv] Livemusik II 1 (19)
lives [laɪvz] Plural von „life" I
living room [ˈlɪvɪŋ ruːm] Wohnzimmer I
°**lobby** [ˈlɒbi] Eingangshalle, Foyer
lock [lɒk] abschließen, zuschließen I • **lock up** abschließen II 5 (81)
°**locomotive** [ˌləʊkəˈməʊtɪv] Lokomotive
long [lɒŋ] lang I • **a long way (from)** weit entfernt (von) I
look [lʊk]
1. schauen, gucken I
2. **look different/great/old** anders/

toll/alt aussehen I
look after sth./sb. sich um etwas/jn. kümmern; auf etwas/jn. aufpassen II 3 (49) • **look at** ansehen, anschauen I • **look for** suchen II 2 (29) • **look left and right** nach links und rechts schauen I • **look round** sich umsehen I • **look up (from)** hochsehen, aufschauen (von) II 2 (29) • °**look up words** Wörter nachschlagen
lose [luːz], **lost, lost** verlieren II 2 (28)
lost [lɒst] siehe **lose**
lot [lɒt]: **a lot (of), lots of** eine Menge, viel, viele I / II 2 (33) • **He likes her a lot.** Er mag sie sehr. • **lots more** viel mehr I • **Thanks a lot!** Vielen Dank! I
loud [laʊd] laut I
love [lʌv] lieben, sehr mögen I • **love sth. very much** etwas sehr lieben II 2 (30) • °**loving care** etwa: liebevolle Fürsorge
love [lʌv] Liebe II 4 (62/165) • **Love …** Liebe Grüße, … (Briefschluss) I
lovely [ˈlʌvli] schön, hübsch, wunderbar II 2 (40)
°**lover** [ˈlʌvə] Freund/in, Liebhaber/in
°**loving care** [ˌlʌvɪŋ ˈkeə] etwa: liebevolle Fürsorge
°**low: be on a low budget** [ləʊ ˈbʌdʒɪt] mit wenig Geld auskommen müssen
luck [lʌk]: **Good luck (with …)!** Viel Glück (bei/mit …)! I
luckily [ˈlʌkɪli] zum Glück, glücklicherweise II 6 (105)
lunch [lʌntʃ] Mittagessen I **lunch break** Mittagspause I

M

machine [məˈʃiːn] Maschine, Gerät II 6 (94)
mad [mæd] verrückt I
made [meɪd] siehe **make**
magazine [ˌmæɡəˈziːn] Zeitschrift, Magazin I
mail sb. [meɪl] jn. anmailen II 3 (46)
make [meɪk], **made, made** machen; bauen I • **make a call** ein Telefongespräch führen, telefonieren II 6 (98) • **make a mess** alles durcheinanderbringen, alles in Unordnung bringen I • °**make comparisons** Vergleiche anstellen, vergleichen • **make friends (with)** Freunde finden; sich anfreunden

Dictionary (English – German)

(mit) II 3 (56) • °**make notes** (sich) Notizen machen
make-up ['meɪkʌp] Make-up II 2 (27)
male [meɪl] Männchen II 3 (49/163)
man [mæn], *pl* **men** [men] Mann I
many ['meni] viele I • **how many?** wie viele? I
map [mæp] Landkarte, Stadtplan II 6 (97)
March [mɑːtʃ] März I
mark sth. up [ˌmɑːk_'ʌp] etwas markieren, kennzeichnen II 5 (79)
market ['mɑːkɪt] Markt II 5 (76)
marmalade ['mɑːməleɪd] Orangenmarmelade I
married (to) ['mærɪd] verheiratet (mit) I
massage ['mæsɑːʒ] Massage II 6 (94) • **have a massage** sich massieren lassen II 6 (94)
match [mætʃ] Spiel, Wettkampf I
°**match sth. (to sth.)** [mætʃ] etwas zuordnen (zu etwas)
material [mə'tɪərɪəl] Material, Stoff II 5 (78)
maths [mæθs] Mathematik I
matter ['mætə]: **What's the matter?** Was ist los? / Was ist denn? II 2 (28)
may [meɪ] dürfen I
▶ S.169 „können" und „dürfen"
May [meɪ] Mai I
maybe ['meɪbi] vielleicht I
°**mayonnaise** [ˌmeɪə'neɪz] Majonäse I
me [miː] mir; mich I • **Me too.** Ich auch. I • **more than me** mehr als ich II 2 (131) • **That's me.** Das bin ich. I • **Why me?** Warum ich? I
mean [miːn], **meant, meant**
1. bedeuten II 4 (65)
2. meinen, sagen wollen I
meaning ['miːnɪŋ] Bedeutung I
meant [ment] *siehe* **mean**
meat [miːt] Fleisch I
mediation [ˌmiːdi'eɪʃn] Vermittlung, Sprachmittlung, Mediation II (3)
meet [miːt], **met, met**
1. treffen; kennenlernen I
2. sich treffen I
men [men] *Plural von „man"* I
°**Merry Christmas.** [ˌmeri 'krɪsməs] Frohe Weihnachten.
mess [mes]: **make a mess** alles durcheinanderbringen, alles in Unordnung bringen I
°**message** ['mesɪdʒ] Nachricht, Botschaft • °**message in a bottle** Flaschenpost
met [met] *siehe* **meet**
metre ['miːtə] Meter II 4 (72)

mice [maɪs] *Plural von „mouse"* I
middle (of) ['mɪdl] Mitte; Mittelteil I
mile [maɪl] Meile (= ca. 1,6 km) II 1 (12) • **for miles** meilenweit II 1 (12)
milk [mɪlk] Milch I
milkshake ['mɪlkʃeɪk] Milchshake I
°**million** ['mɪljən] Million
mime [maɪm] vorspielen, pantomimisch darstellen II 6 (105)
mind: Mind your own business. [maɪnd] Das geht dich nichts an! / Kümmere dich um deine eigenen Angelegenheiten! II 1 (13) • **Never mind.** [ˌnevə 'maɪnd] Kümmere dich nicht drum. / Macht nichts. II 2 (40)
mind map ['maɪnd mæp] Mindmap („Gedankenkarte", „Wissensnetz") I
mine [maɪn] meiner, meine, meins II 2 (28)
°**minister** ['mɪnɪstə] Minister/in
mints *(pl)* [mɪnts] Pfefferminzbonbons I
minute ['mɪnɪt] Minute I • **Wait a minute.** Warte mal! / Moment mal! II 2 (31)
mirror ['mɪrə] Spiegel II 2 (40)
Miss White [mɪs] Frau White (unverheiratet) I
miss [mɪs]
1. vermissen II 3 (56)
2. verpassen II 4 (62)
Miss a turn. Einmal aussetzen. II 5 (76)
missing ['mɪsɪŋ]: **be missing** fehlen II 6 (98) • °**the missing information/words** die fehlenden Informationen/Wörter
mistake [mɪ'steɪk] Fehler I
°**mix (with)** [mɪks] sich vermischen (mit) • °**mix up** durcheinanderbringen
mobile (phone) ['məʊbaɪl] Mobiltelefon, Handy I
model ['mɒdl] Modell(-flugzeug, -schiff usw.) I; (Foto-)Modell II 2 (41)
mole [məʊl] Maulwurf II 3 (45)
moment ['məʊmənt] Augenblick, Moment I • **at the moment** im Moment, gerade, zurzeit I • **for a moment** einen Moment lang II 2 (29)
Monday ['mʌndeɪ, 'mʌndi] Montag I • **Monday morning** Montagmorgen I
money ['mʌni] Geld I
monkey ['mʌŋki] Affe II 3 (49/163)
month [mʌnθ] Monat I
moon [muːn] Mond II 3 (46)

more [mɔː] mehr I • **lots more** viel mehr I • **more boring (than)** langweiliger (als) II 2 (32) • **more quickly (than)** schneller (als) II 3 (49) • **more than me** mehr als ich II 2 (133) • **no more music** keine Musik mehr I • **not (...) any more** nicht mehr II 2 (31) • **one more** noch ein(e), ein(e) weitere(r, s) I
morning ['mɔːnɪŋ] Morgen, Vormittag I • **in the morning** morgens, am Morgen I • **Monday morning** Montagmorgen I • **on Friday morning** freitagmorgens, am Freitagmorgen I
°**mosaic** [məʊ'zeɪɪk] Mosaik
most [məʊst] (der/die/das) meiste ...; am meisten II 2 (130) • **most people** die meisten Leute I • **(the) most boring** der/die/das langweiligste ...; am langweiligsten II 2 (32)
mother ['mʌðə] Mutter I
mountain ['maʊntən] Berg II Welc (6/150)
mouse [maʊs], *pl* **mice** [maɪs] Maus I
mouth [maʊθ] Mund I
move [muːv]
1. bewegen; sich bewegen II 3 (49) **Move back one space.** Geh ein Feld zurück. II 5 (76) • **Move on one space.** Geh ein Feld vor. II 5 (76)
2. **move (to)** umziehen (nach, in) II 3 (56/164) • **move in** einziehen II 3 (56/164) • **move out** ausziehen II 3 (56)
movement ['muːvmənt] Bewegung II 6 (106)
°**movies** *(pl)* ['muːviz] Kino
MP3 player [ˌempiː'θriː ˌpleɪə] MP3-Spieler I
Mr ... ['mɪstə] Herr ... I
Mrs ... ['mɪsɪz] Frau ... I
Ms ... [mɪz, məz] Frau ... I
much [mʌtʃ] viel I • **how much?** wie viel? I • **How much is/are ...?** Was kostet/kosten ...? / Wie viel kostet/kosten ...? I • **like/love sth. very much** etwas sehr mögen/sehr lieben II 2 (30) • **Thanks very much!** Danke sehr! / Vielen Dank! II 2 (30/158)
muesli ['mjuːzli] Müsli I
mum [mʌm] Mama, Mutti; Mutter I
museum [mjuː'ziːəm] Museum I
music ['mjuːzɪk] Musik I
musical ['mjuːzɪkl] Musical I
must [mʌst] müssen I
▶ S.176 must – needn't – mustn't

mustn't do [ˈmʌsnt] nicht tun dürfen II 6 (99)
▶ S.176 must – needn't – mustn't
°**mutineer** [ˌmjuːtəˈnɪə] Meuterer, Meuterin
my [maɪ] mein/e I • **My name is ...** Ich heiße ... / Mein Name ist ... I • **It's my turn.** Ich bin dran / an der Reihe. I
mystery [ˈmɪstri] Rätsel, Geheimnis II 5 (90)

N

name [neɪm] Name I • **My name is ...** Ich heiße ... / Mein Name ist ... I • **What's your name?** Wie heißt du? I
name [neɪm] nennen; benennen II 3 (57/164)
°**national** [ˈnæʃnəl] national
natural [ˈnætʃrəl] natürlich, Natur- II 3 (49) • °**Natural History Unit** Naturkundeabteilung
near [nɪə] in der Nähe von, nahe (bei) I
neat [niːt] gepflegt II 3 (56) • **neat and tidy** schön ordentlich II 3 (56)
°**necessary** [ˈnesəsri] nötig, notwendig
need [niːd] brauchen, benötigen I
needn't do [ˈniːdnt] nicht tun müssen, nicht zu tun brauchen II 6 (98)
▶ S.176 must – needn't – mustn't
neighbour [ˈneɪbə] Nachbar/in I
nervous [ˈnɜːvəs] nervös, aufgeregt I
°**network** [ˈnetwɜːk] (Wörter-)Netz
never [ˈnevə] nie, niemals I • **Never mind.** Kümmere dich nicht drum. / Macht nichts. II 2 (40)
▶ S.166 The present perfect: statements
new [njuː] neu I
news (no pl) [njuːz] Nachrichten I
newspaper [ˈnjuːspeɪpə] Zeitung I
next [nekst]: **be next** der/die Nächste sein I • **the next day** am nächsten Tag I • **the next photo** das nächste Foto I • **What have we got next?** Was haben wir als Nächstes? I
next to [nekst] neben I
nice [naɪs] schön, nett I • **nice and cool/clean/...** schön kühl/sauber/... I
night [naɪt] Nacht, später Abend I • **at night** nachts, in der Nacht I • **on Friday night** freitagnachts, Freitagnacht I
no [nəʊ] nein I

no [nəʊ] kein, keine I • **no more music** keine Musik mehr I • **No way!** [ˌnəʊ ˈweɪ] Auf keinen Fall! / Kommt nicht in Frage! II 1 (14)
nobody [ˈnəʊbədi] niemand II Welc (9)
nod (-dd-) [nɒd] nicken (mit) II 4 (64)
noise [nɔɪz] Geräusch; Lärm I
noisy [ˈnɔɪzi] laut, lärmend II 4 (60)
north [nɔːθ] Norden; nach Norden; nördlich II 4 (62/166) • **north-east** [ˌnɔːθˈiːst] Nordosten; nach Nordosten; nordöstlich II 4 (62/166)
north-west [ˌnɔːθˈwest] Nordwesten; nach Nordwesten; nordwestlich II 4 (62/166)
°**northern** [ˈnɔːðən] Nord-, nördlich
nose [nəʊz] Nase I
not [nɒt] nicht I • **not (...) any** kein, keine I • **not (...) any more** nicht mehr II 2 (31) • **not (...) anybody** niemand II 2 (29/158) • **not (...) anything** [ˈeniθɪŋ] nichts II 2 (29/158) • **not (...) anywhere** nirgendwo(hin) II 2 (29/158) • **not (...) either** auch nicht II 1 (13)
°**not only ... but (also)** nicht nur ..., sondern (auch) • **not (...) yet** noch nicht II 4 (63)
note [nəʊt] Mitteilung, Notiz I • **take notes (on)** sich Notizen machen (über, zu) I • °**make notes** (sich) Notizen machen
nothing [ˈnʌθɪŋ] nichts II 1 (14)
°**notice** [ˈnəʊtɪs] Notiz, Mitteilung
November [nəʊˈvembə] November I
now [naʊ] nun, jetzt I
number [ˈnʌmbə] Zahl, Ziffer, Nummer I

O

o [əʊ] null I
o'clock [əˈklɒk]: **eleven o'clock** elf Uhr I
October [ɒkˈtəʊbə] Oktober I
°**octopus** [ˈɒktəpəs] Krake, Tintenfisch
°**odd** [ɒd]: **What word is the odd one out?** Welches Wort passt nicht dazu? / Welches Wort gehört nicht dazu? I
of [əv, ɒv] von I • **of the summer holidays** der Sommerferien I
of course [əv ˈkɔːs] natürlich, selbstverständlich I
off [ɒf]: **take 10c off** 10 Cent abziehen I
often [ˈɒfn] oft, häufig I
Oh dear! Oje! II 4 (64)

Oh well ... [əʊ ˈwel] Na ja ... / Na gut ... I
OK [əʊˈkeɪ] okay, gut, in Ordnung I
old [əʊld] alt I • **How old are you?** Wie alt bist du? I • **I'm ... years old.** Ich bin ... Jahre alt. I
on [ɒn]
1. auf I
2. **be on** eingeschaltet sein, an sein *(Radio, Licht usw.)* II 1 (19) • **on 13th June** am 13. Juni I • **on Friday** am Freitag I • **on Friday afternoon** freitagnachmittags, am Freitagnachmittag I • **on Friday evening** freitagabends, am Freitagabend I • **on Friday morning** freitagmorgens, am Freitagmorgen I • **on Friday night** freitagnachts, Freitagnacht I • **on the beach** am Strand II Welc (6) • **on the board** an die Tafel I • **on the left** links, auf der linken Seite I • **on the phone** am Telefon I • **on the plane** im Flugzeug II Welc (7/151) • **on the radio** im Radio I • **on the right** rechts, auf der rechten Seite I • **on the train** im Zug I • **on TV** im Fernsehen I • **What page are we on?** Auf welcher Seite sind wir? I • **be on holiday** in Urlaub sein II Welc (6) • **go on holiday** in Urlaub fahren II Welc (6) • **straight on** [streɪt ˈɒn] geradeaus weiter II 6 (97)
°**once** [wʌns] einmal
one [wʌn] eins, ein, eine I • **one day** eines Tages I • **one more** noch ein/e, ein/e weitere(r, s) I • **a new one** ein neuer / eine neue / ein neues II 2 (29/157) • **my old ones** meine alten II 2 (29)
only [ˈəʊnli]
1. nur, bloß I
2. erst II 3 (57)
3. **the only guest** der einzige Gast I
°**Oops!** [uːps] Huch!
open [ˈəʊpən]
1. öffnen, aufmachen I
2. sich öffnen I
open [ˈəʊpən] geöffnet, offen I
open-air concert [ˌəʊpən ˈeə ˌkɒnsət] Open-Air-Konzert, Konzert im Freien II 4 (60)
opposite [ˈɒpəzɪt] gegenüber (von) II 6 (97)
or [ɔː] oder I
orange [ˈɒrɪndʒ] orange(farben) I
orange [ˈɒrɪndʒ] Orange, Apfelsine I • **orange juice** [ˈɒrɪndʒ dʒuːs] Orangensaft I
order [ˈɔːdə] bestellen II 5 (80)

Dictionary (English – German) 191

°**order** [ˈɔːdə] Reihenfolge • °**word order** Wortstellung
°**organ** [ˈɔːgən] Orgel
°**organization** [ˌɔːgənaɪˈzeɪʃn] Organisation
°**organize** [ˈɔːgənaɪz] ordnen, organisieren
other [ˈʌðə] andere(r, s) I • **the others** die anderen I • **the other way round** anders herum II 6 (106)
Ouch! [aʊtʃ] Autsch! I
our [ˈaʊə] unser, unsere I
ours [ˈaʊəz] unserer, unsere, unseres II 2 (128)
out [aʊt] heraus, hinaus; draußen II 1 (22/155) • **be out** weg sein, nicht da sein I • **out of ...** aus ... (heraus/hinaus) I
▶ S.155 out
outfit [ˈaʊtfɪt] Outfit *(Kleidung; Ausrüstung)* II 2 (41)
outside [ˌaʊtˈsaɪd]
1. draußen I
2. nach draußen II 1 (14)
3. **outside the room** vor dem Zimmer; außerhalb des Zimmers I
over [ˈəʊvə]
1. über, oberhalb von I • **from all over the world** aus der ganzen Welt II 5 (81) • **over there** da drüben, dort drüben I • **over to ...** hinüber zu/nach ... II 2 (40)
2. **be over** vorbei sein, zu Ende sein I
own [əʊn]: **our own pool** unser eigenes Schwimmbecken II Welc (7)

P

pack [pæk] packen, einpacken II 3 (56)
packet [ˈpækɪt] Päckchen, Packung, Schachtel I • **a packet of mints** ein Päckchen/eine Packung Pfefferminzbonbons I
page [peɪdʒ] (Buch-, Heft-)Seite I • **What page are we on?** Auf welcher Seite sind wir? I
paid [peɪd] *siehe* **pay**
pain [peɪn] Schmerz(en) I • **cry in pain** vor Schmerzen schreien I
paint [peɪnt] (an)malen I; anstreichen II 1 (19)
painter [ˈpeɪntə] Maler/in II 3 (55)
pair [peə]: **a pair (of)** ein Paar II 2 (27)
paper [ˈpeɪpə] Papier I • °**do a paper round** Zeitungen austragen
°**parade** [pəˈreɪd] Parade, Umzug
paragraph [ˈpærəgrɑːf] Absatz *(in einem Text)* II 4 (62)

paramedic [ˌpærəˈmedɪk] Sanitäter/in II 4 (64)
parcel [ˈpɑːsl] Paket I
parent [ˈpeərənt]: **a single parent** ein(e) Alleinerziehende(r) II 3 (51)
parents [ˈpeərənts] Eltern I
park [pɑːk] Park I
°**parliament** [ˈpɑːləmənt] Parlament
parrot [ˈpærət] Papagei I
part [pɑːt] Teil I
partner [ˈpɑːtnə] Partner/in I
party [ˈpɑːti] Party I
pass [pɑːs] (herüber)reichen, weitergeben I • **pass round** herumgeben I
past [pɑːst] Vergangenheit II 2 (31)
past [pɑːst] vorbei (an), vorüber (an) II 1 (22) • **half past 11** halb zwölf (11.30 / 23.30) I • **quarter past 11** Viertel nach 11 (11.15 / 23.15) I
path [pɑːθ] Pfad, Weg II 6 (96)
pay (for) [peɪ], **paid, paid** bezahlen II 6 (106)
PE [ˌpiːˈiː], **Physical Education** [ˌfɪzɪkəl ˌedʒuˈkeɪʃn] Sportunterricht, Turnen I
pen [pen] Kugelschreiber, Füller I
pence (p) *(pl)* [pens] Pence *(Plural von „penny")* I
pencil [ˈpensl] Bleistift I • **pencil case** [ˈpensl keɪs] Federmäppchen I • **pencil sharpener** [ˈpensl ʃɑːpnə] Bleistiftanspitzer I
penny [ˈpeni] *kleinste britische Münze* I
people [ˈpiːpl] Menschen, Leute I
°**perfect** [ˈpɜːfɪkt] perfekt
°**perhaps** [pəˈhæps] vielleicht
person [ˈpɜːsn] Person I
pet [pet] Haustier I • **pet shop** Tierhandlung I
phone [fəʊn] anrufen I
phone [fəʊn] Telefon I • **on the phone** am Telefon I • **phone number** Telefonnummer I • **pick up the phone** den Hörer abnehmen II 4 (72)
photo [ˈfəʊtəʊ] Foto I • **in the photo** auf dem Foto I • **take photos** Fotos machen, fotografieren I
photographer [fəˈtɒgrəfə] Fotograf/in II 5 (79)
phrase [freɪz] Ausdruck, (Rede-)Wendung II 1 (18)
piano [piˈænəʊ] Klavier, Piano I • **play the piano** Klavier spielen I
pick up the phone [ˌpɪk ˈʌp] den Hörer abnehmen II 4 (72)
picnic [ˈpɪknɪk] Picknick II 4 (62)
picture [ˈpɪktʃə] Bild I • **in the picture** auf dem Bild I

pie [paɪ] Obstkuchen; Pastete II 4 (63)
piece [piːs]: **a piece of** ein Stück I • **a piece of paper** ein Stück Papier I
pink [pɪŋk] pink(farben), rosa I
pirate [ˈpaɪrət] Pirat, Piratin I
pitch [pɪtʃ]: **football/hockey pitch** Fußball-/Hockeyplatz, -feld II 4 (62)
pity [ˈpɪti]: **It's a pity (that ...)** Es ist schade, dass ... II 4 (64)
pizza [ˈpiːtsə] Pizza I
place [pleɪs] Ort, Platz I • **take place** stattfinden II 5 (81)
plan [plæn] Plan I
plan (-nn-) [plæn] planen II 3 (49)
plane [pleɪn] Flugzeug II Welc (6) • **on the plane** im Flugzeug II Welc (7/151)
planet [ˈplænɪt] Planet II 6 (99)
°**plant** [plɑːnt] Pflanze
°**plasticine** [ˈplæstəsiːn] Knetmasse
plate [pleɪt] Teller I • **a plate of chips** ein Teller Pommes frites I
play [pleɪ] spielen I • **play a trick on sb.** jm. einen Streich spielen II 6 (98) • **play football** Fußball spielen I • **play the guitar** Gitarre spielen I • **play the piano** Klavier spielen I
play [pleɪ] Theaterstück I
player [ˈpleɪə] Spieler/in I
please [pliːz] bitte *(in Fragen und Aufforderungen)* I
°**plot** [plɒt] Verschwörung
pm [ˌpiːˈem]: **7 pm** 7 Uhr abends/ 19 Uhr I
pocket [ˈpɒkɪt] Tasche *(an Kleidungsstück)* II 2 (26/156) • **pocket money** [ˈpɒkɪt mʌni] Taschengeld II 2 (26)
poem [ˈpəʊɪm] Gedicht I
°**pohutukawa tree** [pəˌhuːtəˈkɑːwə] Eisenholzbaum
point [pɔɪnt] Punkt II 2 (37) • **11.4 (eleven point four)** 11,4 (elf Komma vier) II 5 (81/172) • **point of view** Standpunkt II 2 (41) • **from my point of view** aus meiner Sicht; von meinem Standpunkt aus gesehen II 2 (41/160)
▶ S.172 Numbers
point (at/to sth.) [pɔɪnt] zeigen, deuten (auf etwas) II 2 (29)
police *(pl)* [pəˈliːs] Polizei I • **police station** Polizeiwache, Polizeirevier II 6 (97)
°**polite** [pəˈlaɪt] höflich
poltergeist [ˈpəʊltəgaɪst] Poltergeist I
pool [puːl] Schwimmbad, Schwimmbecken II Welc (6)

Dictionary (English – German)

poor [pɔː, pʊə] arm I • **poor Sophie** (die) arme Sophie I
popcorn ['pɒpkɔːn] Popcorn II 4 (69)
°**popular** ['pɒpjələ] beliebt, populär
possible ['pɒsəbl] möglich II 5 (80)
post office ['pəʊst ˌɒfɪs] Postamt II 6 (97)
postcard ['pəʊstkɑːd] Postkarte II Welc (6)
poster ['pəʊstə] Poster I
°**pot** [pɒt] Gefäß, Topf
potato [pəˈteɪtəʊ], pl **potatoes** Kartoffel I
pound (£) [paʊnd] Pfund (britische Währung) I
°**powder** ['paʊdə] Pulver
practice ['præktɪs] hier: Übungsteil I
practise ['præktɪs] üben; trainieren I
prepare [prɪˈpeə] vorbereiten; sich vorbereiten II 2 (41) • **prepare for** sich vorbereiten auf II 2 (41/160)
present ['preznt]
1. Gegenwart I
2. Geschenk I
present sth. (to sb.) [prɪˈzent] (jm.) etwas präsentieren, vorstellen I
presentation [ˌpreznˈteɪʃn] Präsentation, Vorstellung I
presenter [prɪˈzentə] Moderator/in II 2 (40)
°**press** [pres] drücken
pretty ['prɪti]
1. hübsch I
2. **pretty cool/good/...** ziemlich cool/gut/... II 5 (80)
°**prevention** [prɪˈvenʃn] Verhütung, Verhinderung
price [praɪs] (Kauf-)Preis I
print sth. out [ˌprɪnt ˈaʊt] etwas ausdrucken II 4 (65)
°**prisoner** ['prɪznə] Gefangene(r)
prize [praɪz] Preis, Gewinn I
probably ['prɒbəbli] wahrscheinlich II 3 (46)
problem ['prɒbləm] Problem II 2 (29)
produce [prəˈdjuːs] produzieren, erzeugen, herstellen II 5 (78)
°**product** ['prɒdʌkt] Produkt
programme ['prəʊgræm] Programm I
project (about, on) ['prɒdʒekt] Projekt (über, zu) I • **do a project** ein Projekt machen, durchführen II 1 (16)
promise ['prɒmɪs] versprechen II 3 (56)
°**pronounce** [prəˈnaʊns] aussprechen

pronunciation [prəˌnʌnsiˈeɪʃn] Aussprache I
proof (no pl) [pruːf] Beweis(e) II 5 (88)
°**Protestant** ['prɒtɪstənt] protestantisch; Protestant/in
proud (of sb./sth.) [praʊd] stolz (auf jn./etwas) II 5 (79)
pub [pʌb] Kneipe, Lokal II 5 (76)
°**public** ['pʌblɪk] öffentliche(r, s)
pull [pʊl] ziehen I
pullover ['pʊləʊvə] Pullover II 2 (27)
punk [pʌŋk] Punker/in II 5 (86)
purple ['pɜːpl] violett; lila I
purse [pɜːs] Geldbörse II 5 (88)
push [pʊʃ] drücken, schieben, stoßen I
put (-tt-) [pʊt], **put, put** legen, stellen, (etwas wohin) tun I • **put sth. on** etwas anziehen (Kleidung); etwas aufsetzen (Hut) II 2 (40)
°**put on a show** eine Show aufführen, zeigen
puzzled ['pʌzld] verwirrt II 2 (41)
pyjamas (pl) [pəˈdʒɑːməz] Schlafanzug II 4 (61)

Q

quarter ['kwɔːtə]: **quarter past 11** Viertel nach 11 (11.15 / 23.15) I • **quarter to 12** Viertel vor 12 (11.45 / 23.45) I
question ['kwestʃn] Frage I • **ask questions** Fragen stellen I
quick [kwɪk] schnell I
quiet ['kwaɪət] leise, still, ruhig I
°**quite** [kwaɪt]: **they don't quite fit** sie passen nicht ganz, nicht richtig
quiz [kwɪz], pl **quizzes** ['kwɪzɪz] Quiz, Ratespiel I

R

rabbit ['ræbɪt] Kaninchen I
radio ['reɪdiəʊ] Radio I • **on the radio** im Radio I
°**raft** [rɑːft] Floß
railway ['reɪlweɪ] Eisenbahn II 4 (62)
rain [reɪn] Regen II Welc (6/150)
rain [reɪn] regnen II Welc (6/150)
°**rainforest** ['reɪnfɒrɪst] Regenwald
rainy ['reɪni] regnerisch II Welc (6/150) • **rainy season** Regenzeit II 2 (30)
ran [ræn] siehe **run**
rang [ræŋ] siehe **ring**
rap [ræp] Rap (rhythmischer Sprechgesang) I

°**rather** ['rɑːðə]: **I'd rather be ...** Ich wäre lieber ...
RE [ˌɑːrˈiː], **Religious Education** [rɪˌlɪdʒəs ˌedʒuˈkeɪʃn] Religion, Religionsunterricht I
read [riːd], **read, read** lesen I • °**read on** weiterlesen • °**read out** vorlesen • °**Read out loud.** Lies laut vor.
reader ['riːdə] Leser/in II 2 (26)
ready ['redi] bereit, fertig I • **get ready (for)** sich fertig machen (für), sich vorbereiten (auf) I • **get things ready** Dinge fertig machen, vorbereiten
real [rɪəl] echt, wirklich I
realize ['rɪəlaɪz] erkennen, merken I
really ['rɪəli] wirklich I
reason ['riːzn] Grund, Begründung I • **for lots of reasons** aus vielen Gründen I
°**recite a poem** [rɪˈsaɪt] ein Gedicht aufsagen, vortragen
recover (from) [rɪˈkʌvə] sich erholen (von) II 5 (79)
recycled [ˌriːˈsaɪkld] wiederverwertet, wiederverwendet, recycelt II 2 (32)
recycling [ˌriːˈsaɪklɪŋ] Wiederverwertung, Recycling II 2 (32)
red [red] rot I
°**reduced** [rɪˈdjuːst] reduziert, (im Preis) heruntergesetzt
°**refer to** [rɪˈfɜː] sich beziehen auf
rehearsal [rɪˈhɜːsl] Probe (am Theater) I
rehearse [rɪˈhɜːs] proben (am Theater) I
relative ['relətɪv] Verwandte(r) II 4 (60)
relax [rɪˈlæks] (sich) entspannen, sich ausruhen II 6 (94)
remember sth. [rɪˈmembə]
1. sich an etwas erinnern I
2. sich etwas merken I
°**Remember ...** Denk dran, ...
°**remind** [rɪˈmaɪnd]: **That reminds me ...** Dabei fällt mir ein ...
°**rent** [rent] leihen, mieten
°**repair** [rɪˈpeə] reparieren
repeat [rɪˈpiːt] wiederholen II 2 (30)
report (on) [rɪˈpɔːt] Bericht, Reportage (über) I
report (to sb.) [rɪˈpɔːt] jm. berichten II 3 (57/164)
reporter [rɪˈpɔːtə] Reporter/in II 4 (74)
°**rescue** ['reskjuː] Rettung(saktion)
rest [rest] Rest II 5 (90)
restart [ˌriːˈstɑːt] neu starten (Computer) II 4 (65)

restaurant ['restrɒnt] Restaurant II 6 (97)
result [rɪ'zʌlt] Ergebnis, Resultat I
revision [rɪ'vɪʒn] Wiederholung (des Lernstoffs) I
rhino ['raɪnəʊ] Nashorn II 3 (49/163)
°**rhyming** ['raɪmɪŋ]: **rhyming pair** Reimpaar • **rhyming words** Reimwörter
rich [rɪtʃ] reich II 5 (77)
ridden [rɪdn] siehe **ride**
ride [raɪd], **rode, ridden** reiten I • **ride a bike** Rad fahren I
ride [raɪd]: **(bike) ride** (Rad-)Fahrt, (Rad-)Tour II 3 (57/164) • **(bus) ride** (Bus-)Fahrt II 3 (57/164)
riding ['raɪdɪŋ] Reiten, Reitsport I • **go riding** ['raɪdɪŋ] reiten gehen I
right [raɪt] richtig I • **all right** [ɔːl 'raɪt] gut, in Ordnung II 1 (23) • **be right** Recht haben I • °**go right** gut laufen, (gut) klappen • **That's right.** Das ist richtig. / Das stimmt. I • **You need a school bag, right?** Du brauchst eine Schultasche, stimmt's? / nicht wahr? I
right [raɪt] rechte(r, s) I • **look right** nach rechts schauen I • **on the right** rechts, auf der rechten Seite I • **turn right** (nach) rechts abbiegen II 6 (97) • °**the right-hand column** die rechte Spalte
right [raɪt]: **right behind you** direkt/genau hinter dir II 1 (14) • **right now** jetzt sofort; jetzt gerade I
ring [rɪŋ] Ring II 5 (88)
ring [rɪŋ], **rang, rung** klingeln, läuten II 4 (72)
river ['rɪvə] Fluss II 4 (60)
road [rəʊd] Straße I • **Park Road** [ˌpɑːk 'rəʊd] Parkstraße I
°**rock** [rɒk] Fels, Felsen
rode [rəʊd] siehe **ride**
roll [rəʊl] Brötchen II 6 (106)
Roman ['rəʊmən] römisch; Römer, Römerin II 6 (94)
roof [ruːf] Dach II Welc (9)
room [ruːm, rʊm] Raum, Zimmer I
round [raʊnd] rund II 6 (94)
round [raʊnd] um ... (herum); in ... umher II Welc (6) • **the other way round** anders herum II 6 (106)
°**roundhouse** ['raʊndhaʊs] Rundhaus
°**route** [ruːt] Route, Weg
°**row** [rəʊ] rudern
royal ['rɔɪəl] königlich, Königs II 6 (96)
°**RSPCA (Royal Society for the Prevention of Cruelty to Animals)** [ˌrɔɪəl səˈsaɪəti fə ðə prɪˈvenʃn ˌəv ˈkruːəlti tuː ˈænɪmlz] britischer Tierschutzverein
rubber ['rʌbə] Radiergummi I
rubbish ['rʌbɪʃ] (Haus-)Müll, Abfall II 3 (46) • **rubbish collection** ['rʌbɪʃ kəˌlekʃn] Müllabfuhr II 3 (48)
rude [ruːd] unhöflich, unverschämt II 1 (13)
°**rule** [ruːl] Regel
ruler ['ruːlə] Lineal I
run [rʌn] (Wett-)Lauf II 3 (49)
run (-nn-) [rʌn], **ran, run** laufen, rennen I
rung [rʌŋ] siehe **ring**
runner ['rʌnə] Läufer/in II 3 (55)

S

sad [sæd] traurig II 2 (28)
safe (from) [seɪf] sicher, in Sicherheit (vor) II 3 (48)
said [sed] siehe **say**
°**sail** [seɪl] Segel
salad ['sæləd] Salat (als Gericht oder Beilage) I
°**sale** [seɪl] Ausverkauf, Schlussverkauf
same [seɪm]: **the same ...** der-/die-/dasselbe ...; dieselben ... I • **be/look the same** gleich sein/aussehen I
°**sand** [sænd] Sand
°**sandbank** ['sændbæŋk] Sandbank
sandwich ['sænwɪtʃ, 'sænwɪdʒ] Sandwich, (zusammengeklapptes) belegtes Brot I • °**sandwich box** Brotdose
sang [sæŋ] siehe **sing**
sat [sæt] siehe **sit**
Saturday ['sætədeɪ, 'sætədi] Samstag, Sonnabend I
sauna ['sɔːnə] Sauna II 6 (94) • **have a sauna** in die Sauna gehen II 6 (94)
sausage ['sɒsɪdʒ] (Brat-, Bock-)Würstchen, Wurst I
save [seɪv]
1. retten II 1 (22)
2. sparen II 2 (26)
°**saved** [seɪvd] gerettet
saw [sɔː] siehe **see**
say [seɪ], **said, said** sagen I • **It says here: ...** Hier steht: ... / Es heißt hier: ... II 4 (65) • **say goodbye** sich verabschieden I • **Say hi to Dilip for me.** Grüß Dilip von mir. I
say sorry sich entschuldigen II 5 (90)
°**saying** ['seɪɪŋ] Sprichwort, Redensart

scan (-nn-) [skæn]: **scan a text** einen Text schnell nach bestimmten Wörtern/Informationen absuchen II 3 (49) • °**scan sth. in** etwas einscannen
scared [skeəd] verängstigt I • **be scared (of)** Angst haben (vor) I
scary ['skeəri] unheimlich; gruselig I
scene [siːn] Szene I
school [skuːl] Schule I • **at school** in der Schule I • **school bag** Schultasche I • **school subject** Schulfach I
science ['saɪəns] Naturwissenschaft I
sea [siː] Meer, (die) See I • **at sea** auf See II 5 (82)
°**seal** [siːl] Robbe, Seehund
season ['siːzn] Jahreszeit II 2 (30) • **rainy season** Regenzeit II 2 (30)
second ['sekənd] Sekunde I
second ['sekənd] zweite(r, s) I
°**second-hand** [ˌsekənd 'hænd] gebraucht; aus zweiter Hand
section ['sekʃn] Abschnitt, Teil II 3 (57)
°**secure** [sɪ'kjʊə] sichern, absichern
see [siː], **saw, seen**
1. sehen I
2. **see sb.** jn. besuchen, jn. aufsuchen II 1 (23) • **See?** Siehst du? I • **See you.** Bis bald. / Tschüs. I
°**seem (to be/do)** [siːm] (zu sein/tun) scheinen
seen [siːn] siehe **see**
selection (of) [sɪ'lekʃn] Auswahl (an) II 2 (31)
sell [sel], **sold, sold** verkaufen I
send [send], **sent, sent** senden, schicken II 2 (30)
sent [sent] siehe **send**
sentence ['sentəns] Satz I
September [sep'tembə] September I
series, pl **series** ['sɪəriːz] (Sende-)Reihe, Serie II 3 (44)
°**servant** ['sɜːvənt] Diener/in
service ['sɜːvɪs] Dienst (am Kunden), Service II 2 (31)
set a trap (for sb.) (-tt-) [set], **set, set** (jm.) eine Falle stellen II 5 (88)
shape [ʃeɪp] Form, Gestalt II 5 (81)
share sth. (with sb.) [ʃeə] sich etwas teilen (mit jm.) I
she [ʃiː] sie I
sheep, pl **sheep** [ʃiːp] Schaf II 4 (60)
shelf [ʃelf], pl **shelves** [ʃelvz] Regal(brett) I
°**shelter (from)** ['ʃeltə] Schutz (vor)

Dictionary (English – German)

shine [ʃaɪn], **shone, shone** scheinen *(Sonne)* II Welc (6)
ship [ʃɪp] Schiff I
shirt [ʃɜːt] Hemd I
shiver [ˈʃɪvə] zittern II 6 (106)
shoe [ʃuː] Schuh I
shone [ʃɒn] *siehe* **shine**
shop [ʃɒp] Laden, Geschäft I
  shop assistant [ˈʃɒp_əˌsɪstənt] Verkäufer/in I
shop (-pp-) [ʃɒp] einkaufen (gehen) I
shopping [ˈʃɒpɪŋ] (das) Einkaufen I • **go shopping** einkaufen gehen I • **shopping list** Einkaufsliste I
°**shore** [ʃɔː] Ufer, Strand
short [ʃɔːt] kurz I
shorts *(pl)* [ʃɔːts] Shorts, kurze Hose I
▶ S.157 Plural words
should [ʃəd, ʃʊd]: **you should ...** du solltest ... / ihr solltet ... I
shoulder [ˈʃəʊldə] Schulter I
shout [ʃaʊt] schreien, rufen I
  shout at sb. jn. anschreien I
show [ʃəʊ] Show, Vorstellung I
show [ʃəʊ], **showed, shown** zeigen I
shower [ˈʃaʊə] Dusche I • **have a shower** (sich) duschen I
shown [ʃəʊn] *siehe* **show**
shut up [ˌʃʌt_ˈʌp], **shut, shut** den Mund halten II 5 (88)
shy [ʃaɪ] schüchtern, scheu II 3 (57)
side [saɪd] Seite II 4 (72)
sights *(pl)* [saɪts] Sehenswürdigkeiten II 1 (12)
°**signal** [ˈsɪɡnəl] Signal, Zeichen
silent letter [ˌsaɪlənt ˈletə] „stummer" Buchstabe *(nicht gesprochener Buchstabe)* II 4 (71)
silly [ˈsɪli] albern, dumm II 5 (80)
°**silver** [ˈsɪlvə] Silber
sing [sɪŋ], **sang, sung** singen I
singer [ˈsɪŋə] Sänger/in II 3 (55)
single [ˈsɪŋɡl] ledig, alleinstehend I • **a single parent** ein(e) Alleinerziehende(r) II 3 (51)
sink [sɪŋk] Spüle, Spülbecken I
°**Sir** [sɜː] Sir *(britischer Adelstitel)*
sister [ˈsɪstə] Schwester I
sit (-tt-) [sɪt], **sat, sat** sitzen; sich setzen I • **sit down** sich hinsetzen II 1 (22/155) • **sit up** sich aufsetzen II 1 (22) • **Sit with me.** Setz dich zu mir. / Setzt euch zu mir. I
size [saɪz] Größe I
skate [skeɪt] Inliner/Skateboard fahren I
skateboard [ˈskeɪtbɔːd] Skateboard I
skates *(pl)* [skeɪts] Inliner I

sketch [sketʃ] Sketch I
skills file [ˈskɪlz faɪl] Anhang mit Lern- und Arbeitstechniken I
°**skin** [skɪn] Haut
skirt [skɜːt] Rock II 2 (27)
sky [skaɪ] Himmel II Welc (7) • **in the sky** am Himmel II Welc (7/151)
slave [sleɪv] Sklave, Sklavin II 5 (77)
sleep [sliːp], **slept, slept** schlafen I
  °**sleep late** lange schlafen
slept [slept] *siehe* **sleep**
slow [sləʊ] langsam II 1 (12/153)
°**slug** [slʌɡ] Nacktschnecke
small [smɔːl] klein II 2 (29)
smell [smel] riechen II 4 (62)
smell [smel] Geruch II 4 (62/165)
smile [smaɪl] lächeln I • **smile at sb.** jn. anlächeln II 3 (57)
smile Lächeln II 4 (62/165)
smoothie [ˈsmuːði] dickflüssiger Fruchtshake mit Milch, Joghurt oder Eiscreme II 5 (80)
snack [snæk] Snack, Imbiss II 5 (76)
snake [sneɪk] Schlange I
snow [snəʊ] Schnee II Welc (6/150)
so [səʊ]
1. also; deshalb, daher I • **So? Und? / Na und?** II 5 (88) • **So what?** [ˌsəʊ ˈwɒt] Und? / Na und? II 1 (22)
2. **so sweet** so süß I • °**so that** sodass
3. **I hope so.** Ich hoffe es. II 2 (30) **I think so.** Ich glaube (ja). I • **I don't think so.** Das finde/glaube ich nicht. I • **Do you really think so?** Meinst du wirklich? / Glaubst du das wirklich? II 1 (14)
soap [səʊp] Seife I
°**society** [səˈsaɪəti] Gesellschaft, Vereinigung
sock [sɒk] Socke, Strumpf I
sofa [ˈsəʊfə] Sofa I
°**soft** [sɒft]: **the softest softboot** der weichste Softboot
software [ˈsɒftweə] Software II 4 (65)
°**solar system** [ˈsəʊlə ˌsɪstəm] Sonnensystem
sold [səʊld] *siehe* **sell**
some [səm, sʌm] einige, ein paar I **some cheese/juice/money** etwas Käse/Saft/Geld I
somebody [ˈsʌmbədi] jemand I **Find/Ask somebody who ...** Finde/Frage jemanden, der ... II 1 (20)
▶ S.158 somebody – anybody
something [ˈsʌmθɪŋ] etwas I
▶ S.158 something – anything
sometimes [ˈsʌmtaɪmz] manchmal I
somewhere [ˈsʌmweə] irgendwo(hin) II 2 (29/158)
▶ S.158 somewhere – anywhere

son [sʌn] Sohn I
song [sɒŋ] Lied, Song I
soon [suːn] bald I • **as soon as** sobald, sowie II 3 (47)
sore [sɔː]: **be sore** wund sein, wehtun II 4 (64) • **have a sore throat** Halsschmerzen haben II 4 (64)
▶ S.167 What's wrong with you?
sorry [ˈsɒri]: **(I'm) sorry.** Entschuldigung. / Tut mir leid. I • **Sorry, I'm late.** Entschuldigung, dass ich zu spät bin/komme. I • **Sorry? Wie bitte?** I • **say sorry** sich entschuldigen II 5 (90)
sort (of) [sɔːt] Art, Sorte II 3 (44)
sound [saʊnd] klingen, sich *(gut usw.)* anhören I
sound [saʊnd] Laut; Klang I
soup [suːp] Suppe II 4 (62)
south [saʊθ] Süden; nach Süden; südlich II 4 (62) • **south-east** [ˌsaʊθˈiːst] Südosten; nach Südosten; südöstlich II 4 (62/166) **south-west** [ˌsaʊθˈwest] Südwesten; nach Südwesten; südwestlich II 4 (62/166)
°**souvenir** [ˌsuːvəˈnɪə] Andenken, Souvenir
space [speɪs]
1. Weltraum II 6 (99)
2. **Move back one space.** Geh ein Feld zurück. II 5 (76) • **Move on one space.** Geh ein Feld vor. II 5 (76)
spaghetti [spəˈɡeti] Spaghetti II Welc (9)
speak (to) [spiːk], **spoke, spoken** sprechen (mit), reden (mit) II Welc (9)
special [ˈspeʃl] besondere(r, s) II 5 (88) • **Did you do anything special?** Habt ihr irgendetwas Besonderes gemacht? I • °**special offer** Sonderangebot
°**speech bubble** [ˈspiːtʃ bʌbl] Sprechblase
spell [spel] buchstabieren I
°**spelling** [ˈspelɪŋ] Schreibung, Schreibweise
spend [spend], **spent, spent: spend money (on)** Geld ausgeben (für) II 2 (26) • **spend time (on)** Zeit verbringen (mit) II 2 (26)
spent [spent] *siehe* **spend**
°**spider** [ˈspaɪdə] Spinne
spoke [spəʊk] *siehe* **speak**
spoken [ˈspəʊkən] *siehe* **speak**
sport [spɔːt] Sport; Sportart I **do sport** Sport treiben I
sports gear *(no pl)* [ˈspɔːts ɡɪə] Sportausrüstung, Sportsachen II 2 (27)

Dictionary (English – German)

spring [sprɪŋ]
1. Frühling I
°2. Quelle
spy [spaɪ] Spion/in I
square [skweə] Platz *(in der Stadt)* II 6 (98)
°**squeeze** [skwiːz]**: they squeeze me so tight** sie drücken mich so sehr *(Schuhe)*
squirrel [ˈskwɪrəl] Eichhörnchen II 3 (45)
stage [steɪdʒ] Bühne I
stairs *(pl)* [steəz] Treppe; Treppenstufen I
stamp [stæmp] Briefmarke I
stand [stænd]**, stood, stood**
1. stehen; sich (hin)stellen II 2 (40)
°**stand 400 metres high** 400 Meter hoch sein
2. ertragen, aushalten, ausstehen II 3 (56) • **I can't stand it.** Ich kann es nicht ertragen/aushalten/ausstehen. II 3 (56)
star [stɑː]
1. Stern II 6 (99)
2. (Film-, Pop-)Star I
start [stɑːt] starten, anfangen, beginnen (mit) I
°**statement** [ˈsteɪtmənt] Aussage, Aussagesatz
station [ˈsteɪʃn] Bahnhof I • **at the station** am Bahnhof I
statue [ˈstætʃuː] Statue II 5 (79)
°**Statue of Liberty** [ˌstætʃuː_əv ˈlɪbəti] Freiheitsstatue
stay [steɪ] bleiben; wohnen, übernachten II Welc (7)
steal [stiːl]**, stole, stolen** stehlen II 5 (81)
step [step] Schritt I
stick on [ˌstɪk_ˈɒn]**, stuck, stuck** aufkleben I
still [stɪl]
1. (immer) noch I
2. trotzdem, dennoch II 6 (99)
stole [stəʊl] *siehe* **steal**
stolen [ˈstəʊlən] *siehe* **steal**
stomach [ˈstʌmək] Magen II 4 (64/167) • **stomach ache** Magenschmerzen, Bauchweh II 4 (64/167)
▶ S.167 What's wrong with you?
stone [stəʊn] Stein II 6 (94)
stood [stʊd] *siehe* **stand**
stop (-pp-) [stɒp]
1. aufhören I
2. anhalten I
Stop that! Hör auf damit! / Lass das! I
storm [stɔːm] Sturm; Gewitter II Welc (6/150)

stormy [ˈstɔːmi] stürmisch II Welc (6/150)
story [ˈstɔːri] Geschichte, Erzählung I
straight on [streɪt_ˈɒn] geradeaus weiter II 6 (97)
strange [streɪndʒ] seltsam, sonderbar I
strawberry [ˈstrɔːbəri] Erdbeere II 5 (80)
street [striːt] Straße I • **at 7 Hamilton Street** in der Hamiltonstraße 7 I
°**stretch** [stretʃ] sich strecken
strong [strɒŋ] stark II 4 (72)
structure [ˈstrʌktʃə] strukturieren, aufbauen II 5 (81)
stuck [stʌk] *siehe* **stick**
student [ˈstjuːdənt] Schüler/in; Student/in I
studio [ˈstjuːdiəʊ] Studio I
°**study** [ˈstʌdi] studieren
study skills *(pl)* [ˈstʌdi skɪlz] Lern- und Arbeitstechniken I
stuff [stʌf] Zeug, Kram I
subject [ˈsʌbdʒɪkt]
1. Subjekt I
2. Schulfach I
subway [ˈsʌbweɪ]**: the subway** *(AE)* die U-Bahn II 1 (12)
suddenly [ˈsʌdnli] plötzlich, auf einmal I
sugar [ˈʃʊɡə] Zucker II 5 (77)
°**suggestion** [səˈdʒestʃən] Vorschlag
°**summarize** [ˈsʌməraɪz] zusammenfassen
summer [ˈsʌmə] Sommer I
sun [sʌn] Sonne II Welc (6/150)
Sunday [ˈsʌndeɪ, ˈsʌndi] Sonntag I
sung [sʌŋ] *siehe* **sing**
sunglasses *(pl)* [ˈsʌnɡlɑːsɪz] (eine) Sonnenbrille I
▶ S.157 Plural words
sunny [ˈsʌni] sonnig II Welc (6/150)
supermarket [ˈsuːpəmɑːkɪt] Supermarkt I
suppose [səˈpəʊz] annehmen, vermuten I
sure [ʃʊə, ʃɔː] sicher I
surf the internet [sɜːf] im Internet surfen II 4 (65/168)
surfboard [ˈsɜːfbɔːd] Surfbrett II Welc (9/152)
surfing [ˈsɜːfɪŋ]**: go surfing** wellenreiten gehen, surfen gehen II Welc (9)
°**surprise** [səˈpraɪz] Überraschung
survey (on) [ˈsɜːveɪ] Umfrage, Untersuchung (über) II 2 (26)
survival [səˈvaɪvl] Überleben II 3 (44/161)
survive [səˈvaɪv] überleben II 3 (44)

°**swallow** [ˈswɒləʊ] verschlucken, hinunterschlucken
swam [swæm] *siehe* **swim**
swap (-pp-) [swɒp] tauschen I
sweatshirt [ˈswetʃɜːt] Sweatshirt I
sweet [swiːt] süß I
sweetheart [ˈswiːthɑːt] Liebling, Schatz II 5 (56)
sweets *(pl)* Süßigkeiten I
swim (-mm-) [swɪm]**, swam, swum** schwimmen I
swimmer [ˈswɪmə] Schwimmer/in II 1 (22)
swimming [ˈswɪmɪŋ] Schwimmen I • **go swimming** schwimmen gehen I
swimming pool [ˈswɪmɪŋ puːl] Schwimmbad, Schwimmbecken II Welc (6)
swum [swʌm] *siehe* **swim**
syllable [ˈsɪləbl] Silbe I

T

table [ˈteɪbl] Tisch I • **table tennis** [ˈteɪbl tenɪs] Tischtennis I
take [teɪk]**, took, taken**
1. nehmen I
2. (weg-, hin)bringen I
°**it takes 50 seconds** es dauert 50 Sekunden • **Take another turn.** hier: Würfel noch einmal. II 5 (76)
take notes sich Notizen machen I
take sth. off etwas ausziehen *(Kleidung)*; etwas absetzen *(Hut)* II 2 (40/160) • **take 10c off** 10 Cent abziehen I • **take sth. out** etwas herausnehmen I • **take photos** Fotos machen, fotografieren I
take place stattfinden II 5 (81)
°**Take turns.** Wechselt euch ab.
I'll take it. *(beim Einkaufen)* Ich werde es (ihn, sie) nehmen. / Ich nehme es (ihn, sie). I
taken [ˈteɪkən] *siehe* **take**
°**talk** [tɔːk] Vortrag, Referat, Rede
talk [tɔːk]**: talk (about)** reden (über), sich unterhalten (über) I • **talk (to)** reden (mit), sich unterhalten (mit) I
°**tall** [tɔːl] groß (gewachsen)
°**task** [tɑːsk] Aufgabe
taught [tɔːt] *siehe* **teach**
tea [tiː] Tee; *(auch:)* leichte Nachmittags- oder Abendmahlzeit I
teach [tiːtʃ]**, taught, taught** unterrichten, lehren I
teacher [ˈtiːtʃə] Lehrer/in I
team [tiːm] Team, Mannschaft I
tear [tɪə] Träne II 3 (57)

°**technology** [tek'nɒlədʒi]: **the latest technology** die neueste Technologie
teenager ['tiːneɪdʒə] Teenager, Jugendliche(r) II 1 (23)
teeth [tiːθ] *Plural von „tooth"* I
telephone ['telɪfəʊn] Telefon I
  telephone number Telefonnummer I
°**telescope** ['telɪskəʊp] Teleskop I
television (TV) ['telɪvɪʒn] Fernsehen I
tell (about) [tel], **told, told** erzählen (von), berichten (über) I • **Tell me your names.** Sagt mir eure Namen. I • **tell sb. the way** jm. den Weg beschreiben II 6 (96/174)
temperature ['temprətʃə] Temperatur II 4 (64) • **have a temperature** Fieber haben II 4 (64)
  ▶ S.167 What's wrong with you?
°**temple** ['templ] Tempel
tennis ['tenɪs] Tennis I
°**tent** [tent] Zelt I
term [tɜːm] Trimester II 6 (105)
terrible ['terəbl] schrecklich, furchtbar I
°**territory** ['terətri] Revier, Gebiet, Territorium
test [test] Klassenarbeit, Test, Prüfung II 2 (28)
text [tekst] Text I
text message ['tekst ˌmesɪdʒ] SMS II Welc (6/151)
text sb. [tekst] jm. eine SMS schicken II Welc (6)
than [ðæn, ðən] als II 2 (31/159)
  more than me mehr als ich II 2 (131)
Thank you. ['θæŋk juː] Danke (schön). I • **Thanks.** [θæŋks] Danke. I • **Thanks a lot!** Vielen Dank! I • **Thanks very much!** Danke sehr! / Vielen Dank! II 2 (30/158)
that [ðət, ðæt]
  1. das (dort) I
  2. jene(r, s) I
  That's me. Das bin ich. I • **That's right.** Das ist richtig. / Das stimmt. I • **that's why** deshalb, darum I
that [ðət, ðæt] dass I • °**so that** sodass
that [ðət, ðæt]: **something that happens in August** etwas, das im August passiert II 5 (78)
the [ðə, ði] der, die, das; die I
theatre ['θɪətə] Theater II 6 (96)
their [ðeə] ihr, ihre *(Plural)* I
theirs [ðeəz] ihrer, ihre, ihrs II 2 (128)
them [ðəm, ðem] sie; ihnen I
  the two of them die beiden; alle beide II 3 (57)

theme park ['θiːm pɑːk] Themenpark II 4 (60)
then [ðen]
  1. dann, danach I
  2. damals II 2 (31)
  Then what? Was dann? II 3 (46)
  just then genau in dem Moment; gerade dann II 3 (48)
there [ðeə]
  1. da, dort I
  2. dahin, dorthin I
  down there (nach) dort unten II 4 (72) • **in there** dort drinnen I • **over there** da drüben, dort drüben I • **there are** es sind (vorhanden); es gibt I • **there's** es ist (vorhanden); es gibt I • **there isn't a ...** es ist kein/e ...; es gibt kein/e ... I
thermometer [θə'mɒmɪtə] Thermometer II 4 (64)
these [ðiːz] diese, die (hier) I
they [ðeɪ] sie *(Plural)* I
thief [θiːf], *pl* **thieves** [θiːvz] Dieb/in II 5 (81)
thing [θɪŋ] Ding, Sache I • **What was the best thing about ...?** Was war das Beste an ...? II 1 (12)
think [θɪŋk], **thought, thought** glauben, meinen, denken I • **Do you really think so?** Meinst du wirklich? / Glaubst du das wirklich? II 1 (14) • **I think so.** Ich glaube (ja). I • **I don't think so.** Das finde/glaube ich nicht. I • **think about**
  1. nachdenken über II 4 (73/170);
  2. denken über, halten von II 4 (73/170) • **think of** 1. denken über, halten von II 4 (73/170);
  2. denken an; sich ausdenken II 4 (73/170)
  ▶ S.170 (to) think
third [θɜːd] dritte(r, s) I
thirsty ['θɜːsti] durstig I • **be thirsty** Durst haben, durstig sein I
this [ðɪs]
  1. dies (hier) I
  2. diese(r, s) I
  This is Isabel. Hier spricht Isabel. / Hier ist Isabel. *(am Telefon)* II 6 (98)
  this morning/afternoon/evening heute Morgen/Nachmittag/Abend I • **this way** hier entlang, in diese Richtung II 5 (89)
those [ðəʊz] die (da), jene (dort) I
thought [θɔːt] *siehe* **think**
thousand ['θaʊznd] tausend I
threw [θruː] *siehe* **throw**
throat Hals, Kehle II 4 (64) • **have a sore throat** [sɔː 'θrəʊt] Halsschmerzen haben II 4 (64)
  ▶ S.167 What's wrong with you?
through [θruː] durch II Welc (9)

throw [θrəʊ], **threw, thrown** werfen I • **throw the dice** würfeln II 5 (76)
thrown [θrəʊn] *siehe* **throw**
Thursday ['θɜːzdeɪ, 'θɜːzdi] Donnerstag I
°**tick** [tɪk] Häkchen
ticket ['tɪkɪt] Eintrittskarte I
°**tickle** ['tɪkl] kitzeln
tide [taɪd] Gezeiten, Ebbe und Flut II 1 (22) • **the tide is in** es ist Flut II 1 (22/155) • **the tide is out** es ist Ebbe II 1 (22/155)
tidy ['taɪdi] aufräumen I
tidy ['taɪdi] ordentlich, aufgeräumt II 3 (56)
tiger ['taɪgə] Tiger II 3 (49/163)
°**tight** [taɪt]: **they squeeze me so tight** sie drücken mich so sehr *(Schuhe)*
till [tɪl] bis *(zeitlich)* I
time [taɪm] Zeit; Uhrzeit I • **in time** rechtzeitig II 1 (23) • **What's the time?** Wie spät ist es? I
time(s) [taɪm(z)] Mal(e); -mal II 1 (12) • **for the first time** zum ersten Mal II 1 (20)
°**timeless** ['taɪmləs] zeitlos
timetable ['taɪmteɪbl] Stundenplan I
tired ['taɪəd] müde I
title ['taɪtl] Titel, Überschrift I
to [tə, tu]
  1. zu, nach I • **an e-mail to** eine E-Mail an I • **to Jenny's** zu Jenny I • **to the front** nach vorn I • **I've never been to Bath.** Ich bin noch nie in Bath gewesen. II 6 (96)
  write to schreiben an I
  2. **quarter to 12** Viertel vor 12 (11.45 / 23.45) I
  3. **try to do** versuchen, zu tun I
  4. **um zu** I
toast [təʊst] Toast(brot) I
today [tə'deɪ] heute I
toe [təʊ] Zeh I
together [tə'geðə] zusammen I
toilet ['tɔɪlət] Toilette I
told [təʊld] *siehe* **tell**
tomato [tə'mɑːtəʊ], *pl* **tomatoes** Tomate II 6 (106)
tomorrow [tə'mɒrəʊ] morgen I
°**tongue-twister** ['tʌŋtwɪstə] Zungenbrecher
tonight [tə'naɪt] heute Nacht, heute Abend I
too [tuː]: **from Bristol too** auch aus Bristol I • **Me too.** Ich auch. I
too much/big/... [tuː] zu viel/groß/ ... I
took [tʊk] *siehe* **take**
°**tool** [tuːl] Werkzeug

Dictionary (English – German)

tooth [tuːθ], pl **teeth** [tiːθ] Zahn I
toothache ['tuːθeɪk] Zahnschmerzen II 4 (64/167)
▶ S.167 What's wrong with you?
top [tɒp]
1. Spitze, oberes Ende I • **at the top (of)** oben, am oberen Ende, an der Spitze (von) I
2. Top, Oberteil I
topic ['tɒpɪk] Thema, Themenbereich I • **topic sentence** Satz, der in das Thema eines Absatzes einführt II 4 (62)
tortoise ['tɔːtəs] Schildkröte I
touch [tʌtʃ] berühren, anfassen I
tour (of the house) [tʊə] Rundgang, Tour (durch das Haus) I
tourist ['tʊərɪst] Tourist/in II 5 (76)
tourist information Fremdenverkehrsamt II 5 (76)
towards Mr Green [tə'wɔːdz] auf Mr Green zu, in Mr Greens Richtung I
towel ['taʊəl] Handtuch II 6 (94)
tower ['taʊə] Turm I
town [taʊn] Stadt I
trade [treɪd] Handel II 5 (77)
°**tradition** [trə'dɪʃn] Tradition I
°**traditional** [trə'dɪʃənl] traditionell I
traffic ['træfɪk] Verkehr II 4 (60)
train [treɪn] Zug I • **on the train** im Zug I
trainers (pl) ['treɪnəz] Turnschuhe II 2 (29)
°**translate** [træns'leɪt] übersetzen I
trap [træp] Falle II 5 (88)
travel (-ll-) ['trævl] reisen II Welc (7)
°**travels** (pl) ['trævlz] Reisen I
tree [triː] Baum I
trick [trɪk]
1. (Zauber-)Kunststück, Trick I • **do tricks** (Zauber-)Kunststücke machen I
2. Streich II 6 (98) • **play a trick on sb.** jm. einen Streich spielen II 6 (98)
trip [trɪp] Reise; Ausflug I • **go on a trip** einen Ausflug/eine Reise machen II Welc (7/151)
trouble ['trʌbl] Schwierigkeiten, Ärger II 1 (14) • **be in trouble** in Schwierigkeiten sein; Ärger kriegen II 1 (14)
°**troubled** ['trʌbld] besorgt, bekümmert I
trousers (pl) ['traʊzəz] Hose II 2 (27)
▶ S.157 Plural words
°**truck** [trʌk] Lastwagen, LKW I
°**true** [truː] wahr II 6 (107) • **come true** wahr werden II 6 (107)
try [traɪ]
1. versuchen I

2. probieren, kosten I
try and do sth. / try to do sth. versuchen, etwas zu tun I • **try sth. on** etwas anprobieren (Kleidung) I
T-shirt ['tiːʃɜːt] T-Shirt I
Tuesday ['tjuːzdeɪ, 'tjuːzdi] Dienstag I
°**tuna (fish)** ['tjuːnə] Thunfisch I
tunnel ['tʌnl] Tunnel II 5 (79)
turn [tɜːn]
1. sich umdrehen II 3 (57) • **turn left/right** (nach) links/rechts abbiegen II 6 (97) • **turn to sb.** sich jm. zuwenden; sich an jn. wenden II 6 (97/175)
2. **turn sth. off** etwas ausschalten I **turn sth. on** etwas einschalten I
▶ S.175 (to) turn
turn [tɜːn]: **(It's) my turn.** Ich bin dran / an der Reihe. I • **Miss a turn.** Einmal aussetzen. II 5 (76) **Take another turn.** hier: Würfel noch einmal. II 5 (76) • °**Take turns.** Wechselt euch ab. I
TV [tiːˈviː] Fernsehen I • **on TV** im Fernsehen I • **watch TV** fernsehen I
twin [twɪn]: **twin brother** Zwillingsbruder I • °**twin-pack** Doppelpack(ung) • **twins** (pl) Zwillinge I • **twin town** Partnerstadt I

U

uncle ['ʌŋkl] Onkel I
unclear [ˌʌn'klɪə] unklar, undeutlich II 1 (21)
uncomfortable [ʌn'kʌmftəbl] unbequem II 1 (21)
unconscious [ʌn'kɒnʃəs] bewusstlos II 4 (73)
under ['ʌndə] unter I
underground [ˌʌndəgraʊnd]: **the underground** die U-Bahn II 1 (12)
°**underline** [ˌʌndə'laɪn] unterstreichen I
°**underneath** [ˌʌndə'niːθ] unter I
°**undersea** ['ʌndəsiː] Unterwasser- I
understand [ˌʌndə'stænd], **understood, understood** verstehen, begreifen I
understood [ˌʌndə'stʊd] siehe **understand**
unfair [ˌʌn'feə] unfair, ungerecht II 1 (21)
unfriendly [ʌn'frendli] unfreundlich II 1 (15)
unhappy [ʌn'hæpi] unglücklich II 1 (15)
uniform ['juːnɪfɔːm] Uniform I

uninteresting [ʌn'ɪntrəstɪŋ] uninteressant II 1 (21)
unit ['juːnɪt] Kapitel, Lektion I
°**university** [ˌjuːnɪ'vɜːsəti] Universität, Hochschule I
unsure [ˌʌn'ʃʊə, ˌʌn'ʃɔː] unsicher II 1 (21)
°**unwanted** [ˌʌn'wɒntɪd] unerwünscht, ungewollt I
up [ʌp] hinauf, herauf, nach oben I • **up the hill** den Hügel hinauf II 4 (73)
°**update** [ˌʌp'deɪt] aktualisieren, auf den neuesten Stand bringen I
upstairs [ˌʌp'steəz] oben; nach oben I
us [əs, ʌs] uns I
use [juːz] benutzen, verwenden I
°**useful** ['juːsfl] nützlich I
usually ['juːʒuəli] meistens, gewöhnlich, normalerweise I

V

valley ['væli] Tal II 4 (60) • **valley floor** Talboden II 4 (72)
°**value** ['væljuː]: **the best value for your money** etwa: das beste Preis-Leistungs-Verhältnis I
°**veggie burger** ['vedʒi ˌbɜːgə] Gemüseburger I
°**verse** [vɜːs] Strophe, Vers I
very ['veri] sehr I • **like/love sth. very much** etwas sehr mögen/ sehr lieben II 2 (30) • **Thanks very much!** Danke sehr! / Vielen Dank! II 2 (30/158)
view [vjuː] Aussicht, Blick II Welc (6) **point of view** [ˌpɔɪnt_əv 'vjuː] Standpunkt II 2 (41) • **from my point of view** aus meiner Sicht; von meinem Standpunkt aus gesehen II 2 (41/160)
villa ['vɪlə] Ferienhaus; Villa II Welc (7)
village ['vɪlɪdʒ] Dorf I
visit ['vɪzɪt] besuchen, aufsuchen II 2 (30)
visit ['vɪzɪt] Besuch II 3 (57/164)
visitor ['vɪzɪtə] Besucher/in, Gast I
vocabulary [və'kæbjələri] Vokabelverzeichnis, Wörterverzeichnis I
voice [vɔɪs] Stimme I
volleyball ['vɒlibɔːl] Volleyball I
°**volunteer** [ˌvɒlən'tɪə] Freiwillige(r) I
°**vowel sound** ['vaʊəl saʊnd] Vokallaut II 1 (17)

W

wait (for) ['weɪt fɔː] warten (auf) I
 I can't wait to see ... ich kann es kaum erwarten, ... zu sehen I
 Wait a minute. Warte mal! / Moment mal! II 2 (31)
walk [wɔːk] (zu Fuß) gehen I
walk [wɔːk] Spaziergang II Welc (7/151) • **go for a walk** spazieren gehen, einen Spaziergang machen II Welc (7/151)
wall [wɔːl] Wand; Mauer II 6 (94)
°**Wallop!** ['wɒləp] Schepper!
want [wɒnt] (haben) wollen I
 want to do tun wollen I
wardrobe ['wɔːdrəʊb] Kleiderschrank I
°**warehouse** ['weəhaʊs] Lagerhaus, -halle
warm [wɔːm] warm II Welc (6/150)
was [wəz, wɒz]: **(I/he/she/it) was** *siehe* **be**
wash [wɒʃ] waschen I • **I wash my hands.** Ich wasche mir die Hände. I
washing machine ['wɒʃɪŋ məˌʃiːn] Waschmaschine II 6 (100)
watch [wɒtʃ] beobachten, sich *etwas* ansehen; zusehen I • **watch TV** fernsehen I
watch [wɒtʃ] Armbanduhr I
water ['wɔːtə] Wasser I
°**waterfall** ['wɔːtəfɔːl] Wasserfall
wave [weɪv] winken II 1 (22)
°**wave** [weɪv] Welle
way [weɪ]
 1. Weg; Strecke II 6 (96) • **a long way (from)** weit entfernt (von) I **ask sb. the way** jn. nach dem Weg fragen II 6 (96/174) • **on the way (to)** auf dem Weg (zu/nach) II 6 (96/174) • **tell sb. the way** jm. den Weg beschreiben II 6 (96/174)
 2. Richtung II 5 (89) • **the other way round** anders herum II 6 (106) **the wrong way** in die falsche Richtung II 5 (89) • **this way** hier entlang, in diese Richtung II 5 (89) **which way?** in welche Richtung? / wohin? II 6 (96/174)
 3. No way! [ˌnəʊ 'weɪ] Auf keinen Fall! / Kommt nicht in Frage! II 1 (14)
 ▶ S.174 way
we [wiː] wir I
weak [wiːk] schwach II 4 (72/169)
wear [weə], **wore, worn** tragen, anhaben *(Kleidung)* I
weather ['weðə] Wetter II Welc (6/150)
webcam ['webkæm] Webcam, Internetkamera II 4 (65)
website ['websaɪt] Website II 3 (47)
Wednesday ['wenzdeɪ, 'wenzdi] Mittwoch I
week [wiːk] Woche I • **days of the week** Wochentage I
weekend [ˌwiːk'end] Wochenende I • **at the weekend** am Wochenende I
welcome ['welkəm]
 1. Welcome (to Bristol). Willkommen (in Bristol). I
 2. You're welcome. Gern geschehen. / Nichts zu danken. I
welcome sb. (to) ['welkəm] jn. begrüßen, willkommen heißen (in) I
 They welcome you to ... Sie heißen dich in ... willkommen I
well [wel] *(gesundheitlich)* gut; gesund, wohlauf II 4 (63)
 ▶ S.167 What's wrong with you?
well [wel] gut II 3 (49) • **go well** gut (ver)laufen, gutgehen II 6 (101) **You looked after them well.** Du hast dich gut um sie gekümmert. II 3 (49) • **Oh well ...** Na ja ... / Na gut ... • **Well, ...** Nun, ... / Also, ... I
Welsh [welʃ] walisisch; Walisisch II 4 (61)
went [went] *siehe* **go**
were [wə, wɜː]: **(we/you/they) were** *siehe* **be**
°**were-rabbit** [ˌweə 'ræbɪt] Werwolf-Kaninchen
west [west] Westen; nach Westen; westlich II 4 (62/166) • °**the West Country** umgangssprachliche Bezeichnung für den Südwesten Englands
wet [wet] feucht, nass II 2 (30)
what [wɒt]
 1. was I
 2. welche(r, s) I
 So what? [ˌsəʊ 'wɒt] Und? / Na und? II 1 (22) • **Then what?** Was dann? II 3 (46) • **What about ...?**
 1. Was ist mit ...? / Und ...? I; **2.** Wie wär's mit ...? I • **What are you talking about?** Wovon redest du? I • **What can I get you?** Was kann/darf ich euch/Ihnen bringen? II 5 (80) • **What colour is ...?** Welche Farbe hat ...? I • **What for?** [ˌwɒt 'fɔː] Wofür? II 2 (29) • **What have we got next?** Was haben wir als Nächstes? I • **What page are we on?** Auf welcher Seite sind wir? I • **What's for homework?** Was haben wir als Hausaufgabe auf? I **What's the time?** Wie spät ist es? I • **What's the matter?** Was ist los? / Was ist denn? II 2 (28)
What's wrong with you? Was fehlt dir? II 4 (64/167) • **What's your name?** Wie heißt du? I • **What was the weather like?** Wie war das Wetter? II Welc (7)
°**wheatgrass** ['wiːtgrɑːs] Weizengras
wheelchair ['wiːltʃeə] Rollstuhl I
°**wheels** *(pl)* [wiːlz] *(umgangssprachlich für:)* fahrbarer Untersatz *(wörtlich:* Räder*)*
when [wen] wann I • **When's your birthday?** Wann hast du Geburtstag? I
when [wen]
 1. wenn I
 2. als I
where [weə]
 1. wo I
 2. wohin I
 Where are you from? Wo kommst du her? I
°**wherever** [weər'evə] wo auch immer
which [wɪtʃ]: **Which picture ...?** Welches Bild ...? I • **which way?** in welche Richtung? / wohin? II 6 (96/174)
which [wɪtʃ]: **a project which starts with a quiz** ein Projekt, das mit einem Quiz beginnt II 5 (78)
°**while** [waɪl] während
whisper ['wɪspə] flüstern I
whistle ['wɪsl] pfeifen II 5 (88)
whistle ['wɪsl] Pfiff; (Triller-)Pfeife II 5 (88/173)
white [waɪt] weiß I
who [huː]
 1. wer I
 2. wen / wem II 1 (15)
 Who did she talk to? Mit wem hat sie geredet? II 1 (15)
who [huː]: **Find/Ask somebody who ...** Finde/Frage jemanden, der ... II 1 (20) • **the people who come to ...** die Menschen, die nach ... kommen II 5 (78)
whole [həʊl] ganze(r, s), gesamte(r, s) II 2 (30) • **the whole of 2006** das ganze Jahr 2006 II 2 (30)
whose [huːz] wessen II 2 (28)
 Whose are these? Wem gehören diese? II 2 (28/157)
whose [huːz]: **the man whose statue ...** der Mann, dessen Statue ... II 5 (79)
why [waɪ] warum I • **Why me?** Warum ich? I • **that's why** deshalb, darum I
wife [waɪf], *pl* **wives** [waɪvz] Ehefrau II 4 (73)
wild [waɪld] wild II 2 (31)

Dictionary (English – German) 199

will [wɪl]: **you'll be cold (= you will be cold)** du wirst frieren; ihr werdet frieren II 3 (46)
win (-nn-) [wɪn], **won, won** gewinnen
wind [wɪnd] Wind I
window ['wɪndəʊ] Fenster I
windy ['wɪndi] windig I
winner ['wɪnə] Gewinner/in, Sieger/in II 3 (55)
winter ['wɪntə] Winter I
°**wisdom** ['wɪzdəm] Weisheit
°**wise** [waɪz] weise
with [wɪð]
  1. mit I
  2. bei I
  Sit with me. Setz dich zu mir. / Setzt euch zu mir. I
without [wɪˈðaʊt] ohne I
wives [waɪvz] *pl von „wife"* II 4 (73)
wolf [wʊlf], *pl* **wolves** [wʊlvz] Wolf II 3 (49/163)
woman ['wʊmən], *pl* **women** ['wɪmɪn] Frau I
won [wʌn] *siehe* **win**
wonder ['wʌndə] sich fragen, gern wissen wollen II 6 (106)
wonderful ['wʌndəfəl] wunderbar II 2 (30)
won't [wəʊnt]: **you won't be cold (= you will not be cold)** du wirst nicht frieren; ihr werdet nicht frieren II 3 (46)
wood [wʊd] Holz II 3 (49/162)
  woods *(pl)* Wald, Wälder II 3 (49)
woodpecker ['wʊdpekə] Specht II 3 (45)
woods *(pl)* [wʊdz] Wald, Wälder II 3 (49)
word [wɜːd] Wort I • **word building** Wortbildung II 1 (21)
  °**word order** Wortstellung
wore [wɔː] *siehe* **wear**
work [wɜːk]
  1. arbeiten I • **work hard** hart arbeiten II 3 (49) • **work on sth.** an etwas arbeiten I
  °**2.** funktionieren
work [wɜːk] Arbeit I • **at work** bei der Arbeit / am Arbeitsplatz I
worker ['wɜːkə] Arbeiter/in II 3 (55)
worksheet ['wɜːkʃiːt] Arbeitsblatt I
world [wɜːld] Welt I • **from all over the world** aus der ganzen Welt II 5 (81) • **in the world** auf der Welt II 2 (31)
°**worm** [wɜːm] Wurm
worn [wɔːn] *siehe* **wear**
worried ['wʌrid]: **be worried (about)** beunruhigt sein, besorgt sein (wegen) I

worry ['wʌri] Sorge, Kummer II 6 (107)
worry (about) ['wʌri] sich Sorgen machen (wegen, um) I • **Don't worry.** Mach dir keine Sorgen. I
worse (than) [wɜːs] schlechter, schlimmer (als) II 2 (31)
worst [wɜːst]: **(the) worst** am schlechtesten, schlimmsten; der/die/das schlechteste, schlimmste II 2 (31/159)
would [wəd, wʊd] würde, würdest, würden II 6 (99) • **I'd like … (= I would like …)** Ich hätte gern … / Ich möchte gern … I • **Would you like …?** Möchtest du …? / Möchten Sie …? I • **I'd like to go (= I would like to go)** Ich würde gern gehen / Ich möchte gehen I • **I wouldn't like to go** ich würde nicht gern gehen / ich möchte nicht gehen I
°**wreck** [rek] Wrack
°**wriggle** ['rɪgl] (herum)zappeln
write [raɪt], **wrote, written** schreiben I • **write down** aufschreiben I • **write to** schreiben an I
writer ['raɪtə] Schreiber/in; Schriftsteller/in II 3 (55)
written ['rɪtn] *siehe* **write**
wrong [rɒŋ] falsch, verkehrt I • °**There was something wrong.** Etwas stimmte nicht. • **the wrong way** in die falsche Richtung II 5 (89) • **What's wrong with you?** Was fehlt dir? II 4 (64/167)
  ▶ S.167 What's wrong with you?
wrote [rəʊt] *siehe* **write**

Y

yard [jɑːd] Hof II 3 (46) • **in the yard** auf dem Hof II 3 (46/161)
yawn [jɔːn] gähnen II 6 (106)
year [jɪə]
  1. Jahr I
  2. Jahrgangsstufe I
yellow ['jeləʊ] gelb I
yes [jes] ja I
yesterday ['jestədeɪ, 'jestədi] gestern I • **the day before yesterday** vorgestern II 1 (20) • **yesterday morning/afternoon/evening** gestern Morgen/Nachmittag/Abend I
yet [jet]: **not (…) yet** noch nicht II 4 (63) • **yet?** schon? II 4 (65/168)
  ▶ S.166 The present perfect: statements
  ▶ S.168 The present perfect: questions
yoga ['jəʊgə] Yoga I

you [juː]
  1. du; Sie I
  2. ihr I
  3. dir; dich; euch I
  How are you? Wie geht es dir/Ihnen/euch? II 1 (21) • **You're welcome.** Gern geschehen. / Nichts zu danken. I • **you two** ihr zwei I
young [jʌŋ] jung I
your [jɔː]:
  1. dein/e I
  2. Ihr I
  3. euer/eure I
yours [jɔːz]
  1. deiner, deine, deins II 2 (128)
  2. eurer, eure, eures II 2 (128)
°**yourself** [jəˈself, jɔːˈself]: **about yourself** über dich selbst
°**Yuck!** [jʌk] Igitt! / Bäh!

Z

zebra ['zebrə] Zebra II 3 (49/163)
zero ['zɪərəʊ] null I
zoo [zuː] Zoo, Tierpark I

Dictionary (German – English)

Das **German – English Dictionary** enthält den **Lernwortschatz** der Bände 1 und 2 von *English G 21*. Es kann dir eine erste Hilfe sein, wenn du vergessen hast, wie etwas auf Englisch heißt.

Wenn du wissen möchtest, wo das englische Wort zum ersten Mal in *English G 21* vorkommt, dann kannst du im **English – German Dictionary** (S. 178–199) nachschlagen.

Im **German – English Dictionary** werden folgende **Abkürzungen** und **Symbole** verwendet:

jm. = jemandem	sb. = somebody	pl = plural (Mehrzahl)	BE = British English
jn. = jemanden	sth. = something	no pl = no plural	AE = American English

▶ Der Pfeil verweist auf Kästchen im Vocabulary (S. 150–177), in denen du weitere Informationen findest.

A

abbiegen: (nach) links/rechts abbiegen turn left/right [tɜːn]
▶ S.175 (to) turn
Abend evening [ˈiːvnɪŋ]; *(später Abend)* night [naɪt] • **am Abend, abends** in the evening
Abendbrot, -essen dinner [ˈdɪnə] **Abendbrot essen** have dinner **zum Abendbrot** for dinner
Abenteuer adventure [ədˈventʃə]
aber but [bət, bʌt]
abfahren *(wegfahren)* leave [liːv]
Abfall rubbish [ˈrʌbɪʃ]
abnehmen: den Hörer abnehmen pick up the phone [pɪk]
Absatz *(in einem Text)* paragraph [ˈpærəɡrɑːf]
abschließen *(Zimmer)* lock up [ˌlɒk ˈʌp]
Abschnitt section [ˈsekʃn]
absetzen: etwas absetzen *(Hut)* take sth. off [ˌteɪk ˈɒf]
Abtei abbey [ˈæbi]
abwaschen: das Geschirr abwaschen do the dishes [ˈdɪʃɪz]
abziehen: 10 Cent abziehen take 10c off [ˌteɪk ˈɒf]
Acker field [fiːld]
addieren (zu) add (to) [æd]
Adresse address [əˈdres]
Affe monkey [ˈmʌŋki]
Aktivität activity [ækˈtɪvəti]
Akzent accent [ˈæksənt]
albern silly [ˈsɪli]
Album album [ˈælbəm]
alle *(die ganze Gruppe)* all [ɔːl]
  alle beide the two of them
allein alone [əˈləʊn]
Alleinerziehende(r) single parent [ˌsɪŋɡl ˈpeərənt]
alleinstehend single [ˈsɪŋɡl]
alles everything [ˈevriθɪŋ]; all [ɔːl]
  alles, was wir jetzt (noch) tun müssen, ... all we have to do now ...
Alphabet alphabet [ˈælfəbet]
als 1. *(zeitlich)* when [wen]; *(während)* as [əz, æz]
2. **größer/teurer als** bigger/more expensive than [ðæn, ðən] • **mehr als** more than • **mehr als ich** more than me
also *(daher, deshalb)* so [səʊ]
  Also, ... Well, ... [wel]
alt old [əʊld]
am 1. **am Bahnhof** at the station • **am Himmel** in the sky • **am oberen Ende (von)** at the top (of) • **am Strand** on the beach • **am Telefon** on the phone • **am unteren Ende (von)** at the bottom (of) [ˈbɒtəm]
2. *(nahe bei)* **am Meer** by the sea
3. *(zeitlich)* **am 13. Juni** on 13th June • **am Morgen/Nachmittag/Abend** in the morning/afternoon/evening • **am Ende (von)** at the end (of) • **am Freitag** on Friday • **am Freitagmorgen** on Friday morning • **am nächsten Morgen/Tag** the next morning/day • **am Wochenende** at the weekend
amüsieren: sich amüsieren have fun [hæv ˈfʌn]
an 1. **an dem/den Tisch (dort)** at that table • **an der Spitze (von)** at the top (of) • **an der/die Tafel** on the board • **schreiben an** write to
2. *(nahe bei)* **an der See** by the sea
3. **Was war das Beste an ...?** What was the best thing about ...?
4. **an sein** *(Radio, Licht usw.)* be on
andere(r, s) other [ˈʌðə] • **die anderen** the others • **ein(e) andere(r, s) ...** another ... [əˈnʌðə]
anderer Meinung sein (als) disagree (with) [ˌdɪsəˈɡriː]
anders (als) different (from) [ˈdɪfrənt]
  anders herum the other way round
anfangen (mit) start [stɑːt]
anfassen touch [tʌtʃ]
anfreunden: sich anfreunden (mit) make friends (with)
anfühlen: sich gut anfühlen feel good [fiːl]
Angst haben (vor) be afraid (of) [əˈfreɪd]; be scared (of) [skeəd]
anhaben *(Kleidung)* wear [weə]
anhalten stop [stɒp]
anhören 1. **sich etwas anhören** listen to sth. [ˈlɪsn]
  2. **sich gut anhören** sound good [saʊnd]
anklicken: etwas anklicken click on sth. [klɪk]
anklopfen (an) knock (on) [nɒk]
ankommen arrive [əˈraɪv]
anlächeln: jn. anlächeln smile at sb. [smaɪl]
Anleitung(en) *(Gebrauchsanweisung(en))* instructions (pl) [ɪnˈstrʌkʃnz]
anmailen: jn. anmailen mail sb. [meɪl]
anmalen paint [peɪnt]
annehmen *(vermuten)* suppose [səˈpəʊz]
anprobieren *(Kleidung)* try on [ˌtraɪ ˈɒn]
Anruf call [kɔːl]; phone call [ˈfəʊn kɔːl]
anrufen call [kɔːl]; phone [fəʊn]
anschauen look at [lʊk]
anschließen: sich jm. anschließen join sb. [dʒɔɪn]
anschreien: jn. anschreien shout at sb. [ʃaʊt]
Anschrift *(Adresse)* address [əˈdres]
ansehen: sich etwas ansehen look at sth. [lʊk]; watch sth. [wɒtʃ]
anstreichen paint [peɪnt]
Antwort (auf) answer (to) [ˈɑːnsə]
antworten answer [ˈɑːnsə]
Anweisung(en) *(Gebrauchsanweisung(en))* instructions (pl) [ɪnˈstrʌkʃnz]
Anzeige *(Inserat)* advert [ˈædvɜːt]
anziehen: etwas anziehen *(Kleidung)* put sth. on [ˌpʊt ˈɒn] • **sich anziehen** get dressed [ɡet ˈdrest]
Apfel apple [ˈæpl]
Apfelsine orange [ˈɒrɪndʒ]
Apotheke chemist [ˈkemɪst]
April April [ˈeɪprəl]

Dictionary (German – English)

Arbeit work [wɜːk] • **bei der Arbeit/ am Arbeitsplatz** at work • **gute Arbeit leisten** do a good job
arbeiten (an) work (on) [wɜːk]
Arbeiter/in worker [ˈwɜːkə]
Arbeitsblatt worksheet [ˈwɜːkʃiːt]
Arbeits- und Lerntechniken study skills [ˈstʌdi skɪlz]
Ärger *(Schwierigkeiten)* trouble [ˈtrʌbl] • **Ärger kriegen** be in trouble
arm poor [pɔː, pʊə]
Arm arm [ɑːm]
Armbanduhr watch [wɒtʃ]
Art *(Sorte)* sort (of) [sɔːt]
Artikel article [ˈɑːtɪkl]
Arzt/Ärztin doctor [ˈdɒktə]
auch: auch aus Bristol from Bristol too [tuː] • **Ich auch.** Me too.
auch nicht not (...) either [ˈaɪðə, ˈiːðə]
auf on [ɒn] • **auf dem Bild/Foto** in the picture/photo • **auf dem Feld** in the field • **auf dem Hof** in the yard • **auf dem Land** in the country • **auf dem Weg (zu/nach)** on the way (to) • **auf der Welt** in the world • **auf einmal** suddenly [ˈsʌdnli] • **auf Englisch** in English **Auf geht's!** Let's go. • **auf jn. zu** towards sb. [təˈwɔːdz] • **Auf keinen Fall!** No way! • **auf See** at sea **Auf welcher Seite sind wir?** What page are we on? • **Auf Wiedersehen.** Goodbye. [ˌɡʊdˈbaɪ]
aufführen *(Szene, Dialog)* act [ækt]
Aufgabe *(im Schulbuch)* exercise [ˈeksəsaɪz]; *(Job)* job [dʒɒb]
aufgeräumt *(ordentlich)* tidy [ˈtaɪdi]
aufgeregt *(nervös)* nervous [ˈnɜːvəs]; *(begeistert)* excited [ɪkˈsaɪtɪd]
aufhören stop [stɒp]
aufkleben stick on [ˌstɪkˈɒn]
auflisten list [lɪst]
aufmachen open [ˈəʊpən]
aufpassen: auf etwas/jn. aufpassen look after sth./sb. [ˌlʊkˈɑːftə]
aufräumen tidy [ˈtaɪdi]
aufregend exciting [ɪkˈsaɪtɪŋ]
Aufsatz essay [ˈeseɪ]
aufschauen (von) look up (from) [ˌlʊkˈʌp]
aufschreiben write down [ˌraɪtˈdaʊn]
aufsetzen: etwas aufsetzen *(Hut)* put sth. on [ˌpʊtˈɒn] • **sich aufsetzen** sit up [ˌsɪtˈʌp]
aufstehen get up [ˌɡetˈʌp]
aufsuchen: jn. aufsuchen see sb. [siː]
aufteilen (in); sich aufteilen (in) divide (into) [dɪˈvaɪd]
aufzählen *(auflisten)* list [lɪst]
Aufzug lift [lɪft] *(BE)*; elevator [ˈelɪveɪtə] *(AE)*

Auge eye [aɪ]
Augenblick moment [ˈməʊmənt]
August August [ˈɔːɡəst]
aus: Ich komme/bin aus ... I'm from ... [frəm, frɒm] • **aus ... (heraus/hinaus)** out of ... [ˈaʊt əv] • **aus dem Zug/Bus aussteigen** get off the train/bus • **aus der ganzen Welt** from all over the world • **aus meiner Sicht** from my point of view • **aus vielen Gründen** for lots of reasons • **Kleider aus den 60ern / aus den 60er Jahren** dresses from the 60s [ˈsɪkstiz]
ausdenken: sich etwas ausdenken think of sth. [θɪŋk]
▶ S.170 (to) think
Ausdruck *((Rede-)Wendung)* phrase [freɪz]
ausdrucken: etwas ausdrucken print sth. out [ˌprɪntˈaʊt]
Auseinandersetzung argument [ˈɑːɡjumənt] • **eine Auseinandersetzung haben** *(sich streiten)* have an argument
Ausflug trip [trɪp] • **einen Ausflug machen** go on a trip
ausgeben: Geld ausgeben (für) spend money (on) [spend]
ausgehen *(weg-, rausgehen)* go out [ˌɡəʊˈaʊt]
ausgezeichnet fine [faɪn]
aushalten *(ertragen)* stand [stænd] **Ich kann es nicht aushalten.** I can't stand it.
Ausland: im Ausland abroad [əˈbrɔːd] **ins Ausland gehen/fahren** go abroad
ausleihen: sich etwas ausleihen borrow sth. [ˈbɒrəʊ]
ausruhen: sich ausruhen relax [rɪˈlæks]
ausschalten: den Computer ausschalten turn off the computer [ˌtɜːnˈɒf]
▶ S.175 (to) turn
aussehen: anders/toll/alt aussehen look different/great/old [lʊk] **gleich aussehen** look the same **außerhalb seines Zimmers** outside his room [aʊtˈsaɪd]
aussetzen: Einmal aussetzen. Miss a turn. [tɜːn]
Aussicht *(Blick)* view [vjuː]
Aussprache pronunciation [prəˌnʌnsiˈeɪʃn]
ausstehen *(ertragen)* stand [stænd] **Ich kann es nicht ausstehen.** I can't stand it.
aussteigen (aus dem Zug/Bus) get off (the train/bus) [ˌɡetˈɒf]

aussuchen: (sich) etwas aussuchen choose sth. [tʃuːz]
Auswahl (an) selection (of) [sɪˈlekʃn]
auswählen choose [tʃuːz]
ausziehen 1. *(aus Wohnung)* move out [ˌmuːvˈaʊt] **2. etwas ausziehen** *(Kleidung)* take sth. off [ˌteɪkˈɒf]
Auto car [kɑː]
Autsch! Ouch! [aʊtʃ]

B

Baby baby [ˈbeɪbi] • **ein Baby bekommen** have a baby
baden *(ein Bad nehmen)* have a bath [bɑːθ]
Badewanne bath [bɑːθ]
Badezimmer bathroom [ˈbɑːθruːm]
Badminton badminton [ˈbædmɪntən]
Bahnhof station [ˈsteɪʃn] • **am Bahnhof** at the station
bald soon [suːn] • **Bis bald.** See you. [ˈsiː juː]
Ball *(im Sport; Tanz)* ball [bɔːl]
Banane banana [bəˈnɑːnə]
Band *(Musikgruppe)* band [bænd]
Bank *(Sparkasse)* bank [bæŋk]
Bankräuber/in bank robber [ˈrɒbə]
Bar bar [bɑː]
Bär bear [beə]
Baseball baseball [ˈbeɪsbɔːl]
Baseballmütze baseball cap [kæp]
Basketball basketball [ˈbɑːskɪtbɔːl]
Bauchweh stomach ache [ˈstʌmək eɪk]
▶ S.167 What's wrong with you?
bauen build [bɪld]
Bauernhof farm [fɑːm]
Baum tree [triː]
beantworten answer [ˈɑːnsə]
bedeuten mean [miːn]
Bedeutung meaning [ˈmiːnɪŋ]
beeilen: sich beeilen hurry [ˈhʌri]; hurry up [ˌhʌriˈʌp]
beenden finish [ˈfɪnɪʃ]
begeistert excited [ɪkˈsaɪtɪd]
beginnen (mit) start [stɑːt]; begin [bɪˈɡɪn]
begreifen understand [ˌʌndəˈstænd]
Begründung reason [ˈriːzn]
bei: bei den Shaws zu Hause at the Shaws' house • **bei der Arbeit** at work • **Englisch bei Mr Kingsley** English with Mr Kingsley
beide both [bəʊθ] • **die beiden / alle beide** the two of them
Beifall klatschen cheer [tʃɪə]
Bein leg [leɡ]
beinahe almost [ˈɔːlməʊst]

Dictionary (German – English)

Beispiel example [ɪɡˈzɑːmpl] • **zum Beispiel** for example
bekommen get [ɡet] • **ein Baby bekommen** have a baby
bellen bark [bɑːk]
benennen name [kɔːl]
benötigen need [niːd]
benutzen use [juːz]
beobachten watch [wɒtʃ]
bequem comfortable [ˈkʌmftəbl]
bereit ready [ˈredi]
bereits already [ɔːlˈredi]
Berg mountain [ˈmaʊntən]
Bericht (über) report (on) [rɪˈpɔːt]
berichten: jm. etwas berichten tell sb. about sth. [tel]; report sth. to sb. [rɪˈpɔːt]
berichtigen correct [kəˈrekt]
beruhigen: jn. beruhigen calm sb. down [ˌkɑːm ˈdaʊn] • **sich beruhigen** calm down
berühmt (für, wegen) famous (for) [ˈfeɪməs]
berühren touch [tʌtʃ]
beschäftigt busy [ˈbɪzi]
Bescheid: über etwas Bescheid wissen know about sth. [nəʊ]
beschließen: (etwas) beschließen decide (on sth.) [dɪˈsaɪd]
beschreiben: (jm.) etwas beschreiben describe sth. (to sb.) [dɪˈskraɪb] • **jm. den Weg beschreiben** tell sb. the way
Beschreibung description [dɪˈskrɪpʃn]
besondere(r, s) special [ˈspeʃl]
besorgen (holen) get [ɡet]
besorgt sein (wegen) be worried (about) [ˈwʌrid]
besser better [ˈbetə]
▶ S.159 good – better – best
beste: am besten (the) best [best] **der/die/das beste …; die besten …** the best … • **Was war das Beste an …?** What was the best thing about …?
▶ S.159 good – better – best
bestellen order [ˈɔːdə]
Besuch visit [ˈvɪzɪt]
besuchen: jn. besuchen visit sb. [ˈvɪzɪt]; see sb. [siː]
Besucher/in visitor [ˈvɪzɪtə]
Bett bed [bed]
beunruhigt sein (wegen) be worried (about) [ˈwʌrid]
Beutel bag [bæɡ]
bevor before [bɪˈfɔː]
bewegen; sich bewegen move [muːv]
Bewegung movement [ˈmuːvmənt]
Beweis(e) proof (no pl) [pruːf]
bewölkt cloudy [ˈklaʊdi]
bewusstlos unconscious [ʌnˈkɒnʃəs]

bezahlen: etwas bezahlen pay for sth. [peɪ]
Bibliothek library [ˈlaɪbrəri]
Bild picture [ˈpɪktʃə] • **auf dem Bild** in the picture
billig cheap [tʃiːp]
Bindewort linking word [ˈlɪŋkɪŋ wɜːd]
Biologie biology [baɪˈɒlədʒi]
bis (zeitlich) till [tɪl] • **Bis bald.** See you. [siː juː]
bisschen: ein bisschen a bit [bɪt]
bitte 1. (in Fragen und Aufforderungen) please [pliːz]
2. Bitte sehr. / Hier bitte. Here you are.
3. Bitte, gern geschehen. You're welcome. [ˈwelkəm]
4. Wie bitte? Sorry? [ˈsɒri]
bitten: jn. um etwas bitten ask sb. for sth. [ɑːsk]
blau blue [bluː]
bleiben stay [steɪ]
Bleistift pencil [ˈpensl]
Bleistiftanspitzer pencil sharpener [ˈpensl ʃɑːpnə]
Blick (Aussicht) view [vjuː]
bloß just [dʒʌst]; only [ˈəʊnli]
Blume flower [ˈflaʊə]
Bluse blouse [blaʊz]
Blüte flower [ˈflaʊə]
Boot boat [bəʊt]
Boss boss [bɒs]
Brand fire [faɪə]
brauchen need [niːd] • **nicht zu tun brauchen** needn't do [ˈniːdnt]
▶ S.176 must – needn't – mustn't
braun brown [braʊn]
brav good [ɡʊd]
brechen break [breɪk]
Brief (an) letter (to) [ˈletə]
Brieffreund/in (im Internet) e-friend [ˈiːfrend]
Briefmarke stamp [stæmp]
Brille: (eine) Brille glasses (pl) [ˈɡlɑːsɪz]
▶ S.157 Plural words
bringen: (mit-, her)bringen bring [brɪŋ] • **(weg-, hin)bringen** take [teɪk] • **Was kann/darf ich euch/Ihnen bringen?** (im Restaurant) What can I get you?
Brite, Britin; britisch British [ˈbrɪtɪʃ]
Broschüre booklet [ˈbʊklət]
Brot bread (no pl) [bred]
Brötchen roll [rəʊl]
Brücke bridge [brɪdʒ]
Bruder brother [ˈbrʌðə]
Buch book [bʊk]
Bücherei library [ˈlaɪbrəri]
Buchstabe letter [ˈletə]
buchstabieren spell [spel]
Bühne stage [steɪdʒ]

Burg castle [ˈkɑːsl]
Bus bus [bʌs]
Busfahrt bus ride [ˈbʌs raɪd]

C

Café café [ˈkæfeɪ]
Cafeteria cafeteria [ˌkæfəˈtɪəriə]
Cartoon cartoon [kɑːˈtuːn]
CD CD [ˌsiːˈdiː] • **CD-Spieler** CD player [ˌsiːˈdiː ˌpleɪə]
Cent cent (c) [sent]
Champion champion [ˈtʃæmpiən]
Chance chance [tʃɑːns]
Chat (Unterhaltung) chat [tʃæt]
chatten chat [tʃæt]
Chef/in boss [bɒs]
Chor choir [ˈkwaɪə]
Clown/in clown [klaʊn]
Cola cola [ˈkəʊlə]
Comedyshow comedy [ˈkɒmədi]
Comic-Heft comic [ˈkɒmɪk]
Computer computer [kəmˈpjuːtə]
cool cool [kuːl]
Cornflakes cornflakes [ˈkɔːnfleɪks]
Cousin, Cousine cousin [ˈkʌzn]

D

da, dahin (dort, dorthin) there [ðeə] **da drüben** over there [ˌəʊvə ˈðeə]
Dach roof [ruːf]
daheim at home [ət ˈhəʊm]
daher (deshalb) so [səʊ]; that's why [ˈðæts ˌwaɪ]
damals then [ðen]
danach (zeitlich) after that [ˌɑːftə ˈðæt]
Danke. Thank you. [ˈθæŋk juː]; Thanks. **Danke sehr!** Thanks very much! **Vielen Dank!** Thanks a lot!
dann then [ðen] • **Was dann?** Then what?
darstellende Kunst drama [ˈdrɑːmə]
darum so [səʊ]; that's why [ˈðæts ˌwaɪ]
das (Artikel) the [ðə, ði]
das (Relativpronomen) **1.** (für Dinge) which; that
2. (für Personen) who, that
das (dort) (Singular) that [ðæt, ðət]; (Plural) those [ðəʊz] • **Das bin ich.** That's me.
dass that [ðət, ðæt]
dasselbe the same [seɪm]
Datum date [deɪt]
decken: den Tisch decken lay the table [ˌleɪ ðə ˈteɪbl]
dein(e) … your … [jɔː]
deiner, deine, deins yours [jɔːz]
denken think [θɪŋk] • **denken an** think of • **Was denkst du über …?**

Dictionary (German – English) 203

What do you think about/of ...?
▶ S.170 (to) think
dennoch still [stɪl]
der *(Artikel)* the [ðə, ðɪ]
der *(Relativpronomen)* **1.** *(für Personen)* who; that
2. *(für Dinge)* which, that
derselbe the same [seɪm]
deshalb so [səʊ]; that's why ['ðæts ˌwaɪ]
dessen *(Relativpronomen)*: **der Mann, dessen Statue ...** the man whose statue ... [huːz]
Detektiv/in detective [dɪ'tektɪv]
deuten (auf etwas) *(zeigen)* point (at/to sth.) [pɔɪnt]
deutlich clear [klɪə]
Deutsch; deutsch; Deutsche(r) German ['dʒɜːmən]
Deutschland Germany ['dʒɜːməni]
Dezember December [dɪ'sembə]
dich you [juː]
die *(Artikel)* the [ðə, ðɪ]
die *(Relativpronomen)* **1.** *(für Personen)* who; that
2. *(für Dinge)* which, that
die (dort) *(Singular)* that [ðɒt, ðæt]; *(Plural)* those [ðəʊz] • **die (hier)** *(Singular)* this [ðɪs]; *(Plural)* these [ðiːz]
Dieb/in thief [θiːf], *pl* thieves [θiːvz]
Diele hall [hɔːl]
Dienst (am Kunden) *(Service)* service ['sɜːvɪs]
Dienstag Tuesday ['tjuːzdeɪ, 'tjuːzdi]
(siehe auch unter „Freitag")
dies (hier); diese(r, s) *(Singular)* this [ðɪs]; *(Plural)* these [ðiːz]
dieselbe(n) the same [seɪm]
Ding thing [θɪŋ]
dir you [juː]
direkt hinter dir right behind you
Disko disco ['dɪskəʊ]
Diskussion discussion [dɪ'skʌʃn]
Doch! ▶ S.160 German „Doch!"
Doktor doctor ['dɒktə]
Dokumentarfilm documentary [ˌdɒkju'mentri]
Donnerstag Thursday ['θɜːzdeɪ, 'θɜːzdi] *(siehe auch unter „Freitag")*
Doppel-, doppelt double ['dʌbl]
Dorf village ['vɪlɪdʒ]
dort, dorthin there [ðeə] • **dort drinnen** in there • **dort drüben** over there • **dort unten** down there
Dossier dossier ['dɒsieɪ]
downloaden download [ˌdaʊn'ləʊd]
Drachen kite [kaɪt]
dran: Ich bin dran. It's my turn. [tɜːn]
draußen outside [ˌaʊt'saɪd]; out [aʊt]
nach draußen outside
▶ S.155 out

drinnen inside [ˌɪn'saɪd] • **dort drinnen** in there [ˌɪn 'ðeə] • **hier drinnen** in here [ˌɪn 'hɪə] • **nach drinnen** inside
dritte(r, s) third [θɜːd]
Drogerie chemist ['kemɪst]
drüben: da/dort drüben over there [ˌəʊvə 'ðeə]
drücken push [pʊʃ]
du you [juː]
dumm *(albern)* silly ['sɪli]
dunkel dark [dɑːk]
durch through [θruː]
durcheinander: alles durcheinanderbringen make a mess [ˌmeɪk ə 'mes]
durchführen: ein Projekt durchführen do a project
dürfen can [kən, kæn]; may [meɪ]; be allowed to [ə'laʊd] • **nicht dürfen** mustn't ['mʌsnt]
▶ S.169 „können" und „dürfen"
▶ S.176 must – needn't – mustn't
Durst haben, durstig sein be thirsty ['θɜːsti]
Dusche shower ['ʃaʊə]
duschen; sich duschen have a shower ['ʃaʊə]
DVD DVD [ˌdiː viː' diː]

E

Ebbe und Flut *(Gezeiten)* tide [taɪd]
es ist Ebbe the tide is out
eben *(flach)* flat [flæt]
echt real [rɪəl]
Ecke corner ['kɔːnə] • **Sand Street, Ecke London Road** on the corner of Sand Street and London Road
Ehefrau wife [waɪf], *pl* wives [waɪvz]
Ehemann husband ['hʌzbənd]
Ei egg [eg]
Eichhörnchen squirrel ['skwɪrəl]
eigene(r, s): unser eigenes Schwimmbad our own pool [əʊn]
Eile: in Eile sein be in a hurry ['hʌri]
eilen *(sich beeilen)* hurry ['hʌri]
eilig: es eilig haben be in a hurry ['hʌri]
ein(e) a, an [ə, ən]; one ['wʌn]
ein(e) andere(r, s) ... another ... [ə'nʌðə] • **eine Menge** a lot (of) [lɒt]; lots (of) [lɒts] • **ein neuer / eine neue / ein neues** a new one [wʌn] • **ein paar** some [səm, sʌm]; *(einige wenige)* a few [fjuː] • **ein Paar** a pair (of) [peə] • **eines Tages** one day
einfach *(nicht schwierig)* easy ['iːzi]
einfach nur just [dʒʌst]
Einfall *(Idee)* idea [aɪ'dɪə]

eingeben: etwas eingeben *(in den Computer)* enter sth. ['entə]
eingeschaltet sein *(Radio, Licht usw.)* be on
einige some [səm, sʌm]; *(einige wenige)* a few [fjuː]
einigen: sich einigen (auf) agree (on) [ə'griː]
einkaufen: einkaufen gehen go shopping [ˌgəʊ 'ʃɒpɪŋ]
Einkaufen shopping ['ʃɒpɪŋ]
Einkaufsliste shopping list
einladen (zu) invite (to) [ɪn'vaɪt]
Einladung (zu) invitation (to) [ˌɪnvɪ'teɪʃn]
einmal: Einmal aussetzen. Miss a turn. [tɜːn] • **auf einmal** suddenly ['sʌdnli]
einpacken pack [pæk]
eins, ein, eine one ['wʌn]
einschalten: den Computer einschalten turn on the computer [ˌtɜːn 'ɒn]
▶ S.175 (to) turn
einschüchtern bully ['bʊli]
einsteigen (in den Zug/Bus) get on (the train/bus) [ˌget 'ɒn]
eintragen: etwas eintragen *(in Formular)* enter sth. ['entə]
eintreffen *(ankommen)* arrive [ə'raɪv]
Eintrittskarte ticket ['tɪkɪt]
einziehen *(in Wohnung)* move in [ˌmuːv 'ɪn]
einzig: der einzige Gast the only guest ['əʊnli]
Eis ice [aɪs]; *(Speiseeis)* ice cream [ˌaɪs 'kriːm]
Eisenbahn railway ['reɪlweɪ]
Elefant elephant ['elɪfənt]
Eltern parents ['peərənts]
E-Mail (an) e-mail (to) ['iːmeɪl]
Ende 1. end [end] • **am Ende (von)** at the end (of) • **zu Ende machen** finish ['fɪnɪʃ] • **zu Ende sein** be over ['əʊvə]
2. oberes Ende *(Spitze)* top [tɒp] • **am oberen Ende (von)** at the top (of)
3. unteres Ende bottom ['bɒtəm] • **am unteren Ende (von)** at the bottom (of) ['bɒtəm]
enden finish ['fɪnɪʃ]
endlich at last [ət 'lɑːst]
Engel angel ['eɪndʒl]
Englisch; englisch English ['ɪŋglɪʃ]
Enkel grandson ['grænsʌn]; grandchild ['græntʃaɪld], *pl* grandchildren ['græntʃɪldrən]
Enkelin granddaughter ['grændɔːtə]; grandchild ['græntʃaɪld], *pl* grandchildren ['græntʃɪldrən]

entdecken discover [dɪˈskʌvə]
Entdecker/in *(Forscher/in)* explorer [ɪkˈsplɔːrə]
entlang der Straße / die Straße entlang along the street [əˈlɒŋ]
entleihen: etwas entleihen *(sich etwas ausleihen)* borrow sth. [ˈbɒrəʊ]
entscheiden: sich entscheiden (für etwas) decide (on sth.) [dɪˈsaɪd]
entschuldigen: sich entschuldigen say sorry [ˈsɒri]
Entschuldigung 1. *(Tut mir leid)* I'm sorry. [ˈsɒri] • **Entschuldigung, dass ich zu spät komme.** Sorry, I'm late.
2. Entschuldigung, … / Entschuldigen Sie, … *(Darf ich mal stören?)* Excuse me, … [ɪkˈskjuːz miː]
entspannen; sich entspannen relax [rɪˈlæks]
entwerfen design [dɪˈzaɪn]
entwickeln *(entwerfen)* design [dɪˈzaɪn]
Enzyklopädie encyclopedia [ɪnˌsaɪkləˈpiːdiə]
er 1. *(männliche Person)* he [hiː]
2. *(Ding, Tier)* it [ɪt]
Erdbeere strawberry [ˈstrɔːbəri]
Erdkunde geography [dʒiˈɒɡrəfi]
Ereignis event [ɪˈvent]
erfahren: etwas über etwas erfahren learn sth. about sth. [lɜːn]
erforschen explore [ɪkˈsplɔː]
ergänzen add (to) [æd]
Ergebnis result [rɪˈzʌlt]
erholen: sich erholen (von) recover (from) [rɪˈkʌvə]
erinnern: sich erinnern (an) remember [rɪˈmembə]
erkältet sein have a cold [kəʊld]
▶ S.167 What's wrong with you?
Erkältung cold [kəʊld] • **eine Erkältung haben** have a cold
▶ S.167 What's wrong with you?
erkennen *(merken)* realize [ˈrɪəlaɪz]
erklären: jm. etwas erklären explain sth. to sb. [ɪkˈspleɪn]
Erklärung explanation [ˌekspləˈneɪʃn]
erkunden explore [ɪkˈsplɔː]
erlauben allow [əˈlaʊ]
erläutern: jm. etwas erläutern explain sth. to sb. [ɪkˈspleɪn]
erraten guess [ɡes]
erst only [ˈəʊnli]
erstaunlich amazing [əˈmeɪzɪŋ]
erste(r, s) first [fɜːst] • **als Erstes** first • **der erste Tag** the first day **der/die Erste sein** be first
ertragen *(aushalten)* stand [stænd]
Ich kann es nicht ertragen. I can't stand it.

erwarten: ich kann es kaum erwarten, … zu sehen I can't wait to see … [weɪt]
erwischen *(fangen)* catch [kætʃ]
erzählen (von) tell (about) [tel]
Erzählung story [ˈstɔːri]
erzeugen *(produzieren)* produce [prəˈdjuːs]
es it [ɪt] • **es gibt** *(es ist vorhanden)* there's; *(es sind vorhanden)* there are
essen eat [iːt] • **Abendbrot essen** have dinner • **Toast zum Frühstück essen** have toast for breakfast
Essen food [fuːd]
Esszimmer dining room [ˈdaɪnɪŋ ruːm]
Etagenbett bunk (bed) [bʌŋk]
etwas something [ˈsʌmθɪŋ]; *(irgendetwas)* anything [ˈeniθɪŋ]; *(ein bisschen)* a bit [bɪt] • **etwas Käse/Saft** some cheese/juice [səm, sʌm]
▶ S.158 something – anything
euch you [juː]
euer, eure … your … [jɔː]
eurer, eure, eures yours [jɔːz]
Euro euro [ˈjʊərəʊ]

F

Fabrik factory [ˈfæktri]
fähig sein, etwas zu tun be able to do sth. [ˈeɪbl]
▶ S.169 „können" und „dürfen"
fahren go [ɡəʊ]; *(ein Auto/mit dem Auto)* drive [draɪv] • **in Urlaub fahren** go on holiday • **mit dem Auto/Zug/Rad/… fahren** go by car/train/bike/… • **Inliner/Skateboard fahren** skate [skeɪt] • **Rad fahren** cycle [ˈsaɪkl]; ride a bike [ˌraɪd ə ˈbaɪk]
Fahrer/in driver [ˈdraɪvə]
Fahrrad bike [baɪk]
Fahrstuhl lift [lɪft] *(BE)*; elevator [ˈelɪveɪtə] *(AE)*
Fahrt: (Rad-/Bus-)Fahrt (bike/bus) ride [raɪd]
fair fair [feə]
Fall 1. *(Kriminalfall)* case [keɪs]
2. Auf keinen Fall! No way! [ˌnəʊ ˈweɪ]
Falle trap [træp] • **(jm.) eine Falle stellen** set a trap (for sb.) [set]
fallen fall [fɔːl]; drop [drɒp]
fallen lassen drop [drɒp]
falls if [ɪf]
falsch wrong [rɒŋ] • **in die falsche Richtung** the wrong way
Familie family [ˈfæməli]
fangen catch [kætʃ]
fantastisch fantastic [fænˈtæstɪk]

Farbe colour [ˈkʌlə] • **Welche Farbe hat …?** What colour is …?
Farm farm [fɑːm]
fast almost [ˈɔːlməʊst]
Februar February [ˈfebruəri]
Federball badminton [ˈbædmɪntən]
Federmäppchen pencil case [ˈpensl keɪs]
fehlen *(nicht da sein)* be missing [ˈmɪsɪŋ] • **Was fehlt dir?** *(bei Krankheit)* What's wrong with you?
▶ S.167 What's wrong with you?
Fehler mistake [mɪˈsteɪk]
Feind/in enemy [ˈenəmi]
Feld 1. field [fiːld] • **auf dem Feld** in the field
2. *(bei Brettspielen)* **Geh ein Feld vor.** Move on one space. [speɪs] • **Geh ein Feld zurück.** Move back one space.
Fenster window [ˈwɪndəʊ]
Ferien holidays [ˈhɒlədeɪz] • **Ferien haben/machen** be on holiday
Ferienhaus villa [ˈvɪlə]
fernsehen watch TV [ˌwɒtʃ tiːˈviː]
Fernsehen television [ˈtelɪvɪʒn]; TV [tiːˈviː] • **im Fernsehen** on TV
fertig *(bereit)* ready [ˈredi] • **sich fertig machen (für)** *(sich vorbereiten)* get ready (for) • **Dinge fertig machen (für)** *(vorbereiten)* get things ready (for)
Fest, Festival festival [ˈfestɪvl]
feucht wet [wet]
Feuer fire [ˈfaɪə]
Feuerwehrfrau firewoman [ˈfaɪəˌwʊmən]
Feuerwehrmann fireman [ˈfaɪəmən]
Fieber haben have a temperature [ˈtemprətʃə]
▶ S.167 What's wrong with you?
Film film [fɪlm]
Filmstar film star [ˈfɪlm stɑː]
Filzstift felt tip [ˈfelt tɪp]
finden *(entdecken)* find [faɪnd] • **Freunde finden** make friends
Finger finger [ˈfɪŋɡə]
Fisch fish, *pl* fish [fɪʃ]
flach *(eben)* flat [flæt]
Flasche bottle [ˈbɒtl] • **eine Flasche Milch** a bottle of milk
Fleisch meat [miːt]
fliegen fly [flaɪ]
Flug flight [flaɪt]
Flugzeug plane [pleɪn] • **im Flugzeug** on the plane
Flur hall [hɔːl]
Fluss river [ˈrɪvə]
Flussdiagramm flow chart [ˈfləʊ tʃɑːt]
Flusspferd hippo [ˈhɪpəʊ]
flüstern whisper [ˈwɪspə]

Dictionary (German – English)

Flut: Ebbe und Flut *(Gezeiten)* tide [taɪd] • **es ist Flut** the tide is in
folgen follow [ˈfɒləʊ]
Football American football [əˌmerɪkən ˈfʊtbɔːl]
Form *(Gestalt)* shape [ʃeɪp]
Forscher/in *(Entdecker/in)* explorer [ɪkˈsplɔːrə]
fort away [əˈweɪ]
Foto photo [ˈfəʊtəʊ] • **auf dem Foto** in the photo • **Fotos machen** take photos
Fotoapparat camera [ˈkæmərə]
Fotograf/in photographer [fəˈtɒɡrəfə]
fotografieren take photos [teɪk ˈfəʊtəʊz]
Frage question [ˈkwestʃn] • **Fragen stellen** ask questions • **Kommt nicht in Frage!** No way!
fragen ask [ɑːsk] • **nach etwas fragen** ask about sth. • **jn. nach dem Weg fragen** ask sb. the way
sich fragen wonder [ˈwʌndə]
Französisch French [frentʃ]
Frau woman [ˈwʊmən], *pl* women [ˈwɪmɪn]; **Frau Brown** Mrs Brown [ˈmɪsɪz]; **Ms Brown** [mɪz, məz] • **Frau White** *(unverheiratet)* Miss White [mɪs]
frei [friː] free • **freie Zeit** free time
Freitag Friday [ˈfraɪdeɪ, ˈfraɪdi] **freitagabends, am Freitagabend** on Friday evening • **freitagnachts, Freitagnacht** on Friday night
Freizeit free time [ˌfriː ˈtaɪm]
Freizeitaktivitäten free-time activities [ˌfriː taɪm ækˈtɪvɪtiz]
Freizeitzentrum, -park leisure centre [ˈleʒə sentə]
Fremdenverkehrsamt tourist information [ˈtʊərɪst ˌɪnfəˌmeɪʃn]
Freund/in friend [frend] • **Freunde finden** make friends
freundlich friendly [ˈfrendli]
frieren be cold [kəʊld]
froh happy [ˈhæpi]
Frosch frog [frɒɡ]
Frucht, Früchte fruit [fruːt]
früh early [ˈɜːli]
Frühling spring [sprɪŋ]
Frühstück breakfast [ˈbrekfəst] **zum Frühstück** for breakfast
frühstücken have breakfast
Frühstückspension Bed and Breakfast (B&B) [ˌbed ən ˈbrekfəst]
Fuchs fox [fɒks]
fühlen; sich fühlen feel [fiːl]
▶ S.167 What's wrong with you?
führen nach *(Straße, Weg)* go to; **ein Telefongespräch führen** make a call [kɔːl]
Füller pen [pen]

für for [fə, fɔː]
furchtbar terrible [ˈterəbl]; awful [ˈɔːfl]
Fuß foot [fʊt], *pl* feet [fiːt]
Fußball football [ˈfʊtbɔːl]
Fußballplatz, -feld football pitch [pɪtʃ]
Fußballschuhe, -stiefel football boots [ˈfʊtbɔːl buːts]
Fußboden floor [flɔː]
Futter food [fuːd]
füttern feed [fiːd]

G

gähnen yawn [jɔːn]
ganze(r, s) whole [həʊl] • **aus der ganzen Welt** from all over the world • **das ganze Jahr 2006** the whole of 2006 • **den ganzen Tag (lang)** all day • **die ganze Zeit** all the time • **Das ist ganz falsch.** This is all wrong.
Garage garage [ˈɡærɑːʒ]
Garten garden [ˈɡɑːdn]
Gast guest [ɡest]; *(Besucher/in)* visitor [ˈvɪzɪtə]
Gebäude building [ˈbɪldɪŋ]
geben give [ɡɪv] • **es gibt** *(es ist vorhanden)* there's; *(es sind vorhanden)* there are
geboren sein/werden be born [bɔːn]
gebrochen *(Arm, Bein)* broken [ˈbrəʊkən]
Geburtstag birthday [ˈbɜːθdeɪ] **Herzlichen Glückwunsch zum Geburtstag.** Happy birthday. **Ich habe im Mai / am 13. Juni Geburtstag.** My birthday is in May / on 13th June. • **Wann hast du Geburtstag?** When's your birthday?
Gedicht poem [ˈpəʊɪm]
Gefahr danger [ˈdeɪndʒə]
gefährlich dangerous [ˈdeɪndʒərəs]
gegen against [əˈɡenst]
gegenüber (von) opposite [ˈɒpəzɪt]
Gegenwart present [ˈpreznt]
Geheimnis *(Rätsel)* mystery [ˈmɪstri]
gehen 1. go [ɡəʊ]; *(zu Fuß gehen)* walk [wɔːk]; *(weggehen)* leave [liːv] • **Auf geht's!** Let's go. • **einkaufen gehen** go shopping • **Geh ein Feld vor.** Move on one space. [speɪs] **Geh ein Feld zurück.** Move back one space. • **in die Sauna gehen** have a sauna [ˈsɔːnə] • **ins Ausland gehen** go abroad [əˈbrɔːd] • **ins Bett gehen** go to bed • **ins Kino gehen** go to the cinema [ˈsɪnəmə] • **nach Hause gehen** go home • **reiten/schwimmen gehen** go riding/swimming • **spazieren**

gehen go for a walk [wɔːk] **2. Es geht mir/ihm gut.** I'm/He's fine. [faɪn] • **Wie geht es dir/Ihnen/euch?** How are you? **3. Es geht um Mr Green.** This is about Mr Green. • **Das geht dich nichts an!** Mind your own business. [ˌmaɪnd jərˌəʊn ˈbɪznəs]
gehören (zu) belong (to) [bɪˈlɒŋ] **Wem gehören diese?** Whose are these? [huːz]
Gelächter laughter [ˈlɑːftə]
gelangen *(hinkommen)* get [ɡet]
gelb yellow [ˈjeləʊ]
Geld money [ˈmʌni] • **Geld ausgeben (für)** spend money (on) [spend]
Geldbörse purse [pɜːs]
genannt werden be called [kɔːld]
genau: genau hinter dir right behind you • **genau in dem Moment** just then • **genau wie du** just like you
genießen enjoy [ɪnˈdʒɔɪ]
genug enough [ɪˈnʌf]
geöffnet open [ˈəʊpən]
Geografie geography [dʒiˈɒɡrəfi]
gepflegt neat [niːt]
gerade at the moment; *(soeben)* just [dʒʌst] • **gerade dann** *(genau in dem Moment)* just then • **jetzt gerade** *(in diesem Moment)* right now [raɪt ˈnaʊ]
▶ S.166 The present perfect: statements
geradeaus weiter straight on [streɪt ˈɒn]
Gerät *(Maschine)* machine [məˈʃiːn]
Geräusch noise [nɔɪz]
gerecht fair [feə]
gern: Ich hätte gern … / Ich möchte gern … I'd like … (= I would like …) [laɪk] • **Ich schwimme/tanze/… gern.** I like swimming/dancing/… **Ich würde gern gehen** I'd like to go **Ich würde nicht gern gehen** I wouldn't like to go • **Gern geschehen.** You're welcome. [ˈwelkəm]
gernhaben like [laɪk]
Geruch smell
gesamte(r, s) whole [həʊl]
Geschäft shop [ʃɒp]
geschehen (mit) happen (to) [ˈhæpən]
Geschenk present [ˈpreznt]
Geschichte 1. story [ˈstɔːri] **2.** *(vergangene Zeiten)* history [ˈhɪstri]
geschieden divorced [dɪˈvɔːst]
Geschirr dishes (pl) [ˈdɪʃɪz] • **das Geschirr abwaschen** do the dishes
Geschirrspülmaschine dishwasher [ˈdɪʃwɒʃə]
geschlossen closed [kləʊzd]

Geschmack(srichtung) flavour ['fleɪvə]
Gesicht face [feɪs]
Gespräch conversation [ˌkɒnvə'seɪʃn]
Gestalt *(Form)* shape [ʃeɪp]
gestern yesterday ['jestədər, 'jestədi] • **gestern Morgen/Nachmittag/Abend** yesterday morning/afternoon/evening
gesund healthy ['helθi]
▶ S.167 What's wrong with you?
Getränk drink [drɪŋk]
Gewinn prize [praɪz]
gewinnen win [wɪn]
Gewinner/in winner ['wɪnə]
Gewitter storm [stɔːm]
gewöhnlich usually ['juːʒuəli]
Gezeiten *(Ebbe und Flut)* tide [taɪd]
Giraffe giraffe [dʒə'rɑːf]
Gitarre guitar [gɪ'tɑː] • **Gitarre spielen** play the guitar
Glas glass [glɑːs] • **ein Glas Wasser** a glass of water
glauben think [θɪŋk] • **Das glaube ich nicht. / Ich glaube nicht.** I don't think so. • **Ich glaube (ja).** I think so. • **Glaubst du das wirklich?** Do you really think so?
gleich sein/aussehen be/look the same [seɪm]
Glocke bell [bel]
Glück: Viel Glück (bei/mit ...)! Good luck (with ...)! [gʊd 'lʌk] • **zum Glück** *(glücklicherweise)* luckily ['lʌkɪli]
glücklich happy ['hæpi]
glücklicherweise luckily ['lʌkɪli]
Grad degree [dɪ'griː]
Grammatik grammar ['græmə]
grau grey [greɪ]
grauenhaft horrible ['hɒrəbl]
Grippe flu [fluː]
groß big [bɪg]
großartig great [greɪt]
Größe *(Schuhgröße usw.)* size [saɪz]
Großeltern grandparents ['grænpeərənts]
Großmutter grandmother ['grænmʌðə]
Großstadt city ['sɪti]
Großvater grandfather ['grænfɑːðə]
grün green [griːn]
Grund reason ['riːzn] • **aus vielen Gründen** for lots of reasons
Gruppe group [gruːp]; *(Musikgruppe)* band [bænd]
gruselig scary ['skeəri]
Gruß: Liebe Grüße, ... *(Briefschluss)* Love ... [lʌv]
Grüß Dilip von mir. Say hi to Dilip for me.
gucken look [lʊk]

gut good [gʊd]; *(okay)* OK [əʊ'keɪ]; *(in Ordnung)* all right [ɔːl 'raɪt]; *(gesundheitlich gut, wohlauf)* well [wel]; fine [faɪn] • **gut (ver)laufen** go well • **Du hast dich gut um sie gekümmert.** You looked after them well. [wel] • **Es geht mir/ihm gut.** I'm/He's fine. • **gute Arbeit leisten** do a good job • **Guten Morgen.** Good morning. • **Guten Tag.** Hello.; *(nachmittags)* Good afternoon.
▶ S.159 good – better – best
▶ S.167 What's wrong with you?
gutgehen *(gut verlaufen)* go well [wel]

H

Haar, Haare hair *(no pl)* [heə]
haben have got ['hæv gɒt]; have [həv, hæv] • **Ich habe keinen Stuhl.** I haven't got a chair. • **Ich habe am 13. Juni/im Mai Geburtstag.** My birthday is on 13th June/in May. • **Wann hast du Geburtstag?** When's your birthday? • **haben wollen** want [wɒnt] • **Was haben wir als Hausaufgabe auf?** What's for homework?
Hähnchen chicken ['tʃɪkɪn]
halbe(r, s) half [hɑːf] • **eine halbe Stunde** half an hour • **halb zwölf** half past 11
Hallo! Hi! [haɪ]; Hello. [hə'ləʊ]
Hals throat [θrəʊt]
Halsschmerzen haben have a sore throat [sɔː 'θrəʊt]
▶ S.167 What's wrong with you?
halten 1. hold [həʊld]
2. **etwas warm/kühl/offen/... halten** keep sth. warm/cool/open/... [kiːp] • **den Mund halten** shut up [ˌʃʌt 'ʌp]
3. **Was hältst du von ...?** What do you think about/of ...?
▶ S.170 (to) think
Hamburger hamburger ['hæmbɜːgə]
Hamster hamster ['hæmstə]
Hand hand [hænd]
Handel trade [treɪd]
Handschuhe gloves *(pl)* [glʌvz]
Handtuch towel ['taʊəl]
Handy mobile (phone) ['məʊbaɪl]
Happyend happy ending [ˌhæpi 'endɪŋ]
hart hard [hɑːd] • **hart arbeiten** work hard
hassen hate [heɪt]
häufig often ['ɒfn]
Haus house [haʊs] • **im Haus der Shaws / bei den Shaws zu Hause** at the Shaws' house • **nach Hause gehen** go home [həʊm] • **nach Hause kommen** come home; get home • **zu Hause** at home
Hausaufgabe(n) homework *(no pl)* ['həʊmwɜːk] • **die Hausaufgabe(n) machen** do homework • **Was haben wir als Hausaufgabe auf?** What's for homework?
Hausmeister/in caretaker ['keəteɪkə]
Haustier pet [pet]
Haustür front door [ˌfrʌnt 'dɔː]
Heim home [həʊm]
heiß hot [hɒt]
heißen 1. *(genannt werden)* be called [kɔːld] • **Ich heiße ...** My name is ... • **Wie heißt du?** What's your name?
2. **Sie heißen dich in ... willkommen** They welcome you to ... ['welkəm]
Heißluftballon balloon [bə'luːn]
Held/in hero ['hɪərəʊ], *pl* heroes ['hɪərəʊz]
helfen help [help]
Helikopter helicopter ['helɪkɒptə]
hell *(leuchtend)* bright [braɪt]
Hemd shirt [ʃɜːt]
herauf up [ʌp]
heraus out [aʊt] • **aus ... heraus** out of ... ['aʊt_əv]
▶ S.155 out
herausfinden find out [ˌfaɪnd 'aʊt]; *(entdecken)* discover [dɪ'skʌvə] • **etwas über etwas herausfinden** learn sth. about sth. [lɜːn]
herausnehmen take out [ˌteɪk 'aʊt]
herbringen bring [brɪŋ]
Herbst autumn ['ɔːtəm]
Herd cooker ['kʊkə]
hereinkommen come in [ˌkʌm 'ɪn]
Herr Brown Mr Brown ['mɪstə]
herstellen *(produzieren)* produce [prə'djuːs]
herum: anders herum the other way round [raʊnd] • **um ... herum** round
herumgeben pass round [ˌpɑːs 'raʊnd]
herunter down [daʊn]
herunterfallen (von) fall off [ˌfɔːl 'ɒf]
Herz heart [hɑːt]
Herzlichen Glückwunsch zum Geburtstag. Happy birthday. [ˌhæpi 'bɜːθdeɪ]
heute today [tə'deɪ] • **heute Morgen/Nachmittag/Abend** this morning/afternoon/evening
heute Nacht tonight [tə'naɪt]
hier here [hɪə] • **Hier bitte.** *(Bitte sehr.)* Here you are. • **hier drinnen** in here [ˌɪn 'hɪə] • **hier entlang** this way [ˌðɪs 'weɪ] • **Hier spricht Isabel. / Hier ist Isabel.** *(am*

Dictionary (German – English)

Telefon) This is Isabel. • **Hier steht: … / Es heißt hier: …** *(im Text)* It says here: …
hierher here [hɪə]
Hilfe help [help]
Himmel sky [skaɪ] • **am Himmel** in the sky
hinauf up [ʌp] • **den Hügel hinauf** up the hill
hinaufklettern (auf) climb [klaɪm] • **Klettere auf einen Baum.** Climb a tree.
hinaus out [aʊt] • **aus … hinaus** out of … ['aʊt_əv]
  ▶ S.155 out
hinein: in … hinein into … ['ɪntə, 'ɪntʊ]
hinfallen fall [fɔːl]; fall down
hinkommen *(gelangen)* get [get]
hinsetzen: sich hinsetzen sit down [,sɪt 'daʊn]
hinstellen: sich hinstellen stand (up) [,stænd_'ʌp]
hinten (im Zimmer) at the back (of the room) [bæk]
hinter behind [bɪ'haɪnd] • **im hinteren Teil (des Zimmers)** at the back (of the room) [bæk]
Hintergrund background ['bækgraʊnd]
Hintertür back door
hinüber zu/nach … over to … ['əʊvə]
hinunter down [daʊn]
hinzufügen (zu) add (to) [æd]
Hirsch deer, *pl* deer [dɪə]
Hobby hobby ['hɒbi], *pl* hobbies
hochsehen (von) look up (from) [,lʊk_'ʌp]
Hockey hockey ['hɒki]
Hockeyplatz, -feld hockey pitch [pɪtʃ]
Hockeyschuhe hockey shoes ['hɒki ʃuːz]
Hof yard [jɑːd] • **auf dem Hof** in the yard
hoffen hope [həʊp] • **Ich hoffe es.** I hope so.
holen *(besorgen)* get [get]
Holz wood [wʊd]
hören hear [hɪə] • **Na hör mal!** Come on. [,kʌm_'ɒn]
Hose trousers *(pl)* ['traʊzəz]
  ▶ S.157 Plural words
Hotel hotel [həʊ'tel]
Hotline hotline ['hɒtlaɪn]
hübsch pretty ['prɪti]; *(schön; wunderbar)* **lovely** ['lʌvli]
Hubschrauber helicopter ['helɪkɒptə]
Hügel hill [hɪl]
Huhn chicken ['tʃɪkɪn]
Hülle cover ['kʌvə]
Hund dog [dɒg]
hundert hundred ['hʌndrəd]
Hunger haben, hungrig sein be hungry ['hʌŋgri]
Hurra! Hooray! [hu'reɪ]
Hut hat [hæt]

I

ich I [aɪ] • **Ich auch.** Me too. [,miː 'tuː] • **Das bin ich.** That's me. **Warum ich?** Why me?
Idee idea [aɪ'dɪə]
Igel hedgehog ['hedʒhɒg]
ihm him; *(bei Dingen, Tieren)* it
ihn him; *(bei Dingen, Tieren)* it
ihnen them [ðəm, ðem]
Ihnen *(höfliche Anrede)* you [juː]
ihr *(Plural von „du")* you [juː]
ihr: Hilf ihr. Help her. [hə, hɜː]
ihr(e) … *(besitzanzeigend) (zu „she")* her … [hə, hɜː]; *(zu „they")* their … [ðeə]
Ihr(e) … *(höfliche Anrede)* your … [jɔː]
ihrer, ihre, ihrs *(zu „she")* hers [hɜːz]; *(zu „they")* theirs [ðeəz]
Ihrer, Ihre, Ihrs *(höfliche Anrede)* yours [jɔːz]
im: im Ausland abroad [ə'brɔːd] • **im Fernsehen** on TV • **im Flugzeug** on the plane • **im Haus der Shaws** at the Shaws' house • **im hinteren Teil (des Zimmers)** at the back (of the room) [bæk] • **im Internet surfen** surf the internet • **im Jahr 2050** in 2050 • **im Mai** in May **im Radio** on the radio • **im Zug** on the train
immer always ['ɔːlweɪz] • **immer noch** still [stɪl]
in in … (**hinein**) into … ['ɪntə, 'ɪntʊ] • **in der …straße** in … Street **in der Hamiltonstraße 7** at 7 Hamilton Street • **in der Nacht** at night • **in der Nähe von** near **in der Pause** *(zwischen Schulstunden)* at break • **in der Schule** at school • **in die falsche Richtung** the wrong way • **in die Sauna gehen** have a sauna • **in Eile sein** be in a hurry • **in den Zug/Bus einsteigen** get on the train/bus **ins Bett gehen** go to bed • **ins Kino gehen** go to the cinema • **in Schwierigkeiten sein** be in trouble ['trʌbl] • **in Urlaub fahren** go on holiday • **in Urlaub sein** be on holiday • **in welche Richtung?** which way? • **Ich bin noch nie in Bath gewesen.** I've never been to Bath.
Infinitiv infinitive [ɪn'fɪnətɪv]
Information(en) (über) information (about/on) *(no pl)* [,ɪnfə'meɪʃn]

Informationstechnologie (IT) information technology (IT) [tek'nɒlədʒi], [,aɪ 'tiː]
Ingenieur/in engineer [,endʒɪ'nɪə]
Inliner skates [skeɪts] • **Inliner fahren** skate
innen (drin) inside [,ɪn'saɪd]
Innenstadt city centre [,sɪti 'sentə]
Insel island ['aɪlənd]
Inserat advert ['ædvɜːt]
Installation installation [,ɪnstə'leɪʃn]
installieren install [ɪn'stɔːl]
interessant interesting ['ɪntrəstɪŋ]
international international [,ɪntə'næʃnəl]
Internet internet ['ɪntənet] • **im Internet surfen** surf the internet
irgendetwas anything ['eniθɪŋ] **Habt ihr irgendetwas Besonderes gemacht?** Did you do anything special?
  ▶ S.158 something – anything
irgendjemand anybody ['enibɒdi]
  ▶ S.158 somebody – anybody
irgendwelche any ['eni]
irgendwo(hin) somewhere ['sʌmweə]; anywhere ['eniweə]
  ▶ S.158 somewhere – anywhere
IT (Informationstechnologie) IT (information technology) [,aɪ 'tiː], [tek'nɒlədʒi]

J

ja yes [jes]
Jacke, Jackett jacket ['dʒækɪt]
Jahr year [jɪə] • **im Jahr 2050** in 2050 • **Kleider aus den 60er Jahren** dresses from the 60s ['sɪkstiz]
Jahreszeit season ['siːzn]
Jahrgangsstufe year [jɪə]
Jahrhundert century ['sentʃəri]
Januar January ['dʒænjuəri]
je? *(jemals?)* ever? ['evə]
  ▶ S.168 The present perfect: questions
Jeans jeans *(pl)* [dʒiːnz]
  ▶ S.157 Plural words
jede(r, s) … *(Begleiter)* **1.** every … ['evri] **2.** *(jeder einzelne)* each … [iːtʃ]
jeder *(alle)* everybody ['evribɒdi]
jemals? ever? ['evə]
  ▶ S.168 The present perfect: questions
jemand somebody ['sʌmbədi]; *(irgendjemand)* anybody ['enibɒdi]
  ▶ S.158 somebody – anybody
jene(r, s) *(Singular)* that [ðət, ðæt]; *(Plural)* those [ðəʊz]
jetzt now [naʊ] • **jetzt gerade, jetzt sofort** right now
Job job [dʒɒb]

jubeln cheer [tʃɪə]
Judo judo [ˈdʒuːdəʊ] • **Judo machen** do judo
Jugend- junior [ˈdʒuːnɪə]
Jugendliche(r) kid [kɪd]; teenager [ˈtiːneɪdʒə]
Juli July [dʒuˈlaɪ]
jung young [jʌŋ]
Junge boy [bɔɪ]
Juni June [dʒuːn]
Junioren- junior [ˈdʒuːnɪə]

K

Käfig cage [keɪdʒ]
Kalender calendar [ˈkælɪndə]
kalt cold [kəʊld]
Kamel camel [ˈkæml]
Kamera camera [ˈkæmərə]
Känguru kangaroo [ˌkæŋgəˈruː]
Kaninchen rabbit [ˈræbɪt]
kapieren: Das kapier ich nicht. I don't get it.
Kappe cap [kæp]
kaputt broken [ˈbrəʊkən] • **kaputt gehen** break [breɪk] • **kaputt machen** break [breɪk]
Karotte carrot [ˈkærət]
Karte (Post-, Spielkarte) card [kɑːd]
Kartoffel potato [pəˈteɪtəʊ], pl potatoes
Kartoffelchips crisps (pl) [krɪsps]
Käse cheese [tʃiːz]
Kästchen, Kasten box [bɒks]
Katze cat [kæt]
kaufen buy [baɪ]
Kaufhaus department store [dɪˈpɑːtmənt stɔː]
Kehle throat [θrəʊt]
kein(e) no; not a; not (...) any • **Ich habe keinen Stuhl.** I haven't got a chair. • **Ich mag kein(e) ...** I don't like ... • **keine Musik mehr** no more music
Keks biscuit [ˈbɪskɪt]
kennen know [nəʊ]
kennenlernen meet [miːt]
kennzeichnen mark up [ˌmɑːkˈʌp]
Kerl guy [gaɪ]
Kind child [tʃaɪld], pl children [ˈtʃɪldrən]; kid [kɪd]
Kino cinema [ˈsɪnəmə] • **ins Kino gehen** go to the cinema
Kirche church [tʃɜːtʃ]
Kiste box [bɒks]
Klang sound [saʊnd]
klar clear [klɪə]
Klasse class [klɑːs]; form [fɔːm]
Klassenarbeit test [test]
Klassenkamerad/in classmate [ˈklɑːsmeɪt]

Klassenlehrer/in class teacher; form teacher
Klassenzimmer classroom [ˈklɑːsruːm]
klatschen: Beifall klatschen cheer [tʃɪə]
Klavier piano [pɪˈænəʊ] • **Klavier spielen** play the piano
kleben: (auf-, ein)kleben glue [gluː]
Klebestift glue stick [ˈgluː stɪk]
Klebstoff glue [gluː]
Kleid dress [dres]
Kleiderschrank wardrobe [ˈwɔːdrəʊb]
Kleidung, Kleidungsstücke clothes (pl) [kləʊðz, kləʊz]
klein little [ˈlɪtl]; small [smɔːl]
Kleinstadt town [taʊn]
klettern climb [klaɪm] • **Klettere auf einen Baum.** Climb a tree.
Klingel bell [bel]
klingeln ring [rɪŋ]
klingen sound [saʊnd]
Klinik clinic [ˈklɪnɪk]
klopfen (an) knock (on) [nɒk]
Klub club [klʌb]
klug clever [ˈklevə]
knapp: Das war knapp. That was close. [kləʊs]
Kneipe pub [pʌb]
Knie knee [niː]
Koch cook [kʊk]
kochen cook [kʊk]
Köchin cook [kʊk]
Koje (Etagenbett) bunk (bed) [bʌŋk]
komisch (witzig) funny [ˈfʌni]
Komma: elf Komma vier (11,4) eleven point four (11.4)
▶ S.172 Numbers
kommen come [kʌm]; (hinkommen) get [get] • **Ich komme aus ...** I'm from ... • **Wo kommst du her?** Where are you from? • **nach Hause kommen** come home; get home • **zu spät kommen** be late • **Kommt nicht in Frage!** No way! • **Ach komm!** Come on. [ˌkʌmˈɒn] • **Na los, komm.** Come on.
Komödie comedy [ˈkɒmədi]
König king [kɪŋ]
königlich, Königs- royal [ˈrɔɪəl]
können can [kən, kæn]; be able to [ˈeɪbl]
▶ S.169 „können" und „dürfen"
konnte(n): ich/er konnte ... I/he could ... [kəd, kʊd]
könnte(n): ich/er könnte ... I/he could ... [kəd, kʊd]
kontrollieren (prüfen) check [tʃek]
Konzert concert [ˈkɒnsət] • **Open-Air-Konzert, Konzert im Freien** open-air concert [ˌəʊpənˈeə ˌkɒnsət]
Kopf head [hed]

Kopfschmerzen headache [ˈhedeɪk]
▶ S.167 What's wrong with you?
kopieren copy [ˈkɒpi]
Korb basket [ˈbɑːskɪt] • **ein Korb Äpfel** a basket of apples
Körper body [ˈbɒdi]
korrekt correct [kəˈrekt]
korrigieren correct [kəˈrekt]
kosten (Essen probieren) try [traɪ]
kosten: Er/Sie/Es kostet 1 Pfund. It's £1. • **Sie kosten 35 Pence.** They are 35p. • **Wie viel kostet/kosten ...?** How much is/are ...?
kostenlos free [friː]
köstlich delicious [dɪˈlɪʃəs]
Kostüm (Verkleidung) costume [ˈkɒstjuːm]
Kram stuff [stʌf]
krank ill [ɪl]
▶ S.167 What's wrong with you?
Krankenhaus hospital [ˈhɒspɪtl]
kreuzen; sich kreuzen cross [krɒs]
kriegen get [get]
Krokodil crocodile [ˈkrɒkədaɪl]
Krug jug [dʒʌg] • **ein Krug Orangensaft** a jug of orange juice
Küche kitchen [ˈkɪtʃɪn]
Kuchen cake [keɪk]
Kugelschreiber pen [pen]
Kuh cow [kaʊ]
kühl cool [kuːl]
Kühlschrank fridge [frɪdʒ]
Kummer worry [ˈwʌri]
kümmern: sich um etwas/jn. kümmern look after sth./sb. [ˌlʊkˈɑːftə] • **Kümmer dich nicht drum.** Never mind. [ˌnevəˈmaɪnd] • **Kümmere dich um deine eigenen Angelegenheiten!** Mind your own business. [ˌmaɪnd jərˌəʊn ˈbɪznəs]
Kunst art [ɑːt]
kurz short [ʃɔːt] • **kurze Hose** shorts (pl) [ʃɔːts]
▶ S.157 Plural words
Küste coast [kəʊst]

L

lächeln smile [smaɪl]
Lächeln smile [smaɪl]
lachen laugh [lɑːf] • **laut lachen** laugh out loud
Laden (Geschäft) shop [ʃɒp]
Lage: in der Lage sein, etwas zu tun be able to do sth. [ˈeɪbl]
▶ S.169 „können" und „dürfen"
Lampe lamp [læmp]
Land (auch als Gegensatz zur Stadt) country [ˈkʌntri] • **auf dem Land** in the country
landen land [lænd]

Dictionary (German – English)

Landkarte map [mæp]
lang long [lɒŋ] • **drei Tage lang** for three days • **einen Moment lang** for a moment
langsam slow [sləʊ]
langweilig boring [ˈbɔːrɪŋ]
Lärm noise [nɔɪz]
lärmend noisy [ˈnɔɪzi]
Lasagne lasagne [ləˈzænjə]
lassen let [let] • **Lass uns ... / Lasst uns ...** Let's ... • **Lass das!** Stop that!
Lauf run [rʌn]
laufen run [rʌn] • **gut laufen** (gutgehen) go well
Läufer/in runner [ˈrʌnə]
laut loud [laʊd]; (lärmend) noisy [ˈnɔɪzi] • **laut lachen** laugh out loud
Laut sound [saʊnd]
läuten ring [rɪŋ]
leben live [lɪv]
Leben life [laɪf], pl lives [laɪvz]
Lebensmittel food [fuːd]
lecker delicious [dɪˈlɪʃəs]
ledig single [ˈsɪŋgl]
leer empty [ˈempti]
legen (hin-, ablegen) put [pʊt]
lehren teach [tiːtʃ]
Lehrer/in teacher [ˈtiːtʃə]
leicht (nicht schwierig) easy [ˈiːzi]
leid: Tut mir leid. I'm sorry. [ˈsɒri]
leider I'm afraid [əˈfreɪd]
leihen: jm. etwas leihen lend sb. sth. [lend] • **sich etwas leihen** borrow sth. [ˈbɒrəʊ]
leise quiet [ˈkwaɪət]
Lektion (im Schulbuch) unit [ˈjuːnɪt]
lernen learn [lɜːn]
Lern- und Arbeitstechniken study skills [ˈstʌdi skɪlz]
lesen read [riːd]
Leser/in reader [ˈriːdə]
letzte(r, s) last [lɑːst]
leuchtend bright [braɪt]
Leute people [ˈpiːpl]; guys [gaɪz]
Lexikon encyclopedia [ɪnˌsaɪkləˈpiːdɪə]
Liebe love [lʌv]
Liebe Grüße, ... (Briefschluss) Love ... [lʌv]
lieben love [lʌv] • **etwas sehr lieben** love sth. very much
lieber: etwas lieber mögen like sth. better
Lieber Jay, ... Dear Jay ... [dɪə]
Liebling dear [dɪə]; sweetheart [ˈswiːthɑːt]
Lieblings-: meine Lieblingsfarbe my favourite colour [ˈfeɪvərɪt]
Lied song [sɒŋ]
lila purple [ˈpɜːpl]
Limonade lemonade [ˌleməˈneɪd]

Lineal ruler [ˈruːlə]
linke(r, s) left [left] • **links, auf der linken Seite** on the left • **(nach) links abbiegen** turn left • **nach links schauen** look left
▶ S.175 (to) turn
Liste list [lɪst]
Livemusik live music [laɪv]
Loch hole [həʊl]
Lokal (Kneipe) pub [pʌb]
Löwe lion [ˈlaɪən]
Luft air [eə]
Luftballon balloon [bəˈluːn]

M

machen do [duː]; make [meɪk] • **die Hausaufgabe(n) machen** do homework • **einen Ausflug machen** go on a trip • **einen Spaziergang machen** go for a walk • **eine Übung machen** do an exercise • **Ferien machen** be on holiday • **Fotos machen** take photos • **Judo machen** do judo **Macht nichts.** Never mind. [ˌnevə ˈmaɪnd] • **sich Notizen machen** take notes • **sich Sorgen machen (wegen, um)** worry (about) [ˈwʌri] • **(Zauber-)Kunststücke machen** do tricks • **Reiten macht Spaß.** Riding is fun.
Mädchen girl [gɜːl]
Magazin (Zeitschrift) magazine [ˌmæɡəˈziːn]
Magen stomach [ˈstʌmək]
Magenschmerzen stomach ache [ˈstʌmək_eɪk]
▶ S.167 What's wrong with you?
Mai May [meɪ]
Make-up make-up [ˈmeɪkʌp]
Mal(e); -mal time(s) [taɪm(z)] • **zum ersten Mal** for the first time
malen paint [peɪnt]
Maler/in painter [ˈpeɪntə]
Mama mum [mʌm]
manchmal sometimes [ˈsʌmtaɪmz]
Mann man [mæn], pl men [men]
Männchen male [meɪl]
Mannschaft team [tiːm]
Mappe (des Sprachenportfolios) dossier [ˈdɒsieɪ]
markieren mark up [ˌmɑːk_ˈʌp]
Markt market [ˈmɑːkɪt]
Marmelade (Orangenmarmelade) marmalade [ˈmɑːməleɪd]
März March [mɑːtʃ]
Maschine machine [məˈʃiːn]
Massage massage [ˈmæsɑːʒ]
massieren: sich massieren lassen have a massage [ˈmæsɑːʒ]

Material material [məˈtɪərɪəl]
Mathematik maths [mæθs]
Mauer wall [wɔːl]
Maulwurf mole [məʊl]
Maus mouse [maʊs], pl mice [maɪs]
Mediation (Sprachmittlung) mediation [ˌmiːdiˈeɪʃn]
Meer sea [siː]
Meerschweinchen guinea pig [ˈgɪni pɪg]
mehr more [mɔː] • **mehr als** more than • **mehr als ich** more than me • **nicht mehr** not (...) any more • **viel mehr** lots more **keine Musik mehr** no more music
Meile (= ca. 1,6 km) mile [maɪl]
meilenweit for miles [maɪlz]
mein(e) ... my ... [maɪ] • **meine neuen** my new ones [wʌnz]
meinen (glauben, denken) think [θɪŋk]; (sagen wollen) mean [miːn] **Meinst du wirklich?** Do you really think so?
meiner, meine, meins mine [maɪn]
Meinung: anderer Meinung sein (als) disagree (with) [ˌdɪsəˈgriː]
meist: (der/die/das) meiste ...; am meisten most [məʊst] • **die meisten Leute** most people
meistens usually [ˈjuːʒuəli]
Meister/in (Champion) champion [ˈtʃæmpiən]
Menge: eine Menge (viel, viele) a lot (of) [lɒt]; lots (of) [lɒts]
Menschen people [ˈpiːpl]
merken 1. (erkennen) realize [ˈrɪəlaɪz]
2. **sich etwas merken** remember sth. [rɪˈmembə]
Meter metre [ˈmiːtə]
mich me [miː]
Milch milk [mɪlk]
Milchshake milkshake [ˈmɪlkʃeɪk]
Mindmap mind map [ˈmaɪnd mæp]
Minute minute [ˈmɪnɪt]
mir me [miː]
mit with [wɪð] • **mit dem Auto/Zug/Rad/... fahren** go by car/train/bike/... • **Mit wem hat sie geredet?** Who did she talk to?
mitbringen bring [brɪŋ]
mitmachen: bei etwas/jm. mitmachen join sth./sb. [dʒɔɪn]
Mitschüler/in classmate [ˈklɑːsmeɪt]
Mittagessen lunch [lʌntʃ] • **zum Mittagessen** for lunch
Mittagspause lunch break [ˈlʌntʃ breɪk]
Mitte centre [ˈsentə]; middle [ˈmɪdl]
Mitteilung (Notiz) note [nəʊt]
Mittwoch Wednesday [ˈwenzdeɪ, ˈwenzdi] (siehe auch unter „Freitag")

Mobiltelefon mobile phone [ˌməʊbaɪl 'fəʊn]; mobile ['məʊbaɪl]
möchte: Ich möchte gern ... (haben) I'd like ... (= I would like ...) [laɪk]
 Ich möchte gehen I'd like to go
 Ich möchte nicht gehen I wouldn't like to go • **Möchtest du / Möchten Sie ...?** Would you like ...?
Mode fashion ['fæʃn]
Modell *(-auto, -schiff; Fotomodell)* model ['mɒdl]
Moderator/in presenter [prɪ'zentə]
mögen like [laɪk]; *(sehr mögen)* love [lʌv] • **etwas lieber mögen** like sth. better • **etwas sehr mögen** like sth. very much
möglich possible ['pɒsəbl]
Möhre carrot ['kærət]
Moment moment ['məʊmənt]
 einen Moment lang for a moment
 im Moment at the moment
 genau in dem Moment just then
 Moment mal! Wait a minute. ['mɪnɪt]
Monat month [mʌnθ]
Mond moon [muːn]
Montag Monday ['mʌndeɪ, 'mʌndi]
 (siehe auch unter „Freitag")
morgen tomorrow [tə'mɒrəʊ]
Morgen morning ['mɔːnɪŋ] • **am Morgen, morgens** in the morning
MP3-Spieler MP3 player [ˌempiː'θriː ˌpleɪə]
müde tired ['taɪəd]
Müll rubbish ['rʌbɪʃ]
Müllabfuhr rubbish collection ['rʌbɪʃ kəˌlekʃn]
Mülltonne bin [bɪn]; dustbin ['dʌstbɪn]
Mund mouth [maʊθ] • **den Mund halten** shut up [ˌʃʌt_'ʌp]
murren grumble ['grʌmbl]
Museum museum [mjuːˈziːəm]
Musical musical ['mjuːzɪkl]
Musik music ['mjuːzɪk]
Müsli muesli ['mjuːzli]
müssen have to; must [mʌst]
 nicht müssen needn't ['niːdnt]
 ▶ S.176 must – needn't – mustn't
Mutter mother ['mʌðə]
Mutti mum [mʌm]
Mütze cap [kæp]

N

Na ja ... / Na gut ... Oh well ... [əʊ 'wel]
Na und? So? [səʊ]; So what? [səʊ 'wɒt]
nach 1. *(örtlich)* to [tə, tu] • **nach draußen** outside • **nach drinnen** inside • **nach Hause gehen** go home • **nach Hause kommen** come home; get home • **nach oben** up; *(im Haus)* upstairs [ˌʌp'steəz] • **nach unten** down; *(im Haus)* downstairs [ˌdaʊn'steəz]
 nach vorn to the front [frʌnt]
 2. *(zeitlich)* after • **Viertel nach 11** quarter past 11 [pɑːst]
 3. **nach etwas fragen** ask about sth. [ə'baʊt] • **jn. nach dem Weg fragen** ask sb. the way
Nachbar/in neighbour ['neɪbə]
nachdem after ['ɑːftə]
nachdenken über think about [θɪŋk]
 ▶ S.170 (to) think
Nachmittag afternoon [ˌɑːftə'nuːn] • **am Nachmittag, nachmittags** in the afternoon
Nachrichten news *(no pl)* [njuːz]
nächste(r, s): am nächsten Tag the next day [nekst] • **der Nächste sein** be next • **Was haben wir als Nächstes?** What have we got next?
Nacht night [naɪt] • **heute Nacht** tonight [tə'naɪt] • **in der Nacht, nachts** at night
nahe (bei) near [nɪə]
Nähe: in der Nähe von near [nɪə]
Name name [neɪm]
Nase nose [nəʊz]
Nashorn rhino ['raɪnəʊ]
nass wet [wet]
natürlich *(selbstverständlich)* of course [əv 'kɔːs]
natürlich, Natur- natural ['nætʃrəl]
Naturwissenschaft science ['saɪəns]
Nebel fog [fɒg]
neben next to [nekst]
neblig foggy ['fɒgi]
nehmen take [teɪk] • **Ich nehme es.** *(beim Einkaufen)* I'll take it.
nein no [nəʊ]
nennen *(rufen, bezeichnen)* call [kɔːl]; *(benennen)* name [neɪm]
nervös nervous ['nɜːvəs]
nett nice [naɪs]
neu new [njuː] • **neu starten** *(Computer)* restart [ˌriː'stɑːt]
nicht not [nɒt] • **auch nicht** not (...) either ['aɪðə, 'iːðə] • **nicht mehr** not (...) any more • **Das glaube ich nicht. / Ich glaube nicht.** I don't think so. • **Du brauchst ein ..., nicht wahr?** You need a ..., right?
noch nicht not (...) yet [jet]
 ▶ S.166 The present perfect: statements
nichts nothing ['nʌθɪŋ]; not (...) anything ['enɪθɪŋ] • **Macht nichts.** Never mind. [ˌnevə 'maɪnd] • **Nichts zu danken.** You're welcome. ['welkəm]
 ▶ S.158 something – anything
nicken (mit) nod [nɒd]

nie, niemals never ['nevə]
 ▶ S.166 The present perfect: statements
niemand nobody ['nəʊbədi]; not (...) anybody ['enibɒdi]
 ▶ S.158 somebody – anybody
nirgendwo(hin) not (...) anywhere ['eniweə]
 ▶ S.158 somewhere – anywhere
noch: noch ein(e) ... another ... [ə'nʌðə]; one more ... [mɔː] • **noch einmal** again [ə'gen] • **noch nicht** not (...) yet [jet] • **noch 70 Meter** another 70 metres • **(immer) noch** still [stɪl]
 ▶ S.166 The present perfect: statements
Norden north [nɔːθ] • **nach Norden** north
nördlich north [nɔːθ]
Nordosten north-east [ˌnɔːθ'iːst]
nach Nordosten north-east
nordöstlich north-east [ˌnɔːθ'iːst]
Nordwest north-west [ˌnɔːθ'west]
nach Nordwesten north-west
nordwestlich north-west [ˌnɔːθ'west]
nörgeln grumble ['grʌmbl]
normalerweise usually ['juːʒuəli]
Notiz note [nəʊt] • **sich Notizen machen** take notes
November November [nəʊ'vembə]
null o [əʊ]; zero ['zɪərəʊ]
Nummer number ['nʌmbə]
nun now [naʊ] • **Nun, ...** Well, ... [wel]
nur only ['əʊnli]; just [dʒʌst] • **nur zum Spaß** just for fun

O

ob if [ɪf]
oben *(an der Spitze)* at the top (of) [tɒp]; *(im Haus)* upstairs [ˌʌp'steəz]
 nach oben up; *(im Haus)* upstairs
Oberbegriff group word ['gruːp wɜːd]
oberhalb von over ['əʊvə]
Oberteil top [tɒp]
Obst fruit [fruːt]
Obstkuchen pie [paɪ]
Obstsalat fruit salad ['fruːt ˌsæləd]
oder or [ɔː]
öffnen open ['əʊpən]
oft often ['ɒfn]
ohne without [wɪ'ðaʊt]
Ohr ear [ɪə]
Ohrenschmerzen earache ['ɪəreɪk]
 ▶ S.167 What's wrong with you?
Ohrring earring ['ɪərɪŋ]
Oje! Oh dear! [əʊ 'dɪə]
okay OK [əʊ'keɪ]
Oktober October [ɒk'təʊbə]
Oma grandma ['grænmɑː]; granny ['græni]
Onkel uncle ['ʌŋkl]

Dictionary (German – English)

Opa grandpa [ˈgrænpɑː]
Open-Air-Konzert open-air concert [ˌəʊpən_ˈeə ˌkɒnsət]
Orange orange [ˈɒrɪndʒ]
orange(farben) orange [ˈɒrɪndʒ]
Orangenmarmelade marmalade [ˈmɑːməleɪd]
Orangensaft orange juice [ˈɒrɪndʒ dʒuːs]
ordentlich tidy [ˈtaɪdi]
Ordnung: in Ordnung all right [ɔːl ˈraɪt]; fine [faɪn]
Ort place [pleɪs]
Osten east [iːst] • **nach Osten** east [iːst]
östlich east [iːst]
Outfit (Kleidung; Ausrüstung) outfit [ˈaʊtfɪt]

P

paar: ein paar some [səm, sʌm]; (einige wenige) a few [fjuː]
Paar: ein Paar a pair (of) [peə]
Päckchen packet [ˈpækɪt] • **ein Päckchen Pfefferminzbonbons** a packet of mints
packen pack [pæk]
Packung packet [ˈpækɪt] • **eine Packung Pfefferminzbonbons** a packet of mints
Paket parcel [ˈpɑːsl]
pantomimisch darstellen mime [maɪm]
Papa dad [dæd]
Papagei parrot [ˈpærət]
Papier paper [ˈpeɪpə]
Park park [pɑːk]
Partner/in partner [ˈpɑːtnə]
Partnerstadt twin town [ˌtwɪn ˈtaʊn]
Party party [ˈpɑːti]
passen fit [fɪt]
passieren (mit) happen (to) [ˈhæpən]
Pastete pie [paɪ]
Pause break [breɪk] • **in der Pause** (zwischen Schulstunden) at break
Pence pence (p) [pens]
Person person [ˈpɜːsn]
Pfad path [pɑːθ]
Pfefferminzbonbons mints [mɪnts]
Pfeife (Trillerpfeife) whistle [ˈwɪsl]
pfeifen whistle [ˈwɪsl]
Pferd horse [hɔːs]
Pfiff whistle [ˈwɪsl]
Pfund (britische Währung) pound (£) [paʊnd] • **Es kostet 1 Pfund.** It's £1.
Piano piano [piˈænəʊ]
Picknick picnic [ˈpɪknɪk]
piepsen bleep [bliːp]
Piepton bleep [bliːp]
pink(farben) pink [pɪŋk]

Pirat/in pirate [ˈpaɪrət]
Pizza pizza [ˈpiːtsə]
Plan plan [plæn]
planen plan [plæn]
Planet planet [ˈplænɪt]
Platz (Ort, Stelle) place [pleɪs]; (in der Stadt) square [skweə]
Plätzchen biscuit [ˈbɪskɪt]
plaudern chat [tʃæt]
plötzlich suddenly [ˈsʌdnli]
Polizei police (pl) [pəˈliːs]
Polizeiwache, Polizeirevier police station [pəˈliːs steɪʃn]
Poltergeist poltergeist [ˈpəʊltəgaɪst]
Pommes frites chips (pl) [tʃɪps]
Popcorn popcorn [ˈpɒpkɔːn]
Postamt post office [ˈpəʊst_ɒfɪs]
Poster poster [ˈpəʊstə]
Postkarte postcard [ˈpəʊstkɑːd]
Präsentation presentation [ˌpreznˈteɪʃn]
präsentieren: (jm.) etwas präsentieren present sth. (to sb.) [prɪˈzent]
Preis (Kaufpreis) price [praɪs]; (Gewinn) prize [praɪz]
Probe (am Theater) rehearsal [rɪˈhɜːsl]
proben (am Theater) rehearse [rɪˈhɜːs]
probieren try [traɪ]
Problem problem [ˈprɒbləm]
produzieren produce [prəˈdjuːs]
Programm programme [ˈprəʊgræm]
Projekt (über, zu) project (on, about) [ˈprɒdʒekt] • **ein Projekt machen, durchführen** do a project
prüfen (überprüfen) check [tʃek]
Prüfung (Test, Klassenarbeit) test [test]
Pullover pullover [ˈpʊləʊvə]
Punker/in punk [pʌŋk]
Punkt (bei Test, Quiz) point [pɔɪnt]
putzen clean [kliːn] • **Ich putze mir die Zähne.** I clean my teeth.
Putzfrau, -mann cleaner [ˈkliːnə]

Q

Quiz quiz [kwɪz], pl quizzes [ˈkwɪzɪz]

R

Rad fahren cycle [ˈsaɪkl]; ride a bike [ˌraɪd ə ˈbaɪk]
Radfahrt bike ride [ˈbaɪk raɪd]
Radiergummi rubber [ˈrʌbə]
Radio radio [ˈreɪdiəʊ] • **im Radio** on the radio
Radtour bike tour [ˈbaɪk tʊə]
Radweg cycle path [ˈsaɪkl pɑːθ]
Rap rap [ræp]
raten guess [ges]

Ratespiel quiz [kwɪz], pl quizzes [ˈkwɪzɪz]
Rätsel (Geheimnis) mystery [ˈmɪstri]
Raum room [ruːm]
Recht haben be right [raɪt]
rechte(r, s) right [raɪt] • **rechts, auf der rechten Seite** on the right **(nach) rechts abbiegen** turn right **nach rechts schauen** look right
▶ S.175 (to) turn
rechtzeitig in time [ɪn ˈtaɪm]
recycelt recycled [ˌriːˈsaɪkld]
Recycling recycling [ˌriːˈsaɪklɪŋ]
reden (mit, über) talk (to, about) [tɔːk]; speak (to, about) [spiːk] • **Wovon redest du?** What are you talking about?
Regal(brett) shelf [ʃelf], pl shelves [ʃelvz]
Regen rain [reɪn]
Regenzeit rainy season [ˈreɪni ˌsiːzn]
regnen rain [reɪn]
regnerisch rainy [ˈreɪni]
Reh deer, pl deer [dɪə]
reich rich [rɪtʃ]
reichen (weitergeben) pass [pɑːs]
Reihe: 1. Du bist an der Reihe. It's your turn. [tɜːn]
2. (Sendereihe, Serie) series, pl series [ˈsɪəriːz]
Reise trip [trɪp] • **eine Reise machen** go on a trip
reisen travel [ˈtrævl]
reiten ride [raɪd] • **reiten gehen** go riding
Religion (Religionsunterricht) RE [ˌɑːrˈiː], Religious Education [rɪˌlɪdʒəs_edʒuˈkeɪʃn]
rennen run [rʌn]
Reportage (über) report (on) [rɪˈpɔːt]
Reporter/in reporter [rɪˈpɔːtə]
Rest rest [rest]
Restaurant restaurant [ˈrestrɒnt]; (Imbissstube, Café) café [ˈkæfeɪ]
Resultat result [rɪˈzʌlt]
retten save [seɪv]
richtig right [raɪt]; (korrekt) correct [kəˈrekt]
Richtung way [weɪ] • **in diese Richtung** this way • **in die falsche Richtung** the wrong way • **in welche Richtung?** which way?
▶ S.174 way
riechen smell [smel]
Ring ring [rɪŋ]
Rock skirt [skɜːt]
Rollstuhl wheelchair [ˈwiːltʃeə]
Römer, Römerin; römisch Roman [ˈrəʊmən]
rosa pink [pɪŋk]
rot red [red]
Ruf call [kɔːl]

Dictionary (German – English)

rufen call [kɔːl]; shout [ʃaʊt] • **die Polizei rufen** call the police
ruhig quiet [ˈkwaɪət]
rund round [raʊnd]
Rundgang (durch das Haus) tour (of the house) [tʊə]
runterladen download [ˌdaʊnˈləʊd]

S

Sache thing [θɪŋ]
Saft juice [dʒuːs]
sagen say [seɪ] • **Sagt mir eure Namen.** Tell me your names. [teɪ]
Salat 1. *(Kopfsalat)* lettuce [ˈletɪs]
2. *(Gericht, Beilage)* salad [ˈsæləd]
sammeln collect [kəˈlekt]
Sammler/in collector [kəˈlektə]
Samstag Saturday [ˈsætədeɪ, ˈsætədi] *(siehe auch unter „Freitag")*
Sandwich sandwich [ˈsænwɪtʃ]
Sänger/in singer [ˈsɪŋə]
Sanitäter/in paramedic [ˌpærəˈmedɪk]
Satz sentence [ˈsentəns]
sauber clean [kliːn] • **sauber machen** clean
Sauna sauna [ˈsɔːnə] • **in die Sauna gehen** have a sauna
Schachtel packet [ˈpækɪt]
schade: Es ist schade, dass … It's a pity (that …) [ˈpɪti]
Schaf sheep, *pl* sheep [ʃiːp]
Schale bowl [bəʊl] • **eine Schale Cornflakes** a bowl of cornflakes
Schatz dear [dɪə]; sweetheart [ˈswiːθɑːt]
schätzen *(erraten)* guess [ges]
schauen look [lʊk]
Schauspiel drama [ˈdrɑːmə]
Schauspieler/in actor [ˈæktə]
scheinen *(Sonne)* shine [ʃaɪn]
scherzen joke [dʒəʊk]
scheu shy [ʃaɪ]
scheußlich horrible [ˈhɒrəbl]
schicken (an) send (to) [send] • **jm. eine SMS schicken** text sb. [tekst]
schieben push [pʊʃ]
Schiff boat [bəʊt]; ship [ʃɪp]
Schildkröte tortoise [ˈtɔːtəs]
Schinkenspeck bacon [ˈbeɪkən]
Schlafanzug pyjamas *(pl)* [pəˈdʒɑːməz]
schlafen sleep [sliːp]; *(nicht wach sein)* be asleep [əˈsliːp]
Schlafzimmer bedroom [ˈbedruːm]
Schlange snake [sneɪk]
schlau clever [ˈklevə]
schlecht bad [bæd] • **schlechter** worse [wɜːs] • **am schlechtesten; der/die/das schlechteste** (the) worst [wɜːst]
▶ S.159 bad – worse – worst

schließen *(zumachen)* close [kləʊz]
schließlich at last [ət ˈlɑːst]
schlimm bad [bæd] • **schlimmer** worse [wɜːs] • **am schlimmsten; der/die/das schlimmste** (the) worst [wɜːst]
▶ S.159 bad – worse – worst
Schlittschuhbahn ice rink [ˈaɪs rɪŋk]
Schloss castle [ˈkɑːsl]
Schlüssel key [kiː]
Schlüsselwort key word [ˈkiː wɜːd]
Schmerz(en) pain [peɪn] • **schreien vor Schmerzen** cry in pain [kraɪ]
schmutzig dirty [ˈdɜːti]
Schnee snow [snəʊ]
schneiden cut [kʌt]
schnell quick [kwɪk]; fast [fɑːst]
Schokolade chocolate [ˈtʃɒklət]
schon already [ɔːlˈredi] • **schon?** yet? [jet] • **schon mal?** ever? [ˈevə] **(vorher) schon mal** before [bɪˈfɔː]
▶ S.166 The present perfect: statements
▶ S.168 The present perfect: questions
schön beautiful [ˈbjuːtɪfl]; *(nett)* nice [naɪs]; *(hübsch; wunderbar)* lovely [ˈlʌvli] • **schön kühl/sauber/… ordentlich** nice and cool/clean/… schön ordentlich neat and tidy
Schrank cupboard [ˈkʌbəd]; *(Kleiderschrank)* wardrobe [ˈwɔːdrəʊb]
schrecklich terrible [ˈterəbl]; awful [ˈɔːfl]
schreiben (an) write (to) [raɪt]
Schreiber/in writer [ˈraɪtə]
Schreibtisch desk [desk]
schreien shout [ʃaʊt]; cry [kraɪ] **schreien vor Schmerzen** cry in pain
Schriftsteller/in writer [ˈraɪtə]
Schritt step [step]
schüchtern shy [ʃaɪ]
Schuh shoe [ʃuː]
Schule school [skuːl] • **in der Schule** at school
Schüler/in student [ˈstjuːdənt]
Schulfach (school) subject [ˈsʌbdʒɪkt]
Schulheft exercise book [ˈeksəsaɪz bʊk]
Schulklasse class [klɑːs]; form [fɔːm]
Schultasche school bag [ˈskuːl bæg]
Schulter shoulder [ˈʃəʊldə]
Schüssel bowl [bəʊl]
schwach weak [wiːk]
schwarz black [blæk]
schwer *(schwierig)* difficult [ˈdɪfɪkəlt]; hard [hɑːd]
Schwester sister [ˈsɪstə]
schwierig difficult [ˈdɪfɪkəlt]; hard [hɑːd]
Schwierigkeiten trouble [ˈtrʌbl] • **in Schwierigkeiten sein** be in trouble
Schwimmbad, -becken swimming pool [ˈswɪmɪŋ puːl]

schwimmen swim [swɪm] **schwimmen gehen** go swimming
Schwimmer/in swimmer [ˈswɪmə]
See 1. *(Binnensee)* lake [leɪk]
2. *(die See, das Meer)* sea [siː] • **auf See** at sea
sehen see [siː] • **Siehst du?** See?
Sehenswürdigkeiten sights *(pl)* [saɪts]
sehr very [ˈveri] • **Danke sehr!** Thanks very much! • **Er mag sie sehr.** He likes her a lot. [ə ˈlɒt] **etwas sehr mögen/sehr lieben** like/love sth. very much
Seife soap [səʊp]
sein *(Verb)* be [biː]
sein(e) … *(besitzanzeigend) (zu „he")* his …; *(zu „it")* its …
seiner, seine, seins his [hɪz]
Seite 1. side [saɪd] • **auf der linken Seite** on the left • **auf der rechten Seite** on the right
2. *(Buch-, Heftseite)* page [peɪdʒ] **Auf welcher Seite sind wir?** What page are we on?
Sekunde second [ˈsekənd]
Selbstbedienungsrestaurant *(Cafeteria)* cafeteria [ˌkæfəˈtɪəriə]
selbstverständlich of course [əv ˈkɔːs]
seltsam strange [streɪndʒ]
senden (an) send (to) [send]
Sendereihe series, *pl* series [ˈsɪəriːz]
September September [sepˈtembə]
Serie *(Sendereihe)* series, *pl* series [ˈsɪəriːz]
Service *(Dienst am Kunden)* service [ˈsɜːvɪs]
Sessel armchair [ˈɑːmtʃeə]
setzen: sich setzen sit [sɪt] • **Setz dich / Setzt euch zu mir.** Sit with me.
Shorts shorts *(pl)* [ʃɔːts]
▶ S.157 Plural words
Show show [ʃəʊ]
sicher 1. *(in Sicherheit)* safe (from) [seɪf]
2. **sicher sein** *(nicht zweifeln)* be sure [ʃʊə, ʃɔː]
Sicherheit: in Sicherheit (vor) safe (from) [seɪf]
Sicht: aus meiner Sicht from my point of view [ˌpɔɪnt əv ˈvjuː]
sie 1. *(weibliche Person)* she [ʃiː] **Frag sie.** Ask her. [hə, hɜː]
2. *(Ding, Tier)* it [ɪt]
3. *(Plural)* they [ðeɪ] • **Frag sie.** Ask them. [ðəm, ðem]
4. **Sie** *(höfliche Anrede)* you [juː]
Sieger/in winner [ˈwɪnə]
Silbe syllable [ˈsɪləbl]
singen sing [sɪŋ]
sitzen sit [sɪt]

Skateboard skateboard [ˈskeɪtbɔːd]
Skateboard fahren skate [skeɪt]
Sketch sketch [sketʃ]
Sklave, Sklavin slave [sleɪv]
SMS text message [ˈtekst ˌmesɪdʒ]
jm. eine SMS schicken text sb. [tekst]
Snack snack [snæk]
so süß so sweet [səʊ] • **so groß/ aufregend wie** as big/exciting as
sobald as soon as [əz ˈsuːn_əz]
Socke sock [sɒk]
soeben just [dʒʌst]
▶ S.166 The present perfect: statements
Sofa sofa [ˈsəʊfə]
Software software [ˈsɒftweə]
sogar even [ˈiːvn]
Sohn son [sʌn]
sollte(n): ich/er sollte ... I/he should [ʃəd, ʃʊd]
Sommer summer [ˈsʌmə]
sonderbar strange [streɪndʒ]
Song song [sɒŋ]
Sonnabend Saturday [ˈsætədeɪ, ˈsætədi] *(siehe auch unter „Freitag")*
Sonne sun [sʌn]
Sonnenbrille: (eine) Sonnenbrille sunglasses *(pl)* [ˈsʌŋglɑːsɪz]
▶ S.157 Plural words
sonnig sunny [ˈsʌni]
Sonntag Sunday [ˈsʌndeɪ, ˈsʌndi] *(siehe auch unter „Freitag")*
Sorge worry [ˈwʌri] • **sich Sorgen machen (wegen, um)** worry (about) • **Mach dir keine Sorgen.** Don't worry.
Sorte sort (of) [sɔːt]
sowie *(sobald)* as soon as [əz ˈsuːn_əz]
sowieso anyway [ˈeniweɪ]
Spaghetti spaghetti [spəˈgeti]
spannend exciting [ɪkˈsaɪtɪŋ]
sparen save [seɪv]
Spaß fun [fʌn] • **Spaß haben** have fun • **nur zum Spaß** just for fun **Reiten macht Spaß.** Riding is fun. **Viel Spaß!** Have fun!
spät late [leɪt] • **Wie spät ist es?** What's the time? • **zu spät sein/ kommen** be late
später later [ˈleɪtə]
spazieren gehen go for a walk [wɔːk]
Spaziergang walk [wɔːk] • **einen Spaziergang machen** go for a walk
Specht woodpecker [ˈwʊdpekə]
Spiegel mirror [ˈmɪrə]
Spiel game [geɪm]; *(Wettkampf)* match [mætʃ]
spielen play [pleɪ]; *(Szene, Dialog)* act [ækt] • **Fußball spielen** play football • **Gitarre/Klavier spielen** play the guitar/the piano • **jm.**

einen Streich spielen play a trick on sb.
Spieler/in player [ˈpleɪə]
Spielstein *(für Brettspiele)* counter [ˈkaʊntə]
Spion/in spy [spaɪ]
Spitze *(oberes Ende)* top [tɒp] • **an der Spitze (von)** at the top (of)
Sport; Sportart sport [spɔːt] • **Sport treiben** do sport
Sportausrüstung, Sportsachen sports gear *(no pl)* [ˈspɔːts gɪə]
Sportunterricht PE [ˌpiːˈiː], Physical Education [ˌfɪzɪkəl_edʒuˈkeɪʃn]
Sprache language [ˈlæŋgwɪdʒ]
Sprachmittlung *(Mediation)* mediation [ˌmiːdiˈeɪʃn]
sprechen (mit) speak (to) [spiːk] **Hier spricht Isabel.** *(am Telefon)* This is Isabel.
springen jump [dʒʌmp]
Spülbecken, Spüle sink [sɪŋk]
Stadt *(Großstadt)* city [ˈsɪti]; *(Kleinstadt)* town [taʊn]
Stadtplan map [mæp]
Stadtzentrum city centre [ˌsɪti ˈsentə]
Stall *(für Kaninchen)* hutch [hʌtʃ]
Stammbaum family tree [ˈfæməli triː]
Standpunkt point of view [ˌpɔɪnt_əv ˈvjuː] • **von meinem Standpunkt aus gesehen** from my point of view
Star *(Film-, Popstar)* star [stɑː]
stark strong [strɒŋ]
starten start [stɑːt] • **neu starten** *(Computer)* restart [ˌriːˈstɑːt]
stattfinden take place [ˌteɪk ˈpleɪs]
Statue statue [ˈstætʃuː]
stehen stand [stænd] • **Hier steht: ...** *(im Text)* It says here: ...
stehlen steal [stiːl]
Steigerung comparison [kəmˈpærɪsn]
Stein stone [stəʊn]
stellen *(hin-, abstellen)* put [pʊt] **Fragen stellen** ask questions **(jm.) eine Falle stellen** set a trap (for sb.) [set] • **sich (hin)stellen** stand [stænd] • **Stell dir vor! / Stellt euch vor!** Guess what! [ˌges ˈwɒt]
sterben (an) die (of) [daɪ]
Stern star [stɑː]
Stichwort *(Schlüsselwort)* key word [ˈkiː wɜːd]
Stiefel boot [buːt]
still quiet [ˈkwaɪət]
Stimme voice [vɔɪs]
stimmen: Das stimmt. That's right. [raɪt] • **Du brauchst ein Lineal, stimmt's?** You need a ruler, right?
Stoff *(Material)* material [məˈtɪəriəl]
stolz (auf jn./etwas) proud (of sb./sth.) [praʊd]

stoßen push [pʊʃ]
Strand beach [biːtʃ] • **am Strand** on the beach
Straße road [rəʊd]; street [striːt]
Strecke way [weɪ]
Streich trick [trɪk] • **jm. einen Streich spielen** play a trick on sb.
Streit argument [ˈɑːgjumənt]
streiten: sich streiten argue [ˈɑːgjuː]; have an argument [ˈɑːgjumənt]
strukturieren structure [ˈstrʌktʃə]
Strumpf sock [sɒk]
Stück piece [piːs] • **ein Stück Papier** a piece of paper
Student/in student [ˈstjuːdənt]
Studio studio [ˈstjuːdiəʊ]
Stuhl chair [tʃeə]
stumm: „stummer" Buchstabe *(nicht gesprochener Buchstabe)* silent letter [ˌsaɪlənt ˈletə]
Stunde hour [ˈaʊə]; *(Schulstunde)* lesson [ˈlesn] • **eine halbe Stunde** half an hour [hɑːf]
Stundenplan timetable [ˈtaɪmteɪbl]
Sturm storm [stɔːm]
stürmisch stormy [ˈstɔːmi]
stürzen *(hinfallen)* fall [fɔːl]
Subjekt subject [ˈsʌbdʒɪkt]
suchen look for [ˈlʊk fɔː]
Süden south [saʊθ] • **nach Süden** south
südlich south [saʊθ]
Südosten south-east [ˌsaʊθˈiːst]
nach Südosten south-east
südöstlich south-east [ˌsaʊθˈiːst]
Südwesten south-west [ˌsaʊθˈwest]
nach Südwesten south-west
südwestlich south-west [ˌsaʊθˈwest]
Supermarkt supermarket [ˈsuːpəmɑːkɪt]
Suppe soup [suːp]
Surfbrett surfboard [ˈsɜːfbɔːd]
surfen gehen go surfing [ˈsɜːfɪŋ] • **im Internet surfen** surf the internet [sɜːf]
süß sweet [swiːt]
Süßigkeiten sweets *(pl)* [swiːts]
Sweatshirt sweatshirt [ˈswetʃɜːt]
Szene scene [siːn]

T

Tafel *(Wandtafel)* board [bɔːd] • **an der/die Tafel** on the board
Tag day [deɪ] • **drei Tage (lang)** for three days • **eines Tages** one day **Guten Tag.** Hello.; *(nachmittags)* Good afternoon. [gʊd_ˌɑːftəˈnuːn]
Tagebuch diary [ˈdaɪəri]
Tal valley [ˈvæli]
Talboden valley floor [ˌvæli ˈflɔː]

Dictionary (German – English)

Talkshow chat show [ˈtʃæt ʃəʊ]
Tante aunt [ɑːnt]; auntie [ˈɑːnti]
Tanz dance [dɑːns]
tanzen dance [dɑːns]
Tänzer/in dancer [ˈdɑːnsə]
Tanzstunden, Tanzunterricht dancing lessons [ˈdɑːnsɪŋ ˌlesnz]
Tasche *(Tragetasche, Beutel)* bag [bæɡ]; *(Hosentasche, Jackentasche)* pocket [ˈpɒkɪt]
Taschengeld pocket money [ˈpɒkɪt ˌmʌni]
Tasse cup [kʌp] • **eine Tasse Tee** a cup of tea
Tätigkeit activity [ækˈtɪvəti]
tausend thousand [ˈθaʊznd]
Team team [tiːm]
Tee tea [tiː]
Teenager teenager [ˈtiːneɪdʒə]
Teil part [pɑːt]; *(eines Textes)* section [ˈsekʃn]
teilen: (sich) teilen (in) divide (into) [dɪˈvaɪd] • **sich etwas teilen (mit jm.)** share sth. (with sb.) [ʃeə]
Telefon (tele)phone [ˈtelɪfəʊn] • **am Telefon** on the phone
Telefongespräch: ein Telefongespräch führen make a call [kɔːl]
Telefonnummer (tele)phone number [ˈtelɪfəʊn ˌnʌmbə]
Teller plate [pleɪt] • **ein Teller Pommes frites** a plate of chips
Temperatur temperature [ˈtemprətʃə]
Tennis tennis [ˈtenɪs]
Termin appointment [əˈpɔɪntmənt]
Terminkalender diary [ˈdaɪəri]
Test test [test]
teuer expensive [ɪkˈspensɪv]
Text text [tekst]
Theater theatre [ˈθɪətə]
Theaterstück play [pleɪ]
Thema, Themenbereich topic [ˈtɒpɪk]
Themenpark theme park [ˈθiːm pɑːk]
Thermometer thermometer [θəˈmɒmɪtə]
Tier animal [ˈænɪml]; *(Haustier)* pet [pet]
Tierhandlung pet shop [ˈpet ʃɒp]
Tierpark zoo [zuː]
Tiger tiger [ˈtaɪɡə]
Tisch table [ˈteɪbl]
Tischtennis table tennis [ˈteɪbl tenɪs]
Titel title [ˈtaɪtl]
Toast(brot) toast [təʊst]
Tochter daughter [ˈdɔːtə]
Toilette toilet [ˈtɔɪlət]
toll fantastic [fænˈtæstɪk]; great [ɡreɪt]
Tomate tomato [təˈmɑːtəʊ], *pl* tomatoes
Top *(Oberteil)* top [tɒp]
Torte cake [keɪk]
tot dead [ded]

töten kill [kɪl]
Tour: (Rad-)Tour (bike) tour [tʊə] **Tour durch das Haus** *(Rundgang)* tour of the house
Tourist/in tourist [ˈtʊərɪst]
tragen *(Kleidung)* wear [weə]
trainieren practise [ˈpræktɪs]
Träne tear [tɪə]
Traum dream [driːm]
Traumhaus dream house
traurig sad [sæd]
treffen; sich treffen meet [miːt]
Treppe(nstufen) stairs *(pl)* [steəz]
Trick *(Zauberkunststück)* trick [trɪk]
Trimester term [tɜːm]
trinken drink [drɪŋk] • **Milch zum Frühstück trinken** have milk for breakfast
trotzdem anyway [ˈeniweɪ]; still [stɪl]
Tschüs. Bye. [baɪ]; See you. [ˈsiː juː]
T-Shirt T-shirt [ˈtiːʃɜːt]
tun do [duː] • **Tue, was ich tue.** Do what I do. • **tun müssen** have to do • **tun wollen** want to do [wɒnt] **Tut mir leid.** I'm sorry. [ˈsɒri]
Tunnel tunnel [ˈtʌnl]
Tür door [dɔː]
Türklingel doorbell [ˈdɔːbel]
Turm tower [ˈtaʊə]
Turnen *(Sportunterricht)* PE [ˌpiː ˈiː], Physical Education [ˌfɪzɪkl ˌedʒuˈkeɪʃn]
Turnschuhe trainers *(pl)* [ˈtreɪnəz]
Tut mir leid. I'm sorry. [ˈsɒri]
Tüte bag [bæɡ]
Typ *(Kerl)* guy [ɡaɪ]
tyrannisieren bully [ˈbʊli]

U

U-Bahn: die U-Bahn the underground [ˈʌndəɡraʊnd] *(BE)*; the subway [ˈsʌbweɪ] *(AE)*
üben practise [ˈpræktɪs]
über about [əˈbaʊt]; *(räumlich)* over [ˈəʊvə]; across [əˈkrɒs]
überall everywhere [ˈevriweə]
übereinstimmen: nicht übereinstimmen (mit) disagree (with) [ˌdɪsəˈɡriː]
überleben survive [səˈvaɪv]
Überleben survival [səˈvaɪvl]
übernachten *(über Nacht bleiben)* stay [steɪ]
überprüfen check [tʃek]
überqueren cross [krɒs]
Überschrift title [ˈtaɪtl]
übrig sein be left [left]
Übung *(Schulbuch)* exercise [ˈeksəsaɪz] **eine Übung machen** do an exercise

Übungsheft exercise book [ˈeksəsaɪz bʊk]
Uhr 1. *(Armbanduhr)* watch [wɒtʃ]; *(Wand-, Stand-, Turmuhr)* clock [klɒk]
2. **elf Uhr** eleven o'clock • **7 Uhr morgens/vormittags** 7 am [ˌeɪ ˈem] **7 Uhr nachmittags/abends** 7 pm [ˌpiː ˈem] • **um 8 Uhr 45** at 8.45
Uhrzeit time [taɪm]
um 1. *(örtlich)* **um ... (herum)** round [raʊnd]
2. *(zeitlich)* **um 8.45** at 8.45
3. **Es geht um Mr Green.** This is about Mr Green.
4. **um zu** to
umdrehen: sich umdrehen turn [tɜːn]
▶ S.175 (to) turn
Umfrage (über) survey (on) [ˈsɜːveɪ]
umher: in ... umher round [raʊnd]
umsehen: sich umsehen look round [ˌlʊk ˈraʊnd]
umziehen (nach, in) *(die Wohnung wechseln)* move (to) [muːv]
unbequem uncomfortable [ʌnˈkʌmftəbl]
und and [ənd, ænd] • **Und? / Na und?** So? [səʊ]; So what? [səʊ ˈwɒt]
undeutlich *(unklar)* unclear [ʌnˈklɪə]
unfair unfair [ʌnˈfeə]
Unfall accident [ˈæksɪdənt]
unfreundlich unfriendly [ʌnˈfrendli]
ungefähr about [əˈbaʊt]
ungerecht unfair [ʌnˈfeə]
unglaublich amazing [əˈmeɪzɪŋ]
unglücklich unhappy [ʌnˈhæpi]
unheimlich scary [ˈskeəri]
unhöflich rude [ruːd]
Uniform uniform [ˈjuːnɪfɔːm]
uninteressant uninteresting [ʌnˈɪntrəstɪŋ]
unklar unclear [ʌnˈklɪə]
unmöglich impossible [ɪmˈpɒsəbl]
Unordnung: alles in Unordnung bringen make a mess [ˌmeɪk ə ˈmes]
uns us [əs, ʌs]
unser(e) ... our ... [ˈaʊə] • **unser eigenes Schwimmbad** our own pool [əʊn]
unserer, unsere, unseres ours [ˈaʊəz]
unsicher unsure [ʌnˈʃʊə, ʌnˈʃɔː]
unten *(im Haus)* downstairs [ˌdaʊnˈsteəz] • **am unteren Ende (von)** at the bottom (of) [ˈbɒtəm] **dort unten** down there • **nach unten** down [daʊn]; *(im Haus)* downstairs
unter under [ˈʌndə]
untere(r, s): am unteren Ende (von) at the bottom (of) [ˈbɒtəm]

unterhalten: sich unterhalten (mit, über) talk (to, about) [tɔːk]
Unterhaltung *(Gespräch)* conversation [ˌkɒnvəˈseɪʃn]
Unterricht lessons *(pl)* [ˈlesnz]
unterrichten teach [tiːtʃ]
unterschiedlich different [ˈdɪfrənt]
Untersuchung (über) *(Umfrage)* survey (on) [ˈsɜːveɪ]
unverschämt rude [ruːd]
Urlaub holiday [ˈhɒlədeɪ] • **in Urlaub fahren** go on holiday • **in Urlaub sein** be on holiday

V

Vater father [ˈfɑːðə]
Vati dad [dæd]
Verabredung appointment [əˈpɔɪntmənt]
verabschieden: sich verabschieden say goodbye [ˌseɪ ɡʊdˈbaɪ]
verängstigt scared [skeəd]
verbessern *(korrigieren)* correct [kəˈrekt]
verbinden *(einander zuordnen)* link [lɪŋk]
verbringen: Zeit verbringen (mit etwas) spend time (on sth.) [spend]
Verein club [klʌb]
verfolgen follow [ˈfɒləʊ]
Vergangenheit past [pɑːst]
Vergleich comparison [kəmˈpærɪsn]
vergleichen compare [kəmˈpeə]
verheiratet (mit) married (to) [ˈmærɪd]
verkaufen sell [sel]
Verkäufer/in shop assistant [ˈʃɒp əˌsɪstənt]
Verkehr traffic [ˈtræfɪk]
verkehrt *(falsch)* wrong [rɒŋ]
Verkleidung *(Kostüm)* costume [ˈkɒstjuːm]
verknüpfen *(einander zuordnen)* link [lɪŋk]
verlassen leave [liːv]
verletzen hurt [hɜːt]
verletzt hurt [hɜːt]
Verletzung injury [ˈɪndʒəri]
verlieren lose [luːz]
vermissen miss [mɪs]
Vermittlung *(Sprachmittlung, Mediation)* mediation [ˌmiːdiˈeɪʃn]
vermuten suppose [səˈpəʊz]
verpassen miss [mɪs]
verrückt mad [mæd]
verschieden different [ˈdɪfrənt]
verschwinden disappear [ˌdɪsəˈpɪə]
versprechen promise [ˈprɒmɪs]
verstecken; sich verstecken hide [haɪd]

verstehen understand [ˌʌndəˈstænd] **Das versteh ich nicht.** I don't get it.
versuchen try [traɪ] • **versuchen zu tun** try and do / try to do
Verwandte(r) relative [ˈrelətɪv]
verwenden use [juːz]
verwirrt puzzled [ˈpʌzld]
viel a lot (of) [lɒt]; lots (of) [lɒts]; much [mʌtʃ] • **viele** a lot (of); lots (of); many [ˈmeni] • **Viel Glück (bei/mit ...)!** Good luck (with ...)! • **viel mehr** lots more • **Viel Spaß!** Have fun! • **wie viel?** how much? **wie viele?** how many? • **Vielen Dank!** Thanks a lot!
vielleicht maybe [ˈmeɪbi]
Viertel: Viertel nach 11 quarter past 11 [ˈkwɔːtə] • **Viertel vor 12** quarter to 12
Villa villa [ˈvɪlə]
violett purple [ˈpɜːpl]
Vogel bird [bɜːd]
Vokabelverzeichnis vocabulary [vəˈkæbjələri]
Vokallaut vowel sound [ˈvaʊəl saʊnd]
voll full [fʊl]
Volleyball volleyball [ˈvɒlibɔːl]
von of [əv, ɒv]; from [frəm, frɒm] • **ein Aufsatz von ...** an essay by ... [baɪ]
vor 1. *(räumlich)* in front of [ɪn ˈfrʌnt əv]
2. *(zeitlich)* **vor dem Abendessen** before dinner [bɪˈfɔː] • **vor einer Minute** a minute ago [əˈɡəʊ] • **Viertel vor 12** quarter to 12
vorbei (an) *(vorüber)* past [pɑːst]
vorbei sein be over [ˈəʊvə]
vorbereiten prepare [prɪˈpeə] • **sich vorbereiten (auf)** prepare (for); get ready (for) [ˈredi] • **Dinge vorbereiten** get things ready
Vordergrund foreground [ˈfɔːɡraʊnd]
vorgestern the day before yesterday
Vormittag morning [ˈmɔːnɪŋ]
vorsichtig careful [ˈkeəfl]
vorspielen *(pantomimisch darstellen)* mime [maɪm]
vorstellen: (jm.) etwas vorstellen *(präsentieren)* present sth. (to sb.) [prɪˈzent] • **Stell dir vor! / Stellt euch vor!** Guess what! [ɡes ˈwɒt]
Vorstellung *(Präsentation)* presentation [ˌpreznˈteɪʃn]; *(Show)* show [ʃəʊ]
vorüber (an) *(vorbei)* past [pɑːst]

W

wachsen grow [ɡrəʊ]
wählen *(auswählen)* choose [tʃuːz]; *(Telefonnummer)* dial [ˈdaɪəl]

wahr true [truː] • **wahr werden** come true
wahrscheinlich probably [ˈprɒbəbli]
Wald forest [ˈfɒrɪst]; woods *(pl)* [wʊdz]
walisisch; Walisisch Welsh [welʃ]
Wand wall [wɔːl]
wann when [wen]
warm warm [wɔːm]
Wärmflasche hot-water bottle [ˌhɒt ˈwɔːtə bɒtl]
warten (auf) wait (for) [weɪt] • **Warte mal!** Wait a minute. [ˈmɪnɪt]
warum why [waɪ] • **Warum ich?** Why me?
was what [wɒt] • **Was dann?** Then what? • **Was fehlt dir?** *(bei Krankheit)* What's wrong with you? • **Was haben wir als Hausaufgabe auf?** What's for homework? • **Was haben wir als Nächstes?** What have we got next? • **Was ist los? / Was ist denn?** What's the matter? [ˈmætə] • **Was ist mit ...?** What about ...? • **Was kann/darf ich euch/Ihnen bringen?** What can I get you? • **Was kostet/kosten ...?** How much is/are ...? • **Was war das Beste an ...?** What was the best thing about ...? • **alles, was wir jetzt (noch) tun müssen, ...** all we have to do now ...
waschen wash [wɒʃ] • **Ich wasche mir das Gesicht.** I wash my face.
Waschmaschine washing machine [ˈwɒʃɪŋ məˌʃiːn]
Wasser water [ˈwɔːtə]
Webcam webcam [ˈwebkæm]
Website website [ˈwebsaɪt]
Wechselgeld change [tʃeɪndʒ]
Wecker alarm clock [əˈlɑːm klɒk]
weg away [əˈweɪ] • **weg sein** *(nicht da sein)* be gone [ɡɒn]; *(aus dem Haus sein)* be out [aʊt]
Weg way [weɪ]; *(Pfad)* path [pɑːθ] • **auf dem Weg (zu/nach)** on the way (to) • **jm. den Weg beschreiben** tell sb. the way • **jn. nach dem Weg fragen** ask sb. the way
▶ S.174 way
Wegbeschreibung(en) directions *(pl)* [dəˈrekʃnz]
weggehen leave [liːv]; *(raus-, ausgehen)* go out
wehtun hurt [hɜːt]; be sore [sɔː]
▶ S.167 What's wrong with you?
Weibchen female [ˈfiːmeɪl]
Weide field [fiːld]
weil because [bɪˈkɒz]
weiß white [waɪt]
weit (entfernt) far [fɑː]; a long way

weiter: geradeaus weiter straight on [streɪt ˈɒn]
weitere(r, s): ein(e) weitere(r, s) one more [mɔː] • **weitere 70 Meter** another 70 metres [əˈnʌðə]
weitergeben pass [pɑːs]
weitergehen continue [kənˈtɪnjuː]
weitermachen go on [ˌɡəʊ ˈɒn]; continue [kənˈtɪnjuː]
weiterreden continue [kənˈtɪnjuː]
welche(r, s) which [wɪtʃ] • **Auf welcher Seite sind wir?** What page are we on? [wɒt] • **Welche Farbe hat ...?** What colour is ...?
wellenreiten gehen go surfing [ˈsɜːfɪŋ]
Wellensittich budgie [ˈbʌdʒi]
Welt world [wɜːld] • **auf der Welt** in the world • **aus der ganzen Welt** from all over the world
Weltraum space [ˈspeɪs]
wem? who? [huː] • **Mit wem hat sie geredet?** Who did she talk to? **Wem gehören diese?** Whose are these? [huːz]
wen? who? [huː]
wenden: sich an jn. wenden turn to sb. [tɜːn]
▶ S.175 (to) turn
wenigstens at least [ət ˈliːst]
wenn 1. *(zeitlich)* when [wen] **2.** *(falls)* if [ɪf]
wer who [huː]
Werbespot advert [ˈædvɜːt]
werden become [bɪˈkʌm] • **geboren werden** be born [bɔːn] • **wütend/heiß/... werden** get angry/hot/... • **wahr werden** come true **du wirst frieren; ihr werdet frieren** you'll be cold (= you will be cold) [wɪl] • **du wirst nicht frieren; ihr werdet nicht frieren** you won't be cold (= you will not be cold) [wəʊnt]
werfen throw [θrəʊ]
wessen? whose? [huːz]
Westen west [west] • **nach Westen** west
westlich west [west]
Wetter weather [ˈweðə]
wichtig important [ɪmˈpɔːtnt]
wie 1. *(Fragewort)* how [haʊ] • **Wie bitte?** Sorry? [ˈsɒri] • **Wie geht es dir/Ihnen/euch?** How are you? [ˌhaʊ ˈɑː juː] • **Wie heißt du?** What's your name? • **Wie spät ist es?** What's the time? • **wie viel?** how much? • **wie viele?** how many? • **Wie war ...?** How was ...? • **Wie war das Wetter?** What was the weather like? • **Wie wär's mit ...?** What about ...?
2. as • **so groß/aufregend wie** as big/exciting as
3. wie ein Filmstar like a film star [laɪk] • **genau wie du** just like you
wieder again [əˈɡen]
wiederholen repeat [rɪˈpiːt]
Wiederholung *(des Lernstoffs)* revision [rɪˈvɪʒn]
Wiedersehen: Auf Wiedersehen. Goodbye. [ɡʊdˈbaɪ]
wiederverwendet/-verwertet recycled [ˌriːˈsaɪkld]
Wiederverwertung recycling [ˌriːˈsaɪklɪŋ]
wild wild [waɪld]
willkommen: Willkommen (in ...). Welcome (to ...). [ˈwelkəm] • **Sie heißen dich in ... willkommen** They welcome you to ...
Wind wind [wɪnd]
windig windy [ˈwɪndi]
winken wave [weɪv]
Winter winter [ˈwɪntə]
wir we [wiː]
wirklich 1. *(Adverb: tatsächlich)* really [ˈrɪəli] • **Meinst du wirklich?/Glaubst du das wirklich?** Do you really think so?
2. *(Adjektiv: echt)* real [rɪəl]
wissen know [nəʊ] • **von etwas wissen; über etwas Bescheid wissen** know about sth. • **..., wissen Sie./..., weißt du.** ..., you know. **Weißt du was, Sophie?** You know what, Sophie? • **Woher weißt du ...?** How do you know ...?
wissen wollen wonder [ˈwʌndə]
Witz joke [dʒəʊk] • **Witze machen** joke
witzig funny [ˈfʌni]
wo where [weə] • **Wo kommst du her?** Where are you from?
Woche week [wiːk]
Wochenende weekend [ˌwiːkˈend] • **am Wochenende** at the weekend
Wochentage days of the week
Wofür? What for? [ˌwɒt ˈfɔː]
Woher weißt du ...? How do you know ...? [nəʊ]
wohin where [weə]; *(in welche Richtung)* which way
Wohlfahrtsorganisation charity [ˈtʃærəti]
Wohltätigkeitsbasar jumble sale [ˈdʒʌmbl seɪl]
wohnen live [lɪv]
Wohnung flat [flæt]
Wohnungstür front door [ˌfrʌnt ˈdɔː]
Wohnwagen caravan [ˈkærəvæn]
Wohnzimmer living room [ˈlɪvɪŋ ruːm]
Wolf wolf, *pl* wolves [wʊlf, wʊlvz]
Wolke cloud [klaʊd]
wollen *(haben wollen)* want [wɒnt] • **tun wollen** want to do
Wort word [wɜːd]
Wortbildung word building [ˈwɜːd ˌbɪldɪŋ]
Wörterbuch dictionary [ˈdɪkʃənri]
Wörterverzeichnis vocabulary [vəˈkæbjələri]; *(alphabetisches)* dictionary [ˈdɪkʃənri]
Wovon redest du? What are you talking about?
wund sein be sore [sɔː]
▶ S.167 What's wrong with you?
wunderbar wonderful [ˈwʌndəfəl]; *(schön, hübsch)* lovely [ˈlʌvli]
würde(n): ich/er würde ... I/he would ... [wəd, wʊd]
Würfel dice, *pl* dice [daɪs]
würfeln throw the dice [ˌθrəʊ ðə ˈdaɪs] **Würfel noch einmal.** Take another turn. [tɜːn]
Wurst, Würstchen sausage [ˈsɒsɪdʒ]
wütend sein (über etwas/auf jn.) be angry (about sth./with sb.) [ˈæŋɡri]

Y

Yoga yoga [ˈjəʊɡə]

Z

Zahl number [ˈnʌmbə]
zählen count [kaʊnt]
Zahn tooth [tuːθ], *pl* teeth [tiːθ] • **Ich putze mir die Zähne.** I clean my teeth.
Zahnschmerzen toothache [ˈtuːθeɪk]
▶ S.167 What's wrong with you?
zanken: sich zanken argue [ˈɑːɡjuː]
Zauberkunststück trick [trɪk] **Zauberkunststücke machen** do tricks
Zebra zebra [ˈzebrə]
Zeh toe [təʊ]
zeigen show [ʃəʊ] • **auf etwas zeigen** point at/to sth. [pɔɪnt]
Zeile line [laɪn]
Zeit time [taɪm] • **Zeit verbringen (mit)** spend time (on) [spend]
Zeitschrift magazine [ˌmæɡəˈziːn]
Zeitung newspaper [ˈnjuːspeɪpə]
Zentrum centre [ˈsentə]
zerbrechen break [breɪk]
zerbrochen broken [ˈbrəʊkən]
Zeug *(Kram)* stuff [stʌf]
ziehen pull [pʊl]
ziemlich cool/gut/... pretty cool/good/... [ˈprɪti]
Ziffer number [ˈnʌmbə]
Zimmer room [ruːm]
zittern shiver [ˈʃɪvə]

Zoo zoo [zu:]
zu 1. *(örtlich)* to [tə, tu] • **zu Jenny** to Jenny's • **zu Hause** at home **Setz dich zu mir.** Sit with me.
2. zum Beispiel for example [ɪɡˈzɑːmpl] • **zum Frühstück/ Mittagessen/Abendbrot** for breakfast/lunch/dinner
3. zu viel too much [tuː] • **zu spät sein/kommen** be late
4. versuchen zu tun try and do / try to do
5. um zu to
zubereiten *(kochen)* cook [kʊk]

Zucker sugar [ˈʃʊɡə]
zuerst first [fɜːst]
Zug train [treɪn] • **im Zug** on the train
Zuhause home [həʊm]
zuhören listen (to) [ˈlɪsn]
Zuhörer/in listener [ˈlɪsnə]
zulassen *(erlauben)* allow [əˈlaʊ]
zumachen close [kləʊz]
zumindest at least [ət ˈliːst]
zurück (nach) back (to) [bæk]
zurückgeben give back [ˌɡɪv ˈbæk]
zurücklassen leave [liːv]
zurzeit at the moment [ˈməʊmənt]

zusammen together [təˈɡeðə]
zusätzlich extra [ˈekstrə]
zusehen watch [wɒtʃ]
zustimmen: jm. zustimmen agree with sb. [əˈɡriː]
zuwenden: sich jm. zuwenden turn to sb. [tɜːn]
▶ S.175 (to) turn
zweite(r, s) second [ˈsekənd]
Zwillinge twins *(pl)* [twɪnz]
Zwillingsbruder twin brother [ˈtwɪn ˌbrʌðə]
zwischen between [bɪˈtwiːn]

English sounds (Englische Laute)

Die Lautschrift in den eckigen Klammern zeigt dir, wie ein Wort ausgesprochen wird. In der folgenden Übersicht findest du alle Lautzeichen.

Vokale (Selbstlaute)

[iː]	gr**ee**n	[eɪ]	sk**a**te
[i]	happ**y**	[aɪ]	t**i**me
[ɪ]	**i**n	[ɔɪ]	b**oy**
[e]	y**e**s	[əʊ]	**o**ld
[æ]	bl**a**ck	[aʊ]	n**ow**
[ɑː]	p**a**rk	[ɪə]	h**ere**
[ɒ]	s**o**ng	[eə]	wh**ere**
[ɔː]	m**o**rning	[ʊə]	t**our**
[uː]	bl**ue**		
[ʊ]	b**oo**k		
[ʌ]	m**u**m		
[ɜː]	T-sh**ir**t		
[ə]	**a** partn**er**		

Konsonanten (Mitlaute)

[b]	**b**ox	[f]	**f**ull
[p]	**p**lay	[v]	**v**ery
[d]	**d**ad	[s]	**s**i**s**ter
[t]	**t**en	[z]	plea**s**e
[ɡ]	**g**ood	[ʃ]	**sh**op
[k]	**c**at	[ʒ]	televi**s**ion
[m]	**m**u**m**	[tʃ]	**t**ea**ch**er
[n]	**n**o	[dʒ]	**G**ermany
[ŋ]	si**ng**	[θ]	**th**anks
[l]	**h**e**ll**o	[ð]	**th**is
[r]	**r**ed	[h]	**h**e
[w]	**w**e		
[j]	**y**ou		

The English alphabet (Das englische Alphabet)

a	[eɪ]	**h**	[eɪtʃ]	**o**	[əʊ]	**v**	[viː]
b	[biː]	**i**	[aɪ]	**p**	[piː]	**w**	[ˈdʌbljuː]
c	[siː]	**j**	[dʒeɪ]	**q**	[kjuː]	**x**	[eks]
d	[diː]	**k**	[keɪ]	**r**	[ɑː]	**y**	[waɪ]
e	[iː]	**l**	[el]	**s**	[es]	**z**	[zed]
f	[ef]	**m**	[em]	**t**	[tiː]		
g	[dʒiː]	**n**	[en]	**u**	[juː]		

List of names

First names (Vornamen)
Alexander [ˌælɪgˈzɑːndə]
Amit [ˈɑːmɪt]
Ananda [əˈnændə]
Angus [ˈæŋgəs]
Barnabas [ˈbɑːnəbəs]
Barry [ˈbæri]
Becky [ˈbeki]
Benjamin [ˈbendʒəmɪn]
Beth [beθ]
Binta [ˈbɪntə]
Bob [bɒb]
Brad [bræd]
Bryn [brɪn]
Caroline [ˈkærəlaɪn]
Catherine [ˈkæθrɪn]
Cid [sɪd]
Dan [dæn]
Daniel [ˈdænjəl]
David [ˈdeɪvɪd]
Dilip [ˈdɪlɪp]
Drew [druː]
Elaine [ɪˈleɪn]
Emily [ˈeməli]
Fiona [fiˈəʊnə]
Grace [greɪs]
Graham [ˈgreɪəm]
Greg [greg]
Griselda [grɪˈzeldə]
Guy [gaɪ]
Gwyneth [ˈgwɪnəθ]
Hannah [ˈhænə]
Harry [ˈhæri]
Henry [ˈhenri]
Isabel [ˈɪzəbel]
Isambard [ˈɪzəmbɑːd]
Jack [dʒæk]
James [dʒeɪmz]
Jay [dʒeɪ]
Jennifer [ˈdʒenɪfə]
Jo [dʒəʊ]
Jody [ˈdʒəʊdi]
Jonah [ˈdʒəʊnə]
Kevin [ˈkevɪn]
Laura [ˈlɔːrə]
Lesley [ˈlezli]
Linda [ˈlɪndə]
Lucy [ˈluːsi]
Mabel [ˈmeɪbl]
Max [mæks]
Meera [ˈmiːrə]
Micky [ˈmɪki]
Mike [maɪk]
Milly [ˈmɪli]
Minnie [ˈmɪni]
Molly [ˈmɒli]
Natale [ˈnætəli]
Nathaniel [nəˈθæniəl]
Nicola [ˈnɪkələ]
Pat [pæt]
Paul [pɔːl]
Pete [piːt]
Prunella [pruˈnelə]
Queenie [ˈkwiːni]
Rachel [ˈreɪtʃəl]
Rebecca [rɪˈbekə]
Richard [ˈrɪtʃəd]
Robinson [ˈrɒbɪnsən]
Ronnie [ˈrɒni]
Rosie [ˈrəʊzi]
Sally [ˈsæli]
Sandra [ˈsɑːndrə]
Shel [ʃel]
Simon [ˈsaɪmən]
Sophie [ˈsəʊfi]
Stephen [ˈstiːvn]
Steve [stiːv]
Susan [ˈsuːzn]
Tamsin [ˈtæmzɪn]
Thomas [ˈtɒməs]
Toby [ˈtəʊbi]
Tony [ˈtəʊni]
Trixie [ˈtrɪksi]
Val [væl]
Valentine [ˈvæləntaɪn]
Vinny [ˈvɪni]
Vortigern [ˈvɔːtɪɡɜːn]
Wallace [ˈwɒlɪs]
Will [wɪl]
William [ˈwɪljəm]
Willy [ˈwɪli]
Zoe [ˈzəʊi]

Family names (Familiennamen)
Baxter [ˈbækstə]
Bean [biːn]
Blake [bleɪk]
Bloggs [blɒgz]
Brooks [brʊks]
Brunel [bruˈnel]
Bute [bjuːt]
Carter-Brown [ˌkɑːtə ˈbraʊn]
Crusoe [ˈkruːsəʊ]
Defoe [dɪˈfəʊ]
Edwards [ˈedwədz]
Ekster [ˈekstə]
Evans [ˈevnz]
Fawkes [fɔːks]
Ghent [gent]
Gupta [ˈgʊptə]
Hanson [ˈhænsn]
Harper [ˈhɑːpə]
Herschel [ˈhɜːʃl]
Hubble [ˈhʌbl]
Kapoor [kəˈpɔː, kəˈpʊə]
Kingdom [ˈkɪŋdəm]
Kingsley [ˈkɪŋzli]
Miller [ˈmɪlə]
Mitton [ˈmɪtn]
Muddles [ˈmʌdlz]
Nichols [ˈnɪkəlz]
Pinney [ˈpɪni]
Selkirk [ˈselkɜːk]
Shaw [ʃɔː]
Silverstein [ˈsɪlvəstiːn]
Smith [smɪθ]
Thompson [ˈtɒmpsən]
Walter [ˈwɔːltə]

Place names (Ortsnamen)
Aardman Studios [ˌɑːdmən ˈstjuːdiəʊz]
Alfred Street [ˌælfrəd striːt]
Aquae Sulis [ˌækwaɪ ˈsuːlɪs]
Bartlett Street [ˈbɑːtlət striːt]
Bath [bɑːθ]
Battersea [ˈbætəsi]
Beauford Square [ˌbəʊfəd ˈskweə]
Berlin [bɜːˈlɪn]
The Brecon Beacons [ˌbrekən ˈbiːkənz]
Bristol [ˈbrɪstl]
Cabot Tower [ˌkæbət ˈtaʊə]
Caerphilly Castle [keəˌfɪli ˈkɑːsl]
Cardiff [ˈkɑːdɪf]
Cardozo High School [kɑːˌdəʊzəʊ ˈhaɪ skuːl]
Central Park [ˌsentrəl ˈpɑːk]
Charlotte Street [ˈʃɑːlət striːt]
Cheap Street [ˈtʃiːp striːt]
Christchurch [ˈkraɪsttʃɜːtʃ]
Clifton Suspension Bridge [ˌklɪftən səˈspenʃn brɪdʒ]
Cologne [kəˈləʊn]
Cornwall [ˈkɔːnwɔːl]
Cotham [ˈkɒtəm]
Crickhowell [krɪkˈhaʊəl]
Delhi [ˈdeli]
Dinas Emrys [ˌdɪnʌs ˈemrɪs]
Doubtful Sound [ˌdaʊtfl ˈsaʊnd]
Dover [ˈdəʊvə]
The Downs [daʊnz]
The Empire State Building [ˌempaɪə ˈsteɪt ˌbɪldɪŋ]
Fiordland [ˈfjɔːdlænd]
George Street [ˈdʒɔːdʒ striːt]
Hamilton Street [ˈhæməltən striːt]
Hanover [ˈhænəʊvə]
Hayle Beach [ˌheɪl ˈbiːtʃ]
Jupiter [ˈdʒuːpɪtə]
Jura [ˈdʒʊərə]
Leeds [liːdz]
Llandoger Trow [hlænˌdɒgə ˈtraʊ]
Llanfoist [hlænˈvɔɪst]
London [ˈlʌndən]
Longleat Safari Park [ˌlɒŋliːt səˈfɑːri pɑːk]
Madrid [məˈdrɪd]
Majorca [məˈjɔːkə]
Manchester [ˈmæntʃɪstə]
Manhattan [mænˈhætn]
Mars [mɑːz]
Milsom Street [ˈmɪlsəm striːt]
Newbridge [ˈnjuːbrɪdʒ]
New York [ˌnjuː ˈjɔːk]
Okarito [ˌɒkəˈriːtəʊ]
Paddington Station [ˌpædɪŋtən ˈsteɪʃn]
Paris [ˈpærɪs]
Pisa [ˈpiːzə]
Portsmouth [ˈpɔːtsməθ]
Queens [kwiːnz]
Queenstown [ˈkwiːnztaʊn]
The River Avon [ˌrɪvər ˈeɪvn]
Saturn [ˈsætɜːn]
The Statue of Liberty [ˌstætʃuː_əv ˈlɪbəti]
St Fagans [sənt ˈfægənz]
St Ives [sənt ˈaɪvz]
St Mary Redcliffe Church [sənt ˌmeəri ˈredklɪf tʃɜːtʃ]
St Nicholas Market [sənt ˌnɪkələs ˈmɑːkɪt]
Stockholm [ˈstɒkhəʊm]
Sussex [ˈsʌsɪks]
Temple Meads Station [ˌtempl ˌmiːdz ˈsteɪʃn]
The Thames [temz]
Theatre Royal [ˌθɪətə ˈrɔɪəl]
Tredegar [trɪˈdiːgə]
Union Street [ˈjuːniən striːt]
Upper Borough Walls [ˌʌpə ˌbʌrə ˈwɔːlz]
Uranus [ˈjʊərənəs]
Valencia [vəˈlenʃə]
Venus [ˈviːnəs]
Warmley [ˈwɔːmli]
York [jɔːk]

Other names (Andere Namen)
Anansi [əˈnænsi]
BBC (British Broadcasting Corporation) [ˌbiː biː ˈsiː], [ˌbrɪtɪʃ ˈbrɔːdkɑːstɪŋ kɔːpəˌreɪʃn]
cawl mamgu [kaʊl ˈmæmgi]
Celtica [ˈkeltɪkə]
Dogwarts University [ˌdɒgwɔːts juːnɪˈvɜːsəti]
Fifi [ˈfiːfiː]
Gromit [ˈgrɒmɪt]
Hogwarts [ˈhɒgwɔːts]
Holi [ˈhəʊli]
Polly [ˈpɒli]
Scruffy [ˈskrʌfi]
Smokey [ˈsməʊki]
Sulis Minerva [ˌsuːlɪs mɪˈnɜːvə]
Techniquest [ˈteknɪkwest]
Travelot [ˈtrævəlɒt]

Countries and continents

Country/Continent	Adjective	Person	People
Africa ['æfrɪkə] *Afrika*	African ['æfrɪkən]	an African	the Africans
America [ə'merɪkə] *Amerika*	American [ə'merɪkən]	an American	the Americans
Asia ['eɪʃə, 'eɪʒə] *Asien*	Asian ['eɪʃn, 'eɪʒn]	an Asian	the Asians
Australia [ɒ'streɪliə] *Australien*	Australian [ɒ'streɪliən]	an Australian	the Australians
Austria ['ɒstriə] *Österreich*	Austrian ['ɒstriən]	an Austrian	the Austrians
Belgium ['beldʒəm] *Belgien*	Belgian ['beldʒən]	a Belgian	the Belgians
Brazil [brə'zɪl] *Brasilien*	Brazilian [brə'zɪliən]	a Brazilian	the Brazilians
(Great) Britain ['brɪtn] *Großbritannien*	British ['brɪtɪʃ]	a Briton ['brɪtn]	the British
the Caribbean [ˌkærə'bi:ən] *die Karibik*	Caribbean [ˌkærə'bi:ən]	a Caribbean	the Caribbeans
Chile ['tʃɪli] *Chile*	Chilean ['tʃɪliən]	a Chilean	the Chileans
China ['tʃaɪnə] *China*	Chinese [ˌtʃaɪ'ni:z]	a Chinese	the Chinese
Croatia [krəʊ'eɪʃə] *Kroatien*	Croatian [krəʊ'eɪʃn]	a Croatian	the Croatians
the Czech Republic [ˌtʃek rɪ'pʌblɪk] *die Tschechische Republik*	Czech [tʃek]	a Czech	the Czechs
Denmark ['denmɑ:k] *Dänemark*	Danish ['deɪnɪʃ]	a Dane [deɪn]	the Danes
England ['ɪŋglənd] *England*	English ['ɪŋglɪʃ]	an Englishman/-woman	the English
Europe ['jʊərəp] *Europa*	European [ˌjʊərə'pi:ən]	a European	the Europeans
Finland ['fɪnlənd] *Finnland*	Finnish ['fɪnɪʃ]	a Finn [fɪn]	the Finns
France [frɑ:ns] *Frankreich*	French [frentʃ]	a Frenchman/-woman	the French
Germany ['dʒɜ:məni] *Deutschland*	German ['dʒɜ:mən]	a German	the Germans
Greece [gri:s] *Griechenland*	Greek [gri:k]	a Greek	the Greeks
Hungary ['hʌŋgəri] *Ungarn*	Hungarian [hʌŋ'geəriən]	a Hungarian	the Hungarians
India ['ɪndiə] *Indien*	Indian ['ɪndiən]	an Indian	the Indians
Ireland ['aɪələnd] *Irland*	Irish ['aɪrɪʃ]	an Irishman/-woman	the Irish
Italy ['ɪtəli] *Italien*	Italian [ɪ'tæliən]	an Italian	the Italians
Jamaica [dʒə'meɪkə] *Jamaika*	Jamaican [dʒə'meɪkən]	a Jamaican	the Jamaicans
Japan [dʒə'pæn] *Japan*	Japanese [ˌdʒæpə'ni:z]	a Japanese	the Japanese
Luxembourg ['lʌksəmbɜ:g] *Luxemburg*	Luxembourg	a Luxembourger ['lʌksəmbɜ:gə]	the Luxembourgers
the Netherlands ['neðələndz] *die Niederlande, Holland*	Dutch [dʌtʃ]	a Dutchman/-woman	the Dutch
New Zealand [ˌnju:'zi:lənd] *Neuseeland*	New Zealand [ˌnju:'zi:lənd]	a New Zealander	the New Zealanders
Norway ['nɔ:weɪ] *Norwegen*	Norwegian [nɔ:'wi:dʒən]	a Norwegian	the Norwegians
Poland ['pəʊlənd] *Polen*	Polish ['pəʊlɪʃ]	a Pole [pəʊl]	the Poles
Portugal ['pɔ:tʃʊgl] *Portugal*	Portuguese [ˌpɔ:tʃʊ'gi:z]	a Portuguese	the Portuguese
Russia ['rʌʃə] *Russland*	Russian ['rʌʃn]	a Russian	the Russians
Scotland ['skɒtlənd] *Schottland*	Scottish ['skɒtɪʃ]	a Scotsman/-woman, a Scot [skɒt]	the Scots, the Scottish
Slovakia [sləʊ'vɑ:kiə, sləʊ'vækiə] *die Slowakei*	Slovak ['sləʊvæk]	a Slovak	the Slovaks
Slovenia [sləʊ'vi:niə] *Slowenien*	Slovenian [sləʊ'vi:niən], Slovene ['sləʊvi:n]	a Slovene, a Slovenian	the Slovenes, the Slovenians
Spain [speɪn] *Spanien*	Spanish ['spænɪʃ]	a Spaniard ['spænɪəd]	the Spaniards
Sweden ['swi:dn] *Schweden*	Swedish ['swi:dɪʃ]	a Swede [swi:d]	the Swedes
Switzerland ['swɪtsələnd] *die Schweiz*	Swiss [swɪs]	a Swiss	the Swiss
Taiwan [taɪ'wɒn, taɪ'wɑ:n] *Taiwan*	Taiwanese [ˌtaɪwə'ni:z]	a Taiwanese	the Taiwanese
Thailand ['taɪlænd] *Thailand*	Thai [taɪ]	a Thai	the Thais
Ukraine [ju:'kreɪn] *die Ukraine*	Ukrainian [ju:'kreɪniən]	a Ukrainian	the Ukrainians
the United Kingdom (the UK) [juˌnaɪtɪd 'kɪŋdəm, ju:'keɪ] *das Vereinigte Königreich (Großbritannien und Nordirland)*	British ['brɪtɪʃ]	a Briton ['brɪtn]	the British
the United States of America (the USA) [juˌnaɪtɪd ˌsteɪts_əv_ə'merɪkə, ju:_es_'eɪ] *die Vereinigten Staaten von Amerika*	American [ə'merɪkən]	an American	the Americans
Vietnam [ˌvjet'næm, ˌvi:et'næm] *Vietnam*	Vietnamese [ˌvjetnə'mi:z, vi:ˌetnə'mi:z]	a Vietnamese	the Vietnamese
Wales [weɪlz] *Wales*	Welsh [welʃ]	a Welshman/-woman	the Welsh

Irregular verbs

Infinitive	Simple past form	Past participle	
(to) be	was/were	been	sein
(to) become	became	become	werden
(to) begin	began	begun	beginnen, anfangen (mit)
(to) break [eɪ]	broke	broken	(zer)brechen; kaputt machen; kaputt gehen
(to) bring	brought	brought	(mit-, her)bringen
(to) build	built	built	bauen
(to) buy	bought	bought	kaufen
(to) catch	caught	caught	fangen; erwischen
(to) choose [uː]	chose [əʊ]	chosen [əʊ]	(aus)wählen; (sich) aussuchen
(to) come	came	come	kommen
(to) cut	cut	cut	schneiden
(to) do	did	done [ʌ]	tun, machen
(to) drink	drank	drunk	trinken
(to) drive [aɪ]	drove	driven [ɪ]	(ein Auto) fahren
(to) eat	ate [et, eɪt]	eaten	essen
(to) fall	fell	fallen	(hin)fallen, stürzen
(to) feed	fed	fed	füttern
(to) feel	felt	felt	(sich) fühlen; sich anfühlen
(to) find	found	found	finden
(to) fly	flew	flown	fliegen
(to) get	got	got	bekommen; holen; werden; (hin)kommen
(to) give	gave	given	geben
(to) go	went	gone [ɒ]	gehen, fahren
(to) grow	grew	grown	wachsen
(to) have (have got)	had	had	haben, besitzen
(to) hear [ɪə]	heard [ɜː]	heard [ɜː]	hören
(to) hide [aɪ]	hid [ɪ]	hidden [ɪ]	(sich) verstecken
(to) hold	held	held	halten
(to) hurt	hurt	hurt	wehtun; verletzen
(to) keep	kept	kept	(warm/offen/...) halten
(to) know [əʊ]	knew [njuː]	known [nəʊn]	wissen; kennen
(to) lay the table	laid	laid	den Tisch decken
(to) leave	left	left	(weg)gehen; abfahren; verlassen; zurücklassen
(to) lend	lent	lent	(ver)leihen
(to) let	let	let	lassen
(to) lose [uː]	lost [ɒ]	lost [ɒ]	verlieren
(to) make	made	made	machen; bauen; bilden
(to) mean [iː]	meant [e]	meant [e]	bedeuten; meinen
(to) meet	met	met	(sich) treffen
(to) pay	paid	paid	bezahlen

Irregular verbs

Infinitive	Simple past form	Past participle	
(to) put	put	put	legen, stellen, *(wohin)* tun
(to) read [iː]	read [e]	read [e]	lesen
(to) ride [aɪ]	rode	ridden [ɪ]	reiten; *(Rad)* fahren
(to) ring	rang	rung	klingeln, läuten
(to) run	ran	run	rennen, laufen
(to) say [eɪ]	said [e]	said [e]	sagen
(to) see	saw	seen	sehen; besuchen, aufsuchen
(to) sell	sold	sold	verkaufen
(to) send	sent	sent	schicken, senden
(to) set a trap	set	set	eine Falle stellen
(to) shine	shone [ɒ]	shone [ɒ]	scheinen *(Sonne)*
(to) show	showed	shown	zeigen
(to) shut up	shut	shut	den Mund halten
(to) sing	sang	sung	singen
(to) sit	sat	sat	sitzen; sich setzen
(to) sleep	slept	slept	schlafen
(to) speak	spoke	spoken	sprechen
(to) spend	spent	spent	*(Zeit)* verbringen; *(Geld)* ausgeben
(to) stand	stood	stood	stehen; sich (hin)stellen
(to) steal	stole	stolen	stehlen
(to) stick on	stuck	stuck	aufkleben
(to) swim	swam	swum	schwimmen
(to) take	took	taken	nehmen; (weg-, hin)bringen
(to) teach	taught	taught	unterrichten, lehren
(to) tell	told	told	erzählen, berichten
(to) think	thought	thought	denken, glauben, meinen
(to) throw	threw	thrown	werfen
(to) understand	understood	understood	verstehen
(to) wear [eə]	wore [ɔː]	worn [ɔː]	tragen *(Kleidung)*
(to) win	won [ʌ]	won [ʌ]	gewinnen
(to) write	wrote	written	schreiben

Classroom English

Was *du* im Klassenzimmer sagen kannst **What *you* can say in the classroom**

Du brauchst Hilfe / You need help

Können Sie mir bitte helfen?	Can you help me, please?
Auf welcher Seite sind wir, bitte?	What page are we on, please?
Was heißt … auf Englisch/Deutsch?	What's … in English/German?
Wie spricht man das erste Wort in Zeile 2 aus?	How do you say the first word in line 2?
Können Sie bitte … buchstabieren?	Can you spell …, please?
Können Sie es bitte an die Tafel schreiben?	Can you write it on the board, please?
Kann ich es auf Deutsch sagen?	Can I say it in German?
Können Sie/Kannst du bitte lauter sprechen?	Can you speak louder, please?
Können Sie/Kannst du das bitte noch mal sagen?	Can you say that again, please?

Beim Zuhören und beim Lesen / Listening and reading

Ich kann die CD nicht hören.	I can't hear the CD.
Ich finde die Geschichte …	I think the story is …
schön/interessant/langweilig/schrecklich/…	nice/interesting/boring/terrible/…
Es war lustig/gruselig/langweilig/…, als …	It was funny/scary/boring/… when …
Ich fand es gut/nicht gut, als …	I liked it/didn't like it when …
Ich finde, Tom hat recht/nicht recht, weil …	I think Tom is right/wrong because …
Ich bin mir nicht sicher. Vielleicht …	I'm not sure. Maybe …

Hausaufgaben und Übungen / Homework and exercises

Tut mir leid, ich habe mein Schulheft nicht dabei, Herr …	Sorry, I haven't got my exercise book, Mr …
Ich habe meine Hausaufgaben vergessen, Frau …	I've forgotten my homework, Mrs/Ms/Miss …
Ich verstehe diese Übung nicht.	I don't understand this exercise.
Ich kann Nummer 3 nicht lösen.	I can't do number 3.
Entschuldigung, ich bin noch nicht fertig.	Sorry, I haven't finished yet.
Ich habe … Ist das auch richtig?	I've got … Is that right too?
Tut mir leid, das weiß ich nicht.	Sorry, I don't know.
Was haben wir (als Hausaufgabe) auf?	What's for homework?

Bei der Partnerarbeit / Work with a partner

Kann ich mit Julian arbeiten?	Can I work with Julian?
Kann ich bitte dein Lineal/deinen Filzstift/… haben?	Can I have your ruler/felt tip/…, please?
Ich bin Lisas Meinung. / Ich bin anderer Meinung.	I agree with Lisa. / I don't agree (with Lisa).
Du bist dran.	It's your turn.

What your *teacher* says / Was dein/e *Lehrer/in* sagt

Open your books at page 24, please.	Schlagt bitte Seite 24 auf.
Look at the picture/line 8/… on page 24.	Seht euch das Bild/Zeile 8/… auf Seite 24 an.
Copy/Complete the chart/network/…	Übertragt/Vervollständigt die Tabelle/das Wörternetz/…
Correct the mistakes.	Verbessert die Fehler.
Fill/Put in the right words.	Setzt die richtigen Wörter ein.
Put the words in the right order.	Bringt die Wörter in die richtige Reihenfolge.
Take notes.	Macht euch Notizen.
Do exercise 3 for homework, please.	Macht bitte Übung 3 als Hausaufgabe.
Bring some photos/… to school.	Bringt ein paar Fotos/… mit in die Schule.
Have you finished?	Seid ihr fertig? / Bist du fertig?
Switch off your mobile phones.	Schaltet eure Handys aus.
Don't send text messages in class.	Verschickt keine SMS während des Unterrichts.
Walk around the class and ask other students.	Geht durch die Klasse und fragt andere Schüler/innen.

Diese Arbeitsanweisungen findest du häufig im Schülerbuch

Act out your dialogue for the class.	Spielt der Klasse euren Dialog vor.
Agree on one place.	Einigt euch auf einen Ort.
Answer the questions.	Beantworte die Fragen.
Ask your partner questions.	Stelle deiner Partnerin/deinem Partner Fragen.
Check with a partner.	Überprüfe das Ergebnis mit deiner Partnerin/deinem Partner.
Check your answers.	Überprüfe deine Antworten.
Collect ideas.	Sammle Ideen.
Compare with a partner.	Vergleiche mit einer Partnerin/einem Partner.
Complete the sentences.	Vervollständige die Sätze.
Copy the chart.	Schreib die Tabelle ab.
Correct your answers.	Verbessere deine Antworten.
Draw a picture.	Zeichne ein Bild.
Fill in the answers.	Trage die Antworten ein.
Find the missing words.	Finde die fehlenden Wörter.
Listen. / Listen again.	Hör zu. / Hör noch einmal zu.
Look at page …	Sieh auf Seite … nach.
Make a chart.	Lege eine Tabelle an.
Make appointments.	Verabrede dich.
Match the letters and numbers.	Ordne die Buchstaben den Nummern zu.
Prepare a dialogue.	Bereitet einen Dialog vor.
Put the sentences in the right order.	Bring die Sätze in die richtige Reihenfolge.
Read the sentences.	Lies die Sätze.
Report to the class.	Berichte der Klasse.
Right or wrong?	Richtig oder falsch?
Scan the text for …	Überfliege den Text und suche nach …
Swap after three questions.	Wechselt euch nach drei Fragen ab.
Take notes.	Mach dir Notizen.
Talk to your partner.	Sprich mit deiner Partnerin/deinem Partner.
Tell your partner about your picture.	Erzähle deiner Partnerin/deinem Partner etwas über dein Bild.
Use ideas from the box.	Verwende Ideen aus dem Kasten.
What's different?	Was ist anders?
Work in groups of four.	Arbeitet in Vierergruppen.
Write down five questions.	Schreib fünf Fragen auf.

Illustrationen

Graham-Cameron Illustration, UK; Fliss Cary, Grafikerin (wenn nicht anders angegeben); **Roland Beier,** Berlin (Vignetten vordere Umschlaginnenseite; S. 14; 18; 21; 33; 35; 37; 52; 54; 58–59; 64; 70–71; 77; 83 unten; 84; 86; 102–103 oben; 111; 112 unten; 113 oben; 114–115 oben; 116 unten–177); **Carlos Borrell,** Berlin (Karten und Stadtpläne: vordere und hintere Umschlaginnenseite; S. 8; 67; 97; 101 (u. 113); 108; 110 oben); **Julie Colthorpe,** Berlin (S. 6; 17; 69 unten re.; 83 oben; 110 unten; 115 Mitte); **Linda Rogers Associates,** London: Gary Rees (S. 91–93); **Michael Teßmer,** Hamburg (S. 94/95 The Roman Baths); **Katherine Wells,** Hamburg (S. 82); **Korinna Wilkes,** Berlin (S. 60/61 Hintergrund)

Fotos

Rob Cousins, Bristol (wenn im Bildquellenverzeichnis nicht anders angegeben)

Bildquellen

AA Guides Ltd, Glenfield (S. 108 Mitte); **AJ Hackett Bungy,** Queenstown (S. 108/109 unten); **Alamy,** Abingdon (S. 6 Bild A: Paul Broadbent; S. 7 Bild D: David Noton Photography; S. 12 oben: Ambient Images Inc./Peter Bennett (M); S. 26 knee elbow guards: Photolibrary; S. 27 oben: Design Pics, Mitte: BananaStock; S. 32 unten: Justin Kase; S. 37: SHOTFILE; S. 45 deer: Vic Pigula; S. 67 Bild 2: The Photolibrary Wales; S. 76: unten: Paul White; S. 77 unten li.: Rolf Richardson; S. 81 unten: Peter Tarry; S. 86: YAY Media AS); At-Bristol science centre (S. 76 li.); Allstar Picture Library (S. 109 Legolas); **Avenue Images,** Hamburg (S. 26 hat: Stock-byte); **Bank of England,** London (S. 26/27 banknotes, reproduced with kind permission); **Camillo Beretta,** Berlin (S. 26 magazine, comic, ticket, book); **Celtic Scene,** Cornwall (S. 6 Bild B: Claire Sellick); **Corbis,** Düsseldorf (S. 24 Bild D: Reuters/Daniel Aguilar; S. 43 unten: Kevin R. Morris; S. 45 hedgehog: Herbert Spichtinger/zefa; S. 85 unten: Bureau L.A. Collection); **Corel Library** (S. 6/7 seagulls; S. 12 oben clouds (M); S. 26 coke; S. 38; S. 50 woodland; S. 53; S. 54 giraffe, tiger); **Cornelsen Verlag,** Berlin (S. 26 Genius); **Cotham School,** Bristol (S. 10/11 Website-Frame, Logo); **Destination Bristol,** Bristol (S. 76/77 map; S. 87: Michaela Norris); **Gareth Evans,** Berlin (S. 8; S. 29 game); Go Orange Limited (S. 109 Mitte re.); **Fiordland Wilderness Experiences – Sea Kayak Fiordland,** Te Anau/ www.fiordlandseakayak.co.nz, info@fiordlandseakayak.co.nz (S. 109 Mitte u. unten re.); **Fotosearch,** Waukesha (S. 29 ice cream); **Georgian House,** Bristol/Bristol Museums & Art Gallery (S. 77); **Getty Images,** München (S. 63 oben: Ryan McVay; S. 75 Railway: Brecon Railway; S. 78: Visit Britain/Britain on View); **Bonnie Glänzer,** Berlin (S. 50 li.; S. 55); **Hassle-free Tours,** Christchurch (S. 108/109 Mitte); The Helicopter Line Ltd, Mt. Cook (S. 108 oben li.); Herschel House, Bristol (S. 99 oben); **Ingram Publishing,** UK (S. 27: gift box); **Keystone,** Hamburg (S. 42 oben: TopFoto/Arena Images/Keith Saunders); **Look,** München (S. 42 unten: Karl Johaentges; S. 99 unten: Photo Researchers); **Marketing for Education,** Nelson (S. 10/11 Bild 1–6); **Mauritius,** Hamburg (S. 10/11 boules (M): Image Source; S. 24, Bild C: Fritz Rauschenbach; S. 30 paperboy: Rubberball; S. 77 oben: Destination Bristol); (S. 99 unten: Photo Researchers); Penguin Group (S. 26 The Adventures of Huckelberry Finn); **Photolibrary Wales,** Cardiff (S. 61 oben; S. 62 unten; S. 63 Welsh flag; S. 67 Bild 1); **Picture-Alliance,** Frankfurt/Main (S. 43 oben: dpa; S. 45 woodpecker, mole (u. S. 120): Okapia/Manfred Danegger, frog: Okapia/Markus Essler; S. 54 monkey: Godong; S. 77 (u. 85) Wallace und Gromit: obs; S. 109 Legolas: KPA Honorar & Belege; PRIVATE EYE magazine (S. 46: Ed McLachlan); **Provincial Pictures,** Bath (S. 7 Bild C: Philip Pierce); **Queenstown Adventure Group,** Queenstown (S. 108 queenstown); **Real Journeys,** Queenstown / www. realjourneys .co.nz (S. 109 oben re.); **Royal Commission on the Ancient and Historical Monument of Wales,** Aberystwyth (S. 75 oben li.: National Monuments Record for Wales, Aberystwyth); **RSPCA Photolibrary,** Horsham (S. 49 Andrew Forsyth); **Shutterstock,** New York (S. 24 Bild B: Jeff Thrower; S. 26 Comic Superman: Vectomart, bottle of water: Nataliya Hora; S. 29 DVDs: Jostein Hauge; S. 44: Mark Simms; S. 45 grey squirrel: John L. Richbourg; S. 120 baby moles: Devin Koob); **Somerfield Stores Ltd,** Bristol (S. 29 juice); **Stills-Online,** Hamburg (S. 26 sweets in bag, pile of sweets, shirt, top, dress, jumper, jacket, trousers, skirt, trainers, CDs; S. 27 unten: mobile, pens, pencils, lipstick, rouge); **Stockfood,** München (S. 26 bottle and glass of orange juice: Christina Peters, chips: Dieter Heinemann, crisps: Kröger & Gross, chocolate: FoodPhotography Eising;); **Techniquest Science Discovery Centre,** Cardiff (S. 67 Bild 3); **Christine Thomas,** Crickhowell (S. 61 sign); Totally Tourism Ltd. (S. 109 Mitte); **ullstein bild,** Berlin (S. 9 CARO/Sorge); Visit Wales Image Centre (S. 67 Bild 4); **V&A Enterprises Ltd.,** London (S. 31: V&A Images/Victoria and Albert Museum); Visum, Hamburg (S. 24 Bild A: Markus Hanke); **Walker Books Ltd.,** London (S. 51: Cover photo © 2005 by Stuart McClymont/Getty Images from NO SMALL THING by Natale Ghent. Reproduced by permission of Walker Books Ltd, London SE11 5HJ); **Wanaka Sightseeing,** Christchurch (S. 108/109 oben); WSW Wuppertaler Stadtwerke GmbH (S. 123 unten)

Titelbild

Rob Cousins, Bristol; **IFA-Bilderteam,** Ottobrunn (Hintergrund Union Jack: Jon Arnold Images); **Mpixel/Achim Meissner,** Krefeld (Himmel)

Textquellen

S. 24: *Sea Timeless Song* by Grace Nichols from: "The Fat Black Woman's Poems". © Virago Press Ltd., London 1984. S. 59: *The Song of a Mole* by Richard Edwards from: "The Word Party", published by Lutterworth Press, Cambridge 1986; *Undersea Tea* by Tony Mitton from: "The Works: Every kind of poem you will ever need for the Literacy Hour", chosen by Paul Cookson. Macmillan Children's Books, A Division of Macmillan Publishers Ltd., London 2000. © Tony Mitton by permission of David Higham Associates; *Early Bird* by Shel Silverstein from: "Where the Sidewalk Ends – the poems and drawings of Shel Silverstein". © Harper & Row, New York 1974

Liedquellen

S. 15: *You've got a friend* (When you're down and). K. & T.: Carole King. 1971 by Screen Gems-EMI Music Inc. © EMI Music Publishing Germany GmbH & Co. KG, Hamburg; S. 32: *Low Budget*. K. & T.: Raymond Douglas Davies © Davray Music Ltd./Sony/ATV Music Publishing (Germany) GmbH, Berlin; S. 58: *I know an old lady*. M. & T.: Rosemary Bedeau, Alan Mills © Peermusic (Germany) GmbH, Hamburg; S. 107: *Summer Holiday*. K. & T.: Bruce Welch, Brian Bennett © Edition Accord Musikverlag GmbH & Co. KG c/o EMI Music Publishing Germany GmbH & KG